S0-BSC-513

MULTIDIMENSIONAL SCALING

VOLUME II
Applications

MULTIDIMENSIONAL SCALING

THEORY AND APPLICATIONS IN THE BEHAVIORAL SCIENCES

EDITED BY

A. Kimball Romney
School of Social Sciences
University of California
Irvine, California

Roger N. Shepard
Department of Psychology
Stanford University
Stanford, California

Sara Beth Nerlove
School of Urban and Public Affairs
Carnegie-Mellon University
Pittsburgh, Pennsylvania

VOLUME II
Applications

SEMINAR PRESS New York San Francisco London 1972
A Subsidiary of Harcourt Brace Jovanovich, Publishers

SEMINAR PRESS, INC.
111 Fifth Avenue, New York, New York 10003

United Kingdom Edition published by
SEMINAR PRESS LIMITED
24/28 Oval Road, London NW1

LIBRARY OF CONGRESS CATALOG CARD NUMBER: 74-187260

PRINTED IN THE UNITED STATES OF AMERICA

CONTENTS

Marketing Research Applications of Nonmetric Scaling Methods

Paul E. Green and Frank J. Carmone

Some Applications of Multidimensional Scaling to Social Science Problems 211

Volney J. Stefflre

A Structural Approach to Predicting Patterns of Electoral Substitution

Gary A. Mauser

Differences in Perceived Similarity of Nations

Myron Wish, Morton Deutsch, and Lois Biener

CONTRIBUTORS TO VOLUME II

Numbers in parentheses indicate the pages on which the authors' contributions begin.

ROY G. D'ANDRADE,* Stanford University, Stanford, California (9)

LOIS BIENER, Teachers College, Columbia University, New York, New York (289)

MICHAEL BURTON, School of Social Sciences, University of California, Irvine, California (55)

FRANK J. CARMONE,† University of Waterloo, Waterloo, Ontario, Canada (183)

NORMAN CLIFF, University of Southern California, Los Angeles, California (163)

MORTON DEUTSCH, Teachers College, Columbia University, New York, New York (289)

SAMUEL FILLENBAUM, University of North Carolina, Chapel Hill, North Carolina (93)

* Present address: Department of Anthropology, University of California, San Diego, California

† Present address: Department of Marketing, Drexel University, Philadelphia, Pennsylvania

PAUL E. GREEN, Wharton School of Finance and Commerce, University of Pennsylvania, Philadelphia, Pennsylvania (183)

GARY A. MAUSER, L'Institut D'Etudes Commerciales, Université de Grenoble, Grenoble, France (245)

SARA BETH NERLOVE, School of Social Sciences, University of California, Irvine, California (1, 9)

NAOMI R. QUINN, Stanford University, Stanford, California (9)

AMNON RAPOPORT, University of North Carolina, Chapel Hill, North Carolina (93)

A. KIMBALL ROMNEY, School of Social Sciences, University of California, Irvine, California (1, 9, 73)

SEYMOUR ROSENBERG, Livingston College, Rutgers University, New Brunswick, New Jersey (133)

ANDREA SEDLAK, Rutgers University, New Brunswick, New Jersey (133)

VOLNEY J. STEFFLRE, School of Social Sciences, University of California, Irvine, California (211)

KENNETH N. WEXLER, School of Social Sciences, University of California, Irvine, California (73)

MYRON WISH, Bell Telephone Laboratories, Inc., Murray Hill, New Jersey (289)

OTHER PARTICIPANTS

James S. Coleman, Department of Social Relations, Johns Hopkins University, Baltimore, Maryland

David G. Hays, Program in Linguistics, State University of New York, Buffalo, New York

Stephen C. Johnson, Bell Telephone Laboratories, Inc., Murray Hill, New Jersey

Paul Kay, Department of Anthropology, University of California, Berkeley, California

Robert Kozelka, Department of Statistics, Williams College, Williamstown, Massachusetts

Kenneth Lutterman, Social Science Section, National Institutes of Health, Bethesda, Maryland

John M. Roberts, Department of Anthropology, Cornell University, Ithaca, New York

Warren S. Torgerson, Department of Psychology, Johns Hopkins University, Baltimore, Maryland

PREFACE

Workers in an increasing variety of behavioral and biomedical sciences are using multidimensional scaling and related methods of clustering and factor analysis in their attempts to discover structures underlying the observed relations among stimuli, concepts, traits, persons, cultures, species, or nations. Indeed, developments have been so rapid since the introduction of the computer-based "nonmetric" methods just ten years ago that workers in one field are often unaware of the emergence of methods that, though developed in a quite different field, may be directly applicable to the very problem with which they are currently struggling.

In an effort to counteract this situation, two of us (Romney and Shepard) jointly organized an advance research seminar on recent theoretical and methodological developments and on substantively significant applications of these developments in a wide range of social and behavioral science fields. The present two volumes are the tangible output of that seminar. The first focuses on the primarily theoretical and methodological developments while the second presents a variety of applications in such diverse fields as anthropology, psychology, political science, and marketing research.

The seminar was sponsored through the auspices of the Mathematical Social Science Board. The Board is financed by a grant from the National Science Foundation (GS-547) through the Center for Advanced Study in the Behavioral Sciences, Stanford. We are grateful to the Mathematical Social Science Board and the National Science Foundation for their support.

David Hays, a member of the Board, who originated the idea for such a conference, had invited Roger Shepard to undertake its organization. Independently, A. Kimball Romney was planning a conference of the same sort specifically oriented toward applications in anthropology. When the two of us learned of each others' plans (by each inviting the other to his own conference!) we decided to integrate our very similar plans into a single Interdisciplinary Advanced Summer Research Seminar. The resulting combined seminar was held near the campus of the University of California, Irvine, in June, 1969.

Copies of the papers initially contributed by the participants were circulated to all participants in advance of the seminar. These papers then served as a basis for the discussions conducted at the seminar. Following the seminar each author revised his paper to take advantage of suggestions and criticisms that arose during the discussions. The final versions of these papers make up the two volumes. Sara Nerlove has taken the major responsibility in working with each author on editorial revisions and in writing the introduction to Volume II. Part of the work of Romney and Nerlove was supported by NIH Grant MH17468-02S1.

It is our impression, shared by all participants, that the seminar was unusually stimulating and productive. We believe that, despite their diversity, the papers form a coherent contribution to the current state of knowledge of multidimensional scaling. Students and researchers concerned with problems of discovering or interpreting patterns or structures in data from diverse fields of social, behavioral, or biomedical science may find them useful.

CONTENTS OF VOLUME I: Theory

INTRODUCTION TO VOLUME II

Sara Beth Nerlove and A. Kimball Romney

SCHOOL OF SOCIAL SCIENCES
UNIVERSITY OF CALIFORNIA
IRVINE, CALIFORNIA

Volume II presents a series of ten papers that illustrate a number of important applications of multidimensional scaling in the behavioral sciences. The various fields represented include anthropology, psycholinguistics, psychology, political science, and market research. It is interesting to note that many of the papers are difficult to categorize strictly within any given traditional discipline. Many of the applications could be better characterized with multiple labels since they lie on the border between fields.

One of the impressive features of these applications is the great variety of empirical methods which have been used to arrive at indices of proximity or subjective distance which may serve as input to programs for multidimensional scaling analyses. In some cases estimates of distance among objects are based on rather straightforward judgments of similarity. In other cases indirect or derived measures of similarity or dissimilarity are used. Some of the papers combine two or more techniques in the collection of a single body of data. The technical description of classes of data which can serve as input to a multidimensional scaling analysis is dealt with at greater length in Volume I.

It is our impression that multidimensional scaling gives the most consistent results when applied to well-defined domains. One of the characteristics of a well-defined domain is that the objects being classified or judged belong to a single conceptual sphere and thus are comparable to one another. The definition of a domain is not a technical problem in multidimensional scaling, but rather a substantive problem for the researcher. The problem of defining a domain is a complicated one. To cite but one example, in a very broad domain, such as that of role terms, the objects tend to be arrayed on the basis of rather general dimensions. An analysis of the general dimensions alone obscures the detailed structure of clusters within the broad picture. In order to elucidate the structure within individual clusters, it may, in some situations, be necessary to analyze each cluster separately. Since this failure to get a complete picture of a domain from a single analysis may be a common phenomenon, let us give a simple example: If one compares kin terms to all other role terms, the resulting overall picture will cluster the kin terms in a single region among other role terms but will not provide a picture of the interrelation among the kin terms. To obtain the structure among kin terms, it is necessary to compare them among themselves and analyze them separately. A possible reason for this phenomenon is that the dimensions relevant for comparison among kin terms are not relevant for comparison of kin terms to other role terms such as, for example, doctor, lawyer, carpenter, etc.

From the various applications, it has become quite clear that the problem of interpreting the multidimensional picture depends in part on considerations independent of the method itself. The considerations include both the nature of the domain under study and the emphasis of the researcher. Some analysts have stressed the interpretation in terms of naming and labeling dimensions, while others impose a less restricted interpretation and speak only in terms of regions in which objects in the same region are interpreted as being similar. The latter category of researchers may make no attempt to interpret overall dimensions and may in fact argue that it would be artificial or fruitless to do so. Many researchers, of course, take a position between these extremes.

Another point upon which there is diversity has to do with the purpose or use of the multidimensional scaling. Some researchers view the technique as a descriptive aid in an inductive sense, while others have various *a priori* models and use scaling for model testing. Like other mathematical and statistical techniques, multidimensional scaling lends itself to both uses.

Closely related to the question of use is that of validation; that is, what are the criteria used in judging how satisfactory a multidimensional scaling result is. In some cases the validation depends upon correlations with outside data, where multidimensional analysis is used to predict some outside phenomenon (or is itself predicted from some outside phenomenon). Other applications depend almost exclusively on internal coherence and related kinds of criteria and do not attempt to relate the multidimensional scaling results to outside independent data.

In the remainder of this introduction, we would like to review very briefly the various fields and applications in terms of some of the above points. We begin with anthropology and the various applications from that field.

Traditionally many anthropologists, while showing a great deal of interest in structure and models, have not shown much interest either in testing their models or in the associated problems of data quantification. In recent years anthropologists have developed methods for the formal analysis of semantic domains such as kinship terms and pronouns and, in part because of these developments, have shown concern with the question of the predictability and replicability of human behavior in general and, in particular, of that related to the formal analyses themselves. Along with these interests came a greater interest in quantitative techniques.

D'Andrade, Quinn, Nerlove, and Romney investigate the conceptual organization of disease categories in American-English and Mexican-Spanish with respect to a wide range of properties. In contrast to the domain of kinship examined by Wexler and Romney, the domain of diseases exhibits a relatively smaller degree of isomorphism between the properties which determine labeling and the properties which determine other behaviors.

By means of three techniques (which are compared and interrelated) i.e., factor analysis, hierarchical clustering, and multidimensional scaling, the distributional similarity of diseases across belief-frames is analyzed in order to determine the structure of the salient properties and categories of disease. One novel application of multidimensional scaling is illustrated by the representation in the same space of the intercorrelations between belief-frames on the one hand and disease terms on the other. The particular way in which this was done here was made possible by the fact that recent nonmetric multidimensional scaling programs (in this case, Kruskal's) can accept a matrix with missing values.

Burton employs multidimensional scaling techniques and Johnson's hierarchical clustering method to achieve a representation of the semantic structure of 60 occupation names in English. Correlating similarity data from paired comparison tests on a scale of prestige with that from a free sorting task which served as input to a scaling program, he tests for the presence of the dimension of prestige in this domain by posing the question as to whether there exists a rotation of axes in the multidimensional representation of the occupation terms such that the projection of points on one of the axes has the same rank order as the rank ordering of points on the prestige scale. This proposition is verified, giving evidence that there is a correspondence between the meaning of occupation names and the judgment of those names on the dimension of prestige. Furthermore the particular axis which maps onto the prestige scale is the longest axis of the representation indicating that prestige is the single most important criterion of the sorting task.

An interest in a quantitative view of human behavior has led to a concern with the nature of individual variations in the paper by Wexler and Romney, who use multidimensional scaling techniques to explore the nature of individual variations in the cognitive structure of American-English kin terms. First a process model, one which specifies how a subject behaves in an experiment (in this case a triads test of judged similarity) assuming any given structural model, is used to isolate the more appropriate structural models from a set of alternatives. Then using multidimensional scaling techniques, individuals are compared with respect to the importance of the dimension of lineality and to how closely they conform to a particular theoretical model. The evidence indicates that individuals may have different or alternative structures; that is, the data appear not to correspond to the anthropological notion that all people in a culture have the same structure.

Rapoport and Fillenbaum, who investigate hierarchical clustering and multidimensional scaling representations as psychological models of data, seek to determine some structural properties of semantic domains. Rapoport and Fillenbaum deal with two *different* domains: color names, which they consider a highly structured and well-defined domain, and the HAVE family of verbs, which they consider a more open domain with unclear boundaries. They collect judged similarity data from various tasks and apply a variety of methods of analysis to both grouped and individual data. One conclusion they draw (involving ideas which are also discussed in Burton's paper) is that the nature of a given domain dictates whether a hierarchical or a multidimensional model is most appropriate. They suggest, for example, that multidimensional scaling is appropriate for paradigmatic structures; while hierarchical clustering is appropriate for taxonomic structures.

Rosenberg and Sedlak obtain co-occurrences among selected samples of personality trait terms and use multidimensional scaling techniques to give these perceived trait co-occurrences a structural representation, for such structure is believed central to everyday social decisions and interactions. A naturalistic description task was used to generate data; the subjects generated the descriptive traits as well as the objects of description and then careful linguistic treatment of the data was employed to group together somewhat different linguistic forms, e.g., intelligent, intelligence, of the same trait.

The measure of co-occurrence between two traits used is one of disassociation or disagreement across subjects, i.e., the number of times those two traits were not assigned to the same person. Their measure includes both direct and indirect co-occurrences for any two traits and is first adjusted for within-subject frequency count of a given trait. Then linear multiple regression is used to interpret the multidimensional scaling configurations by fitting each of nine rated properties (which had also been factor analyzed in this study and compared to the results of a factor analysis of the same properties in a previous study) to each of five multidimensional scaling configurations, representing solutions in from one to five dimensions.

While the results support earlier findings in that evaluation appeared to be a salient dimension in personality perception, the findings in relation to factors of potency and activity are inconsistent with previous studies. The Hard–Soft (potency) dimension, usually orthogonal to Good–Bad (evaluation), was found to correlate with it in this study and the angle between the axes which represent these properties was small in all five spaces examined. Active–Passive (activity) dimension was rather weakly represented in the resultant trait spaces, appearing only in spaces of higher dimensionality, and, even then, with rather low correlations to the spaces. The authors suggest that Osgood's three semantic factors may not hold up strongly with the naturalistic data obtained because of sampling biases in previous trait and semantic differential studies and raise the question whether evaluation is orthogonal to any other dimension in personality perception.

Cliff investigates a substantive model for relating a word combination to its components, reconstructs his original data from the model he develops and uses a test of consistency (for the fit of the model to the data). What he demonstrates is the high degree consistency of a general additive model with data for pair combinations of ten adjectives rated on the dimension of how favorably they apply to executives and technicians. This was done by monotonically transforming the observed scale to maximize consistency with the additive model in a procedure related to ideas of "conjoint measurement," though providing a smooth rather than a step-function transformation. Then he relates the adjective parameters derived from the pair ratings to the mean ratings of the component adjectives and thus is able to specify that the simple averaging form of the additive model is the most appropriate. Finally, he attempts to relate the favorableness data for the pairs to the positions of the component adjectives in a space derived by means of nonmetric multidimensional scaling analysis of a separate set of data. He relates these data in a manner similar to that seen in Burton's paper, comparing the mean ratings of combinations with the projections of the adjectives or coordinate axes as derived from a scaling configuration based on similarity data. Implicit in the approach is that similarity data and preference data have a uniform, simple relationship. The results are interpreted as supporting not only the general additive model of relating the favorableness of adjective to adjective combinations but also multidimensional scaling as a means of yielding valid representations by subjective or cognitive structuring of stimulus sets.

Green and Carmone present an assessment of the applicability of multidimensional scaling techniques to marketing problems, describing typical problem areas in marketing behavior, illustrating their own approach to one such problem by a pilot study they undertook, and finally summarizing in extensive detail both the substantive and methodological problems involved with the use of multidimensional scaling analysis. The basic question Green and Carmone ask is whether the perceptual and preference judgments of "creative experts" in advertising are different or "superior" to those of controls. The subjects ranked ten print ads according to various criteria. The data obtained are analyzed by various methods including Torgerson–Young multidimensional scaling techniques, Thurstonian unidimensional scales, and Carroll–Chang's multidimensional scaling techniques for handling individual data (see Carroll, this book, Volume I). The tentative results of their study show that the experts are neither very different from nor superior to the controls.

One promising area of application of nonmetric scaling methods to market research is the one with which Stefflre deals primarily, i.e., the design of new products for existing markets and the design of new markets for existing products. Basically, Stefflre sees scaling configurations as a heuristic both in representing the structures of similarity and preferences and in determining which features lead items to be located as they are in the structure. He discusses the problem of shifting contexts as well as that of labeling dimensions. Stefflre argues that what is crucial to the problem of shifting criteria is that the same individual will differ in the space treated as relevant to a particular object from context to context.

For Stefflre, the data that are in the main to be fed to multidimensional scaling programs are judged similarity (or dissimilarity) data collected by having each subject rate or rank all pairs of items by degree of intrapair similarity, by having each subject rate or rank some pairs and aggregating these individual data so that they yield a rating or ranking of all pairs, or by having the subjects sort items into groups on the basis of similarity and aggregating these data into an overall similarity measure for the group. In order to be able to build a new product and predict its performance, Stefflre has developed as indexes for product–product substitution: item-by-use matrices, patterns of preference data, and substitution patterns (which involve a combination of similarity-in-use rankings with similarity-in-preference rankings).

Mauser, who has worked closely with Stefflre, applies the general processes and the simulation techniques developed by Stefflre to political campaigns. The first two aims of his paper are to describe the similarity and substitution structures underlying the 1968 Presidential election, and to test the hypothesis that similar candidates substitute for each other. The final aim of Mauser's paper is to discover the features which determine placement in the underlying structures so as to be able to predict for any new candidate of specified features where that candidate would be located in the similarity and substitution structure and what his substitution pattern would be in the election in question.

Three separate samples of California voters were drawn and interviewed prior to the 1968 Presidential election. One sample judged the similarity of a set of politicians who conceivably could be candidates in the contest. The other two samples ranked these politicians (and hypothetical *new* candidates) in terms of their intention to vote for them for President. The rankings were intercorrelated across voters in the second sample to provide a measure of candidates' similarity with respect to preference across the voters. In the third sample, the rankings were used to simulate outcomes of hypothetical elections between selected subsets of candidates. The hypothetical election results are simulated by using frequency with which a candidate was ranked first in any subset to estimate how many votes he would receive in an election between members of the subset alone.

Multidimensional scaling techniques are used to generate models of the similarity and substitution structures which can be adequately displayed in three dimensions. Both similarity and preference correlation can predict relative substitutability in the 1968 Presidential election. Such results strongly suggest that there is an underlying similarity structure which determines how any new candidate will be seen and for whom he will substitute in an election.

Wish, Deutsch, and Biener use Carroll and Chang's INDSCAL (for *IN*dividual *D*ifferences *SCAL*ing) procedure to explore differences in perceptions (or conceptions) of nations among various groups of subjects.

Specifically, they compare the conceptual structures of "doves" with those of "nondoves," of subjects from "developed" countries with those from "underdeveloped" countries, and of males with those of females. In their study 75 Columbia University students from eight different countries judged the pairwise similarities among 21 countries and also rated each of the countries on many different semantic-differential-type scales. They show that there is sufficient communality in the underlying dimensions which different subjects use to characterize nations for meaningful comparisons to be made of how salient the dimensions are to subjects in different subgroups. Moreover, they find consistent differences in conceptual structures of nations which are associated with political orientation, country of origin, and sex of the respondents. Correlations of the INDSCAL dimensions with ratings on the semantic differential scales facilitate and support their interpretations of the dimensions. A great deal of attention is given throughout the paper to methodological as well as to substantive considerations, for example, to circumvent the problem of having an individual subject make too many comparisons, Wish et al. use a balanced design of pairs of "core" countries plus mutually exclusive and exhaustive subsets of pairs.

Readers who desire more technical information about any of the methods are urged to consult Volume I for more extensive treatment. Those interested in theory and methodological issues will find the first volume indispensible.

CATEGORIES OF DISEASE IN AMERICAN-ENGLISH AND MEXICAN-SPANISH

Roy G. D'Andrade,[1] *Naomi R. Quinn,*
Sara Beth Nerlove,[2] *and A. Kimball Romney*[2]

STANFORD UNIVERSITY
STANFORD, CALIFORNIA

This paper presents the results of a study of how English-speaking American and Spanish-speaking Mexican individuals categorize diseases. The notion of categorization is used here in its most general sense. That is, we have focused on how individuals organize diseases with respect to a wide range of properties, rather than concentrating solely on properties which serve to define disease states.

As a lexical domain, disease terms differ in a number of ways from other domains, such as kinship. The distinctive features, or properties, used for defining kin terms are compounded out of a limited number of simple elements. A great variety of properties, however, may serve as distinctive features in defining disease states, such as type of disease agent, body location, source of disease, symptom types and order of appearance, duration

[1] Present address: Department of Anthropology, University of California, San Diego, California.

[2] Present address: University of California, Irvine, California.

of illness, degree of disability, etc. Also, much greater uncertainty exists in the identification of diseases. This uncertainty arises in part from the probabilist nature of many of the properties useful in identifying them (Frake, 1961).

Our early attempts to discover how diseases are categorized were based mainly on analytic models developed to describe domains of kin terms and plant names. Perhaps not surprisingly, these models proved unsatisfactory. Attempts to construct taxonomies resulted in shallow, nonexhaustive, and cross-cutting structures, while attempts to construct paradigms of distinctive features resulted in incomplete definitions and overly complex features. Informant responses tended to be idiosyncratic, and individuals frequently changed their responses from one session to another.

These results suggested that some other analytic techniques more directly related to the informants' actual cognitive structuring of diseases had to be found. Our solution has been to use simple distributional similarity to determine the salient properties and categories of diseases. "Distributional similarity" here refers to the degree to which sets of items are found to co-occur in the same environments. For example, in Table 1, five properties of diseases and five diseases are arranged in a matrix form. A plus indicates that the disease in that row is thought to have the property listed in that column, while a minus indicates that the disease is not considered to have that property.

Any two properties may be said to be similar to the degree that they have pluses (+) in the same columns and minuses (−) in the same columns. Property 1 and property 2, for example, are fairly similar, in that they share pluses for disease 1 and disease 2, and share minuses for disease 3 and disease 5. They disagree only for disease 4, on which property 1 has a plus, and property 2 has a minus. The degree of similarity between property 1 and property 2 is displayed in Table 2. For "all or none" measurements,

TABLE 1

MODEL DISTRIBUTION OF FIVE PROPERTIES ACROSS FIVE DISEASES

		Properties				
		P1	P2	P3	P4	P5
	D 1	+	+	−	+	−
	D 2	+	+	−	−	−
Diseases	D 3	−	−	+	+	−
	D 4	+	−	+	−	+
	D 5	−	−	−	+	+

TABLE 2

SAMPLE 2 × 2 TABLE

		Property 2	
		+	−
Property 1	+	2	1
	−	0	2

such as plus and minus, a correlation coefficient can be calculated from Table 2, representing degree of similarity with a single figure (in this case, $r = +.67$).

The distributional similarity of one disease to another may also be calculated from Table 1. Disease 2 and disease 3, for example, are fairly dissimilar in that for every property where one has a plus the other has a minus, except for property 5, for which both share a minus. The correlation between these two diseases yields a coefficient of $-.67$.

The analysis of distributional similarity offers a very general method for uncovering both those properties that are most salient in categorization and how objects are grouped (V. Stefflre, ms.). This method assumes very little about the nature of the organization of a domain, except that the properties used are relevant to the objects, i.e., that the nature of the object is determined, at least in part, by these properties. However, data gathered in this form require further analysis in order to group the objects and their properties in a meaningful fashion. Techniques for grouping properties and diseases are presented in the following, after discussion of the sample and data gathering procedures.

Sample and Data Gathering Procedures

The sample consists of three groups: 10 English-speaking American undergraduates from Stanford University, 5 Spanish-speaking Ladino adults (Ladinos are people who consider themselves to be non-Indian and a part of Mexican national culture), and 11 bilingual Tzeltal- and Spanish-speaking Indian adults. From ethnographic descriptions of Tzeltal beliefs about illness, it seemed likely that the normative beliefs about illness of the Indian sample would show systematic differences compared to those of the Ladino sample (Metzger & Williams, 1963a). Both Mexican samples are from Villa Las Rosas, in the state of Chiapas, Mexico.

TABLE 3

AMERICAN-ENGLISH BELIEF-FRAMES

(1)	You can catch ______ from other people.
(2)	______ is caused by germs.
(3)	Most people catch ______ in bad weather.
(4)	______ comes from being emotionally upset.
(5)	______ runs in the family.
(6)	When you are overtired, your resistance to ______ is lowered.
(*)	______ comes from not eating the right foods.
(7)	______ can't be cured.
(8)	______ has to run its course.
(9)	______ should be treated with miracle drugs.
(*)	The best cure for ______ is rest.
(10)	______ gets better by itself.
(*)	It's important to catch ______ before it goes too far.
(11)	______ is serious.
(*)	______ should be under a doctor's care.
(12)	______ is a fatal disease.
(13)	You never really get over ______.
(14)	______ is a crippling disease.
(15)	You can have ______ and not know it.
(16)	______ spreads through your whole system.
(*)	______ is painful.
(17)	______ is contagious.
(18)	If a woman comes down with ______ during her pregnancy it harms her child.
(19)	Feeling generally run-down is a sign of ______.
(*)	Dizzy spells are a sign of ______.
(20)	______ affects the heart.
(21)	Your skin breaks out with ______.
(22)	Runny nose is a sign of ______.
(23)	Sore throat comes with ______.
(24)	______ brings on fever.
(25)	Once you've had ______ you can't get it again.
(26)	______ is a children's disease.
(27)	Most people get ______ at some time or other.
(28)	Some people have a tendency to get ______.
(29)	It's safer to have ______ as a child and get it over with.
(30)	______ is a sign of old age.
(*)	______ hits some people harder than others.
(*)	Fat people are more prone to ______.

Work was begun with English-speaking informants. Lists of common diseases were composed, and informants were asked to judge which terms were most common and least ambiguous. At the same time lists of properties relevant to disease states were constructed by using both the informants' and the investigators' folk knowledge about illness. As definitions of disease properties, it was found to be most productive and least ambiguous to use sentence frames approximating ordinary usage, such as "you can catch _____ from other people." (See Metzger & Williams, 1963a; and Frake, 1964; for descriptions of this technique.)

The number of sentences which people know and can use concerning diseases is very large. However, many of these sentences appear to be rephrasings of the same underlying proposition. Sentence frames were selected from the large sample on the basis of their relative independence. The potential generality of the belief across the entire domain of diseases was also used as a criterion in selecting sentences. A sentence frame like "_____ may be carried by anopheles mosquitoes," for example, would be rejected on the basis of its lack of generality since this sentence frame is typically judged to be true for only a very small number of diseases.

In the absence of fully operational guides for the selection of good sentence frames, reliance must be placed on informants' judgments and on the method of analysis. Fortunately, the methods used here do not require that all of the items selected be either unambiguous or especially salient. That is, methods of distrubitional similarity can accept a number of bad items since these items can be identified as poor choices in the course of she analysis itself and then removed. In general, poor items show wide variation in response from individual to individual, little variation across items, and tend to be used differently by the same individual at different times.

For the American sample, it was possible to construct and analyze a pretest. On the basis of the results the poorest items were removed. For the

TABLE 4

AMERICAN-ENGLISH DISEASE TERMS

(1)	Appendicitis	(*)	Arthritis	(*)	Asthma
(2)	Bronchitis	(3)	Cancer	(4)	Chicken pox
(5)	Cold	(6)	Dental cavities	(*)	Dysentery
(7)	Epilepsy	(*)	Gall stones	(8)	Gonorrhea
(*)	Hay fever	(9)	Heart attack	(*)	Hemorrhoids
(*)	Hepatitis	(10)	Influenza	(11)	Laryngitis
(12)	Leukemia	(13)	Malaria	(14)	Measles
(15)	Mononucleosis	(16)	Mumps	(17)	Pneumonia
(18)	Poison ivy	(19)	Polio	(20)	Psychosis
(21)	Rheumatism	(22)	Smallpox	(23)	Strep throat
(24)	Stroke	(25)	Syphilis	(26)	Tonsilitis
(*)	Trench mouth	(27)	Tuberculosis	(28)	Typhoid fever
(29)	Ulcers	(30)	Whooping cough		

TABLE 5

MEXICAN-SPANISH BELIEF-FRAMES

(*) Cuándo una persona ya está desmayada se agarra mas fácilmente ______.
(When a person is already feeling faint he will more easily catch ______.)

(1) ¿Cunde(n) ______ por todo el cuerpo?
(Does ______ spread over the whole body?)

(2) ¿Cuándo tiene ______ la piel le brota granos?
(When you have ______ does the skin break out?)

(*) ¿Se agarra ______ por un desmando?
(Do you get ______ from lack of care?)

(*) ¿Se agarra ______ mas fácilmente por falta de sueño?
(Do you catch ______ more easily because of lack of sleep?)

(3) ¿Hay que descansar en cama especialmente para curar ______?
(Do you need to rest in bed to cure ______?)

(*) ¿Se agarra ______ si está muy caliente el cuerpo?
(Do you catch ______ if your body is hot?)

(4) ¿Cuándo tiene ______ hay hambre?
(When you have ______ do you have your appetite?)

(5) ¿Proviene(n) ______ por ser bilioso?
(Do you get ______ from becoming angry?)

(6) Es difícil sanar ______ luego (rapidmente), dilata(n) para sanar.
(Is it difficult to get well from ______ rapidly?)

(7) Se agarra ______ por mojada (mojadura).
(Do you catch ______ from getting wet?)

(8) ¿Si tiene ______ hay que ir al doctor?
(If you have ______ do you have to go to the doctor?)

(9) ¿Se cura ______ por inyecciónes?
(Is ______ cured by injections?)

(*) ¿Se quita la fuerza con ______?
(Do you lose your strength with ______?)

(10) ¿Indican vágidos ______?
(Do nauseous dizzy spells indicate ______?)

(11) ¿Proviene(n) ______ por los borracheras, viene(n) cuando se embola uno?
(Do you get ______ from getting drunk?)

(12) ¿Es ______ una enfermedad contagiosa? ¿una persona pega ______ a otras?
(Is ______ a contagious disease? Does one person give ______ to another?)

(13) ¿Se puede comer de todo cuando uno tiene ______?
(Can you eat everything when you have ______?)

(14) ¿Se puede morir de ______?
(Can you die from ______?)

(*) ¿Manda Dios ______
(Does God send ______?)

(*) ¿Se agarra ______ mas fácilemente por falta de vitaminas?
(Do you catch ______ more easily because of a lack of vitamins?)

(*) A veces se mejora(n) ______ sin medicina.
(At times can you get better from ______ without medicine?)

(*) ¿Aunque se cura de una vez ______ sigue sufriendo?
(Even after you have gotten over or have been cured from ______ do you continue suffering?)

(15) ¿Da(n) ______ un dolor de garganta?
(Do you have a sore throat with ______?)

(16) ¿Se puede respirar bien cuando tiene ______?
(Can you breathe well when you have ______?)

TABLE 5 (Continued)

(17) ¿Está(n) ______ acompañado(a) (s) con dolores de los huesos?
(Is ______ accompanied by pains in the bones?)
(18) ¿Si tiene ______ necesita tomar cosas frescas (y/o frías)?
(If you have ______ do you need to take cold things?)
(*) ¿Unas personas resisten ______ más y otras resisten ______ menos?
(Do some people resist ______ more and others resist ______ less?)
(19) ¿Proviene(n) ______ por brujería?
(Does ______ come from witchcraft?)
(*) ¿Da(n) ______ un dolor de cabeza?
(Do you get a headache with ______?)
(*) ¿Tienen los hombres ______ más frecuentemente que las mujures?
(Do men have ______ more frequently than women?)
(*) ¿Provienen dolores de las coyunturas por ______?
(Do you get pains in the joints from ______?)
(20) ¿Necesita tomar cosas calientes si una persona tiene ______?
(Do you need to take hot things if you have ______?)
(21) ¿Da(n) ______ mucho escalofrío?
(Do you get lots of chills and fever with ______?)
(22) ¿Es ______ una enfermedad solo de niños?
(Is ______ a sickness only of children?)
(*) ¿Tiene(n) ______ distintas muestras en personas diferentes?
(Does ______ have distinct forms in different persons?)
(*) ¿Hay remedios caseros para ______?
(Are there home remedies for ______?)
(23) ¿Da(n) ______ calentura?
(Does a fever come with ______?)
(24) ¿Les ataca(n) ______ mas frecuentemente a los viejitos?
(Does ______ attack old people more frequently?)
(25) ¿Da(n) ______ un dolor de oídos?
(Do you get an earache with ______?)
(*) ¿Les ataca(n) ______ mas frecuentemente a las personas más gordas?
(Do they attack more frequently people who are fat?)
(*) ¿Trae el aire ______?
(Does the air bring ______?)
(*) ¿Proviene(n) ______ por sangre mala?
(Does ______ come from bad blood?)
(*) ¿A algunas personas les da(n) ______ con más gravedad que a otras?
(Does ______ hit some people harder than others?)
(26) ¿Puede agarrarse como dos, tres mas veces ______?
(Can you catch ______ two, three, or more times?)
(*) ¿______ tiene(n) un solo remedio?
(Does ______ have only one remedy?)
(27) ¿Proviene(n) ______ por microbios?
(Does ______ come from microbes?)
(28) ¿Se agarra ______ si está muy frío el cuerpo?
(Do you catch ______ if your body is cold?)
(29) ¿Si tiene ______ hay que ir al médico?
(If you have ______ is it necessary to go to the curer?)
(30) ¿Se agarra a jovenes ______ más frecuentemente que a viejos?
(Does ______ attack children more frequently than old people?)

TABLE 6

Mexican-Spanish Disease Terms

(*)	Los vichos	Little worms (in stomach)
(*)	La lombrisera	Large worms (in intestines)
(1)	Los bronquios	Bronchitis (very serious, cough)
(*)	La detencíon	Menstrual irregularity
(2)	Dolor de estómago	Stomach ache
(3)	Las diarreas	Diarrhea
(4)	El musuzuelo	Infant bronchitis (up to 1 month old)
(5)	La enlechadura	Illness communicated through mothers' milk (if she had gotten overheated)
(6)	El juego (de la boca)	Sores in the mouth
(7)	La tosferina	Whooping cough
(8)	La costipacíon	Congestion (difficulty breathing, hoarse)
(*)	Dolor de hígado	Liver ailment
(9)	La costipacíon de pecho	Congestion of the chest
(10)	La herida	Wound
(11)	La quemadura	Burn
(12)	La disentería blanca	White dysentery
(13)	La disipela	Shame (infection of the face, from embarrassment or shame)
(*)	El orejon	Swelling behind the ear
(*)	La rasquina	Skin infection
(*)	La nube de ojo	Filming of the eye
(*)	La enritacíon	Irritability (sleeplessness, lack of energy, burning of the body)
(14)	El espanto	Fright
(*)	El aire, el ahigre	Air (strikes the waist)
(15)	Mal parto	Difficult childbirth
(16)	La fiebre	Fever
(*)	Los tumores	Tumors
(17)	El paludismo	Malaria
(*)	Mal de ojo	Conjunctivitis
(18)	Dolor de garganta	Sore throat
(*)	Mal digestíon	Indigestion (swollen stomach, watery feces)
(19)	La pasmasón	Sinus infection (green mucus, facial pain)
(20)	La cruda	Hangover
(21)	La pulmonía	Pneumonia (blood in mucus)
(22)	La viruela	Smallpox
(*)	El cólico de pecho	Illness communicated through mothers' milk (if she gets angry, stomach ache, death)
(23)	La debilidad	Debility
(*)	La quebradura de niño	Inflammation of the testicles, of a child
(24)	La disentería roja	Red dysentery
(*)	Los nacidos	Boils
(25)	El sarampíon	Measles
(26)	La deposicíon	Upset stomach (vomiting)
(27)	El hinchazón	Swelling
(28)	Los ataques	Fits
(*)	Dolor de muela	Toothache
(29)	El catarro	Cold
(30)	El desarollo	Pubescence
(*)	La ventiadura	Air (twists the face to one side)
(*)	El empacho	Loss of appetite
(*)	El comeson	Itching (all over the body)

two Mexican samples, however, there was insufficient time for the administration and analysis of a pretest. Instead a large sample of disease terms were rated by three Mexican informants for familiarity, and the 50 most common diseases were retained. With respect to disease properties, a deliberate attempt was made to translate a number of the American-English sentence frames into Mexican-Spanish, despite some awkwardness and strangeness of the resulting constructions. These translations were done because without some comparability in beliefs, it would be impossible to show that the different cultural groups have different categories of disease. If all the Mexican-Spanish sentence frames were quite divergent in meaning from the American-English frames, any difference in results could be ascribed to the difference in properties used to categorize diseases. Difference in the conceptual organization, while indicated by the very difficulty of obtaining translation equivalents, would remain undemonstrated. However, along with the translations, the majority of sentence frames used were culturally appropriate.

The American-English belief-frames and disease terms are presented in Tables 3 and 4. The Mexican-Spanish belief-frames and disease terms, with translations, are presented in Tables 5 and 6.

The task given to each informant consisted of stating for every one of the sentence frames whether or not the insertion of each of the diseases into the frame would make the sentence true or false. Thus, an informant taking the American-English test would be asked for sentence frame number (1). "You can catch ______ from other people," whether that was true for (1) appendicitis, (2) arthritis, (3) asthma, etc. The test was given orally to the Spanish-speaking informants, while a dittoed form was filled out by the American informants. The pretest indicated that the American informants preferred to answer on a scale, rather than give simple "Yes–No" answers. A five-point scale was therefore developed for the final test form, and administered with the following instructions:

> On the left of each page is a list of illnesses. Each of these illnesses is to be substituted into the blank space in the statement at the top of the page. Indicate how well you think each illness fits into the statement on the scale to the right of that illness. You are given five choices, labeled at the top.

Example:

______ is an allergic reaction.

	definitely:	probably:	possibly:	probably not:	definitely not:
1. Cancer:	________:	________:	________:	___________:	___________:

The Mexican informants, on the other hand, did not seem willing to accept a continuous scale, and so their responses were restricted to "Yes," "At times" (a veces si, a veces no), or "No."

For the final form of the American-English test, 38 diseases and 38 sentence frames were rated by every informant, reduced from the original 56 disease terms and 56 sentence frames given in the pretest. For the Mexican-Spanish test, 50 disease terms and 50 sentence frames were presented to every informant. This means that for an American informant, there were 38 × 38 or 1444 different questions to be answered; for the Mexican informants the number was even larger (50 × 50 or 2500). The time needed for Mexican informants to complete the forms averaged somewhat more than a day since the repitiousness of question forms rapidly builds up a special type of fatique. For their time, informants were paid according to local rates.

Data Analysis: Initial Problems

There are numerous techniques for the analysis of data matrices of the type illustrated in Table 1. Three of these techniques have been used with the American and Mexican disease data: factor analysis, a special form of hierarchical clustering, and nonmetric multidimensional scaling.

Factor Analysis

We begin with an extensive use of factor analysis, hoping to be able to complete our analysis with this technique alone. For each cultural group of informants, and for each individual, two factor analyses were performed; the first based on the intercorrelations of beliefs across diseases, and the second on the intercorrelations of diseases across beliefs. The BMD computer program for factor analysis and the Varimax technique of factor rotations were used (Dixon, 1968). For the group analyses, correlations between items were calculated across all individuals, so that for the American sample, for example, each correlation was based on 30 × 10 or 300 observations. The highest correlation for each variable was used as an estimate of communality. A Varimax rotation of factors was limited in the first ten factors, and from this set of ten, only those factors which contained at least one item with a loading greater than ±.40 were selected for examination.

The results of the factor analyses were not satisfactory. The first ten factors accounted for only 49% of the variance, and the first three factors only 32%. In the Mexican data the proportion of variance accounted for was even lower. The factor analyses of individual protocols and the analyses of disease terms generally accounted for more of the total variance, but yielded less interpretable factors.

Even more discouraging than the low variance proportion of variance accounted for was the instability of factor dimensions. Taking out one or two subjects from the group sample or removing one or two variables from the correlation matrix seemed to have a large effect on changing the composition of the factors, with variables recombining in each different analysis in kaleidoscopic fashion.

Finally, an attempt was made to check back on the way the factor dimensions related to the original scrors. First the factor dimensions were used to partition the disease terms and the belief-frames, respectively, into discrete classes. Then the original data matrices were examined to see if distinct patterns of scores could be found. It was expected that disease terms which belonged to one particular dimension would show similar profiles of scores across factor groupings of belief-frames. Unfortunately, no discernable pattern of score profiles was found.

Since the factor analyses were found so be inadequate, it was felt that some means of simplifying the data was needed so that other techniques of analysis could be applied, and the results could be compared with the input data. An examination of the individual data matrices showed no strong subgroupings of informants either within the American or the Mexican samples. Correlations between all individuals within American and Mexican groups were computed, and no apparent clustering of individuals emerged. (For the Mexican sample this result was surprising, since it was expected that the bilinguals would emerge as a distinct subgroup. Perhaps it could be shown that bilingual informants use Ladino categories when speaking Spanish, but Indian categories when speaking Tzeltal.)

The mean correlation between individuals was +.57 for the American sample and +.31 for the Mexican sample. The variance of the between-individual correlations is very small. The American sample correlations range from +.50 to +.64. The Mexican sample correlations range from +.02 to +.52, with 80% of the correlations between +.26 to +.42. The low variance of the between-individual correlations appears to be a result of a common cultural phenomenon: items or traits tend to either be shared by the entire group, or to be unique to individuals (D'Andrade, 1959). As a result of the high number of items shared by the entire group, the same items tend to affect the degree of similarity between individuals, producing similar correlations between individuals.

To illustrate this sharing phenomenon, imagine a statistician who visits two typical homes in some cultural group. On the basis of these visits, he estimates that roughly 40% of all the household items which he counted were shared by both houses, while 60% were unique to each household. On the basis of this estimate and with the assumption of independent assortment of items, he calculates that if he visits five pairs of houses, he will find on the average only 1% of the items will be shared by all ten houses, i.e., $.4^5$. However, when a census of items across a number of households is actually taken, the results usually do not support the independent assortment of items assumption. Instead, a much larger number than expected are found to be shared by all households, and a larger number than expected are also found to be unique (see Roberts, 1951, for an example of such a census of cultural items).

On the basis of the consistent between-individual correlations and the evidence of cultural sharing, it was decided to use the total group scores for the American and Mexican samples in further analysis of the data.

Using the group scores, the means and standard deviations for each disease term and each belief-frame were calculated. It was found that more belief-frames showed extreme scores on one end of the rating scale than disease terms, with some belief-frames being rated almost "true" across all diseases (e.g., for the American sample, "_____ should be under a doctor's care") and other belief-frames being rated as "false" across almost all disease terms (e.g., for the Mexican sample, "At times can you get better from _____ without medicine"). Disease terms, on the other hand, typically tended to be rated "true" for some belief-frames and rated "false" for others.

One consequence of the high number of individual belief-frames which are rated on only one end of the scale is that the correlations between disease terms are inflated since the extreme scores of the different belief-frames give any two disease terms somewhat similar profiles.

In order to simplify the data, and to correct for the extreme scores of many of the belief-frames, the data were dichotomized by using the mean score for each belief-frame as the basis for deciding whether a score was to be considered a Yes or a No. Thus for an American belief-frame with a mean score across disease terms of 3.2, any score for a disease term on that belief-frame which is equal to or above 3.2 is considered a Yes, while any score below 3.2 is considered a No.

Before dichotomizing the data, for both the American and Mexican samples, a total of 30 belief-frames and 30 disease terms were selected from the original pool of frames and terms. The selection was based on the variance of group scores. A belief-frame, for example, might have low variance for two major reasons: because of a large amount of disagreement between informants on scores, or because the belief-frame elicited the same, usually extreme, score for each informant on each disease term. In

TABLE 7

AMERICAN SAMPLE DICHOTOMIZED DATA

		CATCH 1	GERMS 2	WEATHR 3	EMOTNL 4	INHERI 5	RESIST 6	NOCURE 7	COURSE 8	DRUGS 9	ITSELF 10	SERIOU 11	FATAL 12	NEVER 13	CRIPPL 14	NOTKNO 15	SPREAD 16	CONTAG 17	PREGNA 18	RUNDOW 19	HEART 20	SKIN 21	NOSE 22	THROAT 23	FEVER 24	ONCE 25	CHILDR 26	MOST 27	TENDEN 28	SAFECH 29	OLDAGE 30
appendicitis	1											X	X			X									X	X		X		X	
bronchitis	2		X	X			X			X	X	X				X		X					X	X	X				X		X
cancer	3					X		X				X	X	X	X	X	X		X	X	X	X							X		X
chicken pox	4	X	X				X		X	X	X						X	X	X			X			X	X	X	X		X	
a cold	5	X	X	X			X	X	X		X					X	X	X		X			X	X	X			X	X		
dental cavities	6					X		X						X		X												X	X		
epilepsy	7				X	X		X				X		X	X	X											X				
gonorrhea	8	X	X							X		X	X		X	X		X	X			X									
heart attack	9				X	X	X	X	X			X	X	X	X	X			X		X								X		X
influenza	10	X	X	X			X		X	X	X						X	X	X	X			X	X	X			X			
laryngitis	11	X	X	X			X		X	X	X							X						X	X		X	X	X		
leukemia	12					X		X	X	X		X	X	X	X	X	X		X	X	X					X	X				
malaria	13		X							X		X	X	X			X		X	X	X				X						
measles	14	X	X				X		X		X						X	X	X			X	X		X	X	X	X		X	
mononucleosis	15	X	X	X			X		X	X	X					X	X	X	X	X	X		X		X						
mumps	16	X	X				X		X		X						X	X	X	X				X	X	X	X	X		X	
pneumonia	17	X	X	X			X		X	X	X	X	X				X	X	X	X			X	X	X						
poison ivy	18	X							X		X							X				X						X	X		
polio	19	X	X					X	X	X		X	X	X	X		X	X	X	X	X					X	X				
psychosis	20				X	X	X	X				X		X	X	X													X		X
rheumatism	21			X		X		X	X	X				X	X	X	X			X									X		X
smallpox	22	X	X						X	X		X	X				X	X	X			X			X	X	X			X	
strep throat	23	X	X	X			X		X	X	X							X						X	X		X	X			
stroke	24				X	X	X	X	X			X	X	X	X		X		X		X								X		X
syphilis	25	X	X							X		X	X		X	X	X	X	X		X	X									
tonsilitis	26		X	X			X									X								X	X	X	X	X		X	
tuberculosis	27	X	X				X	X	X	X		X	X	X		X	X	X	X	X						X					
typhoid fever	28	X	X	X			X		X	X		X	X				X	X	X						X	X	X			X	
ulcers	29				X	X								X		X													X		X
whooping cough	30	X	X	X			X			X	X		X					X	X				X	X	X	X	X			X	

either case, low variance was taken to indicate an unsatisfactory item. The reduction of the data to a 30 × 30 matrix was determined in part by the limitations of some of the available computer programs, and by the desire to use only relatively solid data for methodological exploration. Deleted items are indicated in Tables 3, 4, 5, and 6 by an asterisk instead of a number. Tables 7 and 8 present the 30 × 30 dichotomized data matrices for the American and Mexican samples. An X in the intersection of a particular row and column indicates that the disease term in that row has an above average group mean score of "likelihood" for the particular belief-frame in that column. At the top of Tables 7 and 8, each belief-frame is abbreviated by using a single word or part-word. The single word does not represent very accurately the full meaning of the actual belief-frame.

TABLE 8

MEXICAN SAMPLE DICHOTOMIZED DATA

		SPREAD 1	SKIN 2	NEEDREST 3	APPETIT 4	ANGER 5	SLOWLY 6	GET WET 7	DOCTOR 8	INJECTI 9	DIZZY S 10	DRINK 11	CONTAGI 12	CAN EAT 13	CAN DIE 14	THROAT 15	BREATHE 16	BONES 17	COLD ME 18	WITCHCR 19	HOT MED 20	CHILLS 21	CHILDRE 22	CALENTU 23	OLD MOR 24	EARACHE 25	TWO THR 26	MICROBE 27	COLD BO 28	MEDICO 29	KIDS MO 30
bronchitis	1		X	X			X	X	X	X			X		X	X		X			X	X	X	X	X	X	X	X	X		
stomach ache	2			X		X		X			X	X			X					X	X	X					X	X	X	X	
diarrhea	3	X				X			X	X	X	X			X		X			X	X	X			X		X	X	X	X	
infant bronchi	4	X	X	X			X	X	X	X					X			X			X	X	X	X		X		X	X	X	X
enlechadura	5	X	X	X		X	X	X	X	X					X		X	X			X	X	X	X				X	X	X	X
mouth sores	6		X			X			X	X		X	X			X	X		X					X		X	X	X		X	
whooping cough	7				X		X	X	X	X	X		X		X	X			X	X		X	X	X	X	X		X			X
congestion	8	X		X			X	X	X	X	X	X			X	X		X			X	X		X	X	X	X	X	X	X	
chest congesti	9		X	X		X	X	X			X	X			X	X		X			X			X	X	X	X	X	X	X	
wound	10				X		X		X	X	X	X			X				X	X		X		X		X	X				X
burn	11		X	X	X		X		X	X	X	X			X		X		X			X		X			X				X
white dysenter	12				X	X	X		X		X	X					X	X				X			X		X	X	X	X	
shame	13	X	X		X	X								X			X	X	X			X		X			X			X	X
fright	14	X		X	X						X			X	X		X	X	X	X				X			X		X	X	X
diff. childbir	15			X	X	X	X	X	X	X	X				X			X		X	X	X		X					X	X	X
fever	16	X	X	X		X	X	X	X	X	X		X		X			X	X	X		X		X		X					
malaria	17	X	X	X	X		X	X	X	X	X	X	X	X	X		X	X			X	X		X	X			X	X		X
sore throat	18							X	X	X				X		X			X	X	X			X		X	X	X			
sinus infectio	19				X			X	X	X				X		X	X	X	X	X	X					X	X		X		
hangover	20	X										X		X	X	X	X		X						X		X				X
pneumonia	21			X	X		X	X	X	X				X	X			X			X			X	X			X	X		
smallpox	22	X	X	X	X		X		X	X			X		X	X	X		X				X	X		X		X			X
debility	23	X			X	X	X		X	X	X			X	X		X		X						X	X	X		X		
red dysentery	24					X	X				X	X					X	X	X								X	X			
measles	25	X	X	X			X	X	X	X			X			X	X		X				X	X		X		X		X	X
upset stomach	26					X			X	X	X	X			X	X		X			X				X	X	X		X	X	
swelling	27	X		X	X	X	X		X		X			X	X		X			X	X				X		X	X	X	X	
fits	28				X	X	X		X	X	X	X		X	X				X	X	X							X		X	
a cold	29	X						X					X	X		X		X			X			X	X	X	X	X			
pubescency	30			X	X	X	X		X	X	X						X				X									X	

HIERARCHICAL CLUSTERING

The next method to which we turned after the unsatisfactory results of the factor analysis was cluster analysis. A number of different techniques of cluster analysis were developed and tried. At each point, once a technique had been applied to the data, an attempt was made to see how well that techniques ordered the basic data. Given a particular cluster technique, for example, both the belief-frames and the disease terms of each cultural group would be run through the procedure, and the overall result for each group would then be checked by seeing how tightly the Xs within the data matrix were grouped by the row (disease) and column (belief-frame) clustering. The technique which was found to give the best and most interpretable results is a modification of the Johnson (1967) hierarchical clustering technique (although at the time this method was developed, Johnson's work was not known to us).

Table 9, 10, 11, and 12 illustrate how this technique works. The data

TABLE 9

Original Apachean Data (Percentage of Cognate Lexical Items in the One Hundred Basic Word List)

	Na	Ch	SC	Ji	Li
Navaho	—	94	89	89	87
Chiricahua	94	—	91	92	91
San Carlos	89	91	—	87	84
Jicarilla	89	92	87	—	91
Lipan	87	91	84	91	—

in Table 9 consist of the number of cognate items found for a modified one-hundred-word basic vocabulary word list. The linguistic groups are Navaho, Chiricahua, San Carlos, Jicarilla, and Lipan. These groups are considered by linguists to constitute the Southern Athapaskan or Apachean languages spoken in Arizona and New Mexico (Hoijer, 1956).

Generally linguists assume that languages change at a more or less uniform rate. The rate of retention for basic, universal, and noncultural portions of a language's vocabulary has been approximated by empirical study to be about 81% per 1000 years (Lees, 1953; Swadesh, 1952, 1955). Thus the more items of a basic vocabulary shared by any two languages, the more recently these two languages are thought to have separated. Lexicostatistic data have been selected for this example because the underlying model of related languages separating at various times from some original protolanguage fits neatly the rationale behind hierarchical clustering.

The clustering procedure begins by treating every object (language) as a separate entity, as in the original data given in Table 9. Then, based on the similarity scores, the two most similar entities are selected. In Table 9, Navaho and Chiricahau, with a percentage score of 94, are the most similar entities. Using the mean of the original similarity scores, these two languages are treated as a single entity.

Thus in Table 10, .90, the coefficient given for the relation of the new

TABLE 10

First Hierarchical Clustering Modification

	Na–Ch	SC	Ji	Li
Na–Ch	—	90	90.5	89
SC	90	—	87	84
Ji	90.5	87	—	91
Li	89	84	91	—

TABLE 11

SECOND HIERARCHICAL CLUSTERING MODIFICATION

	Na–Ch	SC	Ji–Li
Na–Ch	—	90	89.75
SC	90	—	85.5
Ji–Li	89.75	85.5	—

entity Navaho–Chiricahua to San Carlos is the mean of the two previous scores Navaho to San Carlos (.89) and Chiricahua to San Carlos (.91).

The same process is then repeated with the most similar pair of the new entities selected, and then combined into a new higher level entity. In Table 10, the highest similarity score is between Jicarilla and Lipan (.91); these two are therefore combined into a new entity; and new similarity scores are computed based on the mean scores calculated from the original scores shown in Table 9.

Again, the same procedure is repeated, and Navaho–Chiricahua is grouped in a single third-order entity with San Carlos. The new set of similarity scores for the new table is calculated from the scores in the original table, not from the immediately preceding table of similarities, in order to give equal weight to each of the original objects, and not to overweight the last entity brought into the new grouping.

The final step is to group Navaho–Chiricahua–San Carlos–Jicarilla–Lipan into a single object.

The process described above can be represented as a tree diagram, as in Figure 1.

A second part of this hierarchical clustering procedure calculates the number and percentage of taxonomic errors for each object. A taxonomic error occurs when A has a lower similarity rating with B than with C, but the taxonomic path from object A to object C is longer than the path from object A to object B. For any three objects, the two objects which are dominated by the lowest node are considered closest together. Calculation of taxonomic errors thus does not depend on the coefficient level at which

TABLE 12

THIRD HIERARCHICAL CLUSTERING MODIFICATION

	Na–Ch–Sc	Ji–Li
Na–Ch–Sc	—	88.33
Ji–Li	88.33	—

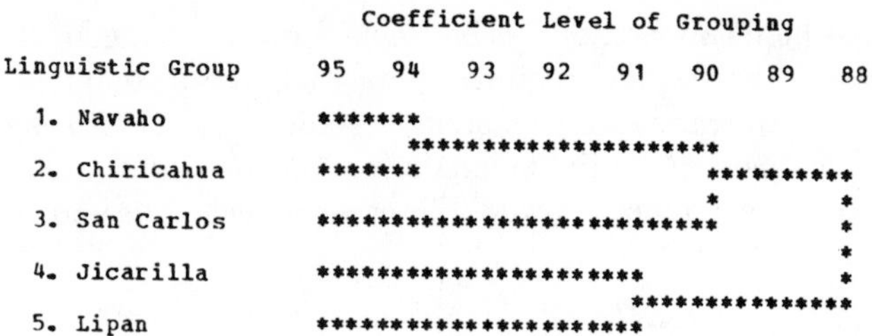

FIG. 1. Taxonomy for Apachean languages based on hierarchical clustering technique.

clustering takes place, but only on the structural form of the taxonomy. In the taxonomy for Apachean languages, there is a taxonomic error between Chiricahua, San Carlos, and Jicarilla. From the tree in Figure 1, it can be seen that Chiricahua is closer in the taxonomy to San Carlos than to Jicarilla, yet Chicircahua has a greater percentage of shared items with Jicarilla (.92) than with San Carlos (.91). A second taxonomic error also occurs between Jicarilla, Lipan, and Chiricahua. Potentially, there are five possible errors for Navaho and Chiricahua, four possible errors for San Carlos, and three possible errors for Jicarilla and Lipan. That is, according to the taxonomic structure in Figure 1, the following rankings of similarity scores are expected:

1. Navaho–Chiricahua	(94)	≧	Navaho–San Carlos	(89)	
2. Navaho–Chiricahua	(94)	≧	Navaho–Jicarilla	(89)	
3. Navaho–Chiricahua	(94)	≧	Navaho–Lipan	(87)	
4. Navaho–San Carlos	(89)	≧	Navaho–Jicarilla	(89)	
5. Navaho–San Carlos	(89)	≧	Navaho–Lipan	(87)	
6. Chiricahua–Navaho	(94)	≧	Chiricahua–San Carlos	(91)	
7. Chiricahua–Navaho	(94)	≧	Chiricahua–Jicarilla	(92)	
8. Chiricahua–Navaho	(94)	≧	Chiricahua–Lipan	(91)	
9. Chiricahua–San Carlos	(91)	≧	Chiricahua–Jicarilla	(92)	ERROR
10. Chiricahua–San Carlos	(91)	≧	Chiricahua–Lipan	(91)	
11. San Carlos–Navaho	(89)	≧	San Carlos–Jicarilla	(87)	
12. San Carlos–Navaho	(89)	≧	San Carlos–Lipan	(84)	
13. San Carlos–Chiricahua	(91)	≧	San Carlos–Jicarilla	(87)	
14. San Carlos–Chiricahua	(91)	≧	San Carlos–Lipan	(84)	
15. Jicarilla–Lipan	(91)	≧	Jicarilla–Navaho	(89)	
16. Jicarilla–Lipan	(91)	≧	Jicarilla–Chiricahua	(92)	ERROR
17. Jicarilla–Lipan	(91)	≧	Jicarilla–San Carlos	(87)	
18. Lipan–Jicarilla	(91)	≧	Lipan–Navaho	(87)	
19. Lipan–Jicarilla	(91)	≧	Lipan–Chiricahua	(91)	
20. Lipan–Jicarilla	(91)	≧	Lipan–San Carlos	(84)	

It should be mentioned that using some form of averaging of similarity ratings, as we have done, requires more than the assumption of monotonicity. The hierarchical clustering technique developed by Johnson (1967), which uses either the minimum or the maximum similarity rating of one subject in the cluster with the other objects, does not require the

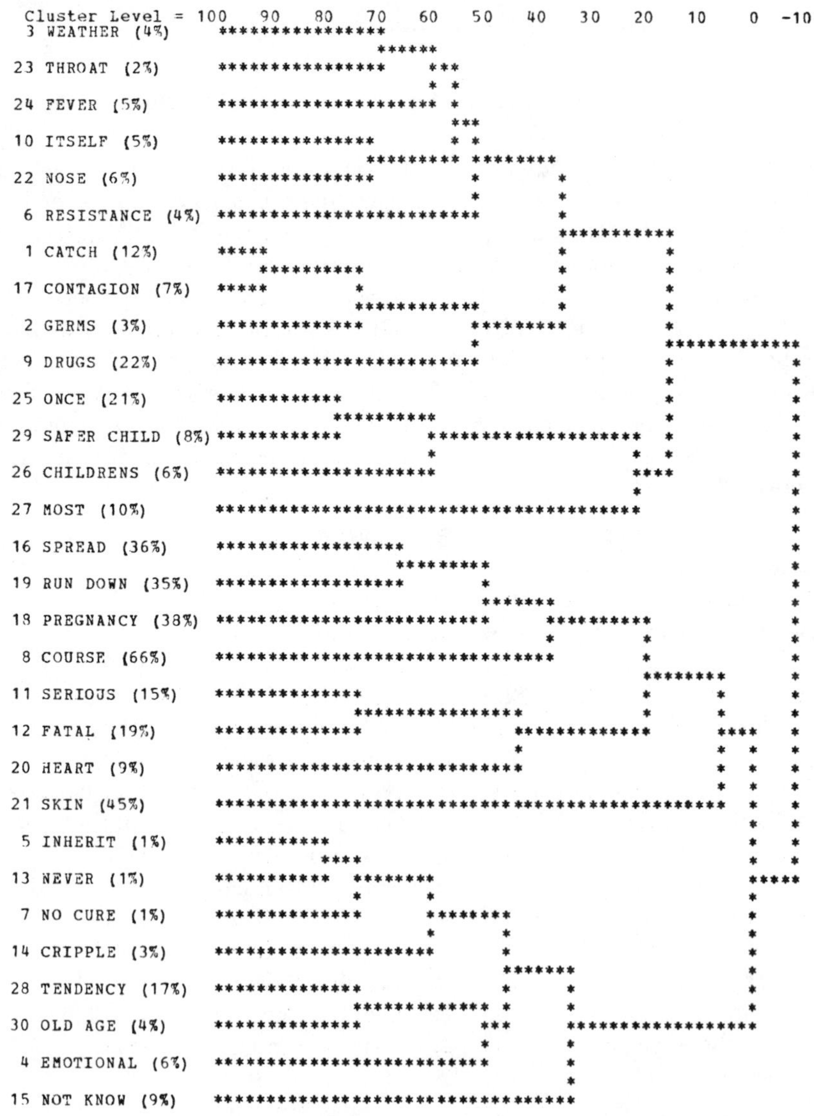

FIG. 2. Taxonomy for American-English belief-frames.

assumption of monotonicity. However, in many cases the maximum methods yield different results, leaving the investigator to face an arbitrary choice between structures. The strategy used here is to make stronger assumptions, but then to test these assumptions by counting taxonomic errors to find out how well the data fit one particular taxonomic organiza-

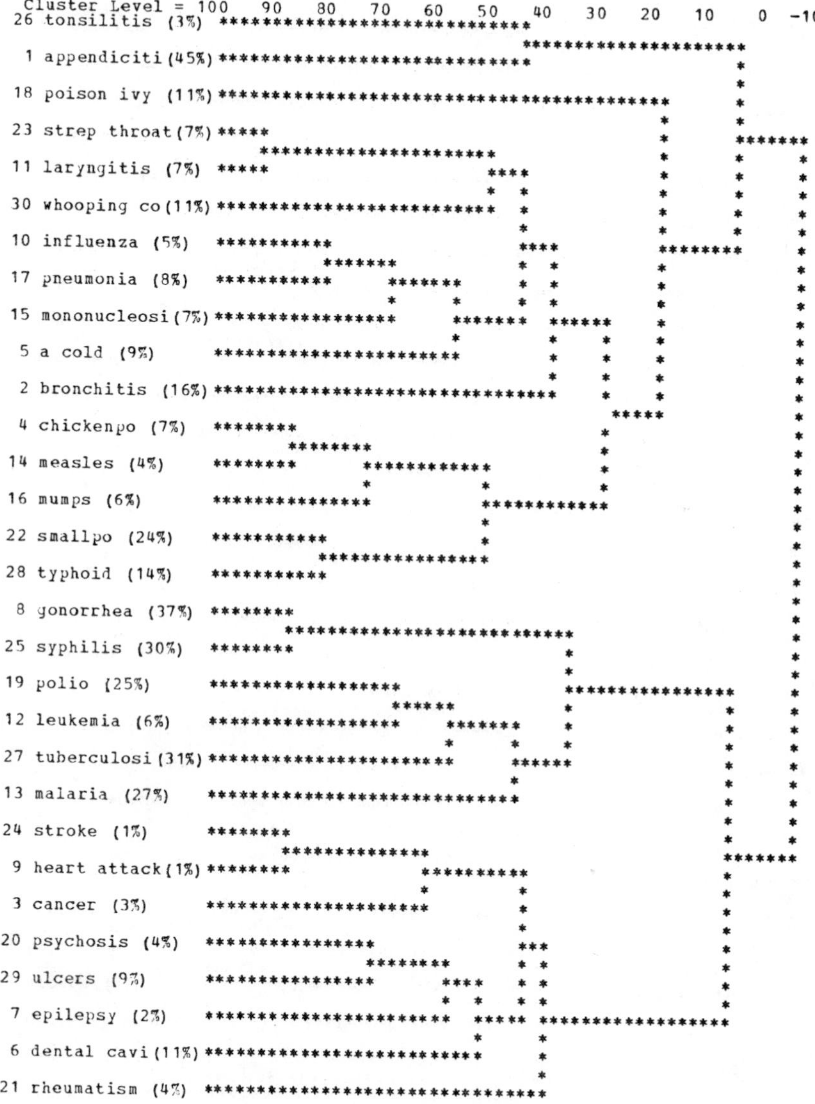

FIG. 3. Taxonomy for American-English disease terms.

tion. For the American and Mexican disease term and belief-frame data, in no case did either the maximum or minimum hierarchical clustering techniques lead to a reduction in total percentage of taxonomic errors over the averaging technique. Of course, other data might give different results. Ideally, one would like to be able to construct the taxonomy which

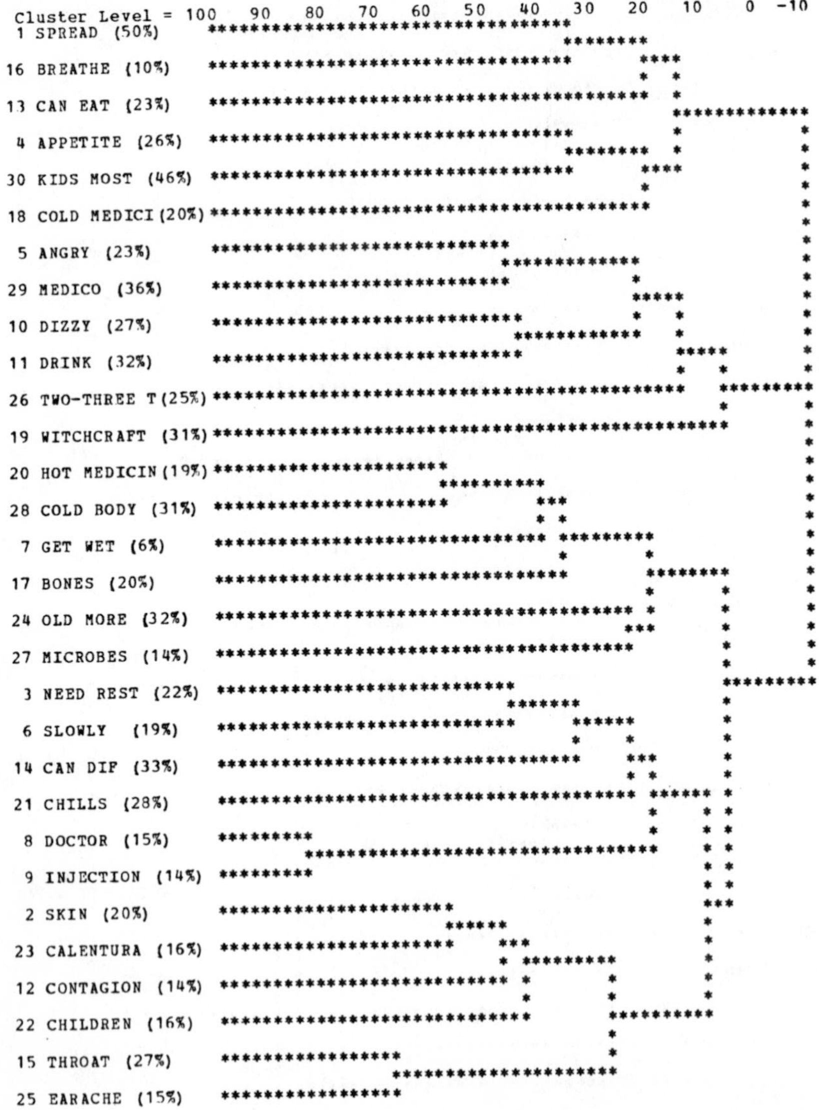

Fig. 4. Taxonomy for Mexican-Spanish belief-frames.

gave the greatest degree of clustering (i.e., number of nodes) and the minimum number of taxonomic errors. At present we have not discovered a direct decision procedure to construct a taxonomy in this way.

To use the hierarchical clustering technique on the disease term and the belief-frame data, it was first necessary to calculate some type of coefficient

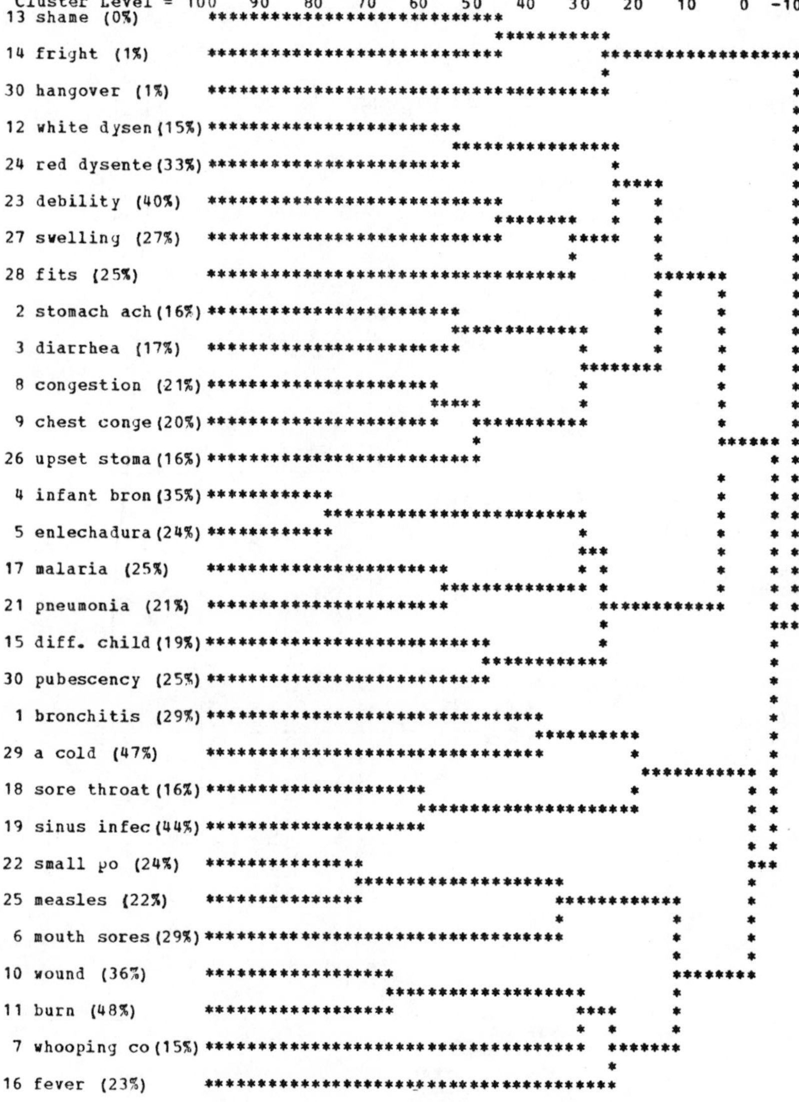

FIG. 5. Taxonomy for Mexican-Spanish disease terms.

which would represent degree of similarity between items. After some experimentation, we selected the Pearsonian correlation coefficient. Correlations between disease terms were calculated across belief-frame scores, while correlations between belief-frames were calculated across disease term scores.

The results of the hierarchical clustering analysis of the American and Mexican data are presented in Figures 2, 3, 4, and 5. The number in parentheses following each item is the percentage of taxonomic errors for that item.

Generally the taxonomic structures given by the hierarchical clustering

TABLE 13

DISTRIBUTIONAL PATTERNING BASED ON HIERARCHICAL CLUSTERING FOR AMERICAN SAMPLE

```
                   |W T F I N R|C C G D|O S C M|S R P C|S F H S|I N N C T O E N
                   |E H E T O E|A O E R|N A H O|P U R O|E A E K|N E O R E L M O
                   |A R V S S S|T N R U|C F I S|R N E U|R T A I|H V C I N D O T
                   |T O E E E I|C T M G|E E L T|E D G R|I A R N|E E U P D A T K
                   |H A R L   S|H A S S|  C D  |A O N S|O L T  |R R R P E G N N
                   |R T   F   T|  G    |  H R  |D W A E|U      |I   E L N E L O
                   |323241022 6 117 2 925292627161918 811122021|513 7142830 415
tonsilitis       26|X X X     X|    X  |X X X X|       |       |              X  **
appendicitis      1|    X      |       |X X   X|       |X X    |              X  *
poison ivy       18|      X    |X X    |      X|      X|      X|        X        *
strep throat     23|X X X X   X|X X X X|    X X|      X|       |                 ***
laryngitis       11|X X X X   X|X X X X|    X X|      X|       |        X        * *
whooping cough   30|X X X X X X|X X X X|X X X  |    X  |  X    |                 * *
influenza        10|X X X X X X|X X X X|      X|X X X X|       |                 ** *
pneumonia        17|X X X X X X|X X X X|       |X X X X|X X    |                 *
mononucleosis    15|X   X X X X|X X X X|       |X X X X|    X  |              X  ***
a cold            5|X X X X X X|X X X  |      X|X X   X|       |    X   X     X  * *
bronchitis        2|X X X X X X|  X X X|       |       |X      |        X X   X  * *
chicken pox       4|    X X   X|X X X X|X X X X|X   X X|      X|                 * *
measles          14|    X X X X|X X X  |X X X X|X   X X|      X|                 * *
mumps            16|  X X X   X|X X X  |X X X X|X X X X|       |                 **** *
smallpox         22|    X      |X X X X|X X X  |X   X X|X X   X|                 *
typhoid FEVER    28|X   X     X|X X X X|X X X  |X   X X|X X    |                 *
gonorrhea         8|           |X X X X|       |    X  |X X   X|      X       X  *
syphilis         25|           |X X X X|       |X   X  |X X X X|      X       X  *
polio            19|           |X X X X|X   X  |X X X X|X X X  |  X X X          **** *
leukemia         12|           |      X|X   X  |X X X X|X X X  |X X X X       X  * *
tuberculosis     27|          X|X X X X|X      |X X X X|X X    |  X X         X  * *
malaria          13|    X      |    X X|       |X X X  |X X X  |  X              ***
stroke           24|          X|       |       |X   X X|X X X  |X X X X X X X    *
heart attack      9|          X|       |       |    X X|X X X  |X X X X X X X X  ** *
cancer            3|           |       |       |X X X  |X X X X|X X X X X X   X  * *
psychosis        20|          X|       |       |       |X      |X X X X X X X X  ***
ulcers           29|           |       |       |       |       |X X     X X X X  *
epilepsy          7|           |       |    X  |       |X      |X X X X     X X  **
dental cavitie    6|           |       |      X|       |       |X X X   X     X
rheumatism       21|X          |      X|       |X X   X|       |X X X X X X   X
                   |
                   |     *         *       *      *        *           *
                   |     ***********       *      **********           *
                   |          *            *           *               *
                   |          **************           *****************
                   |                 *                         *
                   |                 ***************************
```

TABLE 14

DISTRIBUTIONAL PATTERNING BASED ON HIERARCHICAL CLUSTERING FOR MEXICAN SAMPLE

```
                   S B C A K C|A M D D T W|H C G B O M|N S C C D I|S C C C T E
                   P R A P I O|N E I R W I|O O E O L I|E L A H O N|K A O H H A
                   R E N P D L|G D Z I O T|T L T N D C|E O N I C J|I L N I R R
                   E A   E S D|E I Z N   C|  D   E   R|D W   L T E|N E T L O A
                   A T E T    |R C Y K T H|M   W S M O|R L D L O C|  N A D A C
                   D H A I M M|  O     H C|E B E   O B|E Y I S R T|  T G R T H
                     E T T O E|    S   R R|D O T   R E|S   E     I|  U I E   E
                   11613 43018 529101126192028 7172427 3 61421 8 9 22312221525
shame           13|X X X X X X|X X     X  |      X    |      X    |X X
fright          14|X X X X X X|  X X   X X|  X   X    |X   X      |  X          ********
hangover        20|X X X   X X       X X           X         X               X           *
white dysenter  12|  X   X    |X X X X X  |  X   X X X|  X   X X  |                    *
red dysentery   24|  X       X|X   X X X  |      X   X|  X        |             **     *
debility        23|X X X X   X|X   X   X  |  X     X  |  X X   X X|          X   *     *
swelling        27|X X X X    |X X X   X X|X X     X X|X X X   X  |              *     *
fits            28|    X X   X|X X X X   X|X         X|  X X   X X|              ***   *
---------------------------------------------------------------------------
stomach ache     2|           |X X X X X X|X X X     X|X   X X    |              * *   *
diarrhea         3|X X        |X X X X X X|X X     X X|    X X X X|              * *   *
congestion       8|X          |  X X X X  |X X X X X X|X X X X X X|  X     X X  ** *   *
chest congesti   9|           |X X X X X  |X X X X X X|X X X      |X X     X X     *** *
upset stomach   26|           |X X X X X  |X X   X X  |    X   X X|        X X     * * *
---------------------------------------------------------------------------
infant bronchi   4|X       X  |  X        |X X X X   X|X X X X X X|X X   X   X     * * *
enlechadura      5|X X     X  |X X        |X X X X   X|X X X X X X|X X   X         * * *
malaria         17|X X X X X  |    X X    |X X X X X X|X X X X X X|X X X        **** * *
pneumonia       21|    X X    |           |X X X X X X|X X X   X X|  X               ***
diff. childbir  15|      X X  |X X X     X|X X X X    |X X X X X X|  X               *
pubescency      30|  X   X X  |X   X      |X          |X X     X X|                  *
---------------------------------------------------------------------------
bronchitis       1|           |        X  |X X X X X X|X X X X X X|X X X X X X       *
a cold          29|X   X      |        X  |X X X X X X|           |  X X   X X  **** *
sore throat     18|    X     X|        X X|X   X     X|        X X|  X     X X     * *
sinus infectio  19|  X X X   X|        X X|X X X X    |        X X|        X X     ***
---------------------------------------------------------------------------
smallpox        22|X X   X X X|           |          X|X X X   X X|X X X X X X     *
measles         25|X X     X X|  X        |    X     X|X X     X X|X X X X X X  ** *
mouth sores      6|  X       X|X X   X X  |          X|        X X|X X X   X X   ***
---------------------------------------------------------------------------
wound           10|      X X X|    X X X X|           |  X X X X X|  X       X   *
burn            11|  X   X X X|    X X X  |           |X X X X X X|X X          **
whooping cough   7|      X X X|    X     X|    X   X X|  X X X X X|  X X X X X
fever           16|X         X|X   X     X|    X X    |X X X X X X|X X X     X

                        *           *           *           *           *
                        *           *           *           *************
                        *           *           *                 *
                        *           *           *******************
                        *           *                    *
                        **********************************
```

technique appear to be intelligible in terms of our knowledge of the belief systems about illness found in these two cultures. The American data results appear to be more interpretable, and to fit better with subsequent analyses, than the results for the Mexican data, especially the Mexican-Spanish disease terms. In general, the hierarchical clustering technique does not seem able to analyze "noisy" data as well as the other multidimensional scaling methods used here. How well these taxonomic structures do in showing distributional patterning in the dichotomized data can be seen in Tables 13 and 14, which present the disease term and belief-frame matrices, with items grouped into the taxonomic groupings which were given by the hierarchical clustering technique. The overall clustering of Xs is impressive, although it is clear that items fit into taxonomic groupings only in a "more-or-less" fashion.

Nonmetric Multidimensional Scaling

A third method of analysis which can be used with data matrices of similarity (or dissimilarity) scores has recently been developed by Shepard (1962) and Kruskal (1964a, 1964b). Their technique of multidimensional scaling does not require that the original scores form an equal interval or ratio scale, but only that the scores can be treated as constituting an ordinal or rank order scale. The basic accomplishment of the Shepard–Kruskal multidimensional scaling procedure is that it gives a representation of the degree of similarity between every pair of items in terms of distance measures that are monotonically related to the original similarity scores (the greater the distance between any two items, the less the similarity score for those items). Unlike factor analysis, the Shepard–Kruskal procedure makes no assumption about the nature of the function relating the similarity scores to the distance measures, except monotonicity.

A computer program to carry out this procedure, called M-D-SCAL has been developed by Kruskal. The Stanford 3S version of this program has been used throughout this paper. This program accepts as input a matrix of similarity scores for a set of items, and gives an output of Cartesian coordinates for each item. The number of dimensions to be used in calculating the distances is specified by the investigator. Of course, in most cases the number of dimensions which might actually underly the similarity relations of items is unknown. In such cases the investigator can have the program calculate the interpoint distances first for a large number of dimensions, and then repeat the entire procedure for a smaller and smaller number of dimensions, until the data are finally fitted to a single dimension. Each time the program calculates the interpoint distances for some particular number of dimensions, a goodness of fit measure, called "stress," is given—the larger the stress figure, which ranges from .0 to 1.0, the worse the fit between the interpoint distances and the original similarity scores. By plotting the stress figures against the number of dimensions used, the investigator can decide at what point the decrease in the stress score does not appear to warrant the addition of a further dimension.

The use of the M-D-SCAL program can be illustrated by an analysis of American belief-frames. For similarity ratings Pearsonian correlation

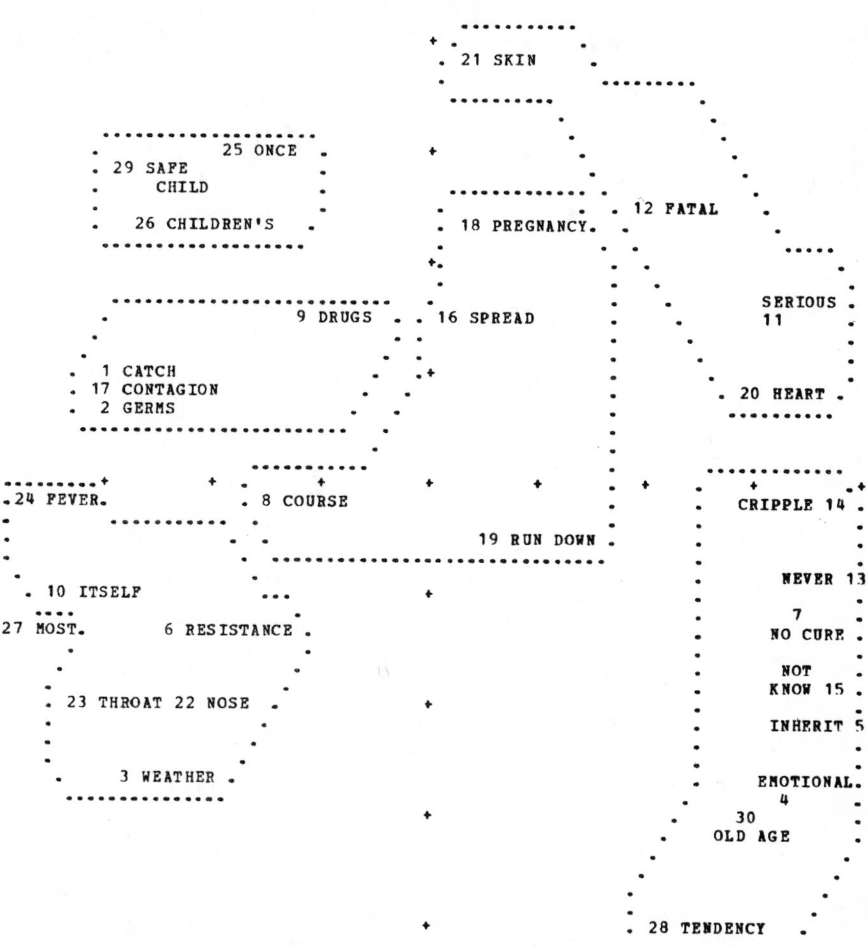

FIG. 6. M-D-SCAL plot for American-English belief-frames with major grouping from hierarchical clustering analysis encircled.

coefficients have been used. The 30 belief-frames were intercorrelated across the binary disease scores, and the complete 30 × 30 symmetrical correlation matrix was used as input. The program was instructed to begin with four dimensions, and reduce by one dimension each cycle until finally a single dimension was reached.

For four dimensions the stress score was .064, for three dimensions .089, for two dimensions .155, and for one dimension .415. Based on the large jump in stress after two dimensions, and the interpretability of the two-

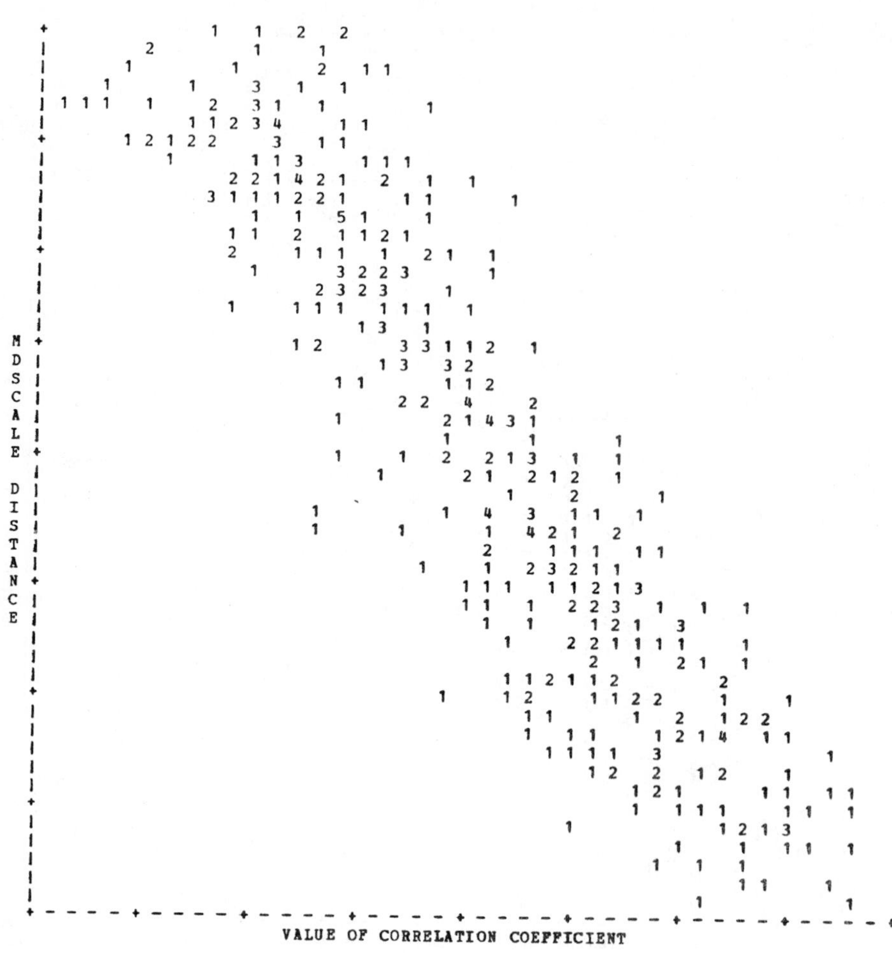

FIG. 7. Frequency plot of M-D-SCAL distances versus original input correlation coefficients for American-English belief-frames.

dimensional results, the two-dimensional distance representation was selected. Figure 6 shows a graphic plot of the 30 belief-frames in two dimensions, with the major groupings from the hierarchical clustering program indicated by dotted outlines.

From the graphic plot of the M-D-SCAL results, it can be seen that the belief-frames relating to contagiousness are close together, flanked on either side by belief-frames relating to children's diseases and to bad-weather colds. Grouped together on the opposite side of the graph are the belief-

TABLE 15

TYPICAL SIMILARITY RATING MATRIX

	1	2	3	4	5	6
1	1.0	.7	.4	.3	.6	.3
2	.7	1.0	.5	.3	.9	.4
3	.4	.5	1.0	.4	.6	.2
4	.8	.3	.4	1.0	.0	.1
5	.6	.9	.6	.0	1.0	.8
6	.3	.4	.2	.1	.8	1.0

frames which involve noncontagion causes of disease, and the related potentially crippling and incurable aspects of such diseases. To the right are the belief-frames which indicate the degree of seriousness of the disease. In the center of the graph are those belief-frames which appear to involve a diffuse internal characteristic of some diseases.

The M-D-SCAL distances between the 30 belief-frames can be compared directly to Pearsonian correlation coefficients which were originally read into the program. A frequency plot of the 435 pairs of M-D-SCAL distances run against the 435 correlation coefficients is presented in Figure 7. It can be seen that the relationship is negative (as the correlations get large, the M-D-SCAL distances get small) and roughly linear. The Pearsonian correlation between the two sets of data is −.912.

Originally we planned to present the M-D-SCAL results for the analysis of all four of the possible sets of intercorrelations: American belief-frames, American disease terms, Mexican belief-frames, and Mexican disease terms. The analyses yielded consistent and interpretable results, and the correlations between the M-D-SCAL distances and the Pearsonian coefficients ranged from −.912 to −.713.

A simpler and more economical means of analyzing the data, suggested by Shepard, is to use the M-D-SCAL program directly on the matrix of original disease term and belief-frame ratings. At first glance, this seems impossible, since the M-D-SCAL program is set up to analyze a square matrix of similarity ratings, where each object is rated against every other. Thus for six objects, the M-D-SCAL program is designed to analyze a matrix of the form shown in Table 15.

However, if we represent items 1 through 3 as diseases, and items 4 through 6 as belief-frames, the original data can be placed in the matrix shown in Table 16.

TABLE 16

THREE DISEASE TERMS RATED FOR THREE BELIEF-FRAMES EMBEDDED IN AN $N \times N$ SIMILARITY MATRIX

		1	2	3	4	5	6
Disease term a	1				6	10	8
Disease term b	2				4	3	9
Disease term c	3				1	5	4
Belief-frame a	4	6	4	1			
Belief-frame b	5	10	3	5			
Belief-frame c	6	8	9	4			

The M-D-SCAL results for American-English diseases are presented in Figure 8. The stress for two dimensions is .176. A check of the frequency plot between the output distances and the input correlation coefficients failed to show any significant degree of nonlinearity.

Since informants were not asked to judge the similarity of diseases or the similarity of belief-frames, there are no values for those sections of the matrix. This would seem to bar a matrix including both disease terms and belief-frames from use in the M-D-SCAL program. However, the M-D-SCAL program has a special feature which permits it to accept matrices with missing values. As a result, the matrix illustrated in Table 16 would be acceptable to the program. The fact that whole sections of the matrix are missing does not affect the action of the program, which is to try to fit all the similarity ratings between pairs of items to distance measures. Of course, in a partial matrix there are some items which have no similarity ratings, and so there is no rating to help directly fix the distance between those pairs of items. The distance measure obtained between such pairs is therefore a result of their distance relations to other items for which ratings are available, so that the distance measure which is calculated for items which are missing similarity ratings is derived by a kind of triangulation method.

Because of the large differences in means and variances for the belief-frames, the original group scores for the American and Mexican samples were normalized by belief-frame so that the overall means and variances across all 30 disease terms for each belief-frame would be equal. (An attempt was made first to use just the dichotomized data, but the results, while encouraging, were much less impressive than the results from the normalized data.) The normalized data was presented as in Table 16 in a 60×60 matrix, with missing scores indicated by negative numbers.

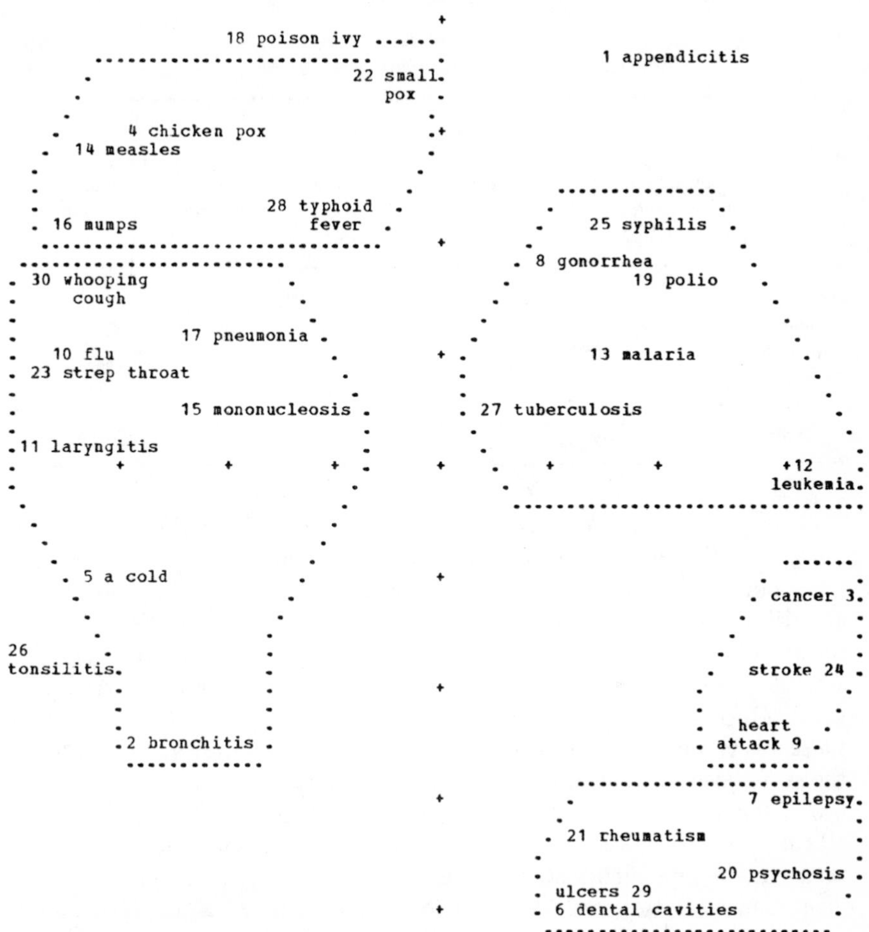

FIG. 8. M-D-SCAL plot for American-English diseases with major grouping from hierarchical clustering analysis encircled.

From the Euclidean coordinates given by the M-D-SCAL analysis of the 60×60 partial data matrix, measures of the distance between every pair of disease terms and belief-frames, between every pair of disease terms, and between every pair of belief-frames can easily be calculated. The M-D-SCAL distances between the disease terms and belief-frames can be compared directly to the normalized group ratings, while the disease term distances and the belief-frame distances can be compared to the relevant correlation coefficient matrices.

TABLE 17

CORRELATIONS BETWEEN OUTPUT M-D-SCAL DISTANCE MEASURES AND PEARSONIAN COEFFICIENTS CALCULATED FROM DICHOTOMIZED DATA

Actual correlation coefficients derived from dichotomized data	Distances from the analyses of the 30 × 30 correlation matrices based on dichotomized scores	Distances from the analyses of the 60 × 60 missing data matrices of normalized scores
American sample		
belief-frame correlations	−.912	−.852
disease term correlations	−.899	−.759
Mexican sample		
belief-frame correlations	−.741	−.601
disease term correlations	−.713	−.523

Given the amount of missing data, the results from the M-D-SCAL analysis of the 60 × 60 matrix are remarkably good. The stress scores are high, but this can be attributed to two factors: the sccondary option, an algorithm for treating tie data, which attempts to equalize the distances for tie scores; and the formula for calculating stress (SFORM 2). The secondary tie option was used because of the large number of tie scores involved in the use of the normalized data (and the even larger number of tie scores involved in the use of the dichotomized data). More importantly, the stress measure SFORM 2 was used for the 60 × 60 matrix because the use of the stress measure SFORM 1 led to a degenerate solution in which all the scores collapsed into two points. SFORM 2, a varaince-based measure, tends to give higher stress scores than SFORM 1. (A reanalysis of the dichotomized data correlation matrices using SFORM 2 was also undertaken, and gave almost identical results to the analysis using SFORM 1.)

For the American sample, the stress for four dimensions was .465, for three dimensions .545, for two dimensions .644, and for one dimension .758. Based primarily on the good results of two-dimensional analyses for the correlation matrices of disease terms and for belief-frames, the two-dimensional representation was selected.

The stress figures for the 60 × 60 partial input of normalized scores for the Mexican sample are slightly higher than for the American sample. For four dimensions the stress figure is .631, for three dimensions .708, for two dimensions .790, and for one dimension .883.

The results of the American sample and Mexican sample 60 × 60 M-D-SCAL analyses compare relatively well with the M-D-SCAL analyses of the correlation coefficient matrices. Table 17 presents the correlations between output M-D-SCAL distance measures and the Pearsonian coefficients, calculated from the dichotomized data. From Table 17, it can be seen that in all instances the correlations are higher when the M-D-SCAL program calculates the distances directly from the input of the correlation coefficients. This is not surprising since for the input of normalized scores, distances between disease terms or distances between belief-frames have to be derived indirectly through the kind of triangulation procedure described above.

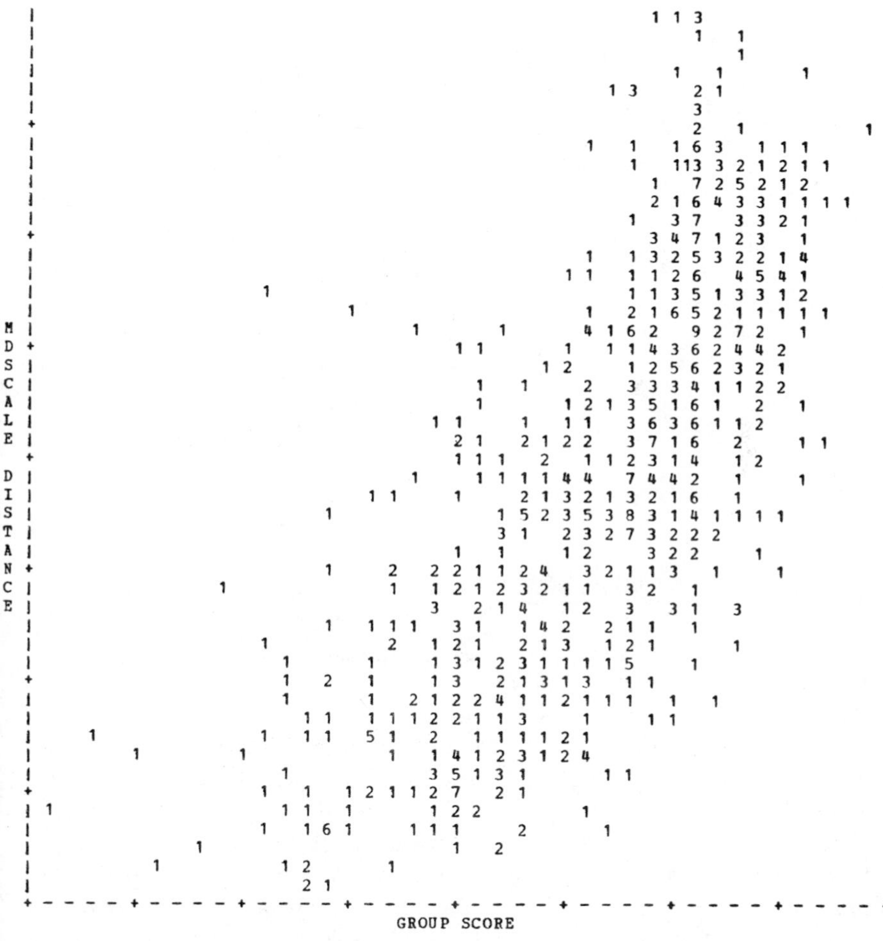

FIG. 9. Plot of M-D-SCAL 60 × 60 disease-belief distances versus normalized American scores.

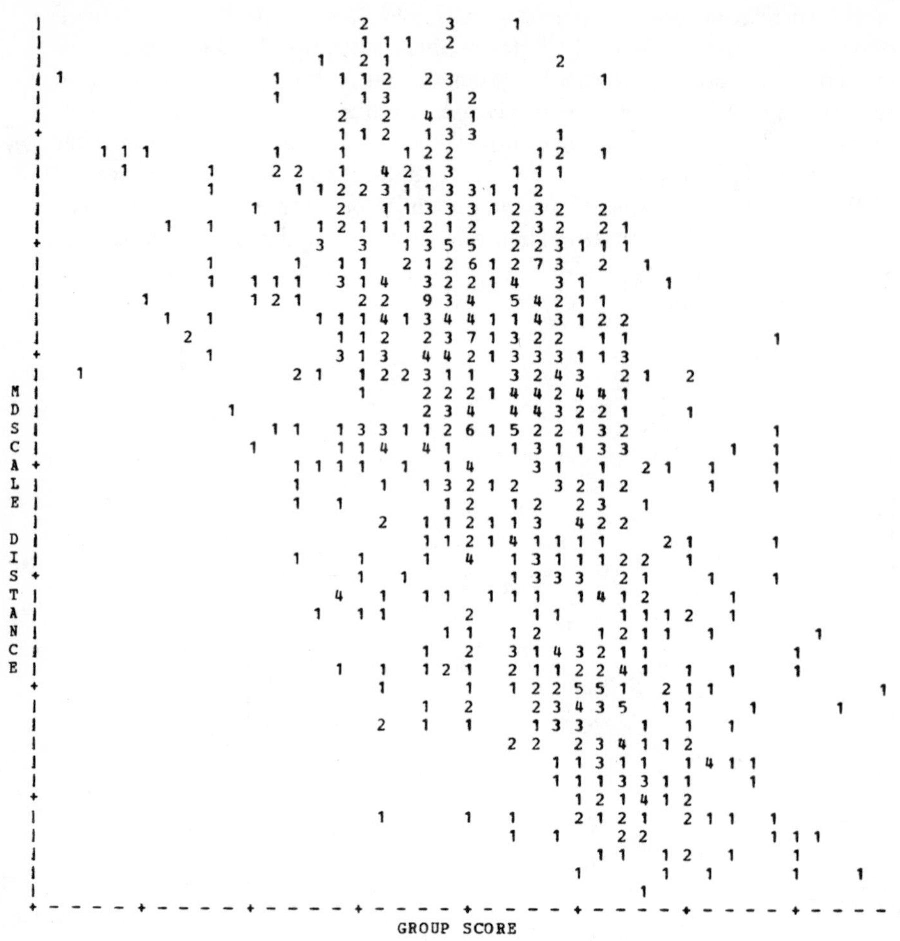

FIG. 10. Plot for M-D-SCAL 60 × 60 disease-belief distances versus normalized Mexican scores.

The great advantage of using the 60 × 60 partial input is that it places both disease terms and belief-frames in the same space. To see how well the M-D-SCAL program has accomplished this, it is possible to compare directly the M-D-SCAL distances between disease terms and belief-frames to the normalized scores. Since these normalized scores indicate the definiteness with which a particular disease term and belief-frame combination is thought to be true, the M-D-SCAL distance measures can be seen as a representation of probability with which a particular belief-frame is perceived as true when a particular disease term is inserted in the frame.

The farther apart the disease term and the belief-frame, the less likely it should be that informants will agree with the belief constituted by the disease term and belief-frame combination.

The relation between the actual normalized scores and the M-D-SCAL distances is displayed for the American sample in Figure 9, and for the Mexican sample in Figure 10. For the American sample there appears to be a slight curvilinear relation between the distance measures and the normalized scores. The correlation for the American sample is +.728, and −.573 for the Mexican sample. (The American coefficient is positive be-

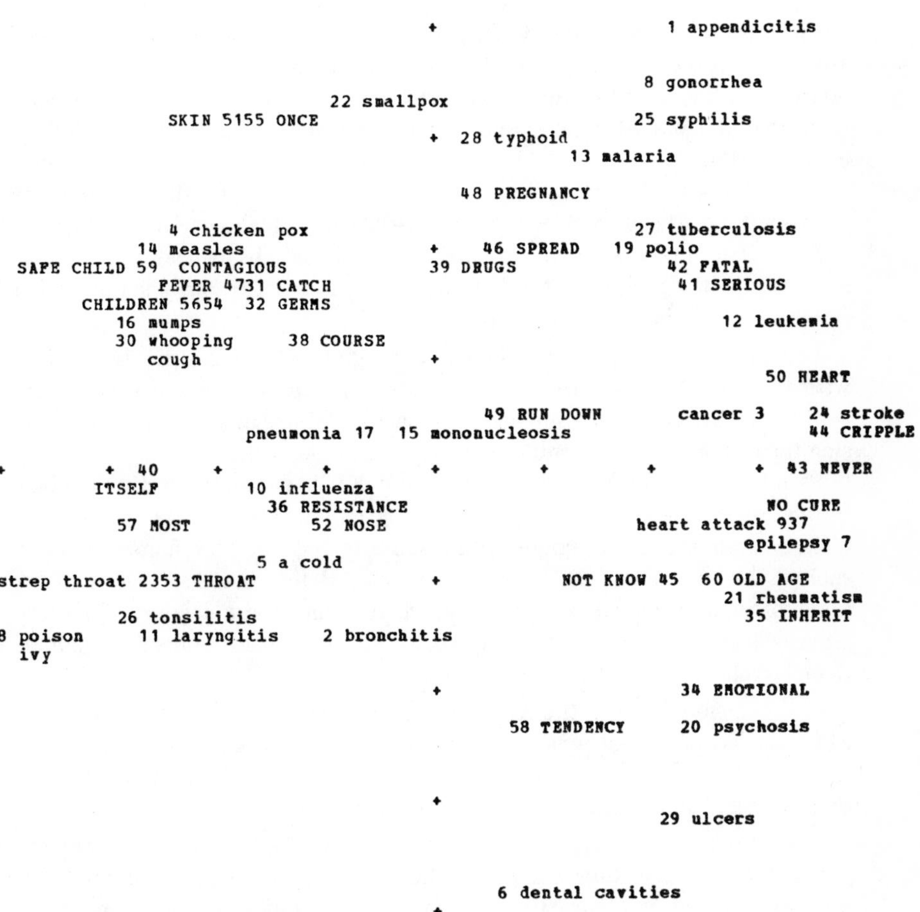

FIG. 11. M-D-SCAL plot for 60 × 60 normalized scores for American-English diseases and belief-frames.

cause the original scale was scored with 1 for definitely, and 5 for definitely not, making a scale of dissimilarity ratings. A dissimilarity rating scale increases with M-D-SCAL distances, while similarity ratings decrease as M-D-SCAL distances increase.

The relation of the dichotomized Yes versus No scores to the M-D-SCAL distances was also examined. The correlation between the dichotomized data and the M-D-SCAL distances for the American sample is −.651 (the American sample data were reversed in direction when they were dichotomized, so that both the Mexican and American sample dichotomized scores could be considered similarity scores), and −.555 for the Mexican sample.

The results of the M-D-SCAL program using the 60 × 60 normalized scores are presented graphically in Figures 10 and 11. For use in these figures, the belief-frames for the American and Mexican samples have been renumbered from 31 to 60, and the belief-frame cover word printed in capital letters.

The M-D-SCAL results are generally comparable to the hierarchical clustering results. The American M-D-SCAL plot shows the contagious bad-weather illnesses, such as colds, strep throat, influenza, pneumonia, and bronchitis grouped together along with belief-frames dealing with resistance, weather, nasal smyptoms, etc.

The next grouping consists of the contagious children's diseases, along with the relevant belief-frames. This cluster shades off toward the serious, contagious, or epidemic, but not necessarily child-related diseases, such as smallpox, malaria, typhoid, gonorrhea, syphilis, tuberculosis, and polio (appendicitis is the exception here). The FATAL and SERIOUS belief-frames mark the watershed point for contagion. The diseases to the left of these frames are contagious, while those to the right are noncontagious, such as luekemia, cancer, heart attack, etc. Below these serious noncontagious diseases which seem to involve internal body degeneracy, there remains a final collection of diseases with special causes: epilepsy, rheumatism, psychosis, ulcers, and dental cavities.

In dimensional terms, the American disease terms and belief-frames seem to be graded on dimensions of contagion and seriousness. It is as if Americans had to make two high-level decisions in order to know how to react to a disease: "Is it contagious?" and "Is it serious?"

The Mexican belief-frames and disease terms show a very different organization than the American data. The results of the Mexican M-D-SCAL program plotted in Figure 12 appear to group the disease terms and associated belief-frames in relation to a hot medicine versus cold medicine dimension (upper right guadrant versus lower left), and a children's epi-

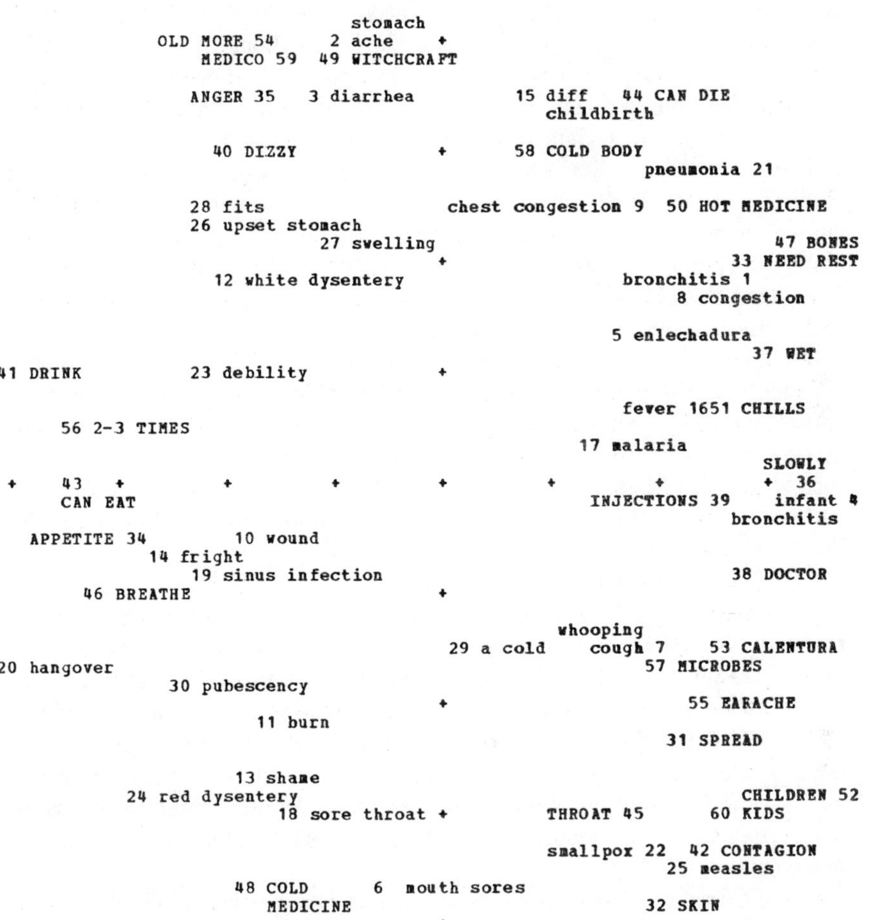

FIG. 12. M-D-SCAL plot for 60 × 60 normalized scores for Mexican-Spanish diseases and belief-frames.

demic versus old people's-witchcraft-gut disorder dimension (lower right quadrant versus upper left). Directly on the hot side of the hot-cold dimension, the belief-frames relating to hot medicines, possible fatality of the disease, getting wet, having a cold body, chills, and pains in the bones group together with a series of disease terms which seem to involve various internal congestive, respiratory, and pulmonary complaints, including problems with milk from nursing mothers.

On the opposite side of this dimension, in the lower left quadrant, is a single belief-frame (cold medicine) adjacent to a number of disease terms which all appear to involve illnesses which are thought to be related to excessive heat, flushing, or burning sensations. (Red dysentery is perhaps included here on the basis of color, and pubescency because it is thought that temperature disorders accompany various stages of aging.)

The second dimension appears to involve a number of contrasts. The children's epidemic side of the dimension, in the lower right quadrant, includes belief-frames relating to contagion, microbes, susceptibility of children, skin eruptions, and throat and ear pains. The illnesses which fail within this cluster of properties are measles, smallpox, whooping cough, and perhaps colds.

On the opposite side of this dimension are the belief-frames which involve the idea that these are diseases which attack older people more frequently, and may also involve witchcraft, or anger (biliousness), with symptoms of nausea and dizzy spells. The illnesses grouped with these properties are mainly gut disorders, such as stomach ache, diarrhea, upset stomach, and white dysentery. However, general swellings (hinchazón) and epilepticlike "fits" are also included.

In between these two dimensions are two other clusters. These two clusters seem almost to form a third dimension, which contrasts illnesses that require injections and doctors and that are difficult to cure rapidly, with those illnesses which do not involve loss of appetite, nor difficulty in in breathing, and which one can have two or more times. The first side of this dimension could be considered to involve serious illnesses which require modern medicine, while the second seems to involve disorders which are not matters of modern medical concern, and do not generally interfere with appetite or breathing, such as hangovers, sinus infections, fright, and wounds.

One difference between the Americans and the Mexicans, which is often commented upon by research workers in health areas in Mexico, is that the range of what is considered contagious is more limited in Mexico than in the United States. Dysenteries, respiratory infections, various kinds of sores, etc., which are considered highly contagious in the U.S. are not reacted to in this fashion in Mexico. These observations agree with the results of the M-D-SCAL and other methods which place the dysenteries and respiratory infections far from the contagious epidemic children's diseases.

M-D-SCAL and Factor Analysis

The results from the M-D-SCAL analysis indicate that two dimensions can account relatively well for the American and Mexican belief data.

The first factor analysis of these same data, however, gave very low figures for the proportion of the variance accounted for by only two dimensions. Since the first factor analyses were not based on group scores, but on individual scores taken across groups, a check was made on the earlier results with a second series of factor analyses. This second series of factor analyses was based on the dichotomized group scores, and rotation was limited to only two factors. As in the first analysis, the BMD computer program was used, with Varimax rotation of factors. Communalities were estimated from the squared multiple correlation coefficients.

The factor analyses were based on the correlation of belief-frames. Factor scores for the two rotated belief-frame dimensions were also obtained for the disease terms. The analysis of the American-English belief-frames showed 33% of the variance accounted for by the first factor, and 15% by the second factor. The analysis of the Mexican-Spanish belief-frames after factor rotation showed 16% of the variance accounted for by the first factor, and 13% by the second factor. Thus in terms of variance, this second analysis also yielded relatively low accountability figures.

In order to compare the effectiveness of the factor analyses with the M-D-SCAL analyses, factor analytic distances between belief-frames were calculated from the two-dimensional factor loading positions. These distances were then correlated with the original matrices of belief-frame Pearsonian coefficients. It was found that correlations for the factor analytic distances were slightly lower than the 60 × 60 M-D-SCAL distances for the American sample (−.841 versus −.852), and slightly higher for the Mexican sample (−.652 versus −.601).

To compare the results of the factor analyses for disease terms with the M-D-SCAL results, the disease factor scores on the two rotated dimensions were used to calculate distances. (The difference between the factor loadings and factor scores may be easier to understand if the belief-frames are thought of as different tests in a battery of IQ tests, and the disease terms are thought of as individuals taking those tests. A factor analysis of the intercorrelations of the tests yields factor loadings for each of the tests on some number of dimensions. A separate procedure is then used to calculate each individual's score on each dimension by using the factor loadings to weight how much each individual test contributes to the person's factor score.) The comparison of the factor score disease term distances to the matrix of disease term intercorrelations shows results similar to the 60 × 60 M-D-SCAL analysis. The correlation for the American sample again shows a slightly lower correlation for the factor analytic distances than for the M-D-SCAL distances (−.726 versus −.759), and for the Mexican sample a slightly higher correlations (−.635 versus −.523). The correla-

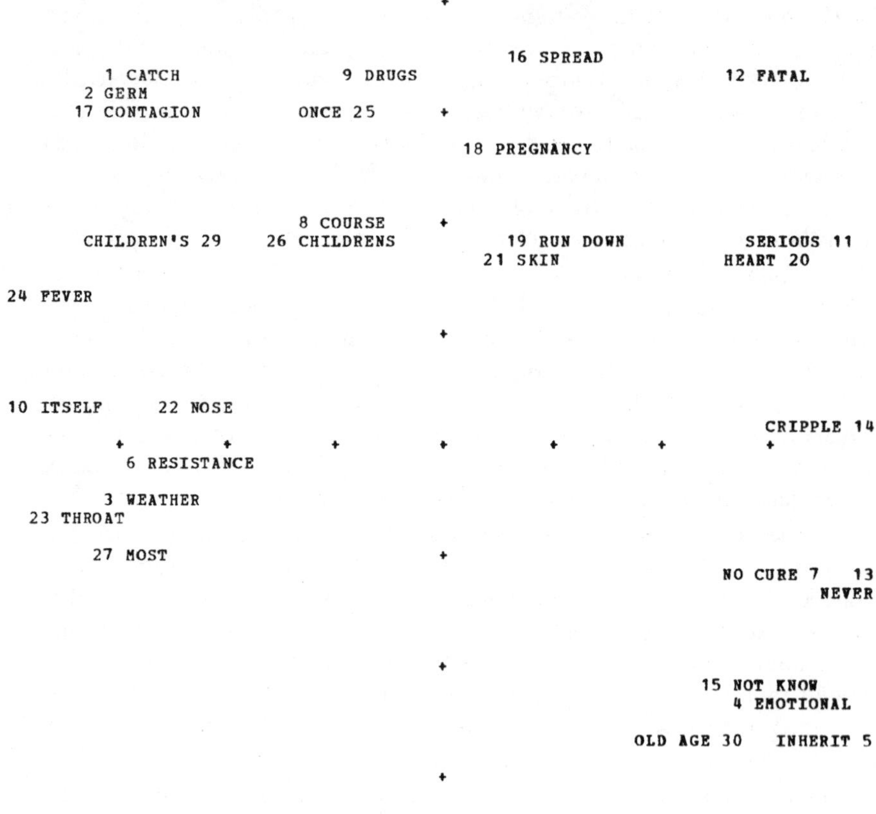

FIG. 13. Factor loadings for American-English belief-frames.

tion between the distances from the 60 × 60 M-D-SCAL analysis and the actual normalized group scores for the American sample is .728, which indicates approximately 50% of the variance has been accounted for. The cumulative proportion of variance accounted for by the factor analysis of American belief-frames is approximately 48%. The results for the Mexican sample are equally close, with a correlation of −.573 for the relation between M-D-SCAL distances and normalized group scores or approximately 32% of the variance accounted for. This figure is again just slightly higher than the factor analytic results, which show the first two factors accounting for 29% of the variance. Furthermore, if the output distances from the factor analyses and the M-D-SCAL analyses are compared directly, even higher correlations are found. For example, for the American-English belief-frames, the M-D-SCAL distances from the 60 × 60 missing data analysis correlate +.835 with distances calculated from the factor loadings. For the Mexican-Spanish belief-frames, the correlation between distances derived from the M-D-SCAL and the factor analysis is +.731. The results from the analyses of disease terms are only slightly lower with +.641 for the American data, and +.721 vor the Mexican data. These figures indicate that both methods of analysis obtain similar structures, and that the cross-method similarity is slightly better than the relation of the structures to the original data, perhaps because the same noisy aspects of the data are being dropped by both methods.

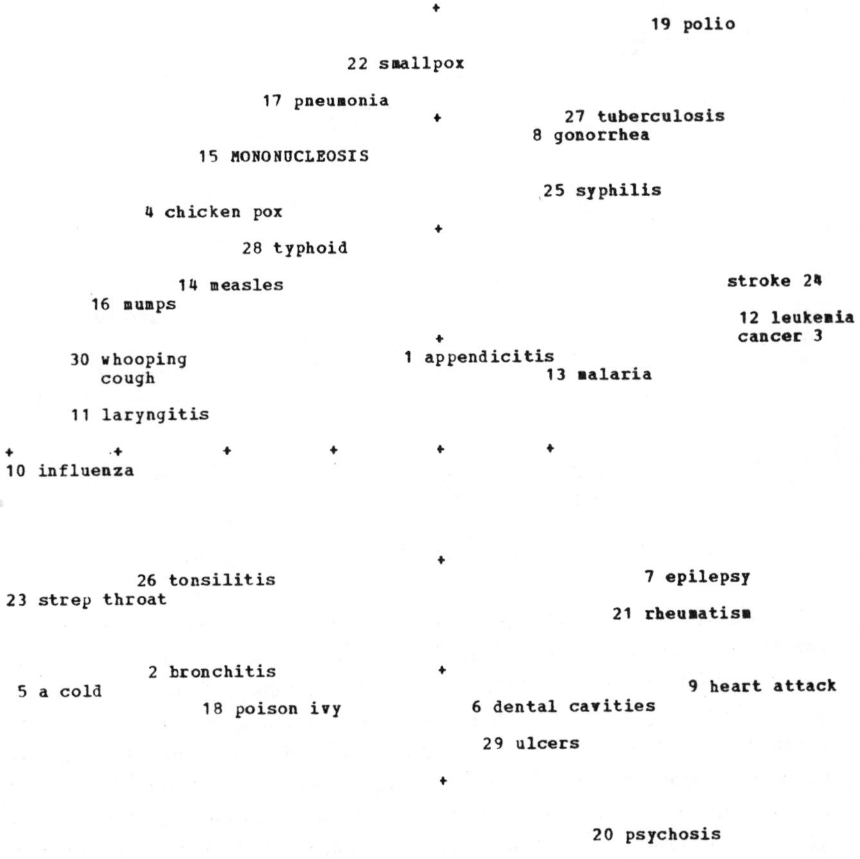

FIG. 14. Factor scores for American-English diseases.

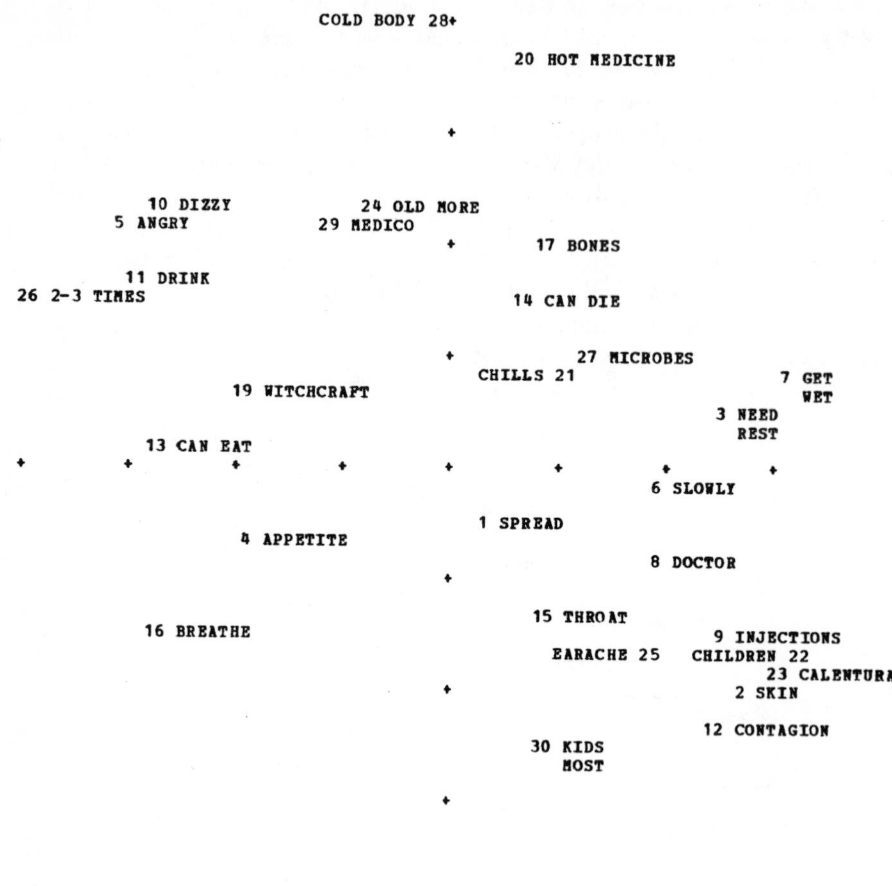

Fig. 15. Factor loadings for Mexican-Spanish belief-frames.

Substantively, the factor analyses also yield results which are similar to the M-D-SCAL results. In Figure 13, the factor loadings for the American-English belief-frames are given for the first two factors. In order to facilitate comparison with the M-D-SCAL results, the axes derived from the Varimax rotation have been rotated an additional 15 degrees. (For the Mexican data, correspondence to the M-D-SCAL results was obtained by rotating axes an additional 16 degrees.) These two factors emerge clearly as a serious versus nonserious dimension and a contagion versus noncontagion dimension.

In Figure 14 the factor scores for American-English disease terms are given, the first factor aligning disease terms on the serious versus nonserious dimension and the second factor aligning disease terms on the contagion versus noncontagion factor.

In Figure 15, the rotated factor loadings for the high variance Mexican-Spanish belief-frames are given for the first two factors.

The results in Figure 15 match the M-D-SCAL results fairly closely, with the first factor contrasting belief-frames relating to children's epidemic diseases to belief-frames involving drink, anger, witchcraft, old people, and diseases which can be caught many times. The second factor contrasts hot medicine-related illness properties to cold medicine-related illness properties.

In Figure 16, the factor scores for disease terms give a similar alignment of illnesses to belief-frames described above for the M-D-SCAL results.

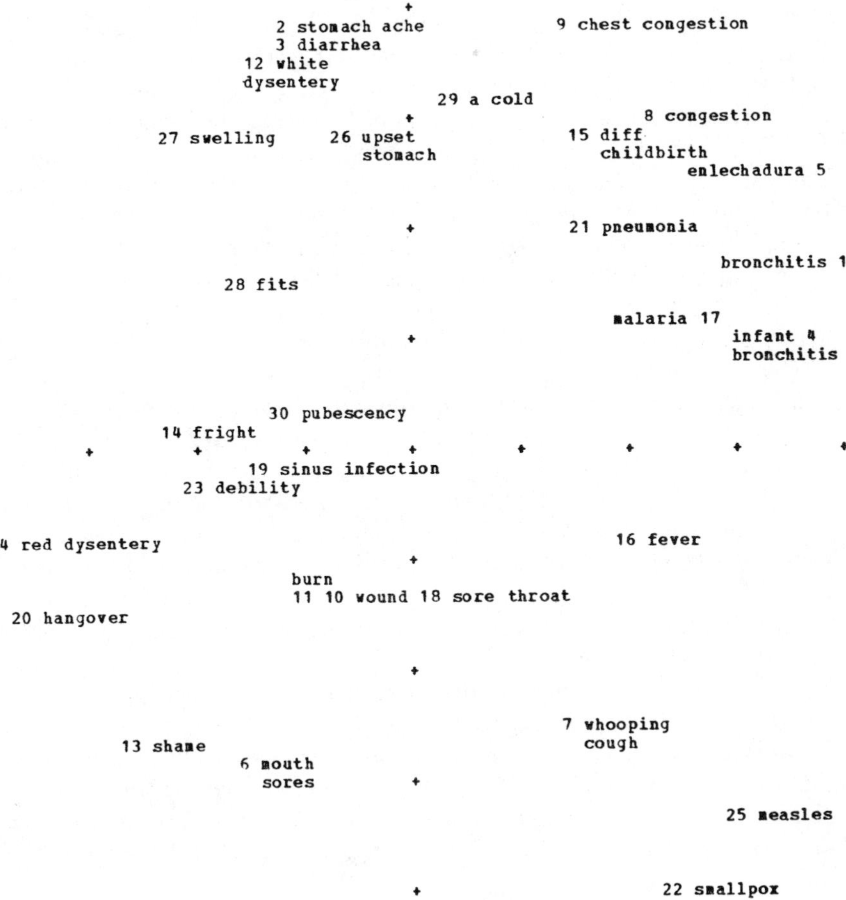

FIG. 16. Factor scores for Mexican-Spanish diseases.

Given the instability of the initial factor analyses, the goodness of fit of the later factor analyses is surprising. It would seem that the robustness of the factor analytic method falls off rapidly as the number of factor dimensions used increases, until at some point the rotation of factors becomes not much more than shadow boxing. In the initial analyses, an attempt was made to rotate as many as ten factors. With somewhat noisy data, a more sensible strategy appears to be to use as few factor dimensions as possible.

Discussion and Conclusions

The results which have been reported here are quite different from typical ethnographic description. Generally, the ethnographic task is to describe as finely and as completely as possible the symbolic and behavioral world of a particular human group. The goal of this study, however, was to find out how a particular symbolic domain is conceptually organized. Certainly the results presented above do not give a complete picture of the total belief system about illness held by any of the sample cultural groups. (For example, contrast the results reported here with the ethnographic descriptions of Mexican beliefs about disease in Rubel, 1960; Metzger & Williams, 1963b; Madsen, 1965; Currier, 1966.) What then, do these results say about the cognitive organization of the disease terms?

The first conclusion drawn from this study is that the defining properties of a set of terms are not always the properties which determine how people categorize or react to those terms. Thus, the categories discovered by the analysis of how disease terms distribute across beliefs do not seem to be related to the features which define these disease terms. Our informants agree that "cancer" is "serious," "noncontagious," and not a "childhood" illness. Based on the three methods of analysis we have used, these properties are major foci for how Americans conceive of diseases. But these are certainly neither necessary nor sufficient conditions for making the decision that someone has cancer.

It might be argued that the disjunction between the salient versus the defining properties is an unusual state of affairs, brought about by the imposition of a scientific theory of disease of a folklike culture. However, the Mexican informants, who appear to be innocent of scientific medicine, also appear to be reacting generally—not to how diseases are to be defined or identified, but rather to their consequences, remedies, and types of victim.

Our claim concerning the lack of cognitive salience for the defining properties of diseases in these two cultures is not meant to imply that in all other domains, defining properties also lack salience. Conklin, for example, has presented data which indicate that the componential structure of Hanunoo kin terms is related to such matters as the amount of fines paid for nonexogamous marriage, while noting that "complete isomorphism between semantic and pragmatic structural relations cannot be anticipated. . ." (Conklin, 1964, p. 47). In the same volume, Pospisil analyzes Nunamuit Eskimo kin terms, and finds that "every genealogical component has a behavioral counterpart" (Pospisil, 1964, p. 401). On the basis of this and other evidence, there seems likely to be a relatively greater degree of isomorphism between the properties which determine labeling and the properties which determine other behaviors in the domain of kinship (Romney & Epling, 1958; Frake, 1960; Goodenough, 1963; Friedrich, 1964; Tyler, 1965).

Second, our experience indicates that the model of lexical domains as organized into taxonomic and paradigmatic relations is not always useful. We have come to conceive of both taxonomies and paradigms as epiphenomena, accounted for by the multiple properties which constitute the meanings of the terms. Thus taxonomic relations occur when one term contains some but not all of the defining properties of another term or set of terms. The terms which are defined by fewer properties are then the "higher" level terms, and the terms which contain additional properties will be the "lower" level terms. For example, the defining properties (distinctive features or criterial attributes) of the American-English kinship term "parent" are identical to those for the kinship terms "father" and "mother," except for the here unspecified value for the property of sex. As a result, "parent" is the higher level term whose denotata, by logical necessity, will include those of the lower level terms. More formally, representing properties by small letters with natural numbers attached to them to indicate various values of these properties, and with the number 0 attached to them when the values are unspecified or indeterminate, a taxonomy has the following form:

term 1: a1 & b0
term 2: a1 & b1
term 3: a1 & b2

Term 1 is here the higher level term, whose denotata are partitioned by term 2 and term 3 on the basis of the different values specified for property h. The a1 property-value is common to all three terms, and is the root meaning which defines the domain (Lounsbury, 1964; Sturtevant, 1964).

A paradigm, from this viewpoint, also results from the structure of the defining properties (Lounsbury, 1964; Kay, 1966b). If a set of terms contains all possible combinations of properties and values then a complete paradigm will result. Thus, a paradigm will have the following form:

term 1: a1 & b1 & c1
term 2: a1 & b1 & c2
term 3: a1 & b2 & c1
term 4: a1 & b2 & c2

It appears that extensive paradigms are most likely to occur when relations are involved, as in kinship, or in the deitic relations of tense, person, mode, etc., perhaps because such relations make possible a great number of combinations from a small number of defining properties. Deep taxonomies, on the other hand, seem to occur when there is utility in sometimes considering a large number of elements abstractly, i.e., with reference to only a few properties, and at other times more concretely, i.e., with reference to many properties. Since humans can hold in mind only seven or so properties at one time (Miller, 1956; Wallace, 1961), and then only a few values for each property, a deep taxonomiclike structure gives an orderly and relatively efficient means of sorting and identifying very large numbers of objects. When such sorting and identification is useful, as with plants in some cultures, or book titles in others, deep taxonomic structure would seem likely to emerge.

However, in the absence of either a relational ordering of properties, or the circumstances under which deep taxonomies are useful, the structure of properties more often seems to consist of a partial subset out of all the possible combinations of properties and values (e.g., Berlin & Romney, 1964).

The final implication suggested by this study concerns the relationship between cognitive operations and belief systems. It seems unlikely that people have stored in their memories huge matrices of the sort presented in miniature in this paper. Such a means of storage would be an extremely wasteful and cumbersome procedure, analogous to trying to learn a language by remembering all possible sequences of words which might be said appropriately. Nor is it apparent that people have an internal representation like the spatial plot produced by multidimensional scaling procedures.

How then are people able to fill out large data matrices of the kind used here? Perhaps a belief system may be represented as a set of propositions, capable of generating such data matrices (Kay, 1966a). At present we have little empirical evidence about the form of such propositions; our initial inclination is to use the symbolic apparatus of logic, especially first-order predicate logic, which remains relatively close to a natural language format. In any case, whatever form these propositions eventually take, the problem will be to develop decision procedures which can economically generate assessments of "truth" and "likelihood" which are the same as those made by informants.

Acknowledgments

Grateful acknowledgment is made to Stanford University for providing funds for computer time.

References

Berlin, B., & Romney, A. K. Descriptive semantics of Tzeltal numeral classifiers. In A. K. Romney & R. G. D'Andrade (Eds.), *Transcultural studies in cognition. American Anthropologist Special Issue*, 1964, **66**(3, Pt. 2), 79–98.

Conklin, H. C. Ethnogenealogical method. In W. H. Goodenough (Ed.), *Explorations in cultural anthropology: Essays presented to George Peter Murdock*. New York: McGraw-Hill, 1964. Pp. 25–66.

Currier, R. L. The hot-cold syndrome and symbolic balance in Mexican and Spanish-American folk medicine. *Ethnology*, 1966, **5**, 251–263.

D'Andrade, R. G. *Memorandum on statistics in social anthropology: F-8*. Laboratory of Social Relations, Harvard University, 1959. Mimeographed report.

Dixon, B. C. *BMD biomedical computer programs*. Berkeley and Los Angeles, California: University of California Press, 1968.

Frake, C. O. The Eastern Subanun of Mindanao. In G. P. Murdock (Ed.), *Social structure in Southeast Asia*. Viking Fund Publications in Anthropology, No. 29. Chicago, Illinois: Quadrangle Books, 1960. Pp. 51–64.

Frake, C. O. The diagnosis of disease among the Subanun of Mindanao. *American Anthropologist*, 1961, **63**, 113–132.

Frake, C. O. Notes on queries in ethnography. In A. K. Romney & R. G. D'Andrade (Eds.), *Transcultural studies in cognition. American Anthropologist Special Issue*, 1964, **66** (3, Pt. 2), 132–145.

Friedrich, P. Semantic structure and social structure: An instance from Russian. In W. H. Goodenough (Ed.), *Explorations in cultural anthropology: Essays presented to George Peter Murdock*. New York: McGraw-Hill, 1964. Pp. 131–166.

Goodenough, W. H. Some applications of Guttman scale analysis to ethnography and culture theory. *Southwestern Journal of Anthropology*, 1963, **19**, 235–250.

Hoijer, H. The chronology of Athapaskan languages. *International Journal of American Linguistics*, 1956, **22**, 219–231.

Johnson, S. C. Hierarchical clustering schemes. *Psychometrika*, 1967, **32**, 241–253.

Kay, P. Comment on ethnographic semantics: A preliminary survey (by B. N. Colby). *Current Anthropology*, 1966, **7**, 20–23. (a)

Kay, P. Ethnography and theory of culture. *Bucknell Review*, 1966, 106–113. (b)

Kruskal, J. B. Multidimensional scaling by optimizing goodness of fit to a nonmetric hypothesis. *Psychometrika*, 1964, **29**, 1–27. (a)

Kruskal, J. B. Nonmetric multidimensional scaling: A numerical method. *Psychometrika*, 1964, **29**, 115–129. (b)

Lees, R. B. The basis of glottochronology. *Language*, 1953, **29**, 113–127.

Lounsbury, F. G. The structural analysis of kinship semantics. In H. G. Lunt (Ed.), *Proceedings of the Ninth International Congress of Linguists*. The Hague: Mouton, 1964.

Madsen, C. A study of change in Mexican folk medicine. *Middle American Research Institute Publication*, No. 25. New Orleans, Louisiana: Tulane University Press, 1965. Pp. 84–139.

Metzger, D., & Williams, G. A formal ethnographic analysis of Tenejapa Ladino weddings. *American Anthropologist*, 1963, **65**, 1076–1101. (a)

Metzger, D., & Williams, G. Tenejapa medicine I: The curer. *Southwestern Journal of Anthropology*, 1963, **19**, 216–234. (b)

Miller, G. A. The magical number seven plus or minus two. *Psychological Review*, 1956, **63**, 81–97.

Pospisil, L. Law and societal structure among the Nunamuit Eskimo. In W. H. Goodenough (Ed.), *Explorations in cultural anthropology: Essays presented to George Peter Murdock*. New York: McGraw-Hill, 1964. Pp. 395–432.

Roberts, J. M. Three Navaho households: A comparative study in small group culture. *Papers of the Peabody Museum*. Vol. 11 (3). Cambridge, Massachusetts: Harvard University, 1951.

Romney, A. K., & Epling, P. J. A simplified model of Kariera kinship. *American Anthropologist*, 1958, **60**, 59–74.

Rubel, A. J. Concepts of disease in Mexican-American culture. *American Anthropologist*, 1960, **62**, 795–814.

Shepard, R. N. The analysis of proximities: Multidimensional scaling with an unknown distance function. *Psychometrika*, 1962, **27**, 125–140, 219–246.

Stefflre, V. Language and behavior. Unpublished manuscript.

Sturtevant, W. C. Studies in ethnoscience. In A. K. Romney & R. G. D'Andrade (Eds.), *Transcultural studies in cognition. American Anthropologist Special Issue*, 1964, **66**(3, Pt. 2), 99–131.

Swadesh, M. J. Lexico-statistic dating of prehistoric ethnic contacts. *American Philo logical Society Publications*, 1952, **96**, 452–463.

Swadesh, M. J. Towards greater accuracy in lexicostatistic dating. *International Journal American Linguistics*, 1955, **21**, 121–137.

Tyler, S. A. Koya language morphology and patterns of kinship behavior. *American Anthropologist*, 1965, **67**, 1428–1440.

Wallace, A. F. C. On being just complicated enough. *Proceedings of the National Academy of Sciences*, 1961, **47**, 458–464.

SEMANTIC DIMENSIONS OF OCCUPATION NAMES

Michael Burton

SCHOOL OF SOCIAL SCIENCES
UNIVERSITY OF CALIFORNIA
IRVINE, CALIFORNIA

This paper is a study of the semantic structure of the domain of occupation names in English, using multidimensional scaling and hierarchical clustering methods. These methods map the occupation terms onto structures which are roughly analogous to the paradigmatic and taxonomical, or tree structure models, of descriptive semantics.

In addition to the nominal scales of the taxonomy or paradigm, however, the multidimensional scaling method also allows for ordinal or interval scale dimensions. A major part of the paper concerns measuring the distance between terms on these dimensions, interpreting the dimensions, and testing for the validity of the interpretation.

Paradigms and Hierarchies in Semantics

Nonmetric multidimensional scaling (Shepard, 1962, 1966) and hierarchial clustering (Johnson, 1967), when applied to data on similarities or dissimilarities among terms in a semantic structure, produce representations which are analogous, respectively, to the paradigmatic (Goodenough, 1956; Harris, 1948; Lounsbury, 1956; Romney and D'Andrade, 1964); and taxonomical (or tree structure) (Berlin, Breedlove, and Raven, 1968; Conklin, 1962; Kay, 1966) models of descriptive semantics.

The paradigmatic model assumes simultaneous assessment of the values (or features) of a lexeme on each of the attributes (or dimensions) of the domain. It is analogous to the multidimensional model, for which the description of an object is a vector of values on axes in a space. The attributes (or dimensions) are unordered, and each one is relevant to every lexeme in the domain.

The taxonomical model assumes an ordering of attributes. A given attribute may not be relevant to every lexeme, but may be only relevant at a single node in the tree structure. Johnson's hierarchical clustering method assigns a metric to such tree structures, so that both nonmetric scaling and hierarchical clustering produce structures with a distance metric from measures of similarity or dissimilarity.

The development of these two methods for scaling and clustering has provided useful tools for students of semantic process and structure. The methods allow precise measurement of variation among structures. They also make possible the testing of alternate hypotheses about the kind of structure in a domain (hierarchical, paradigmatic, etc.) and about the presence or absence of particular attributes within a structure. Testing for kind of structure is a matter of comparing the degree of fit of data in a domain to the multidimensional and hierarchical models. One test for the presence of an attribute (prestige) in a domain (occupations) forms a major part of this paper.

Attributes as Nominal and Ordinal Scales

In the previous section, the term "attribute" was used to refer to a scale. Bruner, Goodnow, and Austin (1956) used "attribute" for a nominal scale and "value" for a category of that scale. Here an attribute may be a nominal classification or it may have ordinal or interval properties.

In anthropology, the terms "component" and "feature" are often used to refer, respectively, to the nominal scale and its categories. The notion of components reflects its origins in phonemics in that binary features, or scales with only two categories, prevail. Behind the preference for binary features is the idea of minimal contrast, as in the phonemic contrast of "bill" and "pill," where two phoneme sequences are identical except for contrast on the feature of voicing. The phoneme "b" is voiced, whereas "p" is unvoiced. A similar example from semantics is the opposition of the lexemes "man" and "woman" which differ only on the sex component. Although such minimal contrasts do occur in semantics, they are far less frequent than in phonemic data. In semantics, it is necessary to allow for multiple category scales and also for ordinal scales.

Whereas nominal scales involve the relation of contrast (A, not-A), ordinal scales involve comparison. It is assumed here that comparison is a general property of semantic process; that is, people order concepts on scales as well as place them in categories. An example of ordering is the scale of power-solidarity. An ordering of a few concepts on this scale is the following: boss, executive, leader, citizen, neighbor, friend, brother. Another role term scale with ordinal properties is ethical evaluation.

In this paper the hypothesis that the ordinal scale of prestige is present in the domain of occupation names is tested through multidimensional scaling. The same data are also analyzed by hierarchical clustering to compare the strengths and weaknesses of the two methods, and to test the appropriateness of the multidimensional model.

Relating Externally Derived Scales to a Semantic Structure

Every cultural system has named attribute scales on which the objects, persons, places, and events of everyday situations are categorized or rated. A productive schema for the description of social behavior in its normative facet is the measurement of these attributes and their relationships both to the semantic system and to the behavioral norms [Frake, 1964]. The measurement of objects on such scales is an important part of cultural description. In this study, persons were asked to perform a paired-comparison task on the attributes "prestige," "social status," and "estimated income" for a set of 60 occupations. Given that people are willing to perform the task, i.e., that they think a given attribute is relevant to the set of words, it is possible by this means to obtain an interval scale for each of the attributes. The next question is whether this attribute is coded in the meaning of the words. Given a complete description of the meaning of each occupation name in the context of the domain of all occupation names, would it be possible to obtain some kind of equation for predicting the ordering of terms on the prestige or status scale from the meanings? This question is handled by testing the following proposition: Is there some rotation of axes in the multidimensional representation of the occupation terms such that the projection of points on one of the axes has the same rank order as the rank ordering of points on the prestige or status scale? If the question is answered in the affirmative, the conclusion that there is a correspondence between the meaning of occupation names and the judgment of those names on the prestige attribute is valid. It tells us that part of the question "How similar are A and B?" (when A and B are occupation names in English) are the questions "Are A and B the same or different on the prestige-status scale? And if they are different, how different?"

Occupation Names as a Subset of Role Terms

This investigation of the domain of occupation names is a continuation of research on English role terms (Burton, 1968). The previous research consisted of a scaling of 58 role terms by the same methods as are used here, and a partitioning of those roles terms into subdomains. One of the subdomains was occupation names. The schema for investigation of semantic structure followed here involved a combination of multidimensional and hierarchical models. There were three highest level dimensions to the role terms (power-solidarity, ethical evaluation, and a binary distinction between occupations and others). These dimensions combined in different ways to produce regions (or clusters) in the space in which there were high concentrations of role terms. The largest such cluster was the occupations, which took up about one-third of the space. The second phase in the schema was to use the information on clustering to produce the first level of a hierarchy (Figure 1). Then a continuation of the research was to do multidimensional analysis within each of the clusters. This was a recursive process, which could continue until the terminal node of each path of the hierarchy was reached.

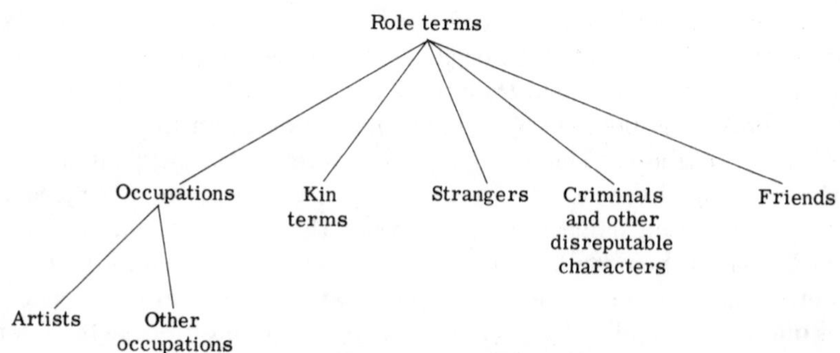

FIG. 1. First level of taxonomy of role terms.

Previously the recursive process of clustering and multidimensional scaling within clusters was done for two of the subdomains: kinship terms and artists (artists, musician, composer, poet, singer, dancer, actor, painter, writer, comedian). The present analysis tackles the occupational subdomain.

The domain of occupational names is very large. Even if only the terms that are likely to be shared by all English speakers are included, the set exceeds the 60-term limit of the version of the Kruskal scaling program (Kruskal 1964a, b) used.

One attempt to define a domain of the appropriate size was to have subjects list occupation terms by free recall, but they tended to list only prestigeful and creative occupations and to omit such terms as MACHINIST, FARMER, MECHANIC, and BAKER, which make up the bulk of things that people actually do. So, a more representative set of terms was chosen from the United States Labor Department *Dictionary of Occupational Titles* (U.S. Dept. of Labor, 1965), which has a classification of occupations into nine major categories. Occupations were selected so as to represent all nine categories.

Data Collection

Fifty-four people who responded to an advertisement in the Harvard student newspaper were used as subjects. They had two tasks, to partition the set of occupation terms and to perform two paired-comparison tests.

For the partitioning task, subjects were given a deck of 60 cards, each having one occupation printed on it. The instructions were to sort the cards "so that occupations which seemed the same were in the same pile." The second task involving the paired comparisons is explained below.

Similarity Measures for the terms

The similarity measure used is derived from principles of information theory. Each subject was allowed to sort the deck of occupation term cards into any number of piles. Each pile of cards is called a cell of the partition. Thus for each subject: Δi is the number of the cells in the partition for subject i, and $C_{i,\alpha}$ is the number of terms in cell α for subject i.

Each cell of a partition can be assigned a probability. Suppose we choose two terms at random from among the 60 occupation names. For a given partition, this probability is the probability that the two terms are contained in a particular cell, given that we have no information about which terms have been placed in which cell. It is clear that this is

$$P_{i,\alpha} = \frac{(C_{i,\alpha})(C_{i,\alpha} - 1)}{60 \cdot 59}$$

That is,

$$P_{i,\alpha} = \frac{\text{number of pairs of terms in cell } \alpha}{\text{number of pairs of terms in all}}$$

If we take the negative of the logarithm to the base 2 of $P_{i,\alpha}$, we have the information that is contained in the event "terms j and k are both in cell α." We can also compute the information in the event "terms j and k are in different cells." This is $-\log_2(Q_i)$, where $Q_i = 1.00 - \sum_{\alpha \neq 1}^{\Delta i} P_{i,\alpha}$. The proposed similarity measure counts the event "j and k are in cell α" as a positive increment to the degree of similarity, and the event "j and k are in different cells" as a decrement. The appropriate factors are

$$X_{j,k,i} = \begin{cases} -\log_2(P_{i,\alpha}) \text{ when items } j \text{ and } k \text{ are in cell } \alpha \\ \\ +\log_2(Q_i) \text{ when items } j \text{ and } k \text{ are in different cells} \end{cases}$$

When a subject places two terms in a very small cell, the event has high information, and there is a relatively large increment to the similarity measure for the two items. Similarly, when a subject places the two terms in different cells, but the Q_i is small (low probability of a given two terms residing in different cells); then there will be a relatively large decrement to the similarity measure. In this manner, the measure compensates for differences among partitions in the sizes of cells.

In order to weight all subjects equally, it is necessary to normalize the proposed increments and decrements. It is simple to compute the mean and standard deviation of these for a subject:

$$E_i = -\sum_{\alpha=1}^{\Delta_i} P_{i,\alpha} \log_2 P_{i,\alpha} + Q_i \log_2 Q_i$$

$$= \text{(mean information of event "}j \text{ and } k \text{ together")}$$
$$- \text{(mean information of event, } j \text{ and } k \text{ apart")}$$

$$\sigma_i^2 = \sum_{\alpha=1}^{\Delta_i} P_{i,\alpha}[\log_2 P_{i,\alpha}]^2 + Q_i[\log_2 Q_i]^2$$

The final similarity measure then is

$$Z_{jk} = \sum_{i=1}^{N} \frac{(X_{j,k,i} - E_i)}{(\sum_{i=1}^{N} \sigma_i^2)^{1/2}}$$

It should be noted that a modification of this measure

$$Z_{jk} = \sum_{i=1}^{N} \frac{X_{j,k,i} - E_i}{\sigma_i}$$

would probably be more in the spirit of the normalization procedure. The present version resulted from the mistaken deduction that it would produce a measure that was asymptotically normal. Since the measure is not a sum of independent events (all trials are sortings of the same two terms, and are thus not independent of one another), that deduction does not hold. In fact the distribution of similarity measures across pairs of terms is highly skewed, with a large concentration at the minimum value (−2.335). Such a distribution reflects the fact that there are many pairs of terms which are so dissimilar in meaning that they are in different cells in each partition.

Multidimensional Scaling of the Data

The Kruskal M-D-SCAL program (in Fortran IV for the IBM 7094) was used for the scaling (Kruskal, 1964a, b). The program was first run in five, four, three, two, and one dimensions, without a starting configuration. The stresses indicated that the three-dimensional solution was the most satisfactory (Figure 4). However, the graphs of the three-dimensional solution were not very easy to interpret. Suspecting that the configuration needed to be rotated to an interpretable alignment, the author recomputed the scaling, using an alternative strategy.

The results of the one-dimensional scaling could be interpreted as a dimension of degree of freedom, or independence (Table 1). At one extreme are people who work alone, or who work for themselves; and at the other extreme are people who work for a large organization. Thinking that this could be the single most important dimension in the structure, the author then computed a two-dimensional scaling with a starting configuration. This starting configuration had the results of the one-dimensional scaling for the first vector. The second vector of the starting configuration was a set of numbers chosen at random.

The resulting scaling preserved the independence dimension along the first axis, and produced a second dimension which could be interpreted as "prestige." Satisfied with this process, the author then computed a three-dimensional scaling with a starting configuration. Here the first two vectors of the starting configuration were the output of the two-dimensional scaling, and the third vector was the same set of random numbers as before.

TABLE 1

One-Dimensional Scaling Solution

Occupation	Scale value	Occupation	Scale value	Occupation	Scale value
Farmer	1.785	Machinist	.408	Librarian	−1.342
Fisherman	1.637	Tool and die maker	.342	Landlord	−1.385
Forest ranger	1.563	Mechanic	.201	Foreman	−1.430
Crop picker	1.515	Carpenter	.188	Salesman	−1.513
Garbage collector	1.373	Social worker	.066	Buyer	−1.538
Sailor	1.336	Locksmith	.025	Clerk	−1.566
Sharecropper	1.221	Bookbinder	−.022	Bank teller	−1.637
Coal miner	1.147	Printer	−.052	Bookkeeper	−1.691
Laborer	1.054	Engraver	−.082	Accountant	−1.706
Priest	1.047	Watchmaker	−.110	Proofreader	−1.738
Longshoreman	1.039	Jeweler	−.130		
Veterinarian	1.020	Leatherworker	−.163		
Chemist	.984	Tailor	−.248		
Truck driver	.972	Embalmer	−.286		
Mechanical engineer	.944	Butcher	−.310		
Optician	.863	Baker	−.385		
Psychologist	.707	Executive	−.474		
Physician	.705	Barber	−.517		
Architect	.654	Stockbroker	−.569		
Lawyer	.580	Draftsman	−.686		
Pipe-fitter	.552	Bartender	−.713		
Professor	.521	Chauffeur	−.742		
Welder	.484	Policeman	−.891		
Bricklayer	.430	Manager	−1.030		
		Building contractor	−1.123		
		Computer programmer	−1.238		

The three-dimensional configuration resulting from this process had identical stress (.167) to the one obtained earlier with no starting configuration, and is the configuration referred to in the following discussion. It is displayed in Figures 2 and 3.

From examination of the graphs of the three-dimensional solution, it is apparent that there are three orthogonal semantic dimensions which are approximately aligned with the axes of the configuration. The first (horizontal axis, Figures 2 and 3) can be called a *dependency* dimension. Most of the occupations to the right of the vertical axis require the employee to punch a time clock and to take orders from a superior in a hierarchy. Many of the occupations to the left of the vertical axis do not require that the employee punch a time clock, and many are independent occupations for which the person does not have a supervisor. Also, many of them involve outdoor work. Thus the COAL MINER, CARPENTER, POLICEMAN, and SOCIAL WORKER all work for a large organization and have some kind of boss or supervisor, but they also work "in the field" or outdoors. It may be that this scale is correlated to the degree of formality of social relations, as expressed by such things as address term usage and off-the-job social activities with co-workers.

The second dimension (vertical in Figure 2), is a scale of *prestige* or status. It appears to be most strongly correlated to the amount of education required to hold the job.

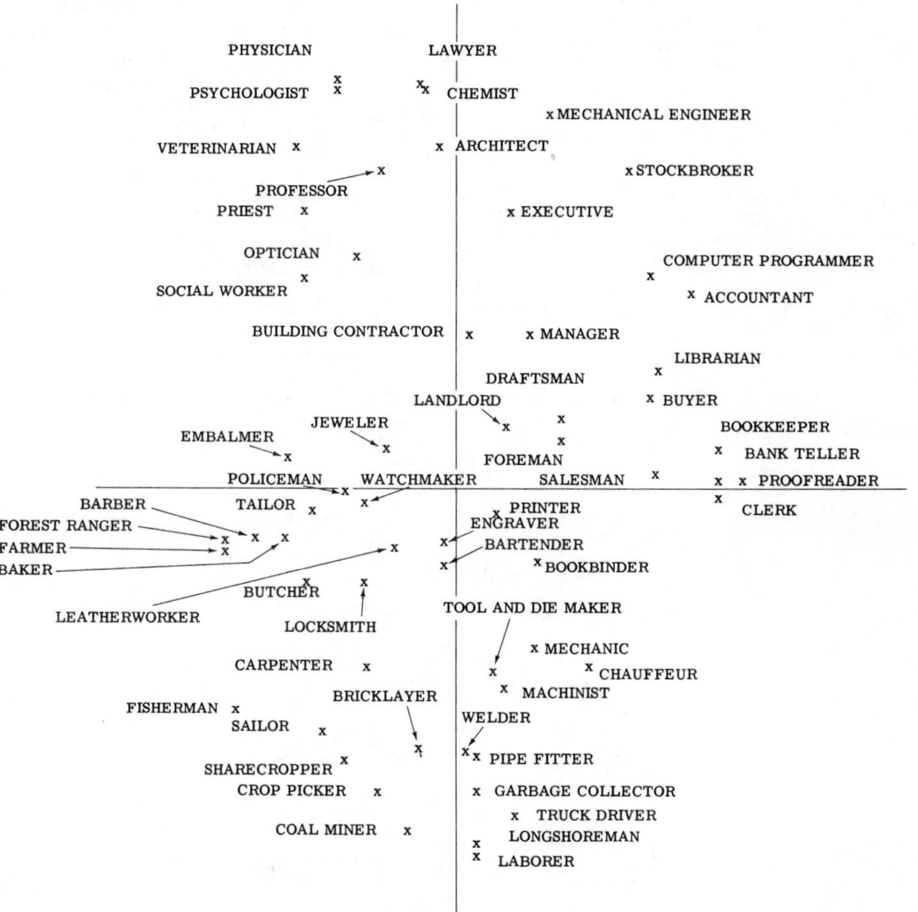

FIG. 2. Three-dimensional configuration: plot of dimensions one and two.

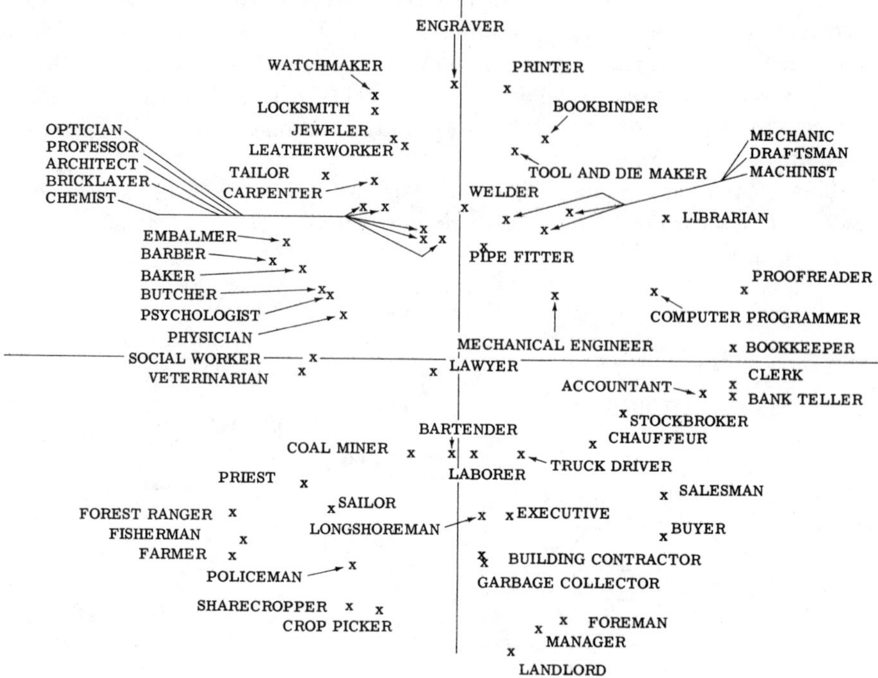

FIG. 3. Three-dimensional configuration: plot of dimensions one and three.

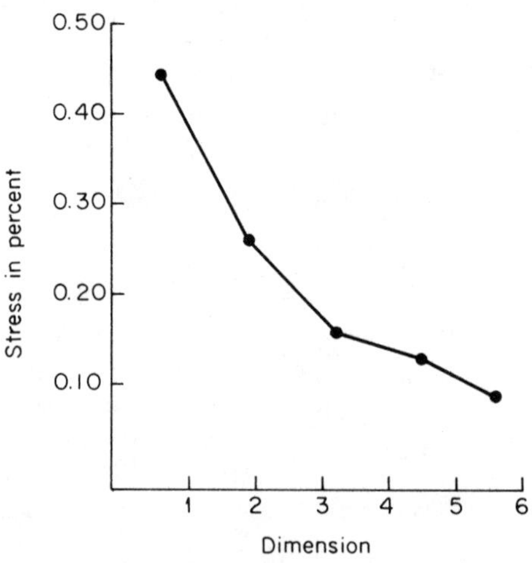

FIG. 4. Goodness of fit of multidimensional solutions obtained from analysis of occupation terms.

The third dimension (vertical in Figure 3) is a *skill* dimension, reflecting the amount of specific training required for the job. This scale of specific training is orthogonal to the scale of general education. Thus EXECUTIVE, MANAGER, and PRIEST are high on the prestige scale, but low on the specific skills scale. Conversely, WELDER, LOCKSMITH, PIPE-FITTER, and MACHINIST are very low on prestige but are high on skill.

External Validation of the Prestige Scale

Following the sorting task, subjects performed a paired-comparison task. Twenty-seven of the subjects did paired comparisons of the occupations on "prestige," followed by the same paired comparisons on "income." The remaining 27 did paired comparisons on "social status" followed by the same paired comparisons on "income." Rather than include all possible pairs (60.59/2 = 1770), 90 pairs were selected in a balanced design such that each term appeared three times and there were two complete cycles through the set of terms. These could then be used with the Gulliksen least-squares solution for incomplete paired comparisons (Torgerson, 1958, pp. 176–179) to produce scales.

The paired-comparisons test was chosen rather than a direct rank-ordering task because it forces the subject to make comparisons which he can easily overlook in a rank-ordering task with as many as 60 terms. Also, paired comparisons are practical for anthropological field research with illiterate informants, whereas complete rank ordering tasks are not.

The three scales from the paired-comparison data were converted to ordinal scales. The resulting rank orderings are listed in the first three columns of Table 2. The Spearman rank correlations among the three scales are Prestige–Status, .910; Prestige–Income, .737; and Status–Income, .789.

It is now possible to test the proposition that there is a monotonic relationship between the three scales derived from the paired-comparison test and some axis of the multidimensional configuration. By using a method suggested by Frederiksen (ms.) which maximizes the quantity

$$F = \sum_{j=1}^{M} \sum_{k=1}^{r} X_{jk} t_k H_j$$

where X_{jk} is the projection of stimulus j on axis k in the original configuration, t_k is the direction cosine of the fitted axis to axis k of the original configuration, and H_j is the rank order of stimulus j on the external scale. This maximization problem has a deterministic solution. It may be that

TABLE 2

RANK ORDERINGS FROM PAIRED COMPARISONS, COMPARED TO RANK ORDERINGS ON AXIS WITH BEST FIT IN THREE DIMENSIONS TO THE STATUS SCALE

Occupation	Status	Prestige	Income	Axis
Lawyer	1	4	2	2
Architect	2	2	8	5
Physician	3	5	1	1
Executive	4	1	4	10
Professor	5	3	10	9
Chemist	6	11	6	4
Psychologist	7	9	5	3
Priest	8	19	56	11
Stockbroker	9	7	3	8
Mechanical engineer	10	6	13	5
Computer programmer	11	12	14	12
Accountant	12	27	21	14
Building contractor	13	10	9	18
Manager	14	16	7	17
Landlord	15	25	18	21
Social worker	16	14	34	15
Optician	17	13	11	13
Veterinarian	18	8	16	7
Buyer	19	28	12	19
Jeweler	20	15	17	24
Librarian	21	18	29	16
Draftsman	22	23	22	20
Farmer	23	22	37	39
Foreman	24	34	19	23
Salesman	25	31	15	27
Tailor	26	33	26	33
Forest ranger	27	17	54	40
Watchmaker	28	20	23	30
Bookkeeper	29	38	41	22
Carpenter	30	30	25	46
Tool and die maker	31	39	32	47
Banker teller	32	35	38	26
Embalmer	33	36	20	28
Engraver	34	21	36	34
Clerk	35	44	44	29
Baker	36	42	42	29
Printer	37	32	27	32
Policeman	38	26	47	31
Sailor	39	29	57	50
Mechanic	40	50	24	45
Proofreader	41	45	43	25

TABLE 2—(Continued)

Occupation	Status	Prestige	Income	Axis
Bricklayer	42	40	28	53
Truck driver	43	52	35	57
Chauffeur	44	47	51	44
Fisherman	45	43	53	49
Bookbinder	46	37	45	38
Barber	47	56	55	35
Locksmith	48	53	33	42
Butcher	49	48	46	43
Machinist	50	41	31	48
Leatherworker	51	24	40	37
Welder	52	49	30	51
Laborer	53	55	50	60
Coal miner	54	51	58	58
Pipe fitter	55	54	48	52
Sharecropper	56	59	59	54
Longshoreman	57	57	39	59
Bartender	58	46	49	41
Garbage collector	59	58	52	55
Crop picker	60	60	60	56

it maximizes the Spearman rank correlation between the external scale and projections of points in the configuration on the fitted axis, although it has not been possible to prove or disprove this conjecture.

The results of this test are shown in Tables 2 and 3.

From these results it is clear that subjects used the criterion of prestige, which is about the same as the criterion of status, in performing the sorting task; and that this criterion is substantially the same as the second dimension of the multidimensional picture. From the pictures it is apparent that the prestige dimension has a much greater spread of values than the other two dimensions. The skill dimension appears to be second in this respect. Thus the prestige–status criterion is a factor in the similarities structure among occupations and is the most important single such factor. The entire similarities structure is a sort of cylinder, with terms falling in a circular pattern on the skill and independence scales, around a long prestige axis.

Hierarchical Clustering of the Similarities Data

Figure 5 shows the first 11 clusters resulting from the application of diameter method hierarchical clustering (Johnson, 1967) to the similarity data on the occupations.

TABLE 3

BEST FITTING AXES TO PRESTIGE, STATUS, AND INCOME SCALES IN TWO, THREE, AND FOUR DIMENSIONS

Dimensions	Prestige	Status	Income
2			
rank corr.	.904	.917	.791
angle 1	86½°	87½°	81°
angle 2	3½°	2½°	9°
3			
rank corr.	.866	.911	.749
angle 1	87½°	87°	76°
angle 2	5½°	2½°	9°
angle 3	85°	89°	79°
4			
rank corr.	.902	.913	
angle 1	89°	85°	
angle 2	22°	19°	Not computed
angle 3	86.5°	89°	
angle 4	68.5°	71.5°	

TABLE 4

THIRTY CLUSTERS FROM DIAMETER METHOD CLUSTERING

1	Building contractor	17	Physician, psychologist
2	Accountant, computer programmer	18	Priest, social worker
3	Draftsman	19	Optician, veterinarian
4	Farmer, fisherman	20	Bartender, chauffeur
5	Sailor	21	Barber, baker, butcher
6	Bank teller, bookkeeper, clerk	22	Embalmer
7	Librarian, proofreader	23	Bookbinder, printer
8	Landlord, foreman, manager	24	Leatherworker, tailor
9	Buyer, salesman	25	Engraver, locksmith, jeweler, watchmaker
10	Crop picker, sharecropper		
11	Coal miner, laborer, longshoreman	26	Machinist, tool and die maker
12	Garbage collector, truck driver	27	Carpenter
13	Architect	28	Mechanic
14	Chemist, mechanical engineer	29	Bricklayer, pipe fitter, welder
15	Executive, stockbroker	30	Forest ranger, policeman
16	Lawyer, professor		

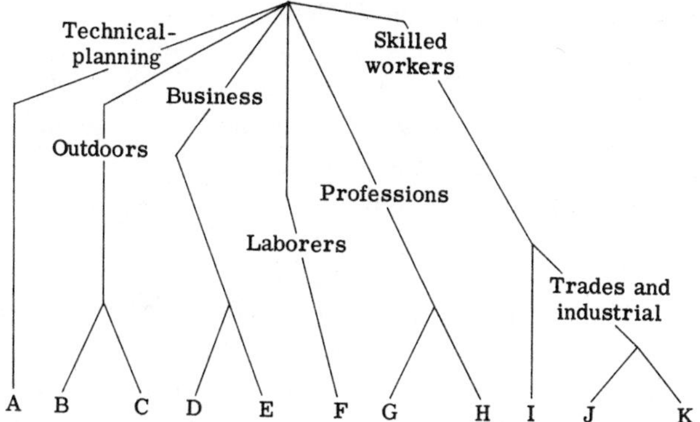

FIG. 5. Hierarchical clustering, diameter method. A. BUILDING CONTRACTOR, ACCOUNTANT, COMPUTER PROGRAMMER, DRAFTSMAN; B. FARMER, FISHERMAN; C. FOREST RANGER, POLICEMAN, SAILOR; D. BANK TELLER, BOOKKEEPER, CLERK, LIBRARIAN, PROOFREADER; E. LANDLORD, FOREMAN, MANAGER, BUYER, SALESMAN; F. CROP PICKER, SHARECROPPER, COAL MINER, LABORER, LONGSHOREMAN, GARBAGE COLLECTOR, TRUCK DRIVER; G. ARCHITECT, CHEMIST, MECHANICAL ENGINEER, EXECUTIVE, STOCKBROKER; H. LAWYER, PROFESSOR, PHYSICIAN, PSYCHOLOGIST, PRIEST, SOCIAL WORKER, OPTICIAN, VETERINARIAN; I. BARTENDER, CHAUFFEUR, BARBER, BAKER, BUTCHER-EMBALMER; J. BOOKBINDER, PRINTER, LEATHER WORKER, TAILOR, ENGRAVER, LOCK, SMITH, JEWLER, WATCHMAKER; K. MACHINIST, TOOL AND DIE MAKER, CARPENTER, MECHANIC, BRICKLAYER, PIPE FITTER, WELDER.

TABLE 5

LOCATIONS OF ELEVEN CLUSTERS IN MULTIDIMENSIONAL SPACE

		Prestige	Skill	Dependence
G	Business profession	++	Irrelevant	+
H	Other professions	++	Irrelevant	–
E	Business	+	–	+
D	Clerks	0, +	0, +	++
A	Technical	+	Irrelevant	+
B, C	Outdoors	–	–	–
J	Crafts	–	++	0
K	Skilled labor	–	+	0
F	Laborers	–	–	0
I	Services	–	Irrelevant	Irrelevant

Table 4 is a list of 30 small clusters that are all on the same hierarchical level in the same structure. Space does permit exposition of the full hierarchy, but it is clear from these two horizontal slices across it that the hierarchical structure corresponds to the multidimensional result (see Table 5). Without exception, terms that are within one of the 30 clusters are also very close in the multidimensional space. With the exception of cluster I, it is also possible to describe the region of the space in which each of the 11 higher level clusters resides.

Although the hierarchical clustering is of no use for finding and validating ordinal scales such as the prestige and skill scales, it does convey useful information about the identity of subdomains within the larger domain. A next step in the scheme for investigation of semantic structure would be a study of the within-cluster structure for a subdomain such as crafts, skilled laborers, laborers, or professions.

Summary

This paper describes the results of multidimensional scaling and hierarchical clustering analyses of a set of 60 names of occupations in the English language. The data for the analyses were obtained from a sorting task which required subjects to induce a partition upon the set of terms. The multidimensional scaling solution produces a three-dimensional representation, which is then used to test the previously formulated hypothesis that the criterion of prestige (status) had been used in the sorting task. The hypothesis is verified. An independently obtained scale of prestige has a strong rank-order correlation with one of the axes of the representation. This is also the longest axis of the representation, indicating that prestige is the single most important criterion of the sorting task.

Acknowledgments

The research on which this paper is based was supported in part by Public Health Service Grant #MH01096-14 to John Whiting at Harvard University.

John Whiting, Beatrice Whiting, Terry Nosanchuck, Klaus Koch, and John Frederiksen contributed valuable advice and criticisms to this paper. Any faults remain my own responsibility.

References

Berlin, B., Breedlove, D. E., & Raven, P. H. Covert categories and folk taxonomies. *American Anthropologist*, 1968, **70**, 290–300.

Bruner, J., Goodnow, J., & Austin, G. *A study of thinking*. New York: Wiley, 1956.

Burton, M. L. *Multidimensional scaling of role terms*. (Doctoral dissertation, Stanford University) Ann Arbor, Michigan: University Microfilms, 1968. No. 69-8160.

Conklin, H. Lexicographical treatment of folk taxonomies. In F. Householder & S. Saporta (eds.), *Problems in lexicography. International Journal of American Linguistics*, 1962, **28**(2), Pt. 4).

Frake, C. O., A structural description of Subanun religious behavior. In W. Goodenough (Ed.), *Explorations in cultural anthropology: Essays presented to George Peter Murdock*. New York: McGraw-Hill, 1964. Pp. 131–166.

Frederiksen, J. Testing hypotheses about the ordering of stimulus projections on a reference axis in multidimensional scaling. Unpublished manuscript.

Goodenough, W. H. Componential analysis and the study of meaning. *Language*, 1956, **32**, 195–216.

Harris, Z. S. Componential analysis of a Hebrew paradigm. *Language*, 1948, **24**, 87–91.

Johnson, S. C. Hierarchical clustering schemes. *Psychometrika*, 1967, **32**, 241–254.

Kay, P. Comment on ethnographic semantics: A preliminary survey (by. B. N. Colby). *Current Anthropology*, 1966, **7**, 20–23.

Kruskal, J. B. Multidimensional scaling by optimizing goodness of fit to a nonmetric hypothesis. *Psychometrika*, 1964, **29**, 1–27. (a)

Kruskal, J. B. Nonmetric multidimensional scaling: A numerical method. *Psychometrika*, 1964, **29**, 115–129. (b)

Lounsbury, F. A semantic analysis of the Pawnee kinship usage. *Language*, 1956, **32**, 158–194.

Romney, A. K., & D'Andrade, R. G. (Eds.). Cognitive aspects of English kin terms. *Transcultural studies in cognition. American Anthropologist Special Issue*, 1964, **66**, (3, Pt. 2) 146–170.

Shepard, R. N. The analysis of Proximities. I. *Psychometrika*, 1962, **27**, 125–140.

Shepard, R. N. Metric structures in ordinal data. *Journal of Mathematical Psychology*, 1966, **3**, 287–315.

Torgerson, W. S. *Theory and methods of scaling*. New York: Wiley, 1958.

United States Labor Department. *Dictionary of occupational titles*. (3rd ed.) Volume 2. *Occupational classification and industry index*. 1965.

INDIVIDUAL VARIATIONS IN COGNITIVE STRUCTURES

Kenneth N. Wexler and A. Kimball Romney

SCHOOL OF SOCIAL SCIENCES
UNIVERSITY OF CALIFORNIA
IRVINE, CALIFORNIA

The major purpose of this paper is to explore the nature of variations among individuals utilizing multidimensional scaling techniques. The data consist of judgments of similarity among kinship terms. Since individuals are compared with respect to how close they approximate a particular theoretical model, the first part of the paper is devoted to process models and their validation.

The Process Models

In recent years anthropologists and linguists have defined methods for the formal analysis of cognitive or semantic structures. These methods have been applied to restricted semantic domains such as pronouns and kinship terms. A semantic domain is defined as a recognized set of words, all on the same level of contrast, that refer to a single conceptual sphere. The words derive their meanings, in part, from their position in an inter-

	C_1	C_2	C_3
b_1	Grandfather		
b_2	Father	Uncle	
b_3	(Ego)	Brother	Cousin
b_4	Son	Nephew	
b_5	Grandson		

FIG. 1. Model A (from Wallace & Atkins, 1960).

dependent system reflecting the way in which a given language classifies the relevant conceptual sphere. The results of these formal analyses are described as possible cognitive or semantic structures. In this paper we refer to the results of such an analysis as structural models.

One problem with these formal methods is that alternative solutions are possible. Later in the paper we introduce the notion of process models in order to isolate the more appropriate structural models from among a set of alternatives. Prior to this, however, we will provide an example from the literature of alternative structural analyses of the same set of English kinship terms (we include only the male terms).

Some years ago Wallace and Atkins (1960) presented the following structural analysis of English kin terms (Figure 1). They referred to their analysis as a componential paradigm. In this analysis, rows and columns represent various dimensions of meaning (these could be referred to as criterial attributes, distinctive features, components, etc.). Wallace and Atkins (1960) hypothesize that the dimensions of meaning are such:

> that three dimensions will be sufficient to define all the terms: sex of relative (A): male (a_1), female (a_2); generation (B): two generations above ego (b_1), one generation above ego (b_2), ego's own generation (b_3), one generation below ego (b_4), two generations below ego (b_5); lineality (C): lineal (c_1), collineal (c_2), ablineal (c_3). We use Goodenough's definition of the values on this dimension of lineality: lineals are persons who are ancestors or descendants of ego; collineals are nonlineals all of whose ancestors include, or are included in, all the ancestors of ego; ablineals are consanguineal relatives who are neither lineals nor collineals (Goodenough, private communication).

We will call the Wallace and Atkins structure "Model A," (for absolute generation).

An alternative analysis presented by Romney and D'Andrade (1964) is shown in Figure 2. These two diagrams represent alternative structural models of English kinship terms. The motivating difference between the two models is that Model A has five generation values, while the second model (Model R) has three generation values and marks the difference between, say, grandfather and grandson by their difference on a third dimension, called the reciprocal dimension. Romney and D'Andrade (1964) observe

> that the general prediction we have made from componential analyses to cognitive measures is that the more components any two terms have in common, the greater will be the similarity of response to these terms. This prediction is derived from the assumption that the components of a term constitute the meaning of that term for an individual; hence, the more components which are shared, the more similar the meaning.

We will now attempt to formalize the above observation by constructing a process model that will enable us to predict from any given structural model, the subjects' performance on a cognitive task involving judgments of similarity or dissimilarity. We will use the following abbreviations for kin terms: Fa = father, So = son, GrFa = grandfather, GrSo = grandson, Br = brother, Un = uncle, Nep = nephew, Cos = cousin.

In order to investigate the above questions, Romney and D'Andrade (1964) used a triads test. In this task a subject (high school student) was presented with a triad consisting of three of the eight kin terms listed above. He was told to select the one of the three which was "most different in meaning from the other two." For example, the subject was presented with three terms, *grandfather*, *uncle*, and *nephew*, and his task was to select the one of the three he thought most different.

Eight terms taken three at a time produce 56 triads. These triads were each presented in written form to 116 subjects. If we look at a triad (A, B, C), we say that the proportion of times term A was chosen as most different is the proportion of times terms B and C are "classed together." Suppose we assume that when two terms are relatively close together on a structural model (e.g., Model R or A), then they will be classed together more often. The results of the experiment suggested that this assumption was more nearly true for Model R than for Model A. On the basis of this finding, Romney and D'Andrade suggested that Model R might be more correct than Model A.

A precise comparison of the two structural models was not possible, however, because no model was available to predict exactly what subjects

	Direct		Collateral	
	−Reciprocal	+Reciprocal	+Reciprocal	−Reciprocal
$G \pm 2$	Grandson	Grandfather		
$G \pm 1$	Son	Father	Uncle	Nephew
$G0$	Brother		Cousin	

FIG. 2. Model R (from Romney & D'Andrade, 1964).

would do in the triad experiment given they held a specified structural model. We introduce here a "process" model which specifies how a subject behaves in the triad experiment assuming any given structural model.

For any structural model, e.g., any grid of the type of Model R or A, we informally define the distance function D on any two points in the model. $D(A, B)$ is the smallest number of steps along the grid it takes to reach B from A (or A from B, of course). For example, for Model A, D(GrFa, Un) = 2, D(GrFa, GrSo) = 4. For Model R, D(GrFa, Un) = 2, D(GrFa, GrSo) = 1. (The two exceptions to this definition are the terms brother and cousin in Model R, which are not given any values on the reciprocity dimension. We could put a third (say, zero) value on this dimension for these terms, but we want to present the structural models in the same form in which they were originally suggested. For these two terms, we define D in the following way. If A = Br or Cos, we calculate D(A, B) twice; once on the basis of A being plus reciprocal, and once on the basis of A being minus reciprocal. D is taken to be the smaller of the two values. Thus, for example in Model R, D(Br, Fa) = 1 and D(Br, So) = 1. By a slight generalization, D(Br, Cos) = 1.) Let $M(A, B, C) = \{\text{pairs } (X, Y) \in \{(\text{A}, \text{B}), (B, C), (A, C)\} \text{ such that } D(X, Y) \leq D(Z, W)$ for all $(Z, W) \in \{(A, B), (\text{B}, \text{C}), (A, C)\}\}$. That is, $M(A, B, C)$ is the closest pair or pairs of points. Let m be the number of elements in $M(A, B, C)$. Let $\Pr(X, Y)$ be the probability of classifying X and Y together. The assumptions of the process model then are:

A1: If $(X, Y) \in M(A, B, C)$, then $\Pr(X, Y) = 1/m$.

A2: If $(X, Y) \notin M(A, B, C)$ then $\Pr(X, Y) = 0$.

As an example, let us make predictions for the triad (GrFa, GrSo, Fa) for both structural models, R and A. In Model A, D(GrFa, GrSo) = 4, D(GrFa, Fa) = 1 and D(Fa, GrSo) = 3. Therefore M(GrFa, GrSo, Fa) = {(GrFa, Fa)}, and thus m = 1. Therefore Pr(GrFa, Fa) = 1 by A1 and Pr(GrFa, GrSo) = 0 and Pr(Fa, GrSo) = 0 by A2. For Model R, D(GrFa, GrSo) = 1, D(GrFa, Fa) = 1 and D(Fa, GrSo) = 2. Therefore, M(GrFa, GrSo, Fa) = {(GrFa, GrSo), (GrFa, Fa)}, and m = 2. Then Pr(GrFa, Fa) = $\frac{1}{2}$ and Pr(GrFa, GrSo) = $\frac{1}{2}$ by A1, and Pr(Fa, GrSo) = 0 by A2.

It should be clear how this process model works. It simply classes together the pair or pairs which are closest together in the structural model. The process model makes very strong predictions which are doubtless wrong in many cases. For example, many probabilities are predicted to be zero (those for all pairs which are not in $M(A, B, C)$).

We will compare the predictions of our models with data from two experiments. Experiment 1 is the triad experiment on high school students described in Romney and D'Andrade (1964) referred to previously. Experiment 2 used the same method on 155 undergraduates at the University of California at Irvine. The students were in an introductory anthropology class and had not studied kinship. They were given sheets of paper containing the 56 triads of the 8 male kin terms and told to pick the word in each triad which was the most different in meaning from the other two. The triads and words within triads were randomly ordered (but were the same for all subjects.) The subjects were told to work quickly but to answer carefully. They were allowed as much time as they needed and none took longer than twenty minutes.

As a first step in comparing the models to data, let us consider the measure that was used by Romney and D'Andrade to determine how "close" two kin terms were. This is the mean number of times the kin terms were classed together over all triads. This is obtained by taking the mean over all subjects of the sum of the times two terms were classed together. Since for each subject a given pair of terms appears in six triads (once for each of the other six terms), this measure can range from zero to six. We will call this sum C. Theoretical predictions for the mean, $E(C)$, are obtained for each structural model by making a prediction for each of the six triads in which the pair appears and summing the six scores. This is easily shown to be correct by the following argument.

For a pair of kin terms (A, B) let X_i, $i = 1, \ldots, 6$, be random variables taking the value 1 if A and B are classed together in triad i (in which A and B appear) and the value 0 if A and B are not classed together. Then, for a given subject $E(X_i) = 1p_i + 0(1 - p_i) = p_i$. Since

$$C = \sum_{i=1}^{6} X_i,$$

$$E(C) = E(\sum_{i=1}^{6} (X_i)) = \sum_{i=1}^{6} E(X_i) = \sum_{i=1}^{6} p_i$$

and

$$E(C) = \sum_{i=1}^{6} p_i$$

which is the basis for our predictions.

In Table 1 are listed the mean C values from Experiments 1 and 2, together with predictions for $E(C)$ from Model A and Model R. There are no parameters in the current models and the models make the same predictions for both sets of data.

TABLE 1[a]

	Observed data		Theoretical predictions	
	Exp. 1	Exp. 2	Model R	Model A
GrSo, Un	.77	.20	0	0
GrFa, Nep	.81	.31	0	0
GrSo, Cos	1.10	.81	0	.33
GrFa, Cos	.62	.27	0	.33
So, Un	.63	.32	.33	0
Fa, Nep	.61	.26	.33	0
So, Cos	1.43	.75	.50	.50
Fa, Cos	.55	.25	.50	.50
GrSo, Nep	1.68	1.38	.67	3.00
GrFa, Un	1.56	.92	.67	3.00
GrSo, Fa	1.62	1.88	.83	.50
GrFa, So	1.43	2.31	.83	.50
GrSo, Br	1.55	1.36	.83	.50
GrFa, Br	1.00	1.01	.83	.50
Br, Nep	1.56	1.63	.83	4.50
Br, Un	1.61	2.47	.83	4.50
So, Fa	3.80	4.02	3.33	1.33
Fa, Un	1.95	2.13	3.50	5.00
So, Nep	1.23	1.02	3.50	5.00
So, Br	3.68	3.01	3.83	1.33
Fa, Br	2.32	2.31	3.83	1.33
GrSo, So	3.17	4.04	4.00	5.50
GrFa, Fa	4.00	4.50	4.00	5.50
Br, Cos	1.75	1.75	4.00	5.00
Un, Nep	3.71	4.27	4.33	2.83
Un, Cos	3.48	3.86	4.33	2.83
Nep, Cos	4.24	4.71	4.33	2.83
GrSo, GrFa	4.10	4.25	5.00	.33

[a] Values of $E(C)$ = mean number of times a pair is classed together; out of a total of six possible.

Inspection of Table 1 makes it clear that Model R does a better job of predicting the data for both experiments than does Model A. As a rough measure of the fit of the models, we calculated the Pearson product moment correlations between the theoretical predictions for each model and the data from both experiments. The value of the correlation coefficients (Table 2) are much larger for Model R than for Model A in both sets of

TABLE 2

CORRELATION OF THEORETICAL $E(C)$ VERSUS OBSERVED $E(C)$

	Model R	Model A
Experiment 1 ($N = 116$)	.86	.33
Experiment 2 ($N = 155$)	.84	.40

data. We do not show significance levels for these coefficients because (1) to do so would require assumptions about distributions that we do not want to make and (2) although there are 28 dyads and thus 28 points in the calculation of each coefficient, these 28 points are not independent, and it is not clear what N should be used in determining significance. We are using the correlation coefficient simply as a rough measure of fit.

It is interesting to observe where Model A fails. For example, Model A predicts $E(C) = .33$ for the pair (GrSo, GrFa), whereas Model R predicts $E(C) = 5$. The small value under Model A is due to the fact that GrSo and GrFa are relatively distant. However experimental values for this pair are $E(C) = 4.3$ for Experiment 1 and $E(C) = 4.2$ for Experiment 2. Table 1 shows other pairs for which Model R is the better predictor. It appears that the reciprocity dimension is a productive one in the structural model.

If we take the absolute difference between the theoretical and observed values of Model A as a measure of the discrepancy between theory and data, we find that for Experiment 1, of the 28 pairs, the three pairs with the largest discrepancy are (Fa, Un), (Br, Cos), and (So, Nep). For Experiment 2, (So, Nep) and (Br, Cos) have the two largest deviations and (Fa, Un) has the sixth largest. These pairs are consistently overpredicted by a large amount. It is interesting to observe that the only difference between the two elements of each pair in Model R is that one is direct and one is collateral. Since the distance between the two terms is 1, according to the model they should be classed together relatively often. But the observed values show that this does not occur. This finding suggests that in a certain sense two terms which differ only on the lineality dimension are not as similar as two terms which differ only on another dimension. This notion may be caught by the construction of a model with parameters related to the various dimensions. Such models are currently under investigation.

Individual Variation

This section explores the nature of individual variations of the cognitive structure of male English kin terms as inferred from the triads test of judged similarity.

There are various implicit and explicit assumptions about individual variations of cognitive structures held by researchers. One common model in the minds of investigators is that there is a single cultural norm around which there is a certain random variation arising from performance and other errors. Another more complicated model envisioned by investigators is that there may be alternative structures present. In this view, one would expect individuals to form a number of tightly grouped clusters. Each cluster of subjects would represent one of the alternative structures. A variety of more complicated assumptions could be imagined.

Below we present a kind of binomial test of the notion that the subjects cluster around a single mode. The binomial test follows from a very simple model. It provides us with an indication that the variation among subjects is clearly not binomially distributed around a single mode. We then present the results of our exploration of individual variation using multidimensional scaling. We present a brief discussion of implications following these two analyses.

A Simple Model

In observing the responses of individual subjects, one difference that we noticed among subjects was the extent to which they classified together pairs that differed on lineality in the theoretical (reciprocal or R) model. That is, one member of the pair is direct, and the other collateral. Some subjects seemed to do this often, others infrequently or even never. Some of these same pairs were drawn to our attention earlier when we noticed that the mean values of the total times the pair was classed together were much lower than the predicted theoretical values.

The pairs noticed earlier were those whose members differed on *only* the lineality dimension; on all other dimensions they had identical values. In the theoretical model, whenever such a pair appears in a triad in which the third member differs from one of the members of the pair only by one step, that is one value on one other dimension, then the predicted probability of classifying the cross-lateral pair together is $\frac{1}{2}$. But in general these mean proportions in the data were much smaller than $\frac{1}{2}$.

In order to ininvestigate individuals' responses, we will consider triads ABC where A and B are identical except that they differ on lineality and

B and *C* are identical except they differ on reciprocity or on one generation value. (In this section all theoretical calculations are for Model R.) Altogether there are 14 of these triads. As an example, let *A* be uncle, *B* be father, and *C* be grandfather. Then *A* and *B* differ only on lineality, and *B* and *C* differ only on generation. If we let *C* be son, then we would have another such triad, where *B* and *C* differed only on reciprocity.

As an index of the extent to which subjects choose to classify cross-laterals together when confronted with a choice of classifying another pair which differs only on another dimension together, we define the statistic *L*, which for each subject is the number of times in the 14 triads he classified together pairs which differ on lineality. *L* is the number of times *A* and *B* or *A* and *C* are classified together, that is, the number of times *C* or *B* is chosen as "most different in meaning."

Now, we have *L* calculated for 155 subjects, and the values, are, of course, different for different subjects. But we always expect variation, and the question is, how do we know whether subjects differ on this process? The process is doubtless probabilistic, and we expect a range of values. To investigate this question, we can set up a very simple model of the subject's behavior. We assume that when the triad *ABC* is presented, the subject chooses *C* or *B* with probability p, independent of all other responses, and with probability $1 - p$, he chooses *A*. (Note that in the original model *B* is never chosen, that is *A* and *C* are never classed together, because the distance between them is 2, and there are smaller distances in the triad). We assume that p is the same for all triads *ABC*. We also assume that p is the same for all subjects. This last assumption is the crucial one. It assumes that there are no underlying differences among subjects, but because it is a probabilistic process, the data will be different for different subjects.

According to the model, for each subject, the *ABC* triads form a sequence of 14 Bernoulli trials with parameter p. *L* is thus distributed binomially with mean $14p$. To the extent that the distribution in the data fits the theoretical distribution, we can say that there is no difference between individuals on this process. It is not clear what an alternative hypothesis would be. One possibility is that there are two types of subjects, each obeying the above model, but with different parameters, p_1 and p_2. But for now we are not interested in an alternative hypothesis, but only in testing the first model.

As an estimate of p, we took the proportion of times *B* or *C* were chosen over all 14 triads and 155 subjects. The value was $p = .30$. For this value of p, Figure 3 shows the theoretical distribution of *L*. The data distribution is also plotted. It is clear that theory and data do not agree (Kolmogoroff–

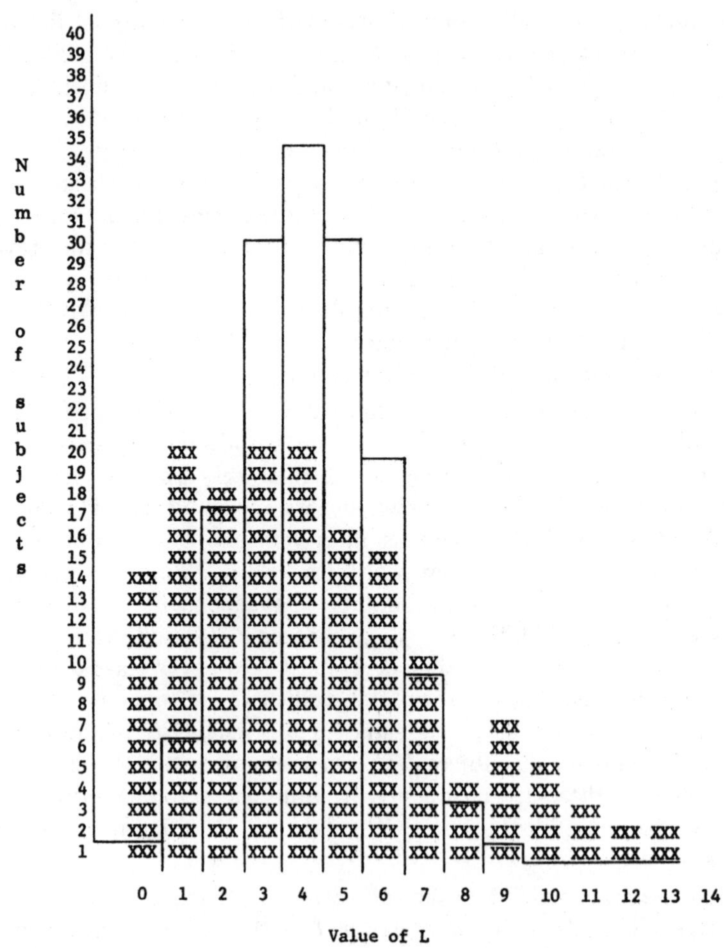

FIG. 3. Theoretical (Binomial $p = .30$) and observed distribution of L for 155 subjects (L defined in text). Bars represent theoretical distribution and X's represent observed distribution.

Smirnov $p < .01$). There are both too many low and too many high values in the data, and the middle is squashed down. This theory predicts that only 1 of the 155 subjects should have an L-value of 9 or greater, but in fact, 19 do. In other words, there is a definite tendency for some subjects to make fewer cross-lateral responses than would be predicted by the model, and for some to make more. We conclude that subjects are not drawn from the same random pool.

Multidimensional Scaling of Individuals

We next wanted to see if we could plot individuals in a multidimensional, space to investigate the nature of individual variation. For one thing could we come up with L as an interpretation in the space? In order to do this we divised a simple proximity measure on pairs of individuals, namely,

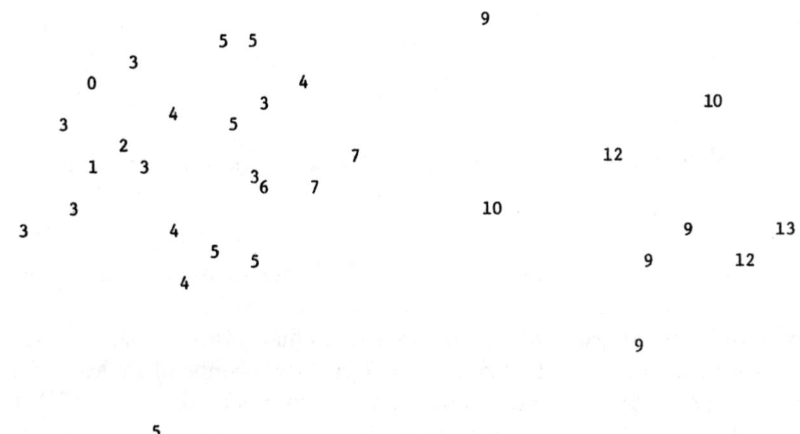

Fig. 4. Multidimensional plot of 35 male subjects. The value plotted is L. Stress = .169.

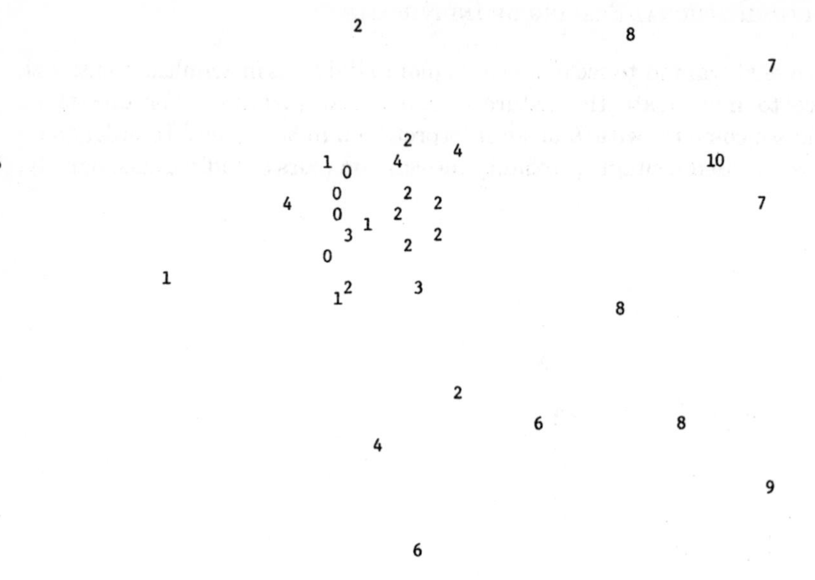

FIG. 5. Multidimensional plot of 35 female subjects. The value plotted is L. Stress = .200.

number of agreements on choices on the 56 triads of the two individuals. This matrix was fed into the Shepard–Kruskal MDS program. We ran a randomly selected group of 35 females and 35 males through the program, in two dimensions only. Figures 4 and 5 plot the groups of males and females, respectively. Instead of points, we have put in the value of L for each subject. In both cases a straight line can be drawn parallel to the y-axis such that subjects with L-values greater than or equal to a given value (8 and 7, respectively) are to the right of the line and subjects with values less than that are to the left. About 70% of the subjects are to the left of this line. These results, we feel, provide a confirmation of the claim that subjects differ on the extent to which they will choose to ignore given dimensions of meaning.

There is a possibility, however, that our finding that L is an interpretation in the multidimensional space is an artifact. This is because the relation between 2 subjects who have similar L-scores is not independent of the distance between the 2 subjects which was fed into the multidimensional program. That is, L was calculated from 14 triads. These 14 were part of the 56 which were used to measure between subject distances for the program. The 2 subjects who had similar L scores would tend to make the same choices on the 14 triads and thus to some extent be close on the overall distance measure for the 56 triads.

In order to check this possibility, we calculated a random statistic L' in

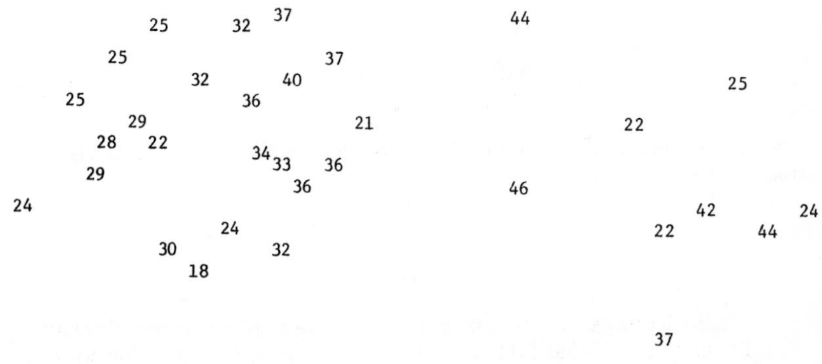

FIG. 6. Multidimensional plot of 35 male subjects. The value plotted is number of agreements with Model A. Stress = .169.

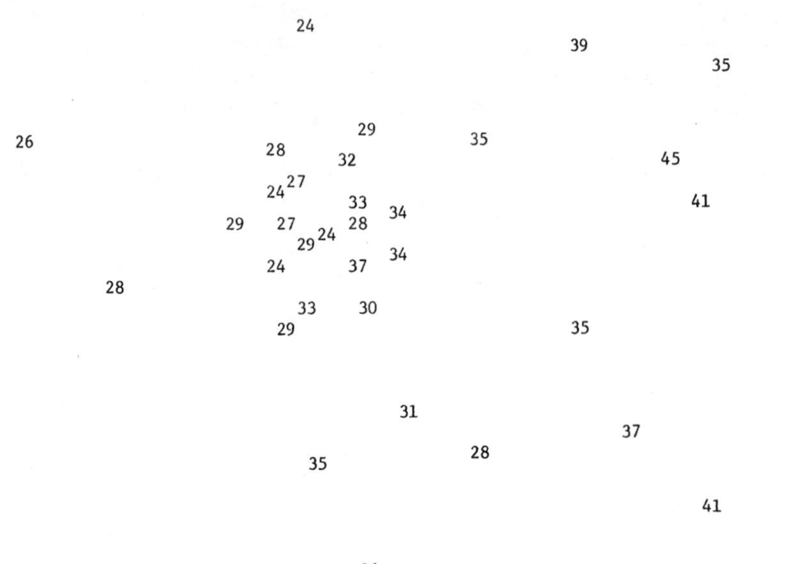

FIG. 7. Multidimensional plot of 35 female subjects. The value plotted is number of agreements with Model A. Stress = .200.

TABLE 3

MEAN NUMBER OF AGREEMENTS WITH EACH MODEL, FOR SUBJECTS DIVIDED INTO THREE GROUPS ACCORDING TO VALUE ON HORIZONTAL DIMENSION OF SCALE[a]

	Group		
	1	2	3
A male	28.8	33.8	41.9
A female	27.3	31.9	38.3
R′ male	47.2	49.6	44.3
R female	48.4	47.3	44.3
A′ male	24.2	22.7	23.2
R′ male	31.0	28.7	28.5

[a] Group 1 represents the left-most subjects and Group 3, the right-most.

the following manner. Of the 56 triads, 14 were picked at random and the 2 responses (of the 3 available) for each triad were chosen randomly. L' for the subject was the number of times in the 14 triads that he made one of these chosen responses. We calculated L' for the group of 35 male subjects. The resulting figures (not shown) have no clear interpretation. We

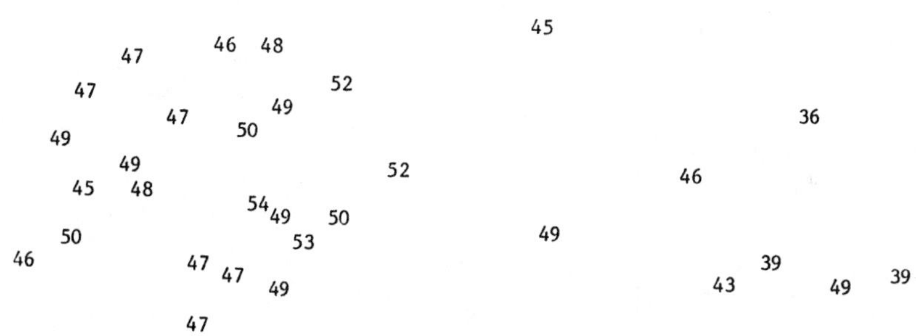

FIG. 8. Multidimensional plot of 35 male subjects. The value plotted is number of agreements with Model R. Stress = .169.

conclude that the finding that L is an interpretation in the multidimensional space is not an artifact.

We next wanted to see if we could find individual variation in amount of compatibility of subject responses with Model R or Model A. In order to do this, we plotted number of agreements with Model R and Model A on the same multidimensional scale separately for males and females (Figures 6 through 9). Recall that the number of agreements with a model for a subject is the number of responses (out of 56) which he made which have probability greater than 0 under that model.

In Figures 6 and 7, it is clear that in general the agreements with Model A increase as one goes from left to right on the graph. Table 3 shows the mean number of agreements with each model for males and females, when we divide the subjects into three groups of equal size depending on their position with respect to the x-axis in the multidimensional plot. Group 1 contains the left-most subjects, Group 2 the middle subjects, and Group 3 the right-most subjects. This phenomenon is true for both males and

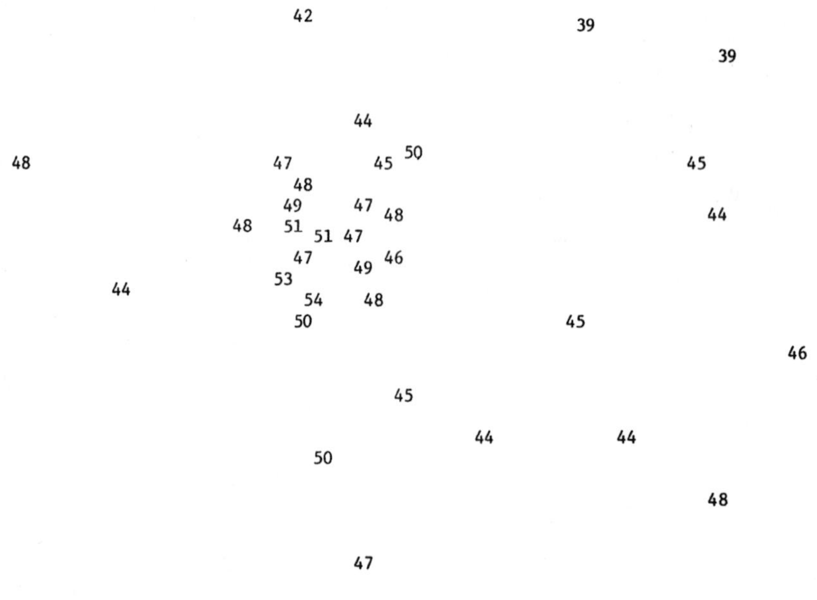

FIG. 9. Multidimensional plot of 35 female subjects. The value plotted is number of agreements with Model R. Stress = .200.

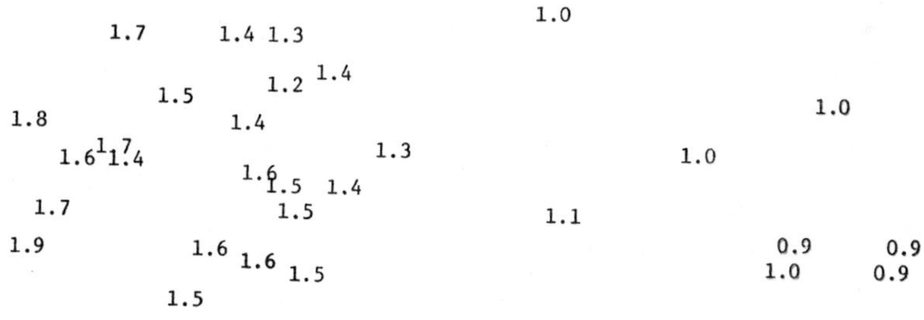

FIG. 10. Multidimensional plot of 35 male subjects. Numbers plotted are number of agreements with Model R divided by number of agreements with Model A. Stress = .169.

females, i.e., the agreements with Model A increasing from left to right. (Of course, the direction of increase does not mean anything, but simply the fact that the dimension can be recovered. We have put all plots in a standard orientation.) Note the two male subjects (Figure 6) most separated from the others, with scores of 25 and 29 respectively, which are the lowest on the graph. Figure 8 shows that these two subjects were also by far the lowest on agreements with Model R (27 and 31, respectively). We assume that they were either deliberately trying to answer aberrantly or they were not paying attention and were simply guessing. At any rate we ignore these two subjects from now on and their values are not included in the computations for Table 3.

Turning now to number of agreements with Model R, Figures 8 and 9

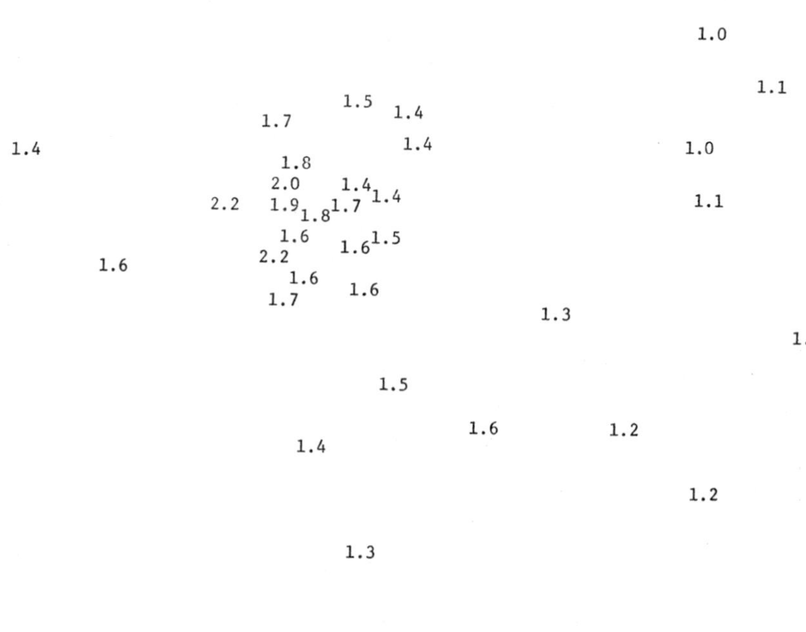

FIG. 11. Multidimensional plot of 35 female subjects. Numbers plotted are number of agreements with Model R divided by number of agreements with Model A. Stress = .200.

show agreements with Model R and Table 3 shows means for the three groups from left to right. The separation is less than for Model A.

In Figures 10 and 11 we plot, for each individual on the same scale, his number of agreements with Model R divided by his number of agreements with Model A. Given our earlier discussion, we, of course, expect the result that for most subjects the values are greater than or equal to 1. These graphs point up very clearly that for both males and females there is a small cluster (of about 10 subjects) on the right who have the smallest values.

Let us summarize what we have seen. First, the outcome for the two groups (males and females) is quite similar, and thus gives us more confidence in our results. We can interpret the x-axis as indicating a higher number of agreements with Model A for higher values of x. This result is very clear. Not quite so clear is the result that higher x-values are related to lower number of agreements with R. In both cases there are two clusters, with about 70% of the subjects in the first and 30% in the second. The smaller (30%) cluster appears to be more spread out on the MDS plot than the larger.

We can ask if the reason that number of agreements with R behaves inversely to the number of agreements with A with respect to the MDS plot is that there is a general negative correlation between the two measures. The Pearson product moment correlation between the two scores is $r = -.14$. Clearly there is almost no relation overall between the two scores.

As was the case when we considered L, we want to consider the possibility that we were able to interpret the number of agreements with a model as values on a dimension simply because the calculation of number of agreements forced subjects who had similar scores to be, on the average, closer on the original distance measures. To check this, we calculated a statistic A' by randomly assigning responses to triads and comparing these to Model A. Then for each subject, the number of agreements with these responses (out of the 56 possible) was calculated. Another statistic R' was also calculated, by using the same method, but by comparing the responses to Model R. Both statistics were calculated for the 35 male subjects.

As expected, the numbers for R' are on the average higher than for A'. Dividing the subjects into thirds, Table 3 shows that R' decreases slightly from left to right, but A' is not even monotonic with x. Clearly, the variation of number of agreements of A with x cannot be explained by this argument.

Our conclusions, then, are that agreements with Model A will vary strongly on an x-dimension while agreements with Model R will vary less clearly, in the opposite direction. Most subjects have a fairly large number of agreements with Model R. A cluster of about 30% of the subjects has large values on agreement with A also, while the other subjects have fewer agreements with A.

Discussion of Individual variation

The approach we have taken to the study of individual variation is a cautious, exploratory one. First, the binomial test together with the scaling results suggest that a simple model of subjects having the same probabilistic parameter is not correct. This simple model also may be interpreted as the anthropological notion that the distribution over people is unimodal. Another possibility is that there is some kind of continuous variation over subjects, with no structures discernible. While this hypothesis is not formulated precisely enough to test exactly, our results regarding agreements with *R* and *A* would seem to not make it very probable.

What we think might be going on is that there are two cognitive structures which are important, roughly, Model R and Model A. Most subjects tend to agree with Model R quite strongly; that is, not many responses are made which are impossible under Model R. However, there is variation in the weighting of dimensions which Model R does not account for. Most subjects (about 70%) do not tend to follow Model A; however, the other 30% do. This result stands out in the two clusters of subjects in the scaling. Even though 30% of the subjects follow Model A, they do not abandon Model R, but agree with it almost as often as the other 70% of the subjects. What seems to happen is that in cases where they do deviate from Model R or where more than one response is permissible under Model R, these subjects (the 30%) tend to pick responses compatible with Model A; whereas, the other subjects pick more randomly.

Summary

By defining a process model and applying it to two different structural models of English kin terms, we have been able to conclude that one model (Model R) is more reasonable than another (Model A). Although neither model fits the data precisely, Model R consistently does better than Model A.

We then studied individual variation in cognitive structure. The most promising hypothesis seems, at least for kin terms, to be that there are a small number of structures (in our case, two) in the population, possibly one of them dominating, the second coming into play for some subjects at some times.

Acknowledgments

We would like to thank Mr. Lee Sailer for doing the programming and helping with the analysis.

References

Romney, A. K., & D'Andrade, R. G. (Eds.). Cognitive aspects of English kin terms. *Transcultural Studies in Cognition. American Anthropologist Special Issue*, 1964, **66** (3, Pt. 2), 146–170.

Wallace, A. F. C., & Atkins, J. The meaning of kinship terms. *American Anthropologist*, 1960, **62,** 58–80.

AN EXPERIMENTAL STUDY OF SEMANTIC STRUCTURES

Amnon Rapoport and Samuel Fillenbaum

UNIVERSITY OF NORTH CAROLINA
CHAPEL HILL, NORTH CAROLINA

This study represents an attempt to determine some structural properties of two different semantic domains (a) color names and (b) the HAVE family of verbs, using as basic data subjects' judgments of proximity (similarity or dissimilarity in meaning) among the terms constituting each domain. It has been suggested (Lyons, 1968) that meaning should be treated as a function of meaning relations, and that the notion of semantic structure be defined in terms of certain relations that hold between the items of particular lexical subsystems. We have followed the logic of this position by seeking to determine what sort of structure is required to accommodate adequately proximity judgments for each of two sets of related terms.

As the terms "semantic structure" and "semantic domain" suggest, our work retains one of the main ideas of the semantic differential method (Osgood, Suci, & Tannenbaum, 1957), i.e., the study of the dimensionality of semantic spaces, but, following Rapoport, Rapoport, Livant, and Boyd (1966), generalizes the idea of "semantic space" in several important ways.

First we have not used bipolar scales to determine the location of concepts in a space and the space we are concerned with is a denotative rather than a connotative, affective space. Second, rather than using factor analysis, the dimensionality of the space has been investigated by means of non-metric multidimensional scaling (MDS) methods, which make considerably weaker assumptions about the data. Third, we have also considered non-Euclidean spaces. Fourth, and most important, we have not confined ourselves to the study of the dimensionality of semantic spaces but we have also used graph and clustering techniques to extract some additional structural properties from the data.

The following considerations governed the selection of lexical items. First, in each study items were chosen in such a fashion as to insure that they formed a structurally related coherent set. Second, the two domains investigated were chosen so as to be quite diverse. Since one of our main purposes is to exemplify and evaluate the uses of various techniques for the analysis of semantic structure, we need to examine not only highly structured or relatively limited, well-defined domains, but also those in which the class of terms is open and the boundaries quite unclear. Third, the domains were chosen so as to represent cases of some intrinsic interest or importance where previous analyses or results were already available, so as to permit comparisons of our results with those of other studies.

Color names constitute a relatively well-defined semantic domain. Several studies have used multidimensional scaling methods to characterize color space or parts of it (e.g., Helm & Tucker, 1962; Shepard, 1962), and there has also been some interest in color names for color space (Chapanis, 1965). We wished to examine the structure that characterizes a set of color names, and to compare it with the color space, for which the underlying dimensionality in terms of physical properties is already known.

The HAVE family of verbs (e.g., including FIND, GAIN, GIVE, HOLD, TAKE, etc.) was chosen because (1) in contrast to color names, these terms constitute a semantic field whose boundaries are rather ill-defined and indefinite; (2) they are intrinsically important and used widely; and (3) a structural analysis has recently been offered for a restricted subset of these verbs by Bendix (1966), who carried out a cross-linguistic study in English, Hindi, and Japanese, requiring subjects to respond to a number of semantic tests including matching and interpretation tasks.

Three procedures were employed in this study to obtain the proximity data: tree construction, complete undirected (linear) graphs, and direct grouping or classification. These methods were chosen for their efficiency, capability of handling a relatively large number of terms in a short time, meaningfulness to the subjects, and amenability to sequential data gathering. The two graph construction methods described below satisfy all of these requirements.

The tree construction method requires subjects to construct "trees" (connected undirected graphs without cycles) by linking words in a given vocabulary set in terms of some specified similarity criterion.[1] The method generates all $M = \binom{N}{2}$ proximity measures among the N words, and it is highly efficient and readily communicable to subjects. One of the purposes of this study was to extend the use of this technique, which had been employed previously in the study of relatively heterogeneous sets of concepts (Rapoport *et al.*, 1966; Rapoport, 1967), to the study of coherent, related sets of terms.

The method of complete undirected graphs requires the rank ordering of all pairs of N words. Like the tree construction method it also allows for the sequential construction of proximity matrices. Whereas the tree construction method yields only the first N–1 ranked pairs of nodes and certain assumptions must be made to obtain the remaining ranks, the complete graphs method yields all M ranked pairs. This is done at a certain cost, however, for the task is tiring, demanding the continuous rescanning of the large subset of remaining pairs.

The method of direct grouping simply requires subjects to sort the words into as many classes as they wish, with any number of words placed in each class (see Clark, 1968, for use of a variant of this procedure in the study of English prepositions; also see Miller, 1967, 1969).

In order to compare various methods for uncovering structural properties of the semantic domains selected, graph, clustering, and nonmetric multidimensional scaling (MDS) methods were used in the analysis of the data. The theory of graphs is employed for detecting "biases," which are hopefully of some psycholinguistic interest, in the proximity data obtained by the two graph construction methods. Examining such properties of graphs as connectivity, cycle size, and distribution of node degree, we shall first determine whether or not the proximity matrices were randomly constructed. Given that they are nonrandom, the complete matrices will be analyzed by a nonmetric MDS technique (Young & Torgerson, 1967) and a hierarchical clustering technique (Johnson, 1967). The MDS and clustering techniques are viewed here mainly as quantitative psycholinguistic models rather than as methods for merely organizing, summarizing, and displaying data. They differ in the assumptions they make about the structure of the semantic domain in question, in their output, and in their appropriateness for the characterization of different semantic domains. The

[1] The terminology currently in use in graph theory is not standardized; in our discussion, we will follow the conventions of Busacker and Saaty (1965).

three methods for data analysis are applied both to proximity matrices averaged over subjects and to randomly selected individual proximity matrices so as to permit some comparisons between averaged and individual data.

Method

Instructions

(a) Tree construction (color names and HAVE verbs studies). The instructions for the tree construction method were as follows:

> You will be given a list of N words arranged in alphabetical order, and a blank sheet of paper. Read the list carefully several times.
>
> From the list of N words pick the two words which you think are *most similar* to each other. Write the pair you have chosen on the blank paper and connect them with a line. Label the connecting line 1. Now you have two options.
>
> *Option 1*
>
> You may go carefully over the remaining words in the list (which now includes N-2 words) and pick the word which you think is most similar to *either* of the *two* words you have already selected. Write this word down on your paper and connect it to the appropriate word already selected. Label the connecting line 2.
>
> *Option 2*
>
> You may look over the remaining words on the list and decide that two of them are more similar to each other than any of them is to either of the two words already selected and joined together. If so, you may select these words and write them down on the paper, just as you did with the first pair. Connect the two new words with a line and label it 2.
>
> After taking option 1 or 2, proceed in exactly the same way. Search carefully the remaining words on the list and continue with option 1 or option 2. When you take option 1, you add a word to an already linked group of words (which is called a tree). When you take option 2 you start a new tree.
>
> *Option 3*
>
> As the experiment proceeds (after your second choice) you have a third option. If you find that you have made several trees you may want to connect any two of them together. If you find two words on two separate trees that are more similar to each other than any other word on the remaining list is to any other word on the trees, you should connect these words (and thus connect the two trees). Label the connecting line according to the sequence already started.
>
> In short, you have the following options:
>
> (1) Adding a new word to one of the trees you have already made,
> (2) starting a new tree with two new words, or
> (3) connecting two separate trees.

> Please continue in this way until all N words have been exhausted and until you have connected *all* separate trees into one tree. When you are finished, you will have made one tree of N words connected by N-1 numbered lines.

The tree construction method allows the subject different ways of constructing a labeled tree. Using just option 1, he can construct one tree only, always adding new nodes to an old tree. Options 2 and 3 allow him considerably more flexibility since at each stage of the construction he can either add new nodes to an old tree, start a new tree, or join two trees together. Whether the subject uses just option 1 or all three options, the end result is one tree. The labeling of the links makes it possible to discover which option was selected at each stage, and the number of subtrees that were constructed.

(b) COMPLETE UNDIRECTED (LINEAR) GRAPHS (COLOR NAMES STUDY). Instructions for constructing a complete graph were considerably more straightforward. Actually, the subject was not asked to construct a complete graph at all but was given the simpler task of filling the entries in the corresponding proximity matrix. The subject was given a list of the N words arranged alphabetically and a list of all the M word pairs arranged randomly, and was asked to decide which was the most similar pair of words in the list, which the next most similar pair, etc. Specifically, he was told.

> You will be given a randomly arranged list of M pairs of words, where each word is paired with every other word. *Go carefully through the list and thoroughly study all the pairs.* Then write 1 by the pair which is least (most) similar, 2 by the next least (most) similar pair, 3 by the next pair. . . and so on until M for the most (least) similar pair. *Work slowly and carefully*; *this is a difficult task*; *take your time.*

(c) DIRECT GROUPING OR CLASSIFICATION (HAVE VERBS STUDY). In the instructions for the direct grouping technique, the subjects were told that they would be required "to sort words in *terms of similarity in meaning.*" Each word was printed on an IBM card, the cards in a deck being arranged alphabetically. Subjects were instructed to

> lay out the cards and look carefully over all the words. Then arrange the words into piles on the basis of similarity or closeness in meaning. *You can use as many piles as you wish and you can have as many or as few words as you like in any pile*— all the way from a large number down to just one. When you have done this look over your piles, make any adjustments or changes you may feel appropriate and then put a rubber band around each pile and around each single card that you may have, and another rubber band around the whole deck. Remember, be sure to look carefully over all the words before starting and then, in terms of similarity or closeness in meaning, sort the words into as many different piles as you feel appropriate.

PROCEDURE

(a) COLOR NAMES. There were four groups of subjects, two of these (Groups CTM and CTF) constructed labeled trees, the other two (Groups CCS and CCD) constructed complete graphs. Groups CTM and CTF consisted of 17 male and 17 female students, respectively, enrolled at the University of North Carolina. (Originally there were 41 subjects, 7 of these unfamiliar with one or more of the color names were discarded.) The subjects in Groups CCS and CCD were 26 male and female American students at the Hebrew University of Jerusalem, all of them native speakers of English.

Groups CTM and CTF were run separately. Every subject received a list of 24 color names arranged alphabetically, a blank sheet, and written instructions for the tree construction method. After the subject had read the instructions, the experimenter exemplified them by constructing a tree on the blackboard and answered questions. The subjects were allowed up to two hours to complete the task but most of them completed it in less than one hour.

The list of 24 color names presented in Table 1 includes words that were assumed to be known by all the subjects and which were judged to provide a wide coverage of the color circle. Several color names such as IVORY and SILVER were deliberately introduced to see whether they would require an additional dimension in the MDS analysis.

The subjects in Groups CCS and CCD were run together in one session that lasted about 90 min. Each subject received a list of 15 color names (the starred words in Table 1) arranged alphabetically, a second list with all 105 pairs of words arranged randomly, and the instructions for constructing a complete undirected graph. The instructions for the two groups were identical with the exception of two words; "more" and "most" were

TABLE 1

COLOR NAMES PRESENTED TO SUBJECTS

1	BEIGE	9	IVORY	17	*RED
2	*BLUE	10	*KHAKI	18	RUST
3	*BRONZE	11	MAGENTA	19	*SCARLET
4	*BROWN	12	MUSTARD	20	SILVER
5	CHARTREUSE	13	*OLIVE	21	*TAN
6	*CRIMSON	14	*ORANGE	22	*TURQUOISE
7	GOLD	15	PINK	23	*VIOLET
8	*GREEN	16	*PURPLE	24	*YELLOW

TABLE 2

HAVE WORDS PRESENTED TO SUBJECTS

1	ACCEPT	11	GET RID OF	21	OWN
2	BEG	12	GIVE	22	RECEIVE
3	BELONG	13	HAVE	23	RETURN
4	BORROW	14	HOLD	24	SAVE
5	BRING	15	KEEP	25	SELL
6	BUY	16	LACK	26	STEAL
7	EARN	17	LEND	27	TAKE
8	FIND	18	LOSE	28	USE
9	GAIN	19	NEED	29	WANT
10	GET	20	OFFER		

substituted in Group CCS for "less" and "least," respectively, in Group CCD. That is, subjects in Group CCS were required to rank-order all 105 pairs in terms of similarity, the subjects in Group CCD in terms of dissimilarity.

A month later, six randomly selected subjects, four from Group CCS and two from Group CCD, were recalled to repeat the same task.

(b) HAVE FAMILY. The subjects were 58 male and female undergraduate students enrolled at the University of North Carolina. There were two groups of subjects, Group HTM, consisting of 17 males who constructed labeled trees, and Group HD, consisting of 41 males and females, who grouped the words directly into clusters.

The list of 29 words employed in this study is presented in Table 2. These words include nine of the ten words used by Bendix (1966) plus 20 more words which we regarded as falling into the same semantic field. Group HTM followed exactly the same procedure as Group CTM. Each subject in Group HD was provided with a large envelope containing four decks of IBM cards. The deck of HAVE words always came either second or third in the series, and most subjects took between 10 and 15 min. to sort the words in this deck.

Results

COLOR NAMES

(a) GRAPH ANALYSIS. By tracing the labeled links the number of distinct subtrees was counted separately for each subject. The mean number of subtrees was 4.76 and 4.94 for Groups CTM and CTF, respectively. With

TABLE 3

OBSERVED AND PREDICTED FREQUENCY DISTRIBUTIONS OF NODE DEGREE (COLOR NAMES)

		Observed	
Node degree	Predicted	Group CTM	Group CTF
1	156	118	105
2	150	222	242
3	72	55	52
4	23	10	8
5+	7	3	1

only three exceptions, the subjects used all three options in constructing the trees. The labeling of the links shows that subtrees were typically connected toward the end of the task; the subjects tended to sort the nodes into separate clusters, and after exhausting the whole list of color names they merged these clusters together. The difference between males and females in terms of the mean number of subtrees was nonsignificant.

The first property examined in comparing random and observed labeled trees is the distribution of node degree (the number of links converging at a node), which was obtained for each subject and then summed over subjects within each of the two groups. Table 3 compares the observed distributions for Groups CTM and CTF to the Poisson distribution (with parameter $\lambda = (N - 1)/N$) which, for a large N, approximates the distribution of node degree in a random tree[2] (Rapoport *et al.*, 1966). The difference between predicted and observed distributions was highly significant in each case ($p < .001$ by the one-sample Kolmogorov–Smirnov test). The difference between the two observed distributions, tested by the two-sample Kolmogorov–Smirnov test, was nonsignificant.

Inspection of Table 3 shows that the observed trees had more nodes with degree $r = 2$ and fewer nodes with degree $r > 2$ or $r = 1$. The observed means for nodes with degree 1 were 6.94 and 6.18 for Groups CTM and CTF, respectively. The expected number of nodes with degree 1 (see Rapoport, 1967) is 9.40 and the standard deviation is 1.42. The difference between observed and predicted mean number of nodes with degree 1 is significant for both groups.

Since trees were not constructed randomly, differences may be expected in the "popularity bias" (the proportion of time two out of N words are

[2] A random tree is a tree selected with equal probability from all the possible N^{N-2} trees that can be formed, each having N labeled nodes and N-1 links.

TABLE 4

OBSERVED AND PREDICTED FREQUENCY DISTRIBUTIONS OF PAIRS OF ADJACENT NODES (COLOR NAMES)

	Group CTM*		Group CTF**	
y	Observed	Predicted	Observed	Predicted
0	171	163	198	181
1	40	41	23	33
2	16	22	13	17
3	12	14	8	11
4	7	9	4	8
5	5	7	3	6
6	5	5	3	4
7	3	4	2	3
8	4	3	4	2
9	4	2	2	2
10	2	2	3	2
11	2	1	2	1
12	2	1	4	1
13	0	1	2	1
14+	3	2	5	4

* $p = .176$, $s = .303$.
** $p = .127$, $s = .206$.

linked together by a sample of Y subjects) of various pairs of adjacent nodes (connected by one link only). Table 4 presents the distributions of the number of pairs of adjacent nodes connected y times, $y = 0, 1, \ldots, 17$; results are presented separately for the two groups. If all Y trees are constructed randomly all pairs of adjacent nodes will have the same popularity bias. Assuming that the popularity bias of different pairs is not constant but is gamma distributed in the population of pairs of nodes, it can be shown (Rapoport *et al.*, 1966) that the distribution of the number of pairs chosen y times is given by the negative binomial distribution with parameters p and s:

$$P(s, y) = \binom{s + y - 1}{y} p^s q^y, \qquad 0 < p < 1, \quad q = 1 - p, \quad s > 0$$

Using the method of moments to estimate the two parameters, the equation above was used to generate the predicted distributions, which are also presented in Table 4.

Inspection of the table shows a fair agreement between the observed and predicted distributions with minor but consistent discrepancies. For both groups, the predicted frequency is smaller than the observed frequency when $y = 0$ and larger when $y = 1, 2, \ldots, 5$. These discrepancies, however, are nonsignificant ($p > .20$) by the one-sample Kolmogorov–Smirnov test, lending support to the assumption that the popularity bias is gamma distributed in the population of pairs of color names. Values of s for Groups CTM and CTF are presented in the lower part of Table 4, suggesting that when the color name space of college students is investigated, the popularity bias is stronger in women than in men.[3]

The results reported thus far reject the hypothesis of random construction of trees. The small values of s suggest that certain pairs of color names are considerably more "popular" than others, and this is more so for females than for males. The small frequency of nodes with degree 1 and the large frequency of nodes with degree 2 relative to the expected frequencies in a random graph, suggest "loose" structures such as a straight line, a curve, or a circle. The difference between the observed distributions of pairs of nodes indicates that results of males and females should be kept separate in further analyses of the data. Before undertaking such analyses, properties of the complete undirected graphs constructed by Groups CCS and CCD will be examined.

Since rank-ordering 105 pairs of words is a demanding task, six subjects were run twice to assess the reliability of the procedure. A Spearman rank-order correlation, computed for each subject between the two separate orderings of the 105 pairs, resulted in correlations of .432, .641, .782, and .635 for the four subjects in Group CCS, and .901, and .792 for the two subjects in Group CCD. All correlations are highly significant, showing a surprisingly high reliability for the procedure.

The following equation was used to compute the cumulative probability, shown in Table 5, that a random graph with N nodes and v_N links, G_{N,v_N}, is completely connected (Erdös & Rényi, 1959, p. 291):

$$P\left(v_N = \left[\frac{N}{2}\log_e N\right] + \mu\right) \sim \frac{2}{N}\exp\left(\left(-\frac{2\mu}{N}\right) - \exp\left(-\frac{2\mu}{N}\right)\right)$$

for $|\mu| = O(N)$, where $[X]$ denotes the integer part of X. The first column of Table 5 gives the predicted cumulative probabilities for $v_N = 14, 15, \ldots, 40, 50, 60$, and the second and third columns show the cumulative proportions of the observed graphs that were completely connected by the

[3] The value of s is related to the variance of the assumed gamma distribution so that the smaller the s the larger the "popularity bias."

TABLE 5

OBSERVED AND PREDICTED CUMULATIVE PROBABILITY THAT G_{N,v_N} IS COMPLETELY CONNECTED (COLOR NAMES)

v_n	Predicted: Cumulative probabilities	Observed: CCS[a]	Observed: CCD[a]	v_n	Predicted: Cumulative probabilities	Observed: CCS[a]	Observed: CCD[a]
14	.0320	0	.0769	29	.6624	.6154	.9230
15	.0689	0	.2307	30	.6893	.7692	.9230
16	.1102	0	.2307	31	.7137	.7692	.9230
17	.1550	0	.2307	32	.7357	.7692	.9230
18	.2025	0	.3076	33	.7554	.8462	.9230
19	.2512	0	.3076	34	.7731	.8462	.9230
20	.3003	.1538	.3846	35	.7888	.8462	1.0000
21	.3490	.2307	.3846	36	.8028	.8462	
22	.3965	.2307	.3846	37	.8153	.8462	
23	.4422	.3076	.5385	38	.8264	.9230	
24	.4857	.3076	.5385	39	.8362	.9230	
25	.5266	.3846	.5385	40	.8449	1.0000	
26	.5649	.3846	.6923	50	.8905		
27	.6002	.4614	.8462	60	.9028		
28	.6327	.5385	.8462				

[a] Cumulative proportions.

first w links, $w \leq v_N$, for Groups CCS and CCD, respectively. The cumulative proportion of completely connected graphs in Group CCS was smaller than predicted for $w < 30$, but larger than predicted for $w \geq 30$. As for Group CCD, the observed cumulative proportion was almost always larger than predicted. The difference between the predicted and each of the two observed distributions, tested by the one-sample Kolmogorov–Smirnov test, and the difference between the two observed distributions, tested by the Mann–Whitney two-tailed test, were nonsignificant ($p >$ .05). The results suggest either that subjects in both groups constructed the graphs randomly, or, more plausibly, that because of the very small number of subjects the comparison between predicted and observed distributions is insensitive to biases operating in the construction of the graphs and to the differences between the two groups.

The next property of random graphs examined is the probability distribution of node degree in a random undirected graph. Table 6 shows the predicted number of nodes with degree r, for 13 random graphs with $N = n = 15$. This distribution was derived from the following equation

TABLE 6

OBSERVED AND PREDICTED FREQUENCY DISTRIBUTIONS OF NODE DEGREE FOR 13 GRAPHS WITH $n = 15$ (COLOR NAMES)

		Observed	
r	Predicted	Group CCS	Group CCD
0	19.2	24	31
1	52.4	45	41
2	61.2	60	69
3	40.2	44	28
4	16.6	17	11
5	4.5	5	10
6	0.8	0	3
7	0	0	1
8	0	0	1
Mean		2.000	2.000
SD		1.236	1.495

(Erdös & Rényi, 1960, p. 58):

$$P(d(v_i) = r) = \frac{\binom{N-1}{r}\binom{\binom{N-1}{2}}{n-r}}{\binom{M}{n}}$$

where $P(d(v_i) = r)$ denotes the probability that a node v_i is connected in $G_{N,n}$ with exactly r other nodes, $r = 0, 1, \ldots, N - 1$, and $d(v_i)$ denotes the degree of node v_i. Presented in the next two columns of Table 6 are the frequency distributions of node degree for the first 15 links summed separately over the subjects in Groups CCS and CCD. The difference between predicted and observed frequencies was tested by chi-square. For $n = 15$ the difference was not significant for Group CCS ($X^2(5) = 2.655$, $p >$ .70), but highly significant for Group CCD ($X^2(5) = 34.070$, $p < .001$). Table 6 shows that the graphs of Group CCD included more nodes with a high degree than expected by chance alone.

Since the distribution of node degree discriminates between the two groups, it may be that other properties of linear graphs are also sensitive to group differences. Examination of the number of cycles of order k in random undirected graphs may also reveal differences. Because the particular color names used in the study may predispose the subject to the early construction of "triangular" cycles, such as RED–SCARLET–CRIMSON, or "rectangular" cycles, such as BRONZE–BROWN–TAN–KHAKI, only the cases $k = 3$ and $k = 4$ are investigated. Let g_k denote the number of cycles of order k, $k \geq 3$, in a random graph, and let $M(g_k)$ denote the expected value of g_k. $M(g_k)$ is given (Erdös & Rényi, 1960, p. 35) by

$$M(g_k) = \frac{(k-1)!\binom{N}{k}\binom{M-k}{n-k}}{2\binom{M}{n}}$$

For $n = N = 15$ we have $M(g_3) = 1.104$ and $M(g_4) = 1.141$.

The means of the observed numbers of "triangular" cycles are 5.231 and 0.231 for Groups CCS and CCD, respectively. The difference between each of the observed means and $M(g_3)$ is significant ($t(12) = 6.06$, $p < .001$ for group CCS and $t(12) = 5.25$, $p < .001$ for Group CCD). The two groups differ from each other with respect to the number of cycles of order 3. Group CCS shows a strong "triangular" bias, while Group CCD shows an opposite bias in the early construction of the graphs. The results show clearly that neither group performed the task randomly, but that subjects in Group CCS, who rank-ordered similarities, had a predisposition for putting color names into groups of three, while subjects in Group CCD had an opposite predisposition.

The two groups did not differ from each other with respect to the mean of the observed cycles of order 4 ($t(24) = .27$, $p > .70$). The means for both groups were, however, significantly greater than expected by chance alone ($t(12) = 2.83$, $p < .02$, for Group CCS, and $t(12) = 2.52$, $p < .05$, for Group CCD). Thus, a "rectangular" bias operated in both groups in the early part of the task.

(b) CLUSTER ANALYSIS. The graph analysis of the group results shows that the proximity data were not generated randomly. Moreover, the fact that subjects in Groups CTM and CTF used all three options in constructing subtrees that later merged into one tree, and the discovery of a popularity bias for color names (Table 1) and pairs of color names (Table 4) suggest that a cluster analysis of the proximity data is in order. We shall consider the clustering results after several of the clustering concepts involved are defined, and reasons provided for using the specific clustering methods employed.

The choice of a particular clustering technique was dictated by the methods used to gather the data and by our wish to compare results from MDS, cluster, and graph analyses of the data. Since the data were gathered either by a direct grouping technique, requiring a subject to put N stimulus objects into an unspecified number of clusters, or by graph construction methods, allowing the investigation of the "evolution" of graphs and since, as can be easily shown, the tree construction method yields directly a hierarchical system of clustering representations, it was decided to apply a hierarchical clustering procedure to our data; in particular, we used the clustering program developed by Johnson (1967). Another reason for applying Johnson's clustering program to our data is its previous use in studies of semantic domains (Miller, 1967, 1969). Miller (1967) has stated that this procedure "seems to offer more promise for semantic theory than any of the other techniques psychologists have used to probe the structure of the subjective lexicon" (p. 70).

Johnson's program is a recursive algorithm which, when applied to a symmetric proximity matrix, constructs a hierarchical system of clustering representations, ranging from a *weak* clustering in which each of the N stimulus objects is represented as a separate cluster to a *strong* cluster in which all N objects are grouped together as a single cluster. The algorithm assumes that there are N stimulus objects $v_1, v_2, \ldots, v_N$, and a sequence of $m + 1$ clusterings, $C_0, C_1, \ldots, C_m$, where each clustering C_h $(h = 1, 2, \ldots, m)$ has associated with it a number α_h, its *value*. C_0 is the weak clustering, with $\alpha_0 = 0$, and C_m is the strong clustering. The values of α_h are assumed to increase, i.e., $\alpha_{h-1} \leq \alpha_h$, and the clusters "increase" too, i.e., $C_{h-1} < C_h$, meaning that every cluster C_h is the *union* of clusters in C_{h-1}. This arrangement of clusterings is called a *hierarchical clustering scheme* (HCS). The values of the clusterings either increase or decrease depending on whether similarities or dissimilarities, respectively, are considered. The program consists of two clustering methods—the Connectedness and the Diameter methods—both described fully in Johnson (1967).

Rejection of the null hypothesis that the proximity data are not random is required before attempts can be made at psychological interpretation of the structural statistics obtained by the two clustering methods. Johnson (1968a) has addressed himself to the problem of finding whether some subset of $k < N$ items make a cluster. He defined a useful cluster statistic:

$$\lambda_{k,N} = \bar{R}_m(k, N) - \bar{R}_i(k, N)$$

where k is the number of items in the cluster, $\bar{R}_m(k, N)$ is the mean of all $\binom{k}{2}$ distances (ranks) within this cluster, and $\bar{R}_i(k, N)$ is the mean of all $k(N - k)$ distances (ranks) from the k items in the cluster to the remaining

$N - k$ items outside this cluster. To test the null hypothesis that an observed value of $\lambda_{k,N}$ is not significantly different from a value expected by chance, the sampling distribution of $\lambda_{k,N}$ is required. Although this distribution is unknown, Johnson has derived the mean $\bar{\lambda}_{k,N}$, and standard deviation, $\sigma_{k,N}$, of $\lambda_{k,N}$, allowing him to compute a "z-score":

$$z_{k,N} = \frac{\lambda_{k,N} - \bar{\lambda}_{k,N}}{\sigma_{k,N}}$$

Since the sampling distribution of $\lambda_{k,N}$ is unknown, Chebyshev's inequality may be used to obtain an upper bound, $1/z_{k,N}$, on the probability of obtaining a cluster of size k which is "better" than a given cluster. Stated differently, the probability of obtaining another cluster of the same size with a larger value of $\lambda_{k,N}$ is less than or equal to $1/z^2_{k,N}$. Fixing the desired level of significance at .05, the critical z-value is $z_{.05} = (20)^{1/2} = 4.47$. Since Chebyshev's inequality is very conservative, the criterion was slightly relaxed and we settled at $z_{.06} = 4$ for testing the hypothesis that an observed cluster differs significantly from one expected by chance alone.

There are several ways to interpret an HCS, depending on the purpose of the investigator. If he wishes to locate the largest number of significant clusters, regardless of the proportion of stimulus objects that they include, he should scan the HCS from top to bottom. If he is interested in finding the largest number of stimulus words which form significant clusters, the HCS should be scanned from bottom to top. Another alternative, which we have adopted, is to consider the largest number of significant clusters, each of which includes a maximum number of stimulus objects. That is, we first find the largest number of significant clusters and then let each of them "increase" to its maximum size (provided it is still significant). A clustering constructed by this procedure will be referred to as a MAXC clustering.

Another notion that we shall make use of is the distance between two clusterings, discussed by Johnson (1968b). Define an *incidence matrix* corresponding to a given clustering C_h as an $N \times N$ matrix of 0s and 1s, where entry i,j in the matrix contains 1 if and only if stimulus objects v_i and v_j are in the same cluster in C_h. A *distance between two clusterings*, C_h and C_h', of size N is defined by $d(C_h, C_h')$ = the number of entries in the incidence matrices of C_h and C_h' that are different, normalized by division by $N(N - 1)$. $d(C_h, C_h')$ is positive, symmetric, it satisfies the triangle inequality, and $0 \leq d(C_h, C_h') \leq 1$. No restrictions are placed on C_h and C_h' except that they should be partitions of the same set of N stimulus objects.

Applying the two clustering methods to the mean proximity matrices

```
Level  IVORY SILVER CHARTREUSE GREEN OLIVE BLUE VIOLET PINK CRIMSON RED SCARLET MAGENTA PURPLE VIOLET BRONZE BROWN RUST KHAKI BEIGE TAN ORANGE GOLD MUSTARD YELLOW      α

  1    . . . . . . . . . XXX . . . . . . . . . . . . .      2.19
  2    . . . . . . . . . XXX . . . . . . . XXX . . . .      2.75
  3    . . . XXX . . . . XXX . . . . . . . XXX . . . .      2.76
  4    . . . XXX . . . XXXXX . XXX . . . . XXX . . . .      2.97
  5    . . . XXX . . . XXXXX . XXX . . . . XXX . . XXX      3.35
  6    . . . XXX . . . XXXXX . XXX XXX . . XXX . . XXX      3.44
  7    . . . XXX XXX . XXXXX . XXX XXX . . XXX . . XXX      3.51
  8    . . . XXX XXX . XXXXX . XXX XXX . . XXX . XXXXX      4.14
  9    . . . XXX XXX . XXXXX . XXX XXXXX . XXX . XXXXX      4.59
 10    XXX . XXX XXX . XXXXX . XXX XXXXX . XXX . XXXXX      5.21
 11    XXX . XXX XXX . XXXXX XXXXX XXXXX . XXX . XXXXX      6.72
 12    XXX . XXX XXX . XXXXX XXXXX XXXXX XXXXX . XXXXX      7.16
 13    XXX . XXX XXX . XXXXX XXXXX XXXXX XXXXX XXXXXXX      7.41
 14    XXX XXXXX XXX . XXXXX XXXXX XXXXX XXXXX XXXXXXX      8.53
 15    XXX XXXXX XXX . XXXXXXXXXXX XXXXX XXXXX XXXXXXX      8.80
 16    XXX XXXXX XXX . XXXXXXXXXXX XXXXXXXXXXX XXXXXXX      9.01
 17    XXX XXXXX XXX XXXXXXXXXXXXX XXXXXXXXXXX XXXXXXX      9,93
 18    XXX XXXXXXXXX XXXXXXXXXXXXX XXXXXXXXXXX XXXXXXX     11.43
 19    XXX XXXXXXXXX XXXXXXXXXXXXX XXXXXXXXXXXXXXXXXXX     12.20
 20    XXX XXXXXXXXXXXXXXXXXXXXXXX XXXXXXXXXXXXXXXXXXX     14.74
 21    XXX XXXXXXXXXXXXXXXXXXXXXXXXXXXXXXXXXXXXXXXXXXX     16.98
 22    XXXXXXXXXXXXXXXXXXXXXXXXXXXXXXXXXXXXXXXXXXXXXXX     19.01
```

Fig. 1. HCS for Group CTM (diameter method).

of Groups CTM and CTF resulted in two HCSs for each group, one for each clustering method. If the proximity data had satisfied the *ultrametric inequality* (see Johnson, 1967) the two HCSs would have been identical. A wide discrepancy between the two solutions indicates that either one is not dealing with a hierarchical conceptual system, or that the proximity data are too noisy for a precise analysis (Miller, 1969). To assess the similarity between the two HCSs, taking into account the significance of the clusters, we measured the distance between the two MAXC clusterings obtained for each group by the two clustering methods. The distances were .1033 and .2572 for Groups CTM and CTF, respectively, indicating a fair similarity.

As the results of the diameter method are more interpretable, they are presented in Figures 1 and 2. The two figures present the HCSs obtained by the diameter method for the mean proximity matrices of Groups CTM and CTF, respectively. The lines connecting the ×'s in the two plots denote significant clusters.

The MAXC clustering for Group CTM included the following three significant clusters:

1. a GREEN–VIOLET cluster [CHARTREUSE, GREEN, OLIVE, BLUE, TURQUOISE, PINK, CRIMSON, RED, SCARLET, MAGENTA, PURPLE, VIOLET];
2. a BROWN cluster [BRONZE, BROWN, RUST, KHAKI, BEIGE, TAN]; and
3. an ORANGE–YELLOW cluster [ORANGE, GOLD, MUSTARD, YELLOW].

The MAXC clustering for Group CTF included the following four significant clusters:

1. a BROWN cluster [IVORY, SILVER, BROWN, KHAKI, BEIGE, TAN];
2. a RED–VIOLET cluster [PINK, RED, CRIMSON, SCARLET, MAGENTA, PURPLE, VIOLET];
3. an ORANGE–YELLOW cluster [ORANGE, BRONZE, RUST, GOLD, MUSTARD, YELLOW]; and
4. a GREEN–BLUE cluster [CHARTREUSE, GREEN, OLIVE, BLUE TURQUOISE].

The two clusterings are essentially the same. Cluster 1 in Group CTM is split into two clusters, 2 and 4, in Group CTF, with color names arranged

```
Level  IVORY SILVER BROWN KHAKI BEIGE TAN CHARTREUSE GREEN OLIVE BLUE TURQUOISE PINK RED CRIMSON SCARLET MAGENTA PURPLE VIOLET ORANGE BRONZE RUST GOLD MUSTARD YELLOW   α

  1    . . . . . . . . . . . . . XXX . . . . . . . . .        0.79
  2    . . . . XXX . . . . . . . XXX . . . . . . . . .        1.27
  3    . . . . XXX . . . . . . XXXXX . . . . . . . . .        1.43
  4    . . . . XXX . . . . . . XXXXX . XXX . . . . . .        1.56
  5    . . . . XXX . . . . . . XXXXX . XXX . . . . XXX        2.02
  6    . . . XXXXX . . . . . . XXXXX . XXX . . . . XXX        2.29
  7    . . . XXXXX . XXX . . . XXXXX . XXX . . . . XXX        2.56
  8    . . . XXXXX . XXX XXX . XXXXX . XXX . . . . XXX        2.62
  9    . . . XXXXX . XXX XXX . XXXXX . XXX . . . XXXXX        2.88
 10    . . XXXXXXX . XXX XXX . XXXXX . XXX . . . XXXXX        3.76
 11    . . XXXXXXX . XXX XXX XXXXXXX . XXX . . . XXXXX        5.30
 12    . . XXXXXXX . XXX XXX XXXXXXX . XXX . XXX XXXXX        5.36
 13    . . XXXXXXX XXXXX XXX XXXXXXX . XXX . XXX XXXXX        5.78
 14    . . XXXXXXX XXXXX XXX XXXXXXX XXXXX . XXX XXXXX        6.69
 15    . . XXXXXXX XXXXX XXX XXXXXXX XXXXX XXXXX XXXXX        6.82
 16    XXX XXXXXXX XXXXX XXX XXXXXXX XXXXX XXXXX XXXXX        6.89
 17    XXX XXXXXXX XXXXX XXX XXXXXXXXXXXXX XXXXX XXXXX        8.50
 18    XXX XXXXXXX XXXXX XXX XXXXXXXXXXXXX XXXXXXXXXXX        9.29
 19    XXX XXXXXXX XXXXXXXXX XXXXXXXXXXXXX XXXXXXXXXXX       10.66
 20    XXXXXXXXXXX XXXXXXXXX XXXXXXXXXXXXX XXXXXXXXXXX       11.93
 21    XXXXXXXXXXX XXXXXXXXX XXXXXXXXXXXXXXXXXXXXXXXXX       17.14
 22    XXXXXXXXXXX XXXXXXXXXXXXXXXXXXXXXXXXXXXXXXXXXXX       18.97
 23    XXXXXXXXXXXXXXXXXXXXXXXXXXXXXXXXXXXXXXXXXXXXXXX       23.48
```

FIG. 2. HCS for Group CTF (diameter method).

in the same order. Clusters 2 and 3 in Group CTM are the same as clusters 1 and 3 in Group CTF, with the exception of BRONZE and RUST, which fall in the BROWN cluster in Group CTM and in the ORANGE–YELLOW cluster in Group CTF, and IVORY and SILVER, which are not included in the Group CTM MAXC clustering. The distance between the two MAXC clusterings is .2174.

The proximity matrices of eight randomly selected subjects, four from each group, were also analyzed by the diameter method, which identified two or three clusters in every MAXC clustering. With few exceptions, the individual MAXC clusterings resembled the group MAXC clusterings. The distances between individual and group MAXC clusterings were .420, .398, .406, and .431 for the four randomly selected male subjects, and .130, .424, .120, and .341 for the four randomly selected female subjects. The difference between Groups CTM and CTF in terms of the distances between individual and group MAXC clusterings is consistent with the difference between the distributions of node degree (Table 4) and the s values, showing a stronger popularity bias for females than for males.

The results yielded by cluster analysis for Group CCS and CCD add very little information and will not be presented here. The relevance of clustering information can best be judged only in terms of the theoretical model(s) that the investigator has in mind, or in terms of the practical purposes for which the classification is intended. Although we have shown that clustering information can be used to differentiate between populations of subjects, additional results and further interpretation of the clusters will serve no theoretical purpose since the obvious model to investigate is a spatial model, postulating that color names lie on the color circle or the color solid. Indeed, the two HCSs for Group CTM and CTF seem consistent with a circular representation, if clusters are properly rearranged. We turn, therefore, to an MDS analysis of the proximity data.

(c) MULTIDIMENSIONAL SCALING ANALYSIS. It is possible to locate colors systematically according to their physical attributes of hue, brightness, and saturation. But what different weights should be assigned to the three dimensions of color to account for the locations of the principal color names in the color name configuration? Chapanis has suggested that "Hue is perhaps the most important of the three fundamental variables of color as a mental phenomenon. It is the main *quality* factor in color and is what the ordinary person means when he says color" (Chapanis, 1965, p. 330). Variations in lightness (brightness) are commonly referred to by terms such as light and dark, and it seems safe to assume that they will have little or no effect on similarity judgments for color names. Variations in saturation, the third dimension of color sensation, are commonly referred

TABLE 7

Stress Values for Euclidean Representations (Color Names)

	Dimensions	No. 1	No. 5	No. 9	No. 13	Mean
Group CTM	3	.050	.028	.015	.096	.064
	2	.079	.053	.021	.169	.156
	1	.206	.141	.059	.356	.280
Group CTF	3	.027	.024	.015	.021	.024
	2	.045	.032	.022	.041	.071
	1	.154	.070	.051	.129	.208
		No. 3	No. 6	No. 7	No. 10	Mean
Group CCS	3	.138	.107	.104	.121	.040
	2	.233	.167	.147	.168	.078
	1	.403	.355	.321	.352	.384
		No. 1	No. 6	No. 9	No. 11	Mean
Group CCD	3	.067	.092	.107	.083	.045
	2	.096	.182	.197	.120	.085
	1	.293	.415	.362	.324	.339

to by words such as weak or strong, pale or deep. The saturation dimension is expected to appear in the representations, particularly in those of Groups CTM and CTF, as the color name list given to them deliberately included words such as BEIGE, TAN, BRONZE (all referring to weakly saturated YELLOW–RED), PINK (a pale RED), and IVORY and SILVER. Most of the names of weakly saturated colors were not included in the word list for Groups CCS and CCD. So one may expect a two-dimensional representation (using polar coordinates) for the first two groups, with hue having a much greater effect than saturation, and a one-dimensional representation for the latter two groups with color names lying in a specified order on the circumference of a circle.

A nonmetric MDS program (Young & Torgerson, 1967) was applied to 16 individual proximity matrices of 16 randomly selected subjects, 4 from each group, and to the 4 mean proximity matrices. Solutions were obtained in one, two, and three dimensions, for both the Euclidean and City-Block metrics. The stress values for the Euclidean solutions, which were always smaller than the corresponding values for the City-Block solutions, are presented in Table 7.

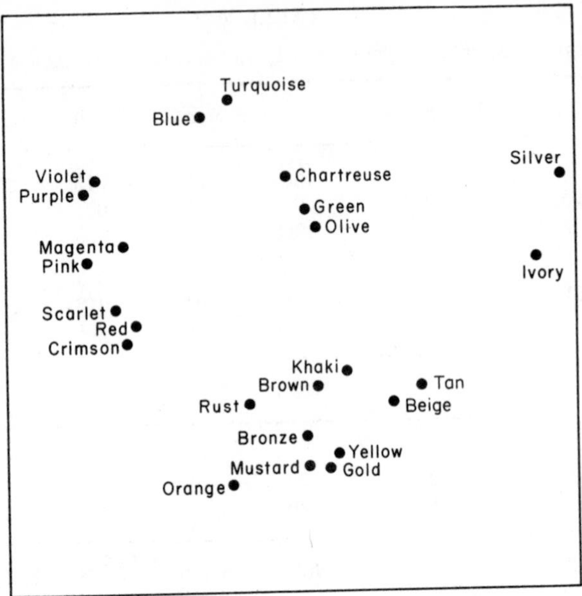

FIG. 3. Two-dimensional Euclidean representation for Group CTM.

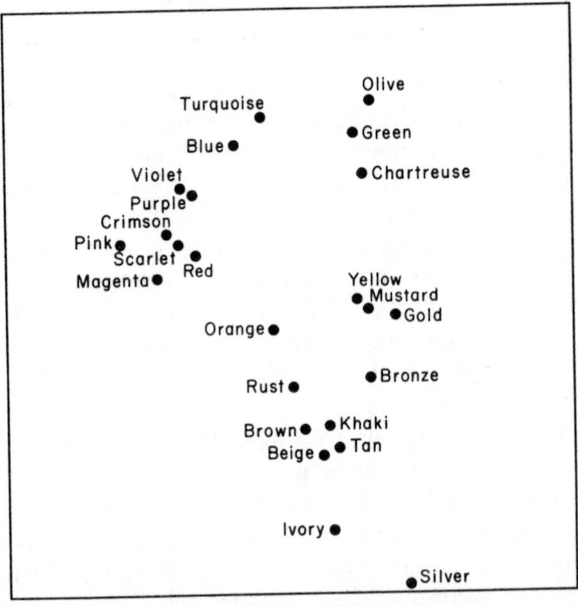

FIG. 4. Two-dimensional Euclidean representation for Group CTF.

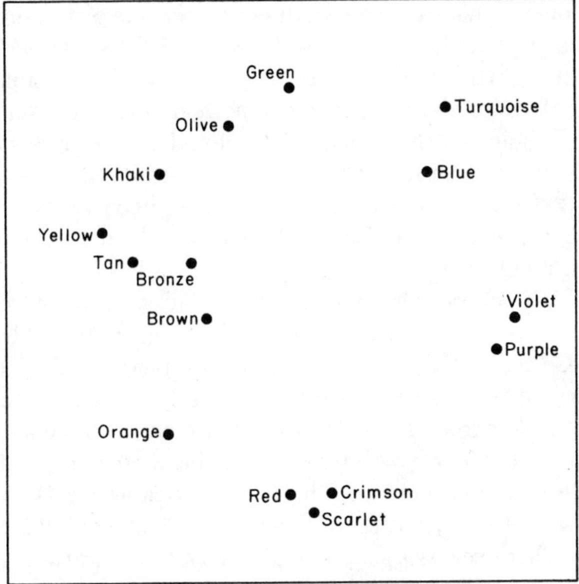

Fig. 5. Two-dimensional Euclidean representation for Group CCS.

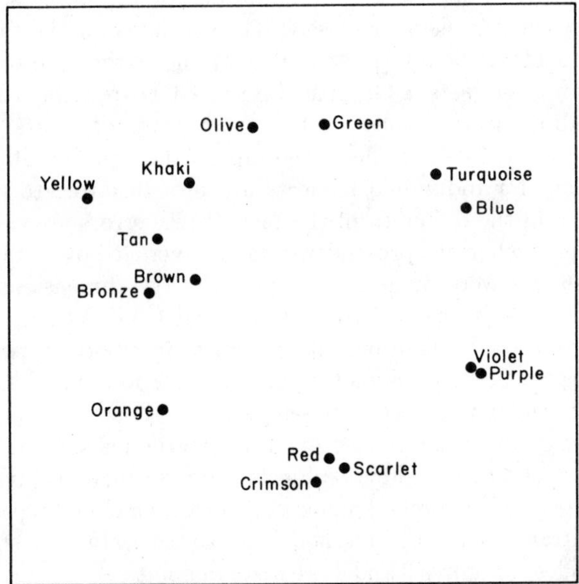

Fig. 6. Two-dimensional Euclidean representation for Group CCD.

First, considering the stress values for the mean proximity data, one notes a sharp break between $m = 1$ and $m = 2$ (where m denotes the dimensionality of the space) for all groups, with the possible exception of Group CTM. Combined with certain methodological considerations determining the choice of the proper dimensionality (see Kruskal, 1964), and the significant departures of the stress values from the critical cutoff points[4] (.22 and .30 for $N = 15$ and $N = 30$, respectively, for $m = 2$), the stress values suggest that the color names can be adequately represented in a two-dimensional Euclidean space.

Figures 3–6 portray the two-dimensional Euclidean representations for the mean proximity matrices of each of the four groups. The solutions for Groups CCS and CCD show a very orderly picture. They are circular in shape, very similar to each other, and closely related to the color circle. The qualitative agreement between the circular arrangement of the color names in each of the representations and the arrangement of colors on the color circle is almost perfect. The representations for Groups CTM and CTF are less orderly, though the somewhat distorted color circle can be identified. There seems to be a small effect of saturation, with names of "weakly saturated" colors such as SILVER, IVORY, PINK, BEIGE, and TAN lying away from the centers of the representations.

With the exceptions of Subject 3 in Group CCS and Subject 9 in Group CCD, the two-dimensional representations of the other six subjects resemble the color circle very closely. The solutions for the two exceptional subjects could not be interpreted. Table 7 shows that the stress values for the individual subjects in Groups CCS and CCD are always larger than the corresponding stress values for the mean proximity data. Inasmuch as this discrepancy does not affect the shape of the representations, the larger stress values for individual subjects are probably due to random errors resulting from the difficulty of the task. These errors are canceled out for the most part when the proximity data are averaged over subjects.

No attempts were made to interpret the two-dimensional solutions of the individual subjects in Groups CTM and CTF. Because the tree construction method does not permit subjects to form circles, two-dimensional circular representations cannot be obtained for individual subjects. When circular, triangular, or other closed configurations are expected on some theoretical grounds, the tree construction method should be avoided when semantic spaces of individual subjects are investigated. Since the restriction imposed by the method amounts to breaking closed representations at some arbitrary point, the method is still serviceable for studying group results. Indeed, Figures 3 and 4 are cases in point.

[4] The critical cutoff points are based on Monte Carlo results reported by Stenson and Knoll (1969).

HAVE FAMILY

(a) GRAPH ANALYSIS. It may be recalled that Group HTM consisted of 17 male subjects constructing labeled trees. All three options were used by the subjects; the mean and standard deviations of the number of subtrees were 6.00 and 2.93, respectively. The labeling of the nodes indicates they were sorted into clusters that merged into larger clusters, and finally into a tree.

Table 8 presents the observed distribution of node degree summed over subjects and the predicted Poisson distribution. The nonsignificant difference between the two distributions suggests either that trees were constructed randomly or that the distribution of node degree, which does not take into account the labeling of links, is not sensitive to judgmental processes operating in the construction of the trees.

Table 9 shows the observed distribution of the number of pairs of adjacent nodes chosen by y subjects, $y = 0, 1, \ldots, 17$, and the predicted negative binomial distribution. The nonsignificant difference between the two distributions confirms again the assumption of a gamma distributed popularity bias, and rejects the hypothesis of randomly constructed trees. A careful inspection of the two distributions shows small discrepancies between observed and predicted frequencies, similar to the ones noted for color names. The predicted frequency is smaller than the observed frequency for $y = 0, 1$, and larger for $y = 2, \ldots, 6$. Because highly skewed distributions are notorious for their insensitivity to extreme values, the small but consistent discrepancies suggest that the assumption of a gamma distribution might prove untenable if a considerably larger amount of proximity data were gathered.

TABLE 8

OBSERVED AND PREDICTED FREQUENCY DISTRIBUTIONS OF NODE DEGREE (HAVE WORDS)

Degree	Observed	Predicted
1	193	187
2	189	181
3	79	87
4	23	28
5	5	7
6+	4	3

TABLE 9

OBSERVED AND PREDICTED DISTRIBUTIONS OF ADJACENT PAIRS OF NODES (HAVE WORDS)

y	Observed	Predicted
0	274	272
1	62	49
2	21	25
3	8	16
4	7	11
5	3	8
6	4	6
7	4	4
8	3	3
9	6	2
10	2	2
11	1	2
12+	11	6

$p = .154$, $s = .214$

(b) CLUSTER ANALYSIS. The data of Group HD were summarized by a proximity matrix in which the entry y_{ij} gives the number of subjects who sorted the words v_i and v_j into the same cluster. Table 10 presents the observed frequency distribution of y, $y = 0, 1, \ldots, 41$. The table shows a fair agreement among the individual clusterings—166 out of 406 pairs of words

TABLE 10

OBSERVED FREQUENCY DISTRIBUTION OF PAIRS OF HAVE WORDS SORTED TOGETHER IN THE SAME CLUSTER

y	Frequency	y	Frequency
0	166	11	4
1	80	12	6
2	28	13	6
3	16	14	4
4	14	15	3
5	16	16	5
6	7	17	1
7	11	18	1
8	7	19	0
9	7	20	0
10	5	21+	19

Items (in order): BELONG, OWN, HAVE, HOLD, KEEP, SAVE, RECEIVE, GET, GAIN, EARN, FIND, ACCEPT, BUY, BEG, BORROW, TAKE, STEAL, BRING, LEND, GIVE, OFFER, RETURN, GET RID OF, SELL, USE, LOSE, LACK, NEED, WANT

Level	α
1	11.53
2	13.59
3	14.88
4	15.12
5	18.00
6	19.88
7	23.59
8	25.35
9	25.88
10	27.24
11	27.71
12	28.94
13	39.29
14	45.65
15	46.12
16	47.18
17	48.18
18	55.41
19	60.88
20	64.12
21	65.53
22	65.76
23	76.71
24	87.35
25	99.53
26	105.06
27	117.12
28	131.47

FIG. 7. HCS for Group HTM (diameter method).

```
Items (left to right): BELONG OWN HAVE HOLD KEEP SAVE USE RECEIVE ACCEPT GET GAIN EARN BUY TAKE STEAL FIND LOSE LEND GIVE OFFER GET RID OF SELL RETURN BRING BEG BORROW LACK NEED WANT

Level                                                                                               α
  1   XXXX  .  .  .  .  .  .  .  .  .  .  .  .  .  .  .  .  .  .  .  .  .  .  .  .  .  .  .  .   36.00
  2   XXXX  .  .  .  .  .  .  .  .  .  .  .  .  .  .  .  .  .  .  .  .  .  .  .  .  .  .  XXXX   35.00
  3   XXXX  .  XXXX  .  .  XXXX  .  .  .  .  .  .  .  .  .  .  .  .  .  .  .  .  .  .  .  XXXX   32.00
  4   XXXX  .  XXXX  .  .  XXXX  .  .  .  .  .  .  .  .  .  XXXX  .  .  .  .  .  .  .  XXXX   30.00
  5   XXXXXXX  XXXXXXX  .  XXXX  .  .  .  .  .  .  .  .  .  XXXX  .  .  .  .  .  .  .  XXXX   29.00
  6   XXXXXXX  XXXXXXX  .  XXXX  .  XXXX  .  XXXX  .  .  .  XXXX  .  .  .  .  .  .  .  XXXX   27.00
  7   XXXXXXX  XXXXXXX  .  XXXX  .  XXXX  .  XXXX  .  .  XXXXXXX  XXXX  .  .  .  .  XXXXXXX   25.00
  8   XXXXXXX  XXXXXXX  .  XXXXXXX  XXXX  .  XXXX  .  .  XXXXXXX  XXXX  .  .  .  .  XXXXXXX   18.00
  9   XXXXXXX  XXXXXXX  .  XXXXXXX  XXXX  .  XXXX  .  .  XXXXXXXXXXXXX  .  .  XXXX  XXXXXXX   12.00
 10   XXXXXXXXXXXXXXXX  .  XXXXXXX  XXXX  .  XXXX  .  .  XXXXXXXXXXXXX  .  .  XXXX  XXXXXXX   11.00
 11   XXXXXXXXXXXXXXXX  .  XXXXXXX  XXXXXXX  XXXX  .  .  XXXXXXXXXXXXX  .  .  XXXX  XXXXXXX   10.00
 12   XXXXXXXXXXXXXXXX  .  XXXXXXX  XXXXXXX  XXXX  .  .  XXXXXXXXXXXXX  XXXX  XXXX  XXXXXXX    9.00
 13   XXXXXXXXXXXXXXXX  .  XXXXXXX  XXXXXXX  XXXXXXX  XXXXXXXXXXXXXXXX  XXXX  XXXX  XXXXXXX    7.00
 14   XXXXXXXXXXXXXXXX  .  XXXXXXX  XXXXXXXXXXXXXXXX  XXXXXXXXXXXXXXXX  XXXX  XXXX  XXXXXXX    5.00
 15   XXXXXXXXXXXXXXXXXXX  XXXXXXXXXXXXXXXXXXXXXXXXX  XXXXXXXXXXXXXXXX  XXXX  XXXX  XXXXXXX    4.00
 16   XXXXXXXXXXXXXXXXXXX  XXXXXXXXXXXXXXXXXXXXXXXXX  XXXXXXXXXXXXXXXXXXXXXX  XXXXXXXXXXXXX    2.00
 17   XXXXXXXXXXXXXXXXXXXXXXXXXXXXXXXXXXXXXXXXXXXXXX  XXXXXXXXXXXXXXXXXXXXXX  XXXXXXXXXXXXX    1.00
 18   XXXXXXXXXXXXXXXXXXXXXXXXXXXXXXXXXXXXXXXXXXXXXXXXXXXXXXXXXXXXXXXXXXXXXXXXXXXXXXXXXXXXXXX     .00
```

Fig. 8. HCS for Group HD (diameter method).

were never clustered together and 108 pairs of words were clustered together by only one or two subjects. The following pairs of words were put in the same cluster by more than 70% of the subjects (the number of subjects who put the pair in the same cluster is given in parentheses); BELONG–OWN (36), NEED–WANT (35), ACCEPT–RECEIVE (32), HAVE–OWN (32), HOLD–KEEP (32), KEEP–SAVE (31), GIVE–OFFER (30), BELONG–HAVE (29), and HOLD–SAVE (29).

Figures 7 and 8 portray the HCSs obtained by applying the diameter method to the mean proximity matrices of Groups HTM and HD, respectively. The MAXC clustering for Group HTM included four significant clusters and that for group HD included six, with a distance of .1921 between them. The difference between the two clustering methods was again quite small; the distances between the MAXC clusterings obtained by the two methods were .0961 and .0616 for Groups HTM and HD, respectively.

It should be noted that significance of the clusters does not necessarily have to be assumed in order to compute a distance between two clusterings. Any two clusterings, i.e., two distinct partitions of the same set of N words, may be used. Indeed, since the significance of clusters depends to some extent on the method used for gathering the proximity data, the MAXC criterion may yield a clustering containing more clusters for one group than for another, and the distance between the two clusterings will then be artificially high. But if the MAXC criterion is rejected in this case, what other criterion might substitute for it in selecting a clustering? Clearly, it is unsatisfactory to pick two rows (clusterings) at random, one from each HCS, and to compute the distance between them, as the distance will depend on the rows selected. When weak or strong clusterings are selected it will be equal to zero. One alternative is to set the number of clusters equal to k, select two clusterings of k clusters each, and compute the distance between them.

On the average, subjects in Group HTM constructed six subtrees; k was therefore set equal to 6, and the distance computed between the two clusterings—C_{20} and C_{15} in the HCSs of Group HTM and HD, respectively. The six clusters for Group HTM C_{20} are as follows:

1. an OWN cluster [BELONG, HAVE, OWN, HOLD, KEEP, SAVE];
2. a BEG cluster [BEG, BORROW];
3. a RECEIVE cluster [BUY, ACCEPT, FIND, EARN, GAIN, GET, RECEIVE];
4. a TAKE cluster [STEAL, TAKE];
5. a GIVE cluster [GIVE, LEND, OFFER, RETURN, GET RID OF, SELL];
6. a NEED cluster [LACK, NEED, WANT];

BRING, LOSE and USE form separate clusters in C_{20}.

The six clusters for Group HD C_{15} are

1. a BRING–RETURN cluster [BRING, RETURN];
2. a GIVE cluster [LOSE, LEND, GIVE, OFFER, GET RID OF, SELL];
3. a RECEIVE–TAKE cluster [ACCEPT, GET, RECEIVE, BUY, EARN, GAIN, FIND, STEAL, TAKE];
4. an OWN cluster [HAVE, BELONG, OWN, HOLD, KEEP, SAVE, USE];
5. a BEG cluster [BEG, BORROW];
6. a NEED cluster [LACK, NEED, WANT].

Neither LOSE nor USE seem to belong to their respective clusters and should perhaps be excluded from Group HD C_{15}. They were the last words to be clustered in Group HD, and they were not clustered with other terms in Group HTM C_{20}.

Group HTM C_{20} and Group HD C_{15} are closely related. The OWN cluster (with the exception of USE), the BEG cluster, the NEED cluster, and the GIVE cluster (with the exception of LOSE and RETURN) are exactly the same in both groups. Clusters 3 and 4 in Group HTM are the same as cluster 3 in Group HD. Moreover, it can be seen that they were formed as two separate clusters and merged together at a later stage. Cluster 1 in Group HD includes two words only, one of which is not included in Group HTM C_{20}. Also, this cluster is the last of the six to be formed, and it is nonsignificant. The distance between the two clusterings is .0764.

The diameter method was also applied to the proximity matrices of five subjects randomly selected from Group HTM. Consistent with the observed frequency distribution presented in Table 9, the individual clusterings were fairly similar to the clustering of the mean proximity data. The distances between the individual and the group MAXC clusterings are .360, .259, .180, .288, and .463, and are of the same order of magnitude as those computed for Groups CTM and CTF.

TABLE 11

STRESS VALUES FOR EUCLIDEAN REPRESENTATIONS (HAVE WORDS)

	Group HTM						GroupHD
Dimensions	No. 3	No. 7	No. 11	No. 15	No. 14	Mean	Mean
3	.084	.083	.062	.039	.043	.068	.110
2	.120	.117	.092	.063	.057	.095	.152
1	.201	.218	.152	.150	.222	.231	.369

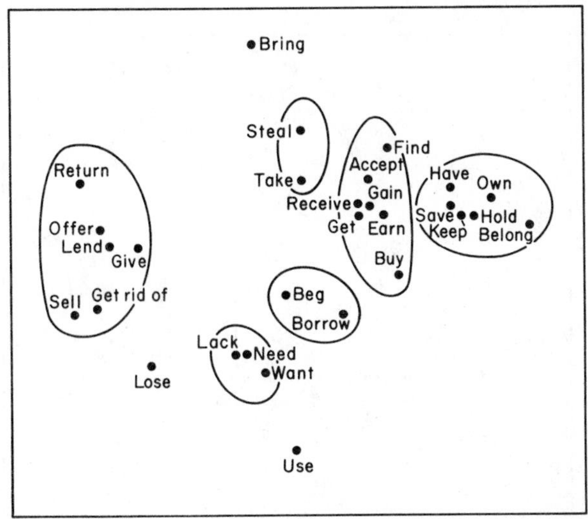

FIG. 9. Two-dimensional Euclidean representation for Group HTM.

(c) MULTIDIMENSIONAL SCALING ANALYSIS. The nonmetric MDS program yielded solutions to the individual and mean proximity data in one, two, and three dimensions, for both Euclidean and City-Block spaces. Table 11 shows the stress values for the Euclidean solutions, which, with the exception of two cases, were always smaller than the corresponding stress values for the City-Block solutions. The break at the stress values between one and two dimensions and the significant departures of these values from the critical cutoff point (.32 for $m = 2$) argue for a two-dimensional Euclidean representation.

Figure 9 portrays the two-dimensional representation for the mean proximity data of Group HTM. The six clusters obtained by the diameter method (C_{20} in Figure 7) are circled in the two-dimensional plot. The two dimensions are difficult to interpret and as the tight clusters appearing on the plot suggest, any attempt at a dimensional representation imposes structure on the data which is not there, and "can easily lead one to overlook special features of the configuration; features which, if noticed, would lead to a vastly different interpretation of the underlying structure" (Torgerson, 1968, pp. 215–216). Attempts to interpret the three-dimensional Euclidean solution yielded similar results: the dimensions seem to be uninterpretable and, more important, the same six clusters identified by the diameter method appear on each of the three two-dimensional plots.

The two-dimensional representations for the five subjects, randomly

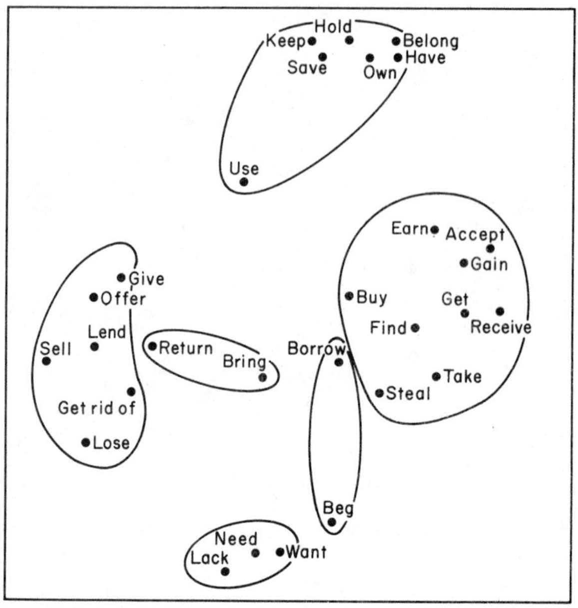

FIG. 10. Two-dimensional Euclidean representation for Group HD.

selected from Group HTM, are similar to the group results: the dimensions seem uninterpretable in almost all cases and the significant clusters identified by the diameter method appear as tight clusters in the two-dimensional plots. This result for individual subjects is expected since subjects used all three options and constructed several subtrees which they then connected into a tree.

Figure 10 portrays the two-dimensional representation for the proximity data of Group HD. The two dimensions are easier to interpret in this case. The horizontal axis is an OFFER–RECEIVE dimension. On the left-hand side of the axis are words such as GIVE, GET RID OF, SELL (but not LOSE), all of which indicate a purposeful activity. On the right side of the axis are words such as RECEIVE, GET, ACCEPT, indicating passive reception, but also words such as TAKE, BUY and EARN, which clearly are not "passive." The vertical axis is a HAVE–LACK dimension, less clearly defined than the horizontal axis because words such as WANT and NEED on the one hand, and SAVE and KEEP on the other hand are not opposites.

The six clusters of C_{15} (Figure 8), which are circled in the two-dimensional plot, suggest again that without carrying out additional analyses a dimensional representation may distort the underlying structure.

Discussion

Color Names

We shall concentrate attention on the results yielded by the method of complete undirected graphs since they were particularly clear and the method imposed fewer constraints on the data than the tree construction method.

Statistics such as the distribution of node degree and the popularity bias of pairs of color names make it clear that neither male nor female subjects constructed trees at random. Similarly, the analysis of graphs obtained by the method of complete undirected graphs revealed that in the early and therefore more meaningful part of the task pairs of color names were not ranked randomly whether a similarity or dissimilarity criterion was employed. These results provide partial justification for applying nonmetric multidimensional scaling techniques to the data.

It is reassuring to find the dimensional representations strikingly similar regardless of whether a similarity or a dissimilarity criterion is used to make the rankings. From the perspective of the subject the similarity criterion presents an easier, more manageable task. If a similarity criterion is employed, the subject must be sensitive to small differences in "distance" where all the "distances" are relatively small. This requirement is most important in his early rankings which were previously noted as the more meaningful and reliable ones. If, on the other hand, a dissimilarity criterion is employed, the subject must be sensitive to small differences in "distance" where all the "distances" are relatively large.

While the placement of colors by individual subjects follows in general the hue circle, the fit in two dimensions is characteristically only fair. However, the two-dimensional color name spaces (CNSs) based on the *mean* proximity matrices yield very similar orderly arrays with almost perfect correspondence between the arrangement of the color names in the CNSs, the space of perceived similarities among colors, and the hue circle (see e.g., Chapanis, 1965, p. 341 for the hue circle, and Shepard, 1962, Figure 13 for a reanalysis of some of Ekman's results based on judged similarities among colors).

The two-dimensional circular representation in Cartesian coordinates is really a one-dimensional closed structure when polar coordinates are employed (the radius is arbitrary and the angle determines the location of each color name). Hue appears to be the principal determinant of the placement of the color names, most of the items falling, as it were, on or near the rim of a circle. There is some slight saturation effect shown in Figures

5 and 6 in which BROWN, BRONZE, and TAN, which refer to relatively desaturated colors, are displaced somewhat toward the center of the CNS. In English there are very few common, single word names which refer to desaturated colors, e.g., pastels. Other than those listed above, PINK is perhaps the only obvious candidate. Given this fact, it is almost inevitable that any study using only common, unqualified single word color names will provide little evidence regarding the saturation dimension, or for that matter, with regard to the brightness dimension either. Thus, necessarily, CNS can only be in partial correspondence to color space, and indeed has to be a collapsed or degenerate version of such a space insofar as common color names principally index the hue of the simply named colors. To discover more complex structures, it might be of interest to determine the CNSs of sophisticated users of a richly differentiated color vocabulary, e.g., interior decorators, painters, etc.

As pointed out earlier the tree construction method imposes certain constraints on the data, namely, cycles are not allowed, circular representations cannot be obtained for individual subjects, and weights are assumed to be additive. An examination of the two-dimensional representations for male and female subjects (Figures 3 and 4) indicates that the general arrangement of the 15 common color names is roughly similar to that obtained by the other graph construction method, although the arrays are hardly circular. For these arrays, note how terms like IVORY and SILVER, whose referents do not fall anywhere on the color circle, are displaced away from the other terms in the array and distort its circular shape.

One can hardly evade the very basic question as to how judgments of similarity can be made at all on color names, and whether the basis for such judgments is the same for color names as for colors. It has been argued (Shepard, 1964, Torgerson, 1965) that one should distinguish between (a) similarity as a basic perceptual relation between instances of a multidimensional attribute where the stimuli are "unitary" and (b) similarity as a derivative cognitive relation between "analyzable" stimuli varying in several distinct components or attributes. It has been suggested that similarity in the latter case may be particularly "sensitive to all of the delicate problems of attitude and strategy involved in decision making in general," (Torgerson, 1965, pp. 389–390) and that the form of the metric may depend upon "the extent to which the different dimensions of the stimuli are perceptually distinct" (Shepard, 1964, p. 59) with the Euclidean metric more appropriate for case (a) and a City-Block metric more appropriate for case (b).

There seems to be agreement that colors fall under case (a) and tend to be reacted to "as homogeneous unanalyzable wholes." But what about color names? When a subject is required to make similarity judgments about a set of color names, he might invoke appropriate (generic) color images, or he might think of objects commonly labeled by the various color names and compare the colors of the objects. If this is how he proceeds then, in principle, similarity judgments based on color names are no different from those based on colors and fall under case (a), and, under this circumstance, it should perhaps not be surprising that CNS corresponds to color space in a collapsed form. On the other hand, for some colors, it is possible that the subject may proceed in a more analytic fashion, defining a given color name descriptively in terms of more primitive color names. Thus, for example, BRONZE might be defined as in Webster's dictionary: "a brown yellowish red-yellow", or even verbally located in a color space in terms analogous to those in the rest of the definition "of low saturation and medium brilliance." If a subject proceeded in some such fashion, a common set of dimensions could hardly be used in the judgment of *all* the stimuli (color names) even if a small set of primitive color names were used as a reference set. In any case this could not be the basis of judgment for terms constituting the primitive reference set. Certainly, some such procedure as the above might well be used in those cases when the color name to be judged is a relatively *rare term* whose referent is "seen" as an amalgam or mix of the referents of some common color names, but this hardly seems likely for more than a few of the color names used in the present study. Thus, it would appear very unlikely that judgments of similarity of color names could constitute a pure case of (b), where all the stimuli are "analyzable," although to some extent there may be some admixture or trace of the (b) case, at least for the rarer color names. As far as our results go, it appears that even if there is some admixture of "analyzable" stimuli the CNS is very similar to the space of perceived similarity judgments of colors, and that both are very similar to the hue circle.

HAVE WORDS

The high skewedness of the distribution of words sorted into the same cluster by different subjects (Table 10), the popularity bias for pairs of words, the significant departure of the stress values from the critical cutoff point, and finally the intuitive plausibility of the clusterings all argue that the proximity data were not generated randomly and thus justify further examination of the results.

The tree construction method and the direct grouping method yield essentially the same results. In each case there is an OWN OR HAVE cluster, a NEED OR LACK cluster, a GIVE OR DISPOSE OF cluster and an ACQUIRE cluster (which breaks down into a passive RECEIVE and more active TAKE cluster for Group HTM), and finally a small BEG–BORROW cluster. In addition, there is a small BRING cluster for Group HD, and the word USE is not clustered by either group.

Examination of Figure 10 suggests some of the bases for the contrasts. In a gross way, the basis for the four principal clusters identified may be found in a cross-classification of the values on two binary dimensions: before versus after some reference time, and possession versus lack of possession. There are two clusters on the horizontal axis—a DISPOSE OF cluster on one side and an ACQUIRE cluster on the other side, which appear to index the difference between (1) presently having and in one way or another being in the process of disposing of, and (2) presently not having and in one way or another being in the process of acquiring. The vertical axis defined by an OWN or HAVE cluster toward one end and a NEED or LACK cluster toward the other end appears to index the difference between (3) having and holding, and (4) not having or lacking. Given this characterization, it makes some sense that BEG falls near the LACK terms and BORROW near the ACQUIRE terms, that RETURN falls near the DISPOSE OF cluster, that BRING falls between the ACQUIRE and DISPOSE OF clusters, and that USE is the most remotely located term since it does not closely share the properties that define the various clusters.

The above comments should not be construed as arguments for a dimensional representation since the same clusters of Group HTM (Figure 9) cannot be accounted for by the same two dimensions, and since the words certainly do not fall in any sensibly graded fashion on the dimensions. The comments should only indicate the heuristic value of such a representation in helping to suggest what may govern the obtained clusterings.

The nine verbs from Bendix (1966) included in our larger set are: BORROW, FIND, GET, GET RID OF, GIVE, KEEP, LEND, LOSE, and TAKE. Bendix defined these in paradigmatic fashion in terms of marked shared features such as possession/nonpossession at given time, status before that time, causal locus or chance determination, and ownership. With respect to our clustering results, GET, FIND, and TAKE fall together in what we have been calling the ACQUIRE cluster; GIVE, LEND, and GET RID OF fall into the DISPOSE OF cluster with LOSE near but somewhat set off from this cluster; KEEP falls into the OWN cluster; and BORROW falls into the BEG–BORROW grouping. Clearly some of the differentiating features, such as possession/nonpossession at a given time, serve to define the clusters while others appear to be rather less important with differences in them having relatively little influence on the location or clustering of the terms. So, in a sense, our procedure provides a weighting of the importance of the various putative features. It should not be surprising that with additional terms a neat paradigmatic structure no longer obtains. Instead, oppositions with regard to some of the features serve as foci for the clustering of the terms, others being much less significant in differentiating them. Furthermore, the structure governing the expanded set of terms is likely to be taxonomic, including some segments which perhaps have componential or paradigmatic properties.

How can judgments of similarity be made for terms like the HAVE verbs? If the judge knows the language he must know how to use these verbs appropriately in a differentiating fashion, assuming that there are no full synonyms in the set. In order to sort the terms into different groups or to build a similarity tree he must ignore some of their distinguishing features. The fewer the features distinguishing two terms or the less important these features, the more likely that the terms will be assigned to the same group or that they will be closely adjacent on a similarity tree. The issue then becomes one of trying "to discover which conceptual features have been ignored and thus, by indirection, what the features are" (Miller, 1969, p. 170), and further of trying to determine the organization of these features—whether the structure is paradigmatic (perfect or incomplete), taxonomic with hierarchic properties and dominance relations obtaining between features, or whatever.

With regard to the present data it seems clear that a dimensional representation is not really appropriate, for the axes of these solutions cannot readily be interpreted and the terms are not distributed in an appropriately graded and intuitively sensible way in the space. On the other hand the cluster analysis does yield intuitively sensible groupings and it has been possible to say something, both about what seems to govern assignment to a particular cluster and what seems to differentiate between clusters. Essentially, it appears that for the HAVE verbs, there is basically a taxonomic structure characterized by inclusion relations of the sort that Bendix described as "B is a kind of A . . ., for example, 'lending,' 'granting,' 'conferring,' 'imparting,' etc. could all be considered as kinds of 'giving' " (1966, p. 6), or what Miller (1969) described in terms of the common presuppositional structure of words where, e.g., both DOCTOR and COOK presuppose PERSON, but with different qualifications, i.e., each is a special kind of person. Thus in our data the terms falling into the ACQUIRE cluster all have this as a common meaning core, and represent different ways in which one may acquire, e.g., FIND where there is the additional feature of chance distinguished by Bendix, TAKE where there is some active causal attribution as contrasted to the passive attribution of RECEIVE, STEAL with the additional feature of illegitimacy as contrasted with BUY which specifies legitimacy and indicates its basis, etc.

Analogous analyses could obviously be performed for the items constituting the other clusters, e.g., SELL disposes of something in a way different from LEND, which in turn differs from GET RID OF, etc. Here we shall make only two observations: (a) While some of the components differentiating items in one cluster may also differentiate items falling in another cluster, e.g., the chance component in LOSE and FIND, or the exchange component in BUY and SELL, there is no reason to expect that these components will recur in all clusters. As Weinreich put it (1963, p. 149): "whereas in the highly patterned or 'terminologized' domains of vocabulary such as kinship or color, distinguishing components recur in numerous sets of signs, the bulk of the vocabulary is of course, more loosely structured and is full of components unique to single pairs, or small numbers of pairs" of signs, thus precluding any paradigmatic system with complete cross-classification. (b) Given that similarities among items, which constitute the input to a cluster analytic routine, are a function of the identity of the items comprising the total set, and given that differences with regard to some features, as say ACQUIRE versus DISPOSE OF, have much greater weight or importance than differences in other features, then it follows that items differing in regard to the former features will be assigned to different clusters and that items with these features in common but differing in other features will fall close together, i.e., in the same cluster, and that paradigmatic, componential distinctions among these items, which would be revealed if one were dealing with limited subsets (as say the subset studied by Bendix), will be masked. However, a detailed examination of the way in which minimal clusters are successively merged into larger and larger clusters should allow one to extract relevant information on the finer details of structure, although this information may sometimes be difficult to interpret if there is a local paradigmatic structure embedded in a larger taxonomic one. Be that as it may, one of the major virtues of a hierarchical clustering procedure is that in addition to yielding clusters it also reveals how these clusters are successively merged, and in so doing provides information about the weighting or importance of the features involved. The later an item is merged with regard to some property, the more significant that property is as a differentiating factor.

Some Comparisons and General Observations

In our comparison of the substantive results of the two studies, the discussion of the color name data was almost entirely concerned with the results of the MDS analysis whereas in that of the HAVE verb data the main emphasis was put on the results of the hierarchic clustering procedure. The reason for these different emphases is simple: the MDS analysis appears to be more appropriate in the first case, the hierarchic one in the second case. In the first case there were strong grounds, based on previous work in color science, for believing that a spatial structure, indeed a dimensional structure of a very specific sort, would provide the most appropriate representation of the data. The results appear to confirm that expectation. In the second case there were grounds for suspecting that a paradigmatic structure would be inappropriate, and somewhat weaker grounds for believing that a looser sort of taxonomic structure would provide a better representation. Again the results appear to confirm expectation, for regardless of how one puts a plane through the points in the dimensional solution no clear structure emerges for the rather tightly clustered terms, while the cluster solution does yield sensible results and permits one to draw some rather plausible inferences as to the basis of the clusters obtained.

How can one decide what is the most appropriate structural representation of a set of proximity measures on words? There are at least two rather different problems involved: (a) delineation of a discovery procedure for underlying structural properties, (b) evaluation or testing of some structural hypothesis. Clearly the second problem is the more tractable one. Given strong constraints from previous findings or some independent theoretical analysis one may follow the sort of rule of thumb suggested by Miller (1969): to use some MDS technique aimed at a dimensional representation, if one believes that the underlying organization is linear or paradigmatic, or to use some hierarchic clustering technique, if one believes that a taxonomic class-inclusion structure is involved. Thus when one is dealing with color terms, as we have done in this study, a dimensional representation would appear to be the natural one. A dimensional representation would also seem appropriate when one is dealing with kin terms or pronominal terms for which there are strong grounds to expect an underlying paradigmatic organization. If, however, one is dealing with a set of names for body parts (e.g., Miller, 1968, pp. 214–217), then a taxonomic class-inclusion organization would appear to be the natural one and one ought to use some hierarchical clustering procedure to analyze and represent the data.

But what if one has no *a priori* structural hypothesis, but instead seeks a discovery procedure for exploring *terra incognita*? If nothing is known about a domain, then it is probably impossible to use the sorts of techniques discussed in this paper as discovery procedures. But characteristically, something is known about verbal domains of interest, because usually concern will be with a relatively coherent set of terms drawn from or constituting a semantic field. If "hierarchical (taxonomic) organization based on relations of class inclusion is a pervasive feature of the (subjective) lexicon" (Miller, 1969, p. 176), and if the presuppositions of even paradigmatically or linearly organized structures may be hierarchic then we have some clues as to how to proceed. What can be done, in any case, is to use concurrently and with safeguards the sorts of techniques outlined in the present paper. They should be used concurrently so that one may compare the adequacy of a dimensional representation with that of a hierarchic representation in order to determine which one appears to be more appropriate. Safeguards of various sorts (such as stress values less than critical cutoff points, significant clusterings, significant graph results, etc.) are obviously necessary to guard against elaborate interpretation of randomly generated data.

Acknowledgment

The work reported here was supported by PHS Research Grant No. MH-10006 from the National Institute of Mental Health. The present work as well as investigations of some seven other semantic domains may now be found fully reported in S. Fillenbaum & A. Rapoport, *Structures in the subjective lexicon*, Academic Press, 1971. That book was written after the present chapter although it appeared in print earlier, and we are indebted to Academic Press for permission to reproduce materials here.

References

Bendix, E. H. Componential analysis of general vocabulary: The semantic structure of a set of verbs in English, Hindi and Japanese. Part II. *International Journal of American Linguistics*, 1966, **32**(2), Publication 41.

Busacker, R. G., & Saaty, T. L. *Finite graphs and networks: An introduction with applications*. New York: McGraw-Hill, 1965.

Chapanis, A. Color names for color space. *American Scientist*, 1965, **53**, 327–346.

Clark, H. H. On the use and meaning of prepositions. *Journal of Verbal Learning and Verbal Behavior*, 1968, **7**, 421–431.

Erdös, P., & Rényi, A. On random graphs I. *Publicationes Mathematicae (Debrecen)*, 1959, **6**, 290–297.

Erdös, P., & Rényi, A. On the evolution of random graphs. *Publications of the Mathematical Institute of the Hungarian Academy of Sciences*, 1960, **5**, 17–61.

Fillenbaum, S., & Rapoport, A. *Structures in the subjective lexicon*. New York: Academic Press, 1971.

Helm, C. E., & Tucker, L. R. Individual differences in the structure of color-perception. *American Journal of Psychology*, 1962, **75**, 437–444.

Johnson, S. C. Hierarchical clustering schemes. *Psychometrika*, 1967, **32**, 241–254.

Johnson, S. C. A simple cluster statistic. 1968, Unpublished manuscript. (a)

Johnson, S. C. Metric clustering. 1968, Unpublished manuscript. (b)

Kruskal, J. B. Multidimensional scaling by optimizing goodness of fit to a nonmetric hypothesis. *Psychometrika*, 1964, **29**, 1–28.

Lyons, J. *Introduction to theoretical linguistics*. London & New York: Cambridge University Press, 1968.

Miller, G. A. Psycholinguistic approaches to the study of communication. In D. S. Arm (Ed.), *Journeys in science: Small steps—great strides*. Albuquerque, New Mexico: University of New Mexico Press, 1967. Pp. 22–73.

Miller, G. A. Algebraic models in psycholinguistics. In C. A. J. Vlek (Ed.), *Algebraic models in psychology*. Proceedings of NUFFIC International Summer Session in Science at "Het Oude Hof," the Hague, August, 1968. Pp. 161–224.

Miller, G. A. A psychological method to investigate verbal concepts. *Journal of Mathematical Psychology*, 1969, **6**, 169–191.

Osgood, C. E., Suci, G. J., & Tannenbaum, P. H. *The measurement of meaning*. Urbana, Illinois: University of Illinois Press, 1957.

Rapoport, A. A comparison of two tree-construction methods for obtaining proximity measures among words. *Journal of Verbal Learning and Verbal Behavior*, 1967, **6**, 884–890.

Rapoport, A., Rapoport, A., Livant, W. P., & Boyd, J. A study of lexical graphs. *Foundations of Language*, 1966, **2**, 338–376.

Shepard, R. N. The analysis of proximities: Multidimensional scaling with an unknown distance function. II. *Psychometrika*, 1962, **27**, 219–246.

Shepard, R. N. Attention and the metric structure of the stimulus space. *Journal of Mathematical Psychology*, 1964, **1**, 54–87.

Stenson, H. H., & Knoll, R. L. Goodness of fit for random rankings in Kruskal's nonmetric scaling procedure. *Psychological Bulletin*, 1969, **71**, 122–126.

Torgerson, W. S. Multidimensional scaling of similarity. *Psychometrika*, 1965, **30**, 379–393.

Torgerson, W. S. Multidimensional representation of similarity structures. In M. M. Katz, J. O. Cole, & W. E. Barton (Eds.), *The role and methodology of classification in psychiatry and psychopathology*. U.S. Department of Health, Education, and Welfare. Washington, D.C.: U.S. Government Printing Office, 1968. Pp. 212–220.

Weinreich, U. On the semantic structure of language. In J. H. Greenberg (Ed.), *Universals of language*. Cambridge, Massachusetts: M.I.T. Press, 1963. Pp. 114–171.

Young, F. W., & Torgerson, W. S. TORSCA, a FORTRAN IV program for Shepard-Kruskal multidimensional scaling analysis. *Behavioral Science*, 1967, **12**, 498.

STRUCTURAL REPRESENTATIONS OF PERCEIVED PERSONALITY TRAIT RELATIONSHIPS

Seymour Rosenberg and Andrea Sedlak

LIVINGSTON COLLEGE
RUTGERS UNIVERSITY
NEW BRUNSWICK, NEW JERSEY

This paper is concerned with (a) discovering, for selected samples of personality traits, those traits that are perceived as going together in the same individual and those that are not, and (b) mapping out these perceived regularities in such a way as to reveal the categories and dimensions underlying personality impressions. The structure underlying such impressions is an important object of research for social psychologists, not only because of the ubiquity with which people think and talk about other people but also because of the central role these impressions are believed to play in everyday social interaction and social decisions.

Perceived trait relationships reveal themselves in at least two different ways in everyday behavior. One is in the personality descriptions that people frequently give of other people, whether as part of a casual conversation, a carefully considered letter of recommendation, a news report, a biography, or even a piece of fiction. Certain trait names and phrases co-occur regularly in such descriptions while others do not. A "bold" person, for example, is also likely to be described as "confident," perhaps as "impulsive," but probably not as "inhibited." A second way in which perceived trait relationships are revealed is in the trait inferences that a listener (or reader) draws from a personality description given to him. If a person is said to be "bold," for example, then a listener may also think of him as "confident," whether or not the speaker says so explicitly.

These two everyday phenomena—trait description and trait inference—have their analogs in the laboratory of the social psychologist. Trait-inference tasks, especially, have been developed and used by a number of investigators to map out the regularities in perceived trait relationships. The first part of this paper summarizes a number of findings that have resulted from the trait-inference approach. Following the section on trait inferences is a brief description of data-gathering techniques involving personality-trait description rather than personality-trait inference. These techniques include trait sorting, the adjective check list, and the trait rating scale—all examples of personality description with vocabularies preselected by the investigator.

The main part of the paper is concerned with the measurement of perceived trait co-occurrences in naturalistic personality descriptions and with the application of multidimensional scaling to the problem of giving these co-occurrences a structural representation. While this approach developed directly out of our experience with trait sorting, it differs from previous methods in that very few constraints are imposed on the subject by the investigator: The subject chooses both the people he will describe and the trait names and phrases he will use to describe them.

Trait-Inference Approach

In the typical trait-inference study, the investigator presents his subject with a personality trait name (or names) as descriptive of some (hypothetical) individual and then asks him to make inferences about the presence of other traits in that individual. The subject usually makes these inferences on one or more rating scales. The scales may be similar in format to that used to obtain similarities judgments; for example, the subject might be instructed as follows:

A person is *warm*. How likely would he be:

	Very likely	Neutral	Very unlikely	
generous	______	______	______	?
intelligent	______	______	______	?

etc.

Alternatively, the scales may resemble the semantic differential; i.e., the bject might be instructed as follows:

A person is *warm*. To what extent is he likely to be:

generous	________________________	*stingy*?
intelligent	________________________	*unintelligent*?

c.

Both types of formats have been used in experiments concerned with apping out the inferential structure of selected samples of trait names. he measures of between-trait relatedness which have been calculated om trait-inference data have varied from study to study, depending to me extent on the format of the inference scales. Also, various psychoetric procedures such as factor analysis and multidimensional scaling ave been used to extract structures from inference data. Three different tudies, each illustrative of a somewhat different combination of methods ill be summarized here.

AYS' TRAIT SIMILARITY STUDY

In a pioneering, albeit small scale study by Hays (1958) the similarities ormat was used with the following eight traits: *warm, cold, dominant, ubmissive, intelligent, stupid, generous, stingy*. That is, each subject was sked to judge the likelihood that trait x is present in an individual given hat he has trait y, and vice versa, for all possible pairs of traits. The reulting 56 judgments were pooled across subjects and then analyzed with multidimensional unfolding technique.

Hays found the following two rank-order dimensions:

Dimension I: *warm, generous, submissive, stupid, intelligent, dominant, tingy, cold;*
Dimension II: *intelligent, dominant, cold, generous, warm, submissive, tingy, stupid.*

He did not name the two dimensions because of the small number of raits involved.

SGOOD–WARE PERSONALITY DIFFERENTIAL

In a more extensive study, Osgood and Ware (Osgood, 1962) constructed wo sets of 40 bipolar scales using personality trait names selected from he Allport and Odbert (1936) lexicon. Subjects rated each scale against every other in a format akin to the semantic differential. According to Osgood, factor analyses of the two samples of "scale-on-scale judgments yielded such large evaluative factors (58% and 69% of total variance, respectively), that little else could be determined." (1962, p. 25)

There are certain disadvantages in scaling trait terms as linked pairs as Osgood and Ware apparently did, as opposed to scaling single terms as Hays did. One problem is that the grammatical opposites which form each pair and which anchor the endpoints of each scale may not correspond to psychological opposites. (See, for example, Wishner, 1960). It would be preferable to determine empirically rather than to decide *a priori* the extent to which two trait terms are at the extremes of some dimension. A second problem is that the psychological distance between polar words may differ for different word pairs; these distances can and probably should be determined empirically. These and other problems associated with the semantic differential format have been summarized by Jackson (1962).

Peabody's Analysis of Individual Terms and a Reanalysis

Peabody (1967) used the semantic differential format but, in contrast to Osgood and Ware, did a factor analysis of individual trait names (as well as of the bipolar inference scales). Peabody's results differed from those of Osgood and Ware in that he found no evidence of an evaluative dimension in his factor analysis of the trait names. However, Peabody inadvertently discarded information about the evaluative component of the traits in his particular use of the correlation coefficient as a measure of between-trait relatedness. Since his treatment of trait-inference data provides an example of a methodological problem of general interest, his study is described here in greater detail than the other trait-inference studies. Also reported here is a reanalysis of Peabody's data by Rosenberg and Olshan (1970) which revealed the presence of a strong evaluative dimension in his data. Their measure of trait relatedness was based on "profile distance" instead of the correlation coefficient.

Peabody's method for selecting traits is relevant to the problems raised by his study and will be described first. He selected sets of four terms according to the 2×2 format shown in Table 1. Thus, each set of four terms was "balanced" for some descriptive attribute and for general favorableness. An example of four such terms is *serious* $(+, X)$, *grim* $(-, X)$, *gay* (+, *antonym of* X), and *frivolous* (−, *antonym of* X). The final list consisted of 90 trait terms derived from 15 sets of 4 terms and 10 incomplete sets of 3 terms.

TABLE 1

SCHEME FOR BALANCING EVALUATION AND A DESCRIPTIVE ATTRIBUTE WITHIN SETS OF FOUR TRAIT TERMS[a]

	Descriptive attribute	
	X	Antonym of *X*
Favorable (+)	Trait term 1	Trait term 2
Unfavorable (−)	Trait term 3	Trait term 4

[a] From Peabody, 1967.

The 90 terms were used to construct a series of inference items, each em consisting of an antecedent trait term and a bipolar scale of two other aits. Subjects were instructed to judge how likely it is that a person ith the antecedent trait has one trait or the other on the ends of the ale.

Each bipolar scale was constructed by pairing the terms on the diagonal Table 1. Thus, descriptive and evaluative elements were in opposition n each scale. The following is a sample scale with an antecedent term:

serious

bold: ____: ____: ____: ____: ____: ____: ____: *timid*

ncomplete sets of three terms yielded one rather than two scales. Since ach trait served as the antecedent term for all bipolar scales, there were 600 items in all. The judging task was subdivided among 240 subjects ho judged 300 items each, 20 subjects judging each item.

Peabody extracted and rotated three factors from the intercorrelations f the antecedent terms. None of the factors could be interpreted as valuative, a finding which is in clear contradiction not only to that of)sgood and Ware but also to our intuitions about the presence of a strong valuative component in personality impressions. The question is why eabody did not find an evaluative dimension in his data.

A close examination of his method revealed the following. Since each ipolar scale contains an evaluative dimension (a favorable trait at one nd and an unfavorable trait at the other end) and since all the scales ere oriented the same way for scoring (seven-step scales with the unavorable end being scored as one), most if not all the information about valuative similarity between any two traits is contained in the difference etween their means over the scales. The product–moment correlation of

TABLE 2

THE 15 BALANCED SETS OF PERSONALITY TRAITS USED IN THE REANALYSIS OF PEABODY'S TRAIT-INFERENCE DATA

Set No.	Traits	
1	Cautious Timid	Bold Rash
2	Self-controlled Inhibited	Uninhibited Impulsive
3	Serious Grim	Gay Frivolous
4	Alert Tense	Relaxed Lethargic
5	Committed Fanatical	Open-minded Noncommital
6	Steady Inflexible	Flexible Vacillating
7	Modest Self-disparaging	Confident Conceited
8	Thrifty Stingy	Generous Extravagant
9	Skeptical Distrustful	Trusting Gullible
10	Selective Choosy	Tolerant Undiscriminating
11	Firm Severe	Lenient Lax
12	Discreet Secretive	Frank Indiscreet
13	Individualistic Uncooperative	Cooperative Conforming
14	Pragmatic Opportunistic	Idealistic Unrealistic
15	Cultivated Artificial	Natural Naive

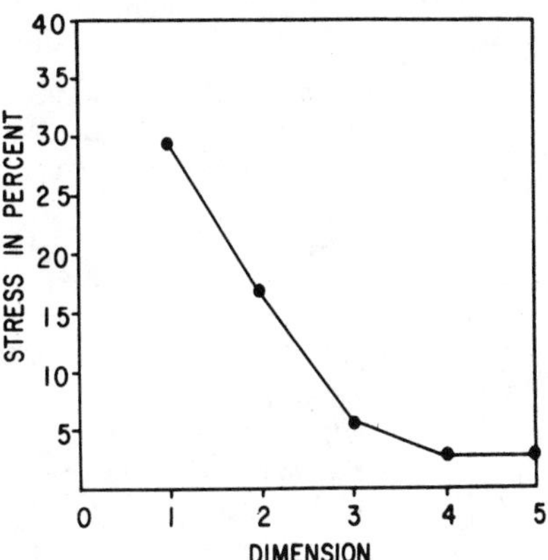

FIG. 1. Goodness of fit of multidimensional solutions obtained by Rosenberg and Olshan (1970) in their reanalysis of Peabody's (1967) trait-inference data.

the average ratings across the scales, which Peabody used in his factor analysis, discards the differences between the means and reflects only the similarity in the profiles. One way to have avoided this difficulty would have been by the use of cross products instead of correlations in the factor analysis.[1]

Another way to avoid any loss of information about the evaluative (or any other) dimension is the use of a "profile distance" measure (Cronbach & Gleser, 1953; Osgood & Suci, 1952). The reanalysis by Rosenberg and Olshan (1970) of Peabody's trait-inference data involved such a profile distance measure in combination with multidimensional scaling. One of the reasons for choosing this method over a factor analysis of the cross products is that it is more consonant with much of the other work to be described in this chapter. The reanalysis was limited to the 60 traits contained in the 15 complete sets of 4 terms each and to the 30 bipolar scales formed from these 60 traits. These traits are shown in Table 2.

The measure used as input for the scaling was actually profile distance squared and was calculated as follows. For any two traits i and j, the squared distance between i and j,

$$D_{ij}^2 = \sum_{k=1}^{30} (x_{ik} - x_{jk})^2 \qquad (1)$$

where x_{ik} and x_{jk} are the subjects' mean ratings of traits i and j, respectively, on bipolar scale k.

[1] We wish to thank Douglas Carroll for helping us clarify the reason why information about a dimension is systematically discarded by the correlation coefficient when the scales are all scored in the same direction with respect to that dimension. Even if the scales were not oriented in the same way, the use of the correlation coefficient is questionable since the size of the r can be fortuitously altered by changing the scoring orientation of *some* (but not all) of the scales.

TABLE 3

MULTIPLE *R*'S BETWEEN EVALUATIVE AND NONEVALUATIVE PROPERTIES AND THE THREE-DIMENSIONAL TRAIT SPACES[a]

Property	MDS of profile distance	Peabody's factor analysis
Evaluative properties		
good–bad	.895†	.354
intellectual good–bad	.887†	.381*
social good–bad	.814†	.474**
Activity properties		
active–passive	.790†	.758†
introverted–extroverted	.667†	.619†
impulsive–inhibited	.796†	.719†
Potency properties		
hard–soft	.872†	.844†
dominant–submissive	.889†	.815†
decided–undecided	.819†	.573†

[a] Based on Peabody's (1967) trait–inference data.
* = $p < .05$.
** = $p < .01$.
† = $p < .001$.

Kruskal's (1964a,b) program was used for scaling. Figure 1 is a plot of the number of dimensions in a configuration versus the stress for each configuration. According to Figure 1, little decrease in stress occurs after three dimensions—and certainly after four dimensions.

Attempts at interpretation, i.e., determining whether the trait space contains an evaluative dimension, were limited to the three-dimensional configuration because a dimensionality of three is comparable to the number of factors that Peabody interpreted in his factor analysis and because the stress decreases very little after three dimensions. Verification of the presence of an evaluative dimension was done empirically using linear multiple regression. Ratings of each of the 60 traits were first obtained on three evaluative scales: good–bad, intellectual good–bad, and social good–bad. The good–bad ratings were obtained by asking a number of persons to use a seven-point scale to rate each trait "according to whether a person who exhibited each of the traits would be a *good* or a *bad* person." Intellectual good–bad ratings were obtained by asking persons to rate the traits "according to whether a person who exhibited each of the traits would be good or bad in his intellectual activities;" for social good–bad ratings, the word "social" was substituted for "intellectual."

The first three rows in Table 3 are the multiple correlations for each of the three evaluative properties versus the multidimensional and the factor analytic solutions. The R values for the multidimensional configuration, based on profile distance, are very large and highly significant for the evaluative properties, whereas the corresponding R values for the factor analysis of correlations are small and, in the case of the general evaluative scale, nonsignificant. These results clearly support the notion that the absence of an evaluative dimension in Peabody's factor analysis was simply the result of his having scored all the bipolar scales in the same direction with respect to evaluation and then correlated across the scales. It seems likely that any dimension, along which a substantial group of traits can be reliably rated and balanced, will be eliminated in this way.

Independent ratings of each of six additional properties were also fitted to the multidimensional and factor analytic solutions. These six nonevaluative properties were suggested by Peabody's interpretation of his space or by the semantic differential. The results, which are summarized in Table 3, indicate that all six properties fit both solutions quite well.

The grouping in Table 3 of the nine properties is based on the results of a factor analysis of the ratings. The factor analysis yielded three factors which we labeled evaluative, activity, and potency, in memory of the semantic differential. The three properties in a given set generally are loaded highly on the same (and only that) factor.

Personality Description with Preselected Vocabularies

A variety of data-gathering methods have been developed for personality research in which a person describes himself and/or other people with a set of trait categories selected by the investigator. This section begins with a description of trait sorting—the most recent addition to this set of techniques. The results of a study using trait sorting will be summarized briefly. The other more traditional methods such as the check list and the rating scale will also be described briefly.

Trait Sorting

In the trait-sorting method each subject is asked to describe several persons of his own choice by sorting personality trait names into different groups, each group representing a different person. The subject is free to distribute the traits given to him among his referent persons in any way he wishes. A "miscellaneous" category may be provided for those traits which do not seem to the subject to go together with any others. The subject may either be restricted to assigning each trait to only one referent person or be free to use any trait to describe as many different referent persons as he wishes.[2]

The trait-sorting method was first used by Rosenberg, Nelson, and Vivekananthan (1968). In their study, each subject used each trait exactly once in his sorting. They used a profile distance measure formally similar to the D^2 measure of Eq. (1) and their distance measure was extracted from the group data as follows: A "disagreement score" was first obtained for each pair of traits by counting the number of subjects who assigned the two traits to two different persons they had in mind. For example, 9 of the 69 subjects assigned *warm* and *intelligent* to the same person so the disagreement score for this pair of traits is 60. Any trait assigned to the miscellaneous category was considered to be in its own category. The disagreement score for any two traits, i and j, is denoted s_{ij}. By definition, $s_{ij} = s_{ji}$, and $s_{ii} = 0$. The input measure for the scaling program, denoted by δ_{ij}, was defined as follows:

$$\delta_{ij} = \sum_{k \in T} (s_{ik} - s_{jk})^2 \tag{2}$$

where T is the set of traits. The main rationale for using the δ-measure (also termed disassociation) rather than the s-measure is that the δ-measure "contains" the s-measure of direct trait co-occurrence *plus* a measure of indirect trait co-occurrence. An indirect trait co-occurrence for any two traits i and j refers to an instance in which i and k co-occur in one description, j and k co-occur in another description, and i and j do not co-occur in either description.

Rosenberg et al. (1968) obtained multidimensional configurations of 60

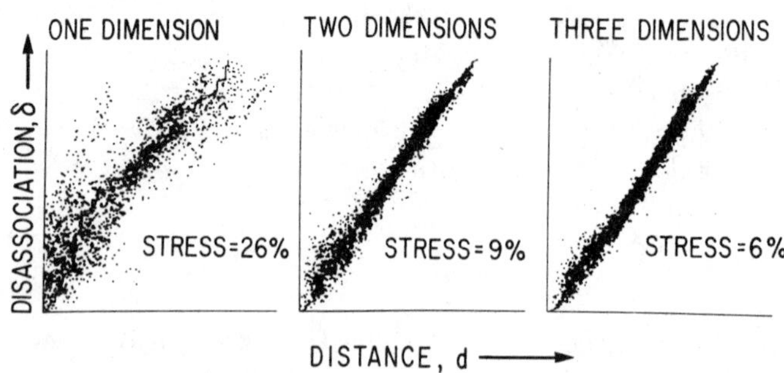

FIG. 2. Scattergram of d versus δ for solutions in one-, two-and three-dimensional spaces. From Rosenberg *et al.* (1968).

[2] For applications of the sorting method to the analysis of semantic structures, see Burton (1968), Miller (1967, 1969), and Steinberg (1967).

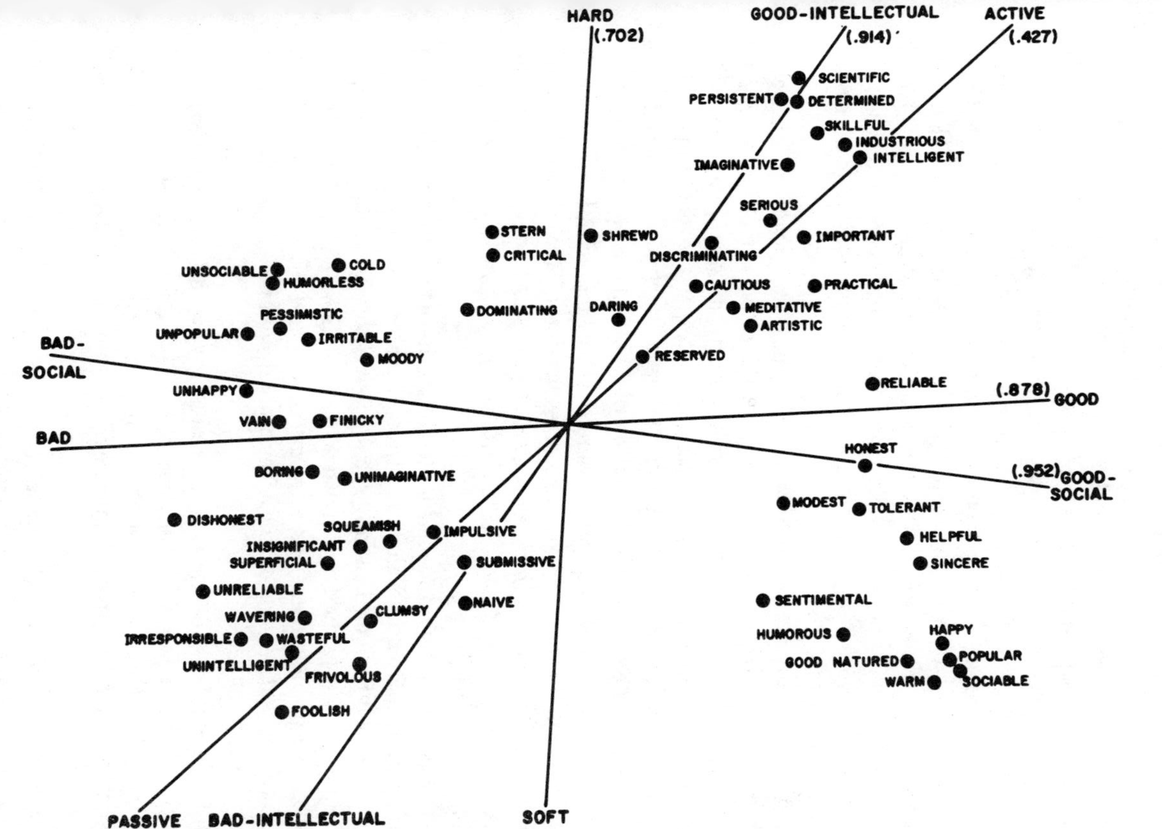

FIG. 3. Two-dimensional configuration of the 60 traits scaled by Rosenberg *et al.* (1968) showing the best-fitting axis for five properties. Each number in parentheses indicates the multiple correlation between projections on the best-fitting axis and property values.

traits with Kruskal's computer program. Because there is no formal rationale for using the δ-measure with sorting data and because, as we shall see, the δ-measure does yield highly meaningful configurations, the empirical relation of input to output distances may be of some interest. The scattergrams from the one-, two-, and three-dimensional configurations which are given in Figure 2, show a nearly linear relation between input and output distances. It would be interesting to know whether this linear relation generally obtains between the δ-measure and output distance. Pursuing the hypothesis that this relation does generally obtain, Carroll (1968) constructed a psychometric model from which such a relation results. In any case, a nonmetric scaling method was apparently not necessary with these particular data.

Some of the substantive results of the study are given in Figure 3, which is a plot of the two-dimensional configuration. It is interesting to note, among other things, that a trait and its antonym are generally located opposite each other in the space. A plot of the one-dimensional configuration is not given because the stress is so high. A stereo transparency of the three-dimensional plot can be obtained from the authors.

The five labeled axes in Figure 3 were obtained empirically using linear multiple regression. That is, ratings of each of the 60 trait names were obtained on each of five bipolar scales. These scales correspond to the labeled dimensions in Figure 3. (The R values associated with each scale are shown in parentheses.)

The three evaluative dimensions fit this trait space quite well and the R values are comparable in magnitude to those found for the multidimensional solution of Peabody's data using the D^2 measure as input (see Table 3). It is also interesting that in Hays' (1958) study, the extreme traits on one of his dimensions were *warm* and *cold* (social desirability?), and on the second dimension they were *intelligent* and *stupid* (intellectual desirability?).

While the R values for the two nonevaluative properties are statistically significant beyond the .01 level, only the R value for hard–soft is at all impressive. The R for active–passive is somewhat more impressive for the three-dimensional solution, increasing in that configuration to .585 ($p < .001$).

The 60 traits used by Rosenberg et al. were drawn mostly from the Asch (1946) and Wishner (1960) studies. One of the reasons for choosing these traits, particularly Asch's study was to reexamine his findings in the light of the multidimensional structure obtained from the trait-sorting data. In his experiments, Asch used a trait-inference method in which a subject was first presented with a short list of trait names descriptive of some hypothetical person; the subject was then given several antonym pairs and asked to select the trait in each pair that best described the person. In one of his experiments, the hypothetical person was described to one group of subjects as *determined, practical, industrious, warm, intelligent, skillful,* and *cautious*; to a second group of subjects, six of the traits in the list were the same but *cold* was substituted for *warm.* According to the two-dimensional solution from the Rosenberg et al. (1968) study (Figure 3), the six traits common to both lists are all on the positive end of the intellectual good–bad axis, whereas *warm* and *cold* are at opposite ends of the social good–bad axis. Traits from nine of the antonym pairs used by the subject in the subsequent inference task are also in the two-dimensional configuration. Of these nine antonym pairs the following five are located on the social desirability axis: *happy–unhappy, popular–unpopular, sociable–unsociable, good-natured–irritable, humorous–humorless.* Choices from these five pairs were strongly affected by the presence of *warm* or *cold* on the stimulus list; that is, subjects given *warm* inferred *happy, popular,* etc., whereas subjects given *cold* inferred *unhappy, unpopular,* etc. Inferences to the remaining four antonym pairs were relatively unaffected by the difference between the two stimulus lists. These pairs are located on the intellectual good–bad axis or between intellectual and social bood–bad; they are *serious–frivolous, important–insignificant, reliable–unreliable, honest–dishonest.* In short, the multidimensional scaling results did provide a new insight into one of Asch's classic experiments on personality impressions. That is, it appears that a trait is influential in a particular list if it brings another dimension into consideration, one not covered by the other traits in the list; it will most affect check-list choices from antonym pairs which fall on this dimension.

Check Lists and Rating Scales

The adjective check list—a variant of trait sorting—has been used in personality research and clinical diagnosis for at least 40 years (e.g., Gough, 1955, 1960; Hartshorne, May, & Maller, 1929; Hartshorne, May, & Shuttleworth, 1930; Hathaway & Meehl, 1951; LaForge & Suczek, 1955; Leary, 1957; Zuckerman, 1960). In a typical application of the check-list method, the respondent is given a list of trait adjectives and asked to check those adjectives descriptive of himself or some person(s) known to him.

Thurstone (1934) was apparently the first investigator to give a structural representation of co-occurrences of items checked on a list of traits. In his study, each subject was given a list of 60 adjectives and asked to describe one person whom he knew well by underlining every adjective descriptive of that person. The tetrachoric r was used as a measure of co-occurrence of each pair of adjectives by pooling the data across subjects.

A factor analysis yielded five factors. The factors were not interpreted making it difficult to compare Thurstone's factors with those obtained in the more recent multidimensional studies summarized in this paper. He did, however, report the following five relatively distinct clusters:

1. *friendly, congenial, broad-minded, generous, cheerful;*
2. *patient, calm, faithful, earnest;*
3. *persevering, hard-working, systematic;*
4. *capable, frank, self-reliant, courageous;*
5. *self-important, sarcastic, haughty, grasping, cynical, quick-tempered.*

Evaluation appears to be one basis for the clustering, along with some finer denotative distinctions among the positive traits.

Aside from Thurstone's original study, there is a little indication in the literature that the check list has been used as a data source for structural studies of personality perception. This paucity is somewhat surprising since the check list is frequently used as a clinical and research tool, is easily administered, is not subject to the criticisms made of bipolar rating scales, and the resulting data readily lend themselves to analyses by a variety of scaling methods. Empirical comparisons of the structures obtained from check-list data with those obtained from other, more laborious, techniques are obviously of methodological interest and are likely to be of substantive interest as well.

By contrast with the small literature on the scaling of check-list data, the literature on factor analyses of rating-scale data is voluminous, too voluminous to summarize here. Moreover, the work is aimed for the most part at the development of a scientific theory of personality rather than at the description of the dimensions of personality perception.

The use of the rating scale, or any lay judgments of personality for that matter, in the construction of a scientific theory of personality has been brought into question, however, by studies which point up the presence, in these observations, of strong semantic factors, as well as stereotypic beliefs and other characteristics of the perceiver (D'Andrade, 1965; Levy & Dugan, 1960; Loehlin, 1961, 1967; Mulaik, 1964; Passini & Norman, 1966). That is, the co-occurrences of trait names in trait-inference data and in personality descriptions may not correspond exclusively (or at all) to co-occurrences in the behavior of the person being judged but may be due instead to similarities in the meaning of the trait names and to the various beliefs of the perceiver. This is not to say that "lay personality theory" may not provide a useful start for the development of a scientific theory of personality. The two systems are likely to be related. The point is that lay judgments of personality contain contaminating effects not of interest to the personality theorist, effects not easily unconfounded. By contrast, when lay judgments are used to study personality perception, the confounding of these various effects is not a serious problem. That is, the lawfulness in perceived co-occurrences of traits is a legitimate and important object of psychological interest, whether such perceptions are valid or not. Of course, if the degree of co-occurrence of trait names in trait-inference data and in personality descriptions reflects only the degree of synonymity of the terms, such data would be of little value in the study of personality perception (although they would be of linguistic interest). The possibility that synonymity alone accounts for the observed co-occurrences of trait names seems very unlikely, however, from a perusal of the co-occurrence patterns obtained in the various studies (see, for example, Figures 3 and 5).

Naturalistic Personality Descriptions

Neither trait inferences nor personality descriptions with preselected vocabularies eliminate the possible biases introduced in the initial selection of trait terms. The number of trait terms, even the commonly used ones, is too large to deal with all at once in an empirical study and we still know too little about the structure of personality impressions to select or eliminate terms which are representative of the various regions of the structure. Thus, the task of mapping perceived trait relationships empirically turns into the task of mapping the structure of modest-sized samples of trait terms.

All the investigators cited so far have chosen their trait samples intuitively, fortuitously, or according to criteria which may have little to do with obtaining a representative trait sample. Thus the interpretation of a multidimensional configuration, even when the interpretation is based on such objective procedures as the multiple regression of independently rated properties, may reflect the trait-sampling biases of the investigator to a greater extent than it does the psychological dimensions of personality impression. While the sample of traits has varied somewhat from one study to another, the variations have not as yet been systematically based on findings from a previous study. Even if they had been, the question of the generality of an interpreted structure would still remain unanswered.

One approach to the problem of obtaining a representative sample of traits can be found in Cattell's (1943, 1945, 1946, 1957) classic work on personality. Although his purpose was to develop a scientific description and measurement of personality rather than a structural description of personality impressions, his "basic trait list" was culled from the vocabulary of everyday language. Cattell (1943) reduced over 4000 trait terms collated by Allport and Odbert (1936) from Webster's *New Unabridged International Dictionary* (1925 edition) to a list of 160 basic terms by instructing two judges, a psychologist and a "student of literature," to group all synonymous terms together with each synonym group under a key term. An objection to this approach, one that was noted by Cattell, is that such judgments may "trespass from semantic into psychological judgments" (Cattell, 1943, p. 487). It is difficult to know whether such an objection has been met in practice. Trait-co-occurrence data for the basic list (plus 17 other traits added by Cattell) were then obtained from bipolar rating scales formed from the basic trait list.

A second approach to the problem of obtaining a representative trait sample is the use of traits and trait co-occurrences generated by subjects themselves in their *ad-lib* descriptions of the personalities of others. The notion of using a free-response approach to the study of person perception is not new, particularly in research on individual differences in person perception (Beach & Wertheimer, 1961; Hastorf, Richardson, & Dornbusch, 1958; Kelly, 1955). However, to our knowledge structural representations of the personality impressions of different individuals or their aggregated data using the free-response method have not appeared in the literature.

In the present study, subjects were asked to list a number of personality traits for each of several people they know. The most frequently occurring traits in the total set of descriptions were selected for analysis. The subjects' data were then aggregated to obtain a co-occurrence measure for each pair of these selected traits. This measure, which served as the input for multidimensional analyses of the trait names, is closely related to the δ-measure used with the trait-sorting data. The details of the method, including the coding of the protocols and a precise definition of the co-occurrence measure, will be given first. This will be followed by a description of the results obtained to date.

Data Collection

One hundred students, 50 men and 50 women, enrolled in introductory psychology courses at Rutgers University were used as subjects. Each subject was given a page of instructions and a test booklet of ten blank numbered pages. Half the male sample and half the female sample received the following instructions:

> The purpose of this study is to find out what traits you use to describe people whom you know or have heard about. First of all, think of five people whom you

> *know* rather *well.* Try to draw these people from different aspects of your life. Then describe each of these people as accurately as possible using a simple list (words or short phrases) of traits. Next, think of five people whom you *know* mainly or wholly by *reputation.* Describe them in the same fashion. For each of the ten descriptions, try to include at least five adjectives, and use as many as necessary. Pick some people whom you like, some who you dislike, and some about whom you are ambivalent. We are not interested in a description of their physical features.

The remaining subjects were given similar instructions in which they were asked to describe first the five persons known to them by reputation. All the subjects were also asked not to identify themselves anywhere in their booklets.

Coding of Protocols

Two editing processes, the second following the completion of the first, were performed by the authors on the set of descriptions. They were as follows:

(a) *Extraction of linguistic units.* One-word trait names such as *intelligent, perceptive, resourceful, mature* were readily identified. Where a subject used a trait phrase, however, a judgment was frequently necessary as to whether the particular phrase referred to a single trait or could, in fact, be divided into two or more linguistic units, each descriptive of a different trait. Phrases which were coded as single units were those in which the trait name was simply preceded or followed by some modifier or modifying phrase; for example, *very intelligent, rather cold, great amount of determination, a bit conceited, inconsiderate sometimes but not deliberately, patient with work but not with people, shy until known well,* and *sensitive to criticism.* Phrases which were coded as more than one linguistic unit were those in which each subpart could stand alone as a description of a different aspect of personality; for example, *knowledgable* but *doesn't try to impress anyone, inexperienced in life* but *open-minded to new situations,* and *fun to watch* because he *appears so stupid.* The total number of linguistic units extracted from the protocols was 7057.

(b) *Grouping linguistic units into trait categories.* Linguistic units which were judged as referring to the same trait were grouped into one trait category, provided they contained the same basic morpheme. (Note that this method is much more restrictive than Cattell's method of grouping "synonyms" regardless of their morphological dissimilarities.) The reason for this step was to reduce the total number of linguistic tokens to a small number of trait "types" and hence include a larger number of linguistic tokens in the analyses of the most frequently occurring traits. The following categorization rules were used.

1. Descriptions which were different grammatical forms of the same words were placed in a single category; for example, *lies* and *liar*, *snob* and *snobbish.*

2. Descriptions which were accompanied by the following modifiers were placed in the same trait category as the unmodified descriptions: *very, most, extremely, incredibly, completely, wholly, truly, quite, rather, fairly, constantly, often,* and *always.* The only exceptions to this rule were *very friendly* and *very intelligent* which, because of the high frequency with which they occurred, were placed in categories of their own.

3. Traits which were judged by the authors as negative and which were modified with the following terms were placed in the same trait category as the unmodified description: *at times, sometimes, slightly, a trifle, a bit, tends to be, a little,* and *somewhat.* For example, *inconsiderate at times* was included in the category *inconsiderate.* The reason for not grouping positive traits so modified with their respective single-word traits was that a positive trait modified in any of these ways was judged to be considerably less positive than the unmodified trait, or even negative. For example, *considerate at times* was not categorized with *considerate.*

4. Any trait adjective modifying the terms *personality, person, mind,* and *nature* was included in the same category as its single-word trait. For example, *domineering personality, sincere person, brilliant mind,* and *warm nature* were included in the categories *domineering, sincere, brilliant,* and *warm,* respectively.

5. Traits preceded by the verbs *appears* and *seems* were included in the unmodified trait category only if the person so described was one known by reputation.

6. The negation of a trait with *not* or *never* was categorized with the trait prefixed by *un-, in-,* or *im-.* For instance, *not intelligent* was categorized with *unintelligent.* In addition, *selfless* was categorized with *unselfish.*

7. Traits which were otherwise qualified or modified were not included in the same category as the unmodified single-word trait. Examples of phrases in which the meaning of the trait is made too specific by the qualification are *sensitive to criticism, shy until well known, stubborn in a quiet way, thoughtful about important things,* and *hard-working only when interested;* these descriptive phrases were not categorized with their respective single-word traits *sensitive, shy, stubborn, thoughtful,* and *hard-working.*

TABLE 4

TRAITS OCCURRING WITH A FREQUENCY OF TEN OR GREATER IN THE PERSONALITY DESCRIPTION PROTOCOLS

Traits	Frequency	Traits	Frequency
Intelligent	143	Egotistical	20
Friendly	80	Liberal[b]	20
Hard-worker	54	Witty	20
Helpful	51	Proud	19
Honest	50	Domineering	18
Kind[b]	47	Easy to get along with[b]	18
Self-centered	37	Idealistic	18
Sense of humor	36	Nervous	18
Sincere	36	Sarcastic	18
Generous[b]	34	Trustworthy[b]	18
Sensitive	34	Dedicated	17
Conceited	31	Extrovert	17
Ambitious[b]	30	Happy	17
Very Intelligent	30	Liar	17
Stubborn	29	Warm	17
Understanding	29	Bigot	16
Athletic	28	Brilliant	16
Outgoing	27	Confident	16
Considerate	26	Conscientious	15
Quiet	26	Fun-loving[b]	15
Shy	26	Independent	15
Easy-going	25	Individualistic[b]	15
Selfish	25	Loving	15
Conservative[b]	24	Loyal	15
Thoughtful	24	Insecure[b]	14
Emotional	23	Active	14
Interesting	23	Aggressive	14
Moody	23	Concerned	14
Religious[b]	23	Inconsiderate	14
Talkative	23	Dependable	14
Determined[b]	22	Very friendly[b]	14
Humorous	22	Snobbish	14
Immature	22	Narrow-minded	13
Smart	22	Open-minded	13
Lazy	21	Outspoken[b]	13

TABLE 4 (Continued)

Traits	Frequency	Traits	Frequency
Pleasant[b]	13	Phony	11
Polite	13	Unselfish	11
Affectionate	12	Sophisticated	11
Cold	12	Talented	11
Considerate of others[b]	12	Untrustworthy	11
Cool	12	Two-faced	11
Courageous	12	Carefree[a]	10
Cynical	12	Concerned about others[a]	10
Good-natured	12	Forceful[a]	10
Introvert	12	Interested inothers[a]	10
Responsible	12	Likeable[a]	10
Sweet	12	Nice[a]	10
Arrogant	11	Optimistic	10
Calm	11	Popular[a]	10
Cheerful[b]	11	Reliable[a]	10
Demanding[b]	11	Irresponsible	10
Drinker[b]	11	Self-sacrificing[a]	10
Hypocritical[b]	11	Sloppy[a]	10
Unintelligent	11	Sympathetic	10
Naive	11	Quick-tempered[a]	10

[a] Not included in the 99 traits rated.
[b] Not included in the 80 traits used in the multidimensional scaling.

Trait categories with at least 10 tokens are listed in Table 4 and are identified by the unmodified trait name. Table 4 contains 110 trait categories, of which 99 were selected for analysis by randomly removing 11 categories with frequency of 10.

Measure

The measure of disassociation between the 99 traits analyzed in the present study was based on the δ-measure (Eq. (2)) developed by Rosenberg et al. (1968) and then adapted by Wing and Nelson (1972) to the trait-sorting task in which a subject is free to use any trait on the list to describe as many different persons as he wishes. That is, in the Rosenberg et al. study, with each subject permitted to use each trait only once, s_{ij} was simply an index of the number of subjects who ascribed the two traits i and j to two different persons (see page 142). In the present study and in the Wing and Nelson study, the s_{ij} measure was adjusted for the frequency with which a given subject used traits i and j. The more frequently a subject used a particular trait, the less effect a given co-occurrence of that trait with another trait would have on the s_{ij} value.

A disagreement score between traits i and j was first obtained for each subject in the study. A subject l's disagreement score between traits i and j was defined as follows:

$$s_{ijl} = \sum_{p=1}^{m} f_p(r_{il}, r_{jl}) \Big/ m \tag{3}$$

where m is the number of persons described by the subject (generally 10 in this study), r_{il} and r_{jl} are the number of times he used i and j, respectively, in all m descriptions, and p is an index for the person being described. If i and j never co-occur in any of the m persons described by l, then $s_{ijl} = 1$. If i and j co-occur in at least one person, then

$$f_p = \begin{cases} 0 & \text{if neither } i \text{ nor } j \text{ occur in } p \\ 1 & \text{if either } i \text{ or } j \text{ but not both occur in } p \\ \left| \dfrac{1}{r_{il}} - \dfrac{1}{r_{jl}} \right| & \text{if both } i \text{ and } j \text{ occur in } p \end{cases}$$

The s_{ij} value was defined as the average of all s_{ijl} values. That is,

$$s_{ij} = \sum_{l=1}^{N} s_{ijl} \Big/ N$$

where N is the number of subjects. The disassociation score δ was then computed from s in a manner analogous to that used by Rosenberg et al. (1968). Note that when $r_{il} = r_{jl} = 1$ for all subjects and all traits, i.e., all subjects use each trait exactly once, the resulting δ-measure is proportional to the one described by Eq. (2).

Trait Ratings

Ratings were obtained on each of the nine properties used by Rosenberg and Olshan (1970). The purpose of these ratings, as in previous studies, was to interpret the multidimensional configurations.

The raters were 99 men and 99 women enrolled in introductory psychology courses at Rutgers University. None of the subjects had any previous experience with trait studies. Each subject was required to rate the 99

TABLE 5

FACTOR ANALYSIS OF THE NINE RATED PROPERTIES

Property	Factor 1	Factor 2	Factor 3
Good–bad	.94	.07	.21
Social good–bad	.92	.18	.20
Hard–soft	−.88	.14	.32
Active–passive	.20	.77	.46
Introverted–extroverted	.02	−.92	−.15
Impulsive–inhibited	.04	.92	.06
Intellectual good–bad	.47	.17	.68
Dominant–submissive	−.40	.47	.73
Decided–undecided	.06	.11	.88

Note: Underlined numbers are the highest loading for the given property.

traits on only one scale. A median rating of each trait for each scale was calculated and was based on the ratings of 11 men and 11 women.

To determine whether the 9 properties group into 3 subsets for this set of 99 traits, as they did for the set of 60 traits used by Rosenberg and Olshan, a factor analysis of the intercorrelations of the median ratings was performed. A principal axis factor analysis was applied and the first three factors were rotated by a varimax rotation. The resulting factor matrix is shown in Table 5.

According to Table 5, three somewhat distinct clusters of three properties each emerged from the factor analysis. These clusters are not as distinct, however, as those found by Rosenberg and Olshan, nor are they the same if we use factor loading as the criterion of cluster membership. One of the main differences is that hard–soft and intellectual good–bad exchange clusters. That is, in the present study hard–soft clusters with good–bad and social good–bad instead of with dominant–submissive and decided–undecided; and intellectual good–bad clusters more closely with the latter two properties here than with the other two evaluative properties. The activity cluster remains unchanged. In short, the findings in Table 5 suggest that the three "semantic" clusters, evaluation, potency, and activity, are not orthogonal to each other when the trait sample is selected from naturalistic descriptions. We shall return to this issue in a later section.

Results and Discussion

(a) *Dimensionality of the trait space.* Since the capacity of the scaling program available to us is limited to 80 objects, multidimensional configurations were obtained for 80 trait categories randomly selected from the 99 trait categories for which δ_{ij} values had been obtained. Kruskal's (1964a,b) procedure was used to obtain solutions for dimensionalities one through five. Figure 4 is a plot of the stress for each configuration versus the number of dimensions in a configuration.

The dimensionality of the space required to satisfy the input values is considerably higher in this study than that of previous studies. Even at five dimensions the stress in this study is noticeably above the value of (a) 9% found by Rosenberg et al. (1968) in their two-dimensional configuration of 60 traits (see Figure 2), and (b) 6% found by Rosenberg and Olshan (1970) in their three-dimensional configuration of 60 traits (see Figure 1). The relatively high stress here may be due to any or all of a variety of factors such as:

1. 80 traits were scaled instead of 60;
2. naturalistic descriptions yield a less stable measure of between-trait disassociation than either trait sorting or trait inference, for a given sample size of subjects;
3. the dimensionality of a set of traits extracted from naturalistic descriptions is simply larger than that of a set of traits fortuitously selected by an investigator for trait sorting or trait inference.

Research is currently being planned to discover which of these factors might be responsible for the relatively high stress. If, for example, the set

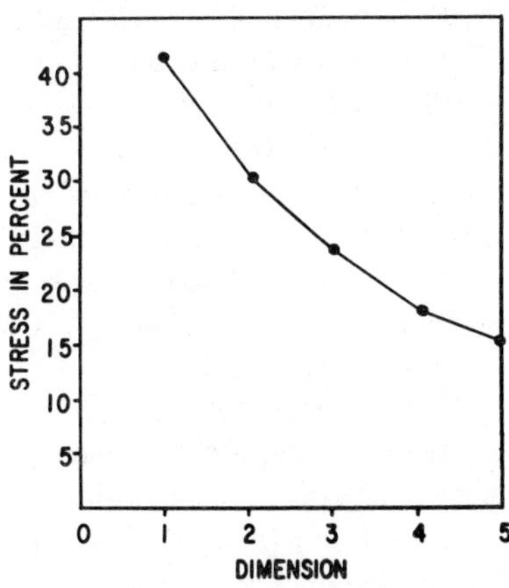

Fig. 4. Goodness of fit of the multidimensional configurations of 80 trait categories selected from the personality descriptions.

TABLE 6

MULTIPLE *R*'S BETWEEN NINE PROPERTIES AND EACH OF THE FIVE MULTIDIMENSIONAL CONFIGURATIONS OF EIGHTY TRAIT CATEGORIES

Property	Dimensionality				
	1	2	3	4	5
Good–bad	.678†	.777†	.775†	.780†	.834†
Social good–bad	.651†	.734†	.723†	.724†	.772†
Hard–soft	.589†	.691†	.660†	.732†	.727†
Active–passive	.096	.186	.165	.417**	.506†
Introverted–extroverted	.143	.196	.218	.433**	.518†
Impulsive–inhibited	.080	.121	.216	.498**	.518†
Intellectual good–bad	.365†	.385**	.396**	.408**	.465**
Dominant–submissive	.266*	.328*	.291	.580†	.612†
Decided–undecided	.126	.179	.227	.340	.480**

Note: Properties are grouped in sets of three based on the factor analysis summarized in Table 5.
* $p < .05$.
** $p < .01$.
† $p < .001$.

of traits selected from Table 4 is simply of higher dimensionality than that found in previous studies, this fact should be revealed by using these traits in a trait-sorting task.

In spite of the relatively high stress, there is obviously a considerable amount of lawfulness in the data in the sense that the stress values appear to be substantially below that of a random input (Stenson & Knoll, 1969). Thus, the configurations may be at least partly interpretable in terms of a subset of the rated properties of the traits.

(b) *Interpretation of the configurations.* The five configurations were interpreted by fitting each of the nine rated properties to each configuration with linear multiple regression. The results are summarized in Table 6.

According to Table 6, only good–bad, social good–bad, and hard–soft fit all five spaces with $p < .001$ *and* with R values comparable in magnitude to those found in the studies described in previous sections of this chapter. The magnitudes of the R values of the other six properties, although statistically significant for several of the fits, are small, particularly for the spaces of low dimensionality.

A question that arises is whether another set of solutions could be obtained which are more clearly interpretable by these six properties. That

TABLE 7

MULTIPLE R'S BETWEEN NINE PROPERTIES AND EACH OF THE FOUR MULTIDIMENSIONAL CONFIGURATIONS OBTAINED IN A RESCALING OF EIGHTY TRAIT CATEGORIES

	Dimensionality			
Property	1	2	3	4
Good–bad	.750†	.820†	.823†	.826†
Social good–bad	.696†	.762†	.766†	.770†
Hard–soft	.639†	.658†	.676†	.698†
Active–passive	.112	.395**	.504†	.506†
Introverted–extroverted	.113	.371**	.488†	.470†
Impulsive–inhibited	.100	.151	.449†	.507†
Intellectual good–bad	.387†	.426†	.436**	.462**
Dominant–submissive	.323**	.430†	.568†	.554†
Decided–undecided	.096	.340†	.419**	.469**

Note: Properties are grouped in sets of three based on the factor analysis summarized in Table 5.
* $p < .05$.
** $p < .01$.
† $p < .001$.

is, it is possible for two or more nonmetric scaling solutions of a given dimensionality to have about the same stress but differ in their configurations and, hence, in how well a set of external properties fit these solutions.

In order to check this possibility, another set of solutions was obtained as follows. The "best" four dimensions of the five-dimensional solution were used as the initial configuration for the four-dimensional solution; then, the best three dimensions of the five-dimensional solution were used as the initial configuration for the three-dimensional solution; and so on until the one-dimensional solution was obtained. The "best n dimensions" are defined here as those n dimensions in the five-dimensional configuration with the largest regression coefficients, according to the multiple regression of each of the various properties and the five-dimensional configuration.[3] Obviously, this procedure cannot improve the solution with which it starts or any solution of higher dimensionality than the starting solution. In the present case, the five-dimensional solution was chosen as the starting solution. (Unless otherwise programmed, the initial configuration in Kruskal's program is either random or the first n dimensions of the $n + 1$

[3] We wish to thank Myron Wish for suggesting this procedure.

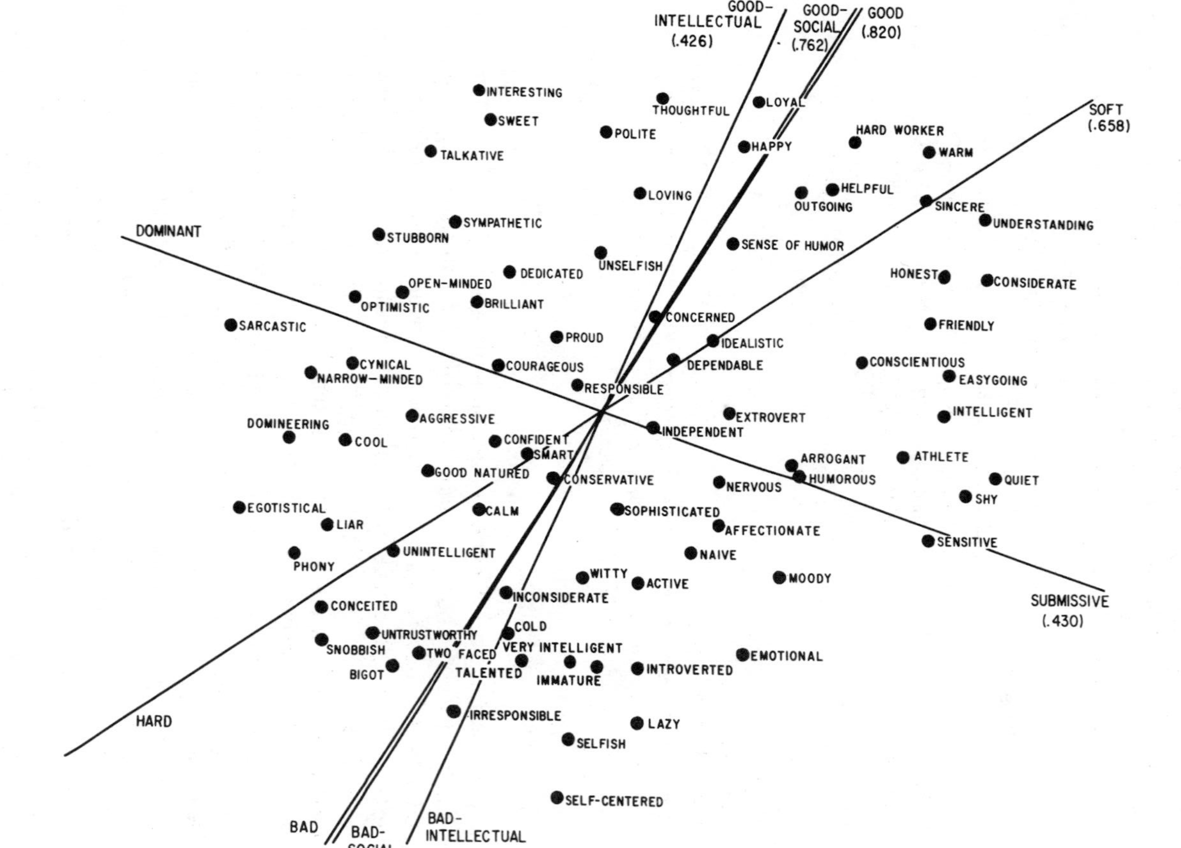

FIG. 5. Two-dimensional configuration obtained from a rescaling (see text) of the 80 trait categories selected from the personality descriptions. Also shown is the best-fitting axis for each of the five properties with multiple R's significant beyond the .001 level. Each

dimensional solution provided such a solution was obtained in the same run.)

The stress values obtained from the procedure described above are almost indistinguishable from those shown in Figure 4. There is, however, a noticeable increase in the magnitude of the R values associated with several of the rated properties according to Table 7.

The results obtained from this rescaling of the naturalistic descriptions confirm a number of findings obtained from the more structured tasks described earlier in this paper. There are also several interesting differences.

We shall summarize these similarities and differences briefly using as a point of departure the comparison of the two-dimensional space obtained from trait sorting (Figure 3) with that obtained from the naturalistic descriptions (Figure 5). Figure 5 is the rescaled two-dimensional solution and shows the best-fitting axes for the five properties whose R values in Table 7 (dimensionality of two) are significant beyond the .001 level.

First, evaluation appears to be a strong dimension in personality perception regardless of the data-gathering technique. It should be noted, however, that good–bad and social good–bad virtually coincide in the naturalistic descriptions whereas in the trait-sorting results in Figure 3 they are distinguishable properties.

Second, although the hard–soft dimension is strongly represented in naturalistic descriptions, the angle between it and the two evaluative dimensions is approximately 25°—far short of the near orthogonality shown in Figure 3 and usually found in semantic differential studies. Nor does hard–soft differentiate itself from evaluation in the spaces of higher dimensionality. The angle between it and good–bad is 22° in the five-dimensional solution. These properties are also closely related according to the factor analysis of the ratings in Table 5.

Third, intellectual good–bad, which emerged clearly in Figure 3, makes little sense for interpreting the two-dimensional configuration in Figure 5 even though the R is significant beyond the .001 level. Significance beyond the .001 level is obviously not yet significance beyond cavil. The traits which refer to intellectual functioning, i.e., *brilliant, sophisticated, very intelligent,* and *talented* are located almost indiscriminately in the space both with respect to each other and with respect to the evaluative properties of the other traits. This may not be as true with *smart* because it may have been used in the sense of "smart-assed." The weakness of intellectual good–bad is particularly surprising in view of the fact that *intelligent* is the most frequently occurring trait in the protocols. A possible reason for this dimension failing to appear clearly is that subjects are reluctant to describe "unintelligent persons."

Fourth, in contrast to Figure 3, the configuration in Figure 5 does not seem capable of being *completely* interpreted satisfactorily. That is, although evaluation shows up clearly as one dimension, the dimension orthogonal to it appears to defy a consistent interpretation. As already suggested, the data may be noisy or require a space of higher dimensionality and, hence, give a distorted picture when forced into a space of lower dimensionality. The best-fitting axis for dominant–submissive, for example, which seems as good an interpretation as any for the upper-left to lower-right dimension, is not very convincing; a small but compelling number of traits at either end of the axis violates common sense, e.g., *sweet, open-minded, good-natured,* and *arrogant.*

Fifth, the activity set—active–passive, introverted–extroverted, impulsive–inhibited—emerges from the naturalistic descriptions only in the spaces of higher dimensionality. Even at five dimensions, however, the R's for these three properties are smaller than those found for three-dimensional configurations of trait-sorting and trait-inference data.

In summary, while Osgood's three "semantic" factors—evaluation, potency, and activity—provide at least *one* interpretive scheme (albeit a general one) for the structures obtained from trait inference, trait sorting, and trait ratings (see, e.g., Mulaik, 1964; Peterson, 1965; Vernon, 1964), they do not hold up as strongly in naturalistic descriptions. Except for evaluation, the factors are either weakly represented and/or not orthogonal to evaluation. Whether previous trait studies and semantic differential studies, which found hard–soft and good–bad orthogonal, were due to the way investigators sampled concepts and traits is not yet clear. The question is certainly worth pursuing, however. It may be the case that evaluation is not orthogonal to any other dimension of personality perception. If this is true, a novel type of structure will be needed to represent this feature adequately.

Acknowledgment

This work was supported in part by NIH Research Scientist Award #1-K5-MH-29, 326-02 to Seymour Rosenberg and in part by NSF Grant GS-2552.

References

Allport, G. W., & Odbert, H. S. Trait names: A psycholexical study. *Psychological Monographs*, 1936, **47**, (1, Whole No. 211).

Asch, S. E. Forming impressions of personality. *Journal of Abnormal and Social Psychology*, 1946, **41**, 258–290.

Beach, L., & Wertheimer, M. A free-response approach to the study of person cognition. *Journal of Abnormal and Social Psychology*, 1961, **62,** 367–374.

Burton, M. L. Multidimensional Scaling of Role Terms. Doctoral dissertation, Stanford University, Ann Arbor, Michigan: University Microfilms, 1968. No. 69-8160.

Carroll, J. D. Parametric mapping of similarity data. Paper presented at the Symposium in Mathematical Psychology, Stanford University, 1968.

Cattell, R. B. The description of personality: Basic traits resolved into clusters. *Journal of Abnormal and Social Psychology*, 1943, **38,** 476–506.

Cattell, R. B. The description of personality: Principles and findings in a factor analysis. *American Journal of Psychology*, 1945, **58,** 69–90.

Cattell, R. B. *Description and measurement of personality*. London: Harrap, 1946.

Cattell, R. B. *Personality and motivation: Structure and measurement*. Yonkers-on-Hudson, New York: World Book, 1957.

Cronbach, L. J., & Gleser, G. C. Assessing similarity between profiles. *Psychological Bulletin*, 1953, **50,** 456–473.

D'Andrade, R. G. Trait psychology and componential analysis. In E. A. Hammel (Ed.), *Formal American semantic analysis. Anthropologist Special Issue*, 1965, **67** (5, Pt. 2), 215–228.

Gough, H. G. *Reference handbook for the Gough Adjective Check-List*. Berkeley, California: University of California Institute for Personality Assessment and Research, 1955.

Gough, H. G. The adjective check list as a personality assessment research technique. *Psychological Reports*, 1960, **6,** 107–122.

Hartshorne, H., May, M. A., & Maller, J. B. *Studies in the nature of character:* II. *Studies in service and self-control*. New York: Macmillan, 1929.

Hartshorne, H., May, M. A., & Shuttleworth, F. K. *Studies in the nature of character:* III. *Studies in the organization of character*. New York: Macmillan, 1930.

Hastorf, A. H., Richardson, S. A., & Dornbusch, S. M. The problem of relevance in the study of person perception. In R. Tagiuri and L. Petrullo (Eds.), *Person perception and interpersonal behavior*. Stanford, California: Stanford University Press, 1958. Pp. 54–62.

Hathaway, S. R., & Meehl, P. E. The Minnesota Multiphasic Personality Inventory. *Military clinical psychology*. Washington, D.C.: Government Printing Office, 1951. Pp. 71–111.

Hays, W. L. An approach to the study of trait implication and trait similarity. In R. Tagiuri and L. Petrullo (Eds.), *Person perception and interpersonal behavior*. Stanford, California: Stanford University Press, 1958.

Jackson, D. N. The measurement of perceived personality trait relationships. In N. F. Washburne (Ed.), *Decisions, values, and groups*. Oxford: Pergamon Press, 1962.

Kelly, G. A. *The psychology of personal constructs*. Vol. 1. New York: Norton, 1955.

Kruskal, J. B. Multidimensional scaling by optimizing goodness of fit to a nonmetric hypothesis. *Psychometrika*, 1964, **29,** 1–27. (a)

Kruskal, J. B. Nonmetric multidimensional scaling: A numerical method. *Psychometrika*, 1964, **29,** 115–129. (b)

LaForge, R., & Suczek, R. F. The interpersonal dimension of personality: III. An interpersonal check list. *Journal of Personality*, 1955, **24,** 94–112.

Leary, T. F. *Interpersonal diagnosis of personality*. New York: Ronald Press, 1957.

Levy, L. H., & Dugan, R. D. A constant error approach to the study of dimensions of social perception. *Journal of Abnormal and Social Psychology*, 1960, **61,** 21–24.

Loehlin, J. C. Word meanings and self-descriptions. *Journal of Abnormal and Social Psychology*, 1961, **62,** 28–34.

Loehlin, J. C. Word meanings and self-descriptions: A replication and extension. *Journal of Personality and Social Psychology,* 1967, **5,** 107–110.

Miller, G. A. Psycholinguistic approaches to the study of communication. In D. L. Arm (Ed.), *Journeys in science: Small steps—great strides.* Albuquerque: The University of New Mexico Press, 1967.

Miller, G. A. A psychological method to investigate verbal concepts. *Journal of Mathematical Psychology,* 1969, **6,** 169–191.

Mulaik, S. A. Are personality factors raters' conceptual factors? *Journal of Consulting Psychology,* 1964, **28,** 506–511.

Osgood, C. E. Studies on the generality of the affective meaning systems. *American Psychologist,* 1962, **17,** 10–28.

Osgood, C. E., & Suci, G. J. A measure of relation determined by both mean differences and profile information. *Psychological Bulletin,* 1952, **49,** 251–262.

Passini, F. T., & Norman, W. T. A universal conception of personality structure? *Journal of Personality and Social Psychology,* 1966, **4,** 44–49.

Peabody, D. Trait inferences: Evaluative and descriptive aspects. *Journal of Personality and Social Psychology,* 1967, 7 (4, Whole No. 644).

Peterson, D. R. Scope and generality of verbally defined personality factors. *Psychological Review,* 1965, **72,** 48–59.

Rosenberg, S., Nelson, C., & Vivekananthan, P. S. A multidimensional approach to the structure of personality impressions. *Journal of Personality and Social Psychology,* 1968, **9,** 283–294.

Rosenberg, S., & Olshan, K. Evaluative and descriptive aspects in personality perception. *Journal of Personality and Social Psychology,* 1970, **16,** 619–626.

Steinberg, D. D. The word sort: An instrument for semantic analysis. *Psychonomic Science,* 1967, **12,** 541–542.

Stenson, H. H., & Knoll, R. L. Goodness of fit for random rankings in Kruskal's nonmetric scaling procedure. *Psychological Bulletin,* 1969, **71,** 122–126.

Thurstone, L. L. The vectors of mind. *Psychological Review,* 1934, **41,** 1–32.

Vernon, P. E. *Personality assessment: A critical survey.* London: Methuen, 1964.

Wing, H., & Nelson, C. E. The perception of personality through trait sorting: A comparison of trait sampling techniques. *Multivariate Behavioral Research,* 1972, in press.

Wishner, J. Reanalysis of "Impressions of personality." *Psychological Review,* 1960, **67,** 96–112.

Zuckerman, M. The development of an affect adjective check list for the measurement of anxiety. *Journal of Consulting Psychology,* 1960, **24,** 457–462.

CONSISTENCIES AMONG JUDGMENTS OF ADJECTIVE COMBINATIONS

Norman Cliff

UNIVERSITY OF SOUTHERN CALIFORNIA
LOS ANGELES, CALIFORNIA

Introduction

Models and Measurement

A model may be defined as the specification of one or more relations among two or more theoretical variables that are presumed to have real-world counterparts. If the correspondence between theoretical variables and their empirical counterparts is specifiable sufficiently directly and completely, then the model may be *tested* by seeing if the empirical variables bear the relations to each other that are required by the model. On the other hand, if some variables are incompletely specified, then it is possible that they can be *scaled* by making use of the equations or other relations relating them to other variables in the model. The norm in psychology is to separate models into substantive models which are tested and scaling models which are used to measure variables, but this is an artificial bifurcation, and in numerous instances a "substantive" model has been used to "measure" variables or a "scaling" model has been "tested." The former procedure is frequently employed in physical systems when direct measurement methods are impractical, as in astronomy, and it is as old as the use of the Pythagorean theorem to solve for the unknown length of one leg of a triangle from the known lengths of the other two, as in surveying. In psychology, models of choice or betting behavior which are used in conjunction with stimulus and response to solve for subjective probability or utility scales are perhaps the most common instances. It is hardly necessary to point out that psychometric or measurement models are frequently tested for their validity as models for the data on which they are employed. (Compare Bock & Jones, 1968; Lord & Novick, 1968.)

If a given set of data contains enough degrees of freedom, it may be possible both to test the model and scale some of the variables. In the field of word combination, the subject of the present paper, Cliff (1959) provided an early example of a case where a model for adverb–adjective combinations is tested and values for the words on psychological scales are defined using the same data. In view of the fact that the distinction between a substantive and a scaling model is often a hazy or even an arbitrary one, the most appropriate strategy seems to be to ignore the distinction, and employ a model in either role, testing it or scaling with it as the occasion demands. As noted above, this dual role for models is not a new development, the common tendency in psychology to separate measurement from substantive models notwithstanding.

A recent innovation, which does seem to be more unique in the history of science, is the development of ordinal models, where variables with interval or ratio scale properties are derived from stimulus scales which are only nominal and response scales which are only ordinal in their properties. Moreover, if enough ordinal relations are available, it is possible to evaluate the appropriateness of the models. Important examples here are the nonmetric multidimensional scaling models of Shepard (1962a,b), Kruskal (1964a,b), Young and Torgerson (1967), and Guttman and Lingoes (Lingoes, 1965; Guttman, 1968); although perhaps the earliest example is Helm (1960). Also important are the developments of conjoint measurement (Luce & Tukey, 1964; Krantz, 1964), and monotonic rescaling in analysis of variance (Anderson, 1962a, Kruskal, 1965). An earlier example of monotonic rescaling of an observed variable to make it more consistent with a model is provided by the method of successive intervals. (See Bock & Jones, 1968). In all these cases, a response variable, even one which might ordinarily be treated as an interval variable, is subjected to monotonic transformation to maximize its consistency with a model. Subsequently, or concurrently, the model is used to scale one or more independent or stimulus variables. In some cases the model may also be tested for goodness of fit.

The study which is to be described here follows a procedure of this kind, monotonically transforming an observed scale to maximize consistency with a model, but the model used is a substantive one for the relation of a word combination to its components.

Additive Models for Adjective Combinations

The data to be studied are the favorableness ratings of pairs of adjectives. While some form of additive combination model relating favorableness of pairs to effects of the component adjectives has been found to be appropriate for some time (Cf. Anderson, 1962b), the exact nature of the additive model has been subject to controversy. Anderson (1968a) discusses several possibilities, and prefers one particular form.

The present study will attempt to shed light on the nature of this relationship by considering several kinds of data for the same adjectives, to make use of the technique of monotonically transforming the data to increase the consistency of each kind of data with a model appropriate for it, and finally to interrelate the numbers derived from the various models.

First, the general model

$$x_{ijk} = \alpha_j + \beta_k + \mu + e_{ijk} \tag{1}$$

will be considered. In it, the favorableness rating that person i gives to the adjective pair j-followed-by-k is described as an effect for the first adjective plus one for the second and no interaction. If the data depart from the model of Eq. (1), then we will attempt to find a monotonic transformation of the observed scale such that the model does hold on the transformed scale. It is hoped that relating the transformed data to the similarly-transformed ratings of the component adjectives rated singly will yield a simple model for accounting for both kinds of data. In spite of his early espousal of the principle of transformation to fit a model, Anderson has not apparently made use of this procedure. This may be because he has not found it necessary, but in at least one case (Sidowski & Anderson, 1967), it would appear that transformation might have eliminated an apparent interaction effect. Some of the other complicating effects described by him (Anderson, 1968a) might also be eliminated when the data are transformed.

Luce and Tukey (1964) did not provide methods for transforming the data in a conjoint measurement study. Lingoes (1968a,b) provided a computer method for dealing with the problem, his CM-II program being the most relevant. The MONANOVA procedure of Kruskal (1965) is also designed for essentially the same purpose. Anderson's (1962a) suggestion concerning a series expansion has the drawback of not constraining the transformation to be monotonic. The procedure actually used here was a straightforward graphical one which should have the same effect as MONANOVA, but the resulting transformation is continuous rather than a step-function.

The adjectives used in this study have also been used in one employing nonmetric multidimensional scaling, the other main type of model which has allowed monotonic transformation of the response scale in order to increase conformity to the model. It was felt that very useful information on the validity of the transformation procedures might be provided if the data-numbers derived from the monotonic transformation to additivity analysis just described were compared to those from the nonmetric multidimensional scaling analysis. In another paper, Young (this book, Volume I) discussed a set of computer programs built around the notion that both conjoint measurement and nonmetric multidimensional scaling are special cases of what he calls "polynomial conjoint analysis."

TABLE 1

ADJECTIVES USED AND FAVORABLENESS RATINGS

	Adjective	Favorableness		
		Executive[a]	Technician[a]	Anderson[b]
1	Able	7.9	7.8	4.4
2	Talented[c]	7.8	7.9	4.8
3	Energetic[c]	7.6	7.3	4.6
4	Bold[c]	6.0	6.2	3.4
5	Cautious[c]	5.1	6.1	3.3
6	Timid[c]	3.3	3.5	2.2
7	Indecisive	2.4	2.4	not rated
8	Ineffective	2.0	1.6	not rated
9	Incompetent[c]	1.8	1.4	1.1
10	Sloppy	2.3	1.5	not rated

[a] Mean ratings of single adjectives on 1–9 scale in present study.
[b] "Likeableness" ratings on a 0–6 scale as reported by Anderson (1968b).
[c] Adjectives included in the 7-adjective subset.

The present study has several aims. First, it tests to see if data on the favorableness of adjective pairs are, or can be made to be, consistent with a model which is additive in the sense of nonsignificant interaction in an analysis of variance. Then it compares the data for combinations with the data for the same adjectives judged singly in order to see which particular form of the additive model is most appropriate. Finally, it attempts to relate the favorableness data for the pairs to the positions of the component adjectives in a space derived by means of nonmetric multidimensional scaling analysis of a separate set of data.

Ellis (1966) has emphasized that the crucial quality of data numbers (the property that raises numbers from the status or mere "working numbers" to that of measurements) is the number, closeness, and simplicity of the relationships among them. We are attempting here to demonstrate a network of relationships, first among favorableness ratings of pairs of adjectives, second, between numbers derived from these relationships and the ratings of single adjectives, and third, between both of these numbers derived from similarity ratings of pairs of adjectives.

Method

Stimulus Sets

The adjectives used were the ten listed in Table 1. They are a subset of those used by Cliff and Young (1968) in a multidimensional scaling study, which was selected because these particular adjectives were found to lie in two dimensions, roughly falling around the circumference of an ellipse. (See Figure 1.)

Stimuli in the study consisted of the ten single adjectives plus all possible pairs of these adjectives. Two hypothetical target persons were used. In one set of directions, the subjects were told to think of the pairs as being used to describe a *skilled technician*, and in the other, they were told the pairs were being used to describe a high-level business *executive*. Some pairs were included twice in order to permit the use of the unreliability of the mean judgments to define an error term which could be used to test goodness of fit.

The stimuli were presented in booklets, and the subject indicated his judgment by circling the appropriate number on a scale from 1 to 9. One end of the scale was defined as "highly unfavorable" and the other "highly favorable."

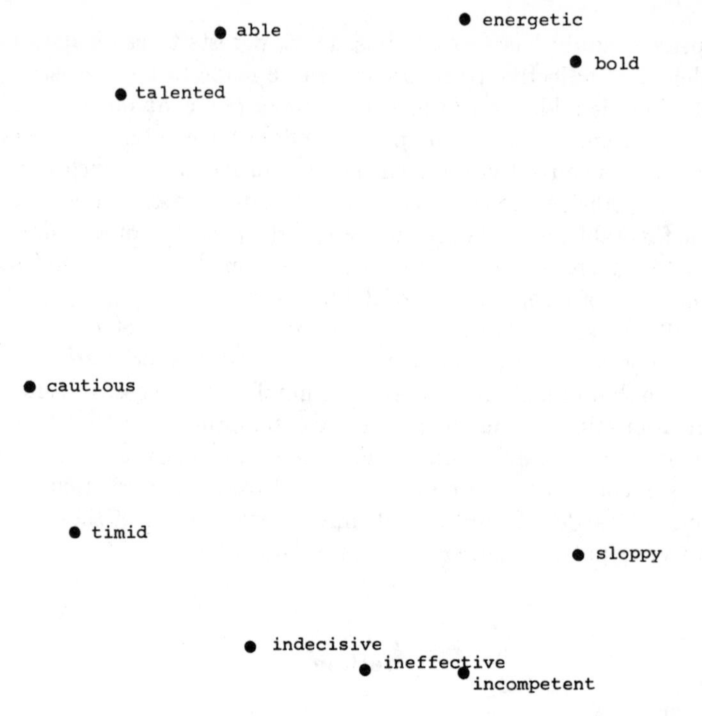

Fig. 1. Locations of adjectives in two-dimensional space. From Cliff and Young (1968).

Subjects and Administration

Two questionnaire forms were used, and each consisted of two parts. In the first part of each form, all pairs and singles of the complete set of ten adjectives were included. In the second part, only the pairs and singles of a subset of seven adjectives were included. The two forms of the questionnaire differed as follows. One had the *executive* as the target for the ten-adjective first part and the *technician* as the target for the seven-adjective second part. The reverse was true in the second form. Thus there were four sets of data. These will be referred to as the Executive-10, Technician-7, Executive-7, and Technician-10 sets. The ten-adjective part always came first, the shorter sections being considered supplementary. There were 15 repeated pairs in the ten-adjective data and 12 in the seven-adjective data.

There were two groups of subjects, one for each form, with subjects and forms randomized. There were 31 subjects in all, 16 for one form and 15 for the other. The subjects were introductory psychology students fulfilling a course requirement of participation in studies. The data were gathered in several small group sessions, *E* reading the directions to the *S*s.

Tests of Fit

The repeated items form the basis for the test of goodness of fit. Let x_{jk} and x'_{jk} represent the means across subjects for two repetitions of the same adjective pair. For all stimuli, the two are assumed to differ only because of differences in errors of measurement ($e_{.jk}$ and $e'_{.jk}$, respectively) on the two occasions, and the errors are assumed to be independently distributed with mean zero and constant variance σ^2. Then the differences between the mean values for repetitions of identical pairs can be used to estimate σ^2, even though not all pairs are repeated. The variance estimate thus derived corresponds to what would be a within-pairs mean square in a subjects by first adjectives by second adjectives analysis of variance with two replications per cell, if all the pairs had been repeated. Thus the test of the general additive model is to compute the ratio of interaction mean square to within-pairs mean square. Also, closeness of relations of the mean ratings of the pairs to the mean ratings of single adjectives will be evaluated by comparing the errors of estimating pair ratings from the ratings of the component single adjectives to this within-pairs mean square. The same thing will be done with respect to predicting the ratings of the pairs from the positions of the component adjectives in the multidimensional space.

The test of the *simple* averaging model, the one which states that the mean rating of a scale value should be the average of the ratings of the component adjectives, can be made by computing the regression coefficients for the pairs on the mean ratings of their component adjectives. If the simple averaging model holds, then the regression coefficients will be .5 for both the first and second adjective of the pair and the intercept should be zero. Also, the error of estimate using the single adjectives as predictors should not be significantly greater than the error variance estimated from repeated items. If this is the case while the regression coefficients differ from .5, this will be evidence for a weighted rather than a simple averaging model.

The adequacy of the relation between the pairs and the results of the multidimensional scaling for single adjectives can be tested in a similar way, comparing the mean square deviations from regression on the dimensions for the two adjectives to the error mean square. If the fit is adequate, then this result will support the view presented by Cliff and Young (1968) that multidimensional scaling solutions constitute a rather general representation of how subjects perceive the stimuli and that other responses to the same stimuli are relatable to this representation by the operation of simple mathematical rules.

Each of the latter two analyses will be performed using both the transformed and untransformed favorableness ratings. Insofar as the transformed ratings are found to be more closely related to the single adjective ratings and the multidimensional scaling data, the importance of the transformation procedure will be further supported.

Results

General Additive Model

The four sets of mean ratings of the pairs were arranged in 10 × 10 or 7 × 7 tables and the row, column, and grand means computed. (The diagonal entries, which would conceptually correspond to the values for the same adjective repeated twice, were treated as missing data and estimated iteratively.) Then an estimate, $\hat{x}_{jk}$, of cell jk was made for all values of j and k in the 10 × 10 or 7 × 7 tables according to the general linear model by adding the row mean to the column mean and subtracting the grand mean.

$$x_{jk} = \bar{x}_{j.} + \bar{x}_{.k} - \bar{x}_{..} \tag{2}$$

These estimates were then plotted against the corresponding obtained cell means. Both sets of data for a given group of subjects were plotted on the same graph. The resulting plots were the strikingly ogival shapes shown in Figure 2.

In the plots, the ordinate is the obtained mean rating of the pair. The abscissa is the value for the cell estimated as a sum of row and column effects, i.e., Eq. (2). The curve for both groups is of the same form, although the parameters of the curves appear to be slightly different.

Now, the transformations were made by simply drawing in the curves by hand and reading off the transformed values from the abscissa. That is, for each point on the ordinate (the original scale), a horizontal line was drawn across until it intersected the curve. Then a vertical line was drawn down to the abscissa. The value at this point on the abscissa was then substituted for the starting ordinate value. The process is illustrated in Figure 2, where in the upper graph it is shown that in Sample 1 (Executive-10, Technician-7) a mean of 3.0 was transformed into 3.4, and in the lower graph it is shown that in Sample 2 (Technician-10, Executive-7) a

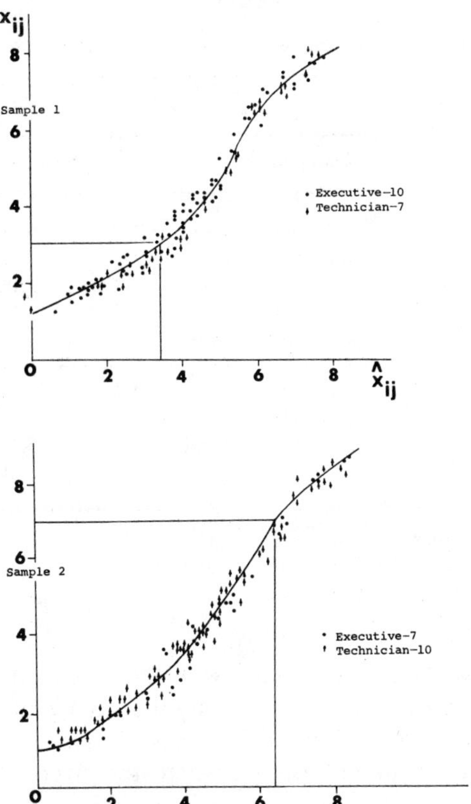

FIG. 2. Plots of observed mean ratings of combinations (ordinate) against ratings predicted on the basis of the zero-interaction model. Curves are the transformations used in an attempt to make the model fit more closely.

mean of 7.0 was transformed into 6.5. It may be noted that the overall effect of the transformation was to stretch out the ends of the scale while compressing the middle.

Then the test of the validity of the general additive model for the pair means on the transformed scale was performed by means of the analyses of variance shown in Table 2. The "error" term was the estimate derived from the data for the repeated pairs. As can be seen, the main effects are enormously significant, the second adjective effect being slightly the larger in all four cases, indicating a mild recency effect. The interactions, however, are nonsignificant in three of the four cases, indicating that in these three

TABLE 2

ANALYSIS OF VARIANCE OF TRANSFORMED RATINGS OF PAIRS

Source	*df*	Executive-10 Mean square	Executive-10 *F*	Technician-10 Mean square	Technician-10 *F*
First adj.	9	19.966	136.75**	20.094	717.64**
Second adj.	9	20.418	139.85**	23.087	824.54**
Interaction	71	.121	<1	.094	3.36*
Error[a]	15	.146		.028	
		Executive-7		Technician-7	
First adj.	6	20.485	163.88**	18.363	176.57**
Second adj.	6	23.718	189.74**	19.623	188.68**
Interaction	29	.117	<1	.175	1.68
Error[a]	12	.125		.104	

[a] Estimated from repeated items.
* Significantly greater than "error" at $p < .01$.
** Significantly greater than "error" at $p < .001$.

cases the model is about as consistent with the data as the means for two repetitions of the same pair are with each other. It may be noted that the model fits just about equally in all four sets of data; the one case where the departures are significant is that where the error term is unusually small.

The goodness of fit is also illustrated by the correlations given in Table 3. The correlations in Table 3 are simply those between the observed pair means and the ones predicted from the additive model. The correlations are quite high, even for the untransformed data, summarizing the strong

TABLE 3

CORRELATIONS OF ADDITIVE MODEL WITH DATA BEFORE AND AFTER TRANSFORMATION

	Exec.-10	Tech.-10	Exec.-7	Tech.-7
r before trans.	.977	.982	.982	.970
r after trans.	.988	.991	.994	.989
Reliability	.979	.997	.990	.989

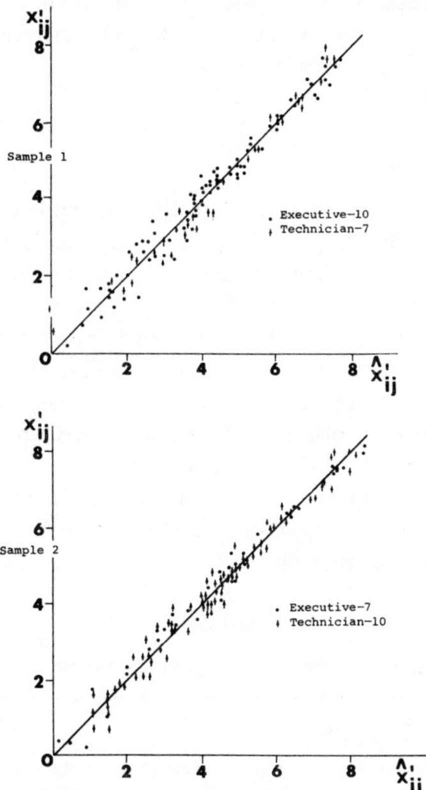

FIG. 3. Transformed mean ratings (ordinate) plotted against ratings predicted on the basis of the zero-interaction model. Straight lines are the 45° line.

monotonic trends in Figure 2. They are still higher for the transformed data, being comparable to the reliabilities except in the one case where the latter is extremely high.

The closeness of the fit of the model to data is also illustrated in Figure 3, which is analogous to Figure 2 except that the ordinate is now the transformed obtained data and the abscissa is the expected means derived from the main effects in the analyses of variance of the transformed data. The data appear to represent straight lines, and the points lie very close to them. The straightness of the lines indicates that the transformation was successful in just a single iteration. The smallness of the interaction mean square is reflected by the small horizontal distances of the points to the 45° line.

These results suggest very strongly that we have succeeded in transforming the response scale to one on which the general additive model holds within a high degree of exactness.

Specific Form of the Additive Model

Next, the consistency of the pairs with the single adjectives was studied, and the adequacy of the simple averaging model was tested by computing the regression of the favorableness of the combinations on the favorableness of the component single adjectives. That is, a regression equation of the form $x_{jk} = b_1x_j + b_2x_k$ was derived, in which b_1 and b_2 are regression weights, and x_j and x_k are the favorablenesses of the first and second adjectives, respectively, in the pair when they were presented singly. Analyses were done for both the transformed and untransformed data. In the case of the transformed data, the values of both the single adjectives and of the pairs were transformed according to the curves of Figure 2. The results of the analyses are summarized in Table 4. There, the columns labeled R give the multiple correlations. These are clearly very high,

TABLE 4

Pairs Predicted as Linear Combinations of Single Adjectives

Target and pair set	From pairs repeated		Linear combination-fit statistics					
	Est.σ_e^2	df	R	[a]Est.σ_e^2	df	b_j	b_k	Intercept
Executive-10								
untransformed	.146	15	.960	.183	87	.54	.55	−.95
transformed			.975	.111		.56*	.58*	−.10
Technician-10								
untransformed	.028	15	.957	.245	87	.55	.58*	−.87
transformed			.961	.185		.54	.58*	−.05
Executive-7								
untransformed	.125	12	.963	.208	39	.58*	.64*	−1.67
transformed			.976	.155		.67*	.73*	−.20
Technician-7								
untransformed	.104	12	.945	.349	39	.68*	.69*	−2.15
transformed			.952	.260		.64*	.67*	−.13

[a] Estimated as $\frac{2}{3}$ of mean square deviations from regression in order to take account of error of measurement in the predictors.

* Significantly greater than .5, $p < .01$.

although not quite as high as those in the previous table. The mean square deviations from fit were estimated in a rather complicated way in order to take into account the error of measurement in the predictors, which in this case are the single adjectives. Again, for the transformed data, the deviations are quite comparable to the corresponding error variances estimated from the repeated pairs, again except in the case of highly reliable Technician-10 data. No significance tests were computed, however, because of the complications in the variance estimation procedures.

The regression weights are in all cases greater than .5; in some cases the differences are significant. The consistency with which this happens is quite convincing evidence that a combination of two positive characteristics is better than either characteristic alone. For example, it is better to be talented and energetic than either talented alone or energetic alone.

It is also true in all four cases that the fit using the transformed data is slightly better than that using the untransformed. The goodness of fit pattern is much the same as in Table 2, markedly poorer than the stability of repeated items only in the one case where the stability is very high. It is also worthy of note that the intercept values are very close to zero, around .10 on a scale where the data run from around zero to 8.5. The results of these regression analyses are partially independent confirmation of the validity of the transformation to procedure.

Comparisons to Multidimensional Scale Values

The mean ratings of the combinations, both transformed and untransformed, were also remarkably consistent with the projections of the adjectives on coordinate axes as derived from the earlier study (Cliff & Young, 1968). Here, we are attempting to predict the mean ratings of the combinations from the projections of the two adjectives on two dimensions, treating the problem first as a straightforward four variable linear regression problem, and then testing to see whether there were any nonlinearities in the regressions and also any interactions between either the dimensions or the adjectives. With the present data, this was done through the use of a multiple regression program, BMD 02R (Dixon, 1964). The predictor variables were the projections of both adjectives on the two dimensions. In addition, in order to test for nonlinearities, the predictor variables included all the squares of the projections and the products of projections, both between adjectives and between dimensions for the same adjective. The analytic approach was to compute the multiple regression, using linear components only, and then to examine for significance the residual relations (i.e., partial correlations) between the favorableness of the pair and

TABLE 5

PAIRS RELATED TO MULTIDIMENSIONAL SCALING RESULTS

Target	After transformation				Before transformation			
	R	Est.σ_e^2	*df*	F	R	Est.σ_e^2	*df*	F
Executive-10								
linear	.976	.166	85	1.14	.965	.278	85	1.90
nonlinear	[a]				.975	.174	77	1.19
Technician-10								
linear	.980	.147	85	5.31*	.968	.288	85	10.41*
nonlinear	.981	.139	77	5.02*	.979	.184	77	6.64*
Executive-7								
linear	.982	.184	37	1.60	.975	.254	37	2.21
nonlinear	.992	.097	29	<1	.988	.142	29	1.23
Technician-7								
linear	.975	.291	37	2.10	.954	.461	37	4.44*
nonlinear	.979	.189	29	1.82	.969	.322	29	3.10

[a] No improvement using nonlinear terms.

* Deviations from regression on coordinates significantly greater than "error" derived from repeated items, $p < .01$.

the nonlinear variables. Again, we compared the goodness of fit to the reliability of the data, and performed the analyses first on the untransformed mean ratings and then on the transformed values. The results of the analyses are summarized in Table 5. Examining first the data for the untransformed means, we find multiple R's greater than .95 in the case of all four sets of data. In two of the four cases, mean squares estimated from errors of estimate are not significantly greater than mean squares estimated from errors of measurement. This procedure leaves little room for the operation of interactions and nonlinearities, but there did seem to be some small but perhaps reliable influences of this kind. Clearly, the consistency of these data, which are from two different samples of subjects and were gathered about two years apart, is very great, almost the maximum we could expect it to be.

Identical analyses performed on the transformed data improved the fit in all four cases, the correlations being raised one or two points. Now only one set of data (again Technician-10) significantly departs from the best expectable fit.

The already small degree of nonlinearity is virtually eliminated; when nonlinear terms are included, one multiple R stays the same to three decimals, two to two decimals, and the remaining one goes up by a single point in the second decimal. While in each of these last three cases there was at least one "significant" nonlinear variable, the nonlinear influences are clearly very small. Moreover, there was no consistency across the four sets of data in the nature of nonlinearity. The implication of these results showing the tightening and simplification of relationships is that transformation of the scale in order to enhance the fit of a linear model of one kind improves the fit of a linear model of a second, independent kind.

Discussion

The discovery of a high degree of consistency in judgments of word combinations, while interesting, is not new, as several researchers, e.g., Cliff (1959), Morikawa, Hatano, Shimizu, Nemoto, Sasaki, and Kinoshita (1960), Howe (1963), Kristof (1966), Anderson (1968a,b,c), Gollob (1968), have demonstrated such relations for various sorts of words in the past. What the present study provides in addition is support for the utility of an approach similar to that of conjoint measurement in which data are "scaled" in such a way as to maximize consistency with an additive model, and a demonstration that the numbers so derived are "better" in the sense of being more closely related to others, though they were independently gathered That. is, it was not simply found that the data scale could be bent to make a model fit; it was found that two independent sets of data needed to be bent in almost the identical way. Moreover, the numbers derived from the data so bent were found to fit more tightly with two other kinds of data, the single adjective ratings and the multidimensional scaling results.

While one may very well be uncomfortable at the seemingly arbitrary transformation of the data, the procedure employed goes beyond a simple choice of model over data. The fits suggest that the choice was the correct one. Moreover, the transformations required for the two sets of data were highly similar, indicating that the distortion introduced into the data by rating scale procedure is a consistent one. It would be desirable and interesting to evolve a model for the distortion.

In the present study, the analyses were performed on simple averages of ratings, and it was found that the resulting scale needed to be transformed. Perhaps the use of a different scaling method would have made the transformation unnecessary. Cliff (1959), in his studies of adverb–adjective combinations, used successive intervals scale values as his basic data and did not need to employ further transformations of the data. In cases where the scale is bipolar, such as with words, successive intervals scaling tends to stretch the ends of it relative to the middle. This tendency may explain why the transformation was not found to be necessary in those earlier studies, since this is the kind of transformation that was applied here. A third possibility would have been to employ a magnitude scaling method (Stevens, 1957) as the judgment procedure. This, too, might have removed the need for transformation, although the logarithmic relation between successive intervals and magnitude scales implies that transformation would have been necessary in one of these cases or the other. It should be emphasized, though, that even if a more formal method such as successive intervals or magnitude scaling had been used to derive the original scale values for the combinations, those scales, too, would still have been transformed if transformation had been found necessary in order to make the additive model hold. That is, the substantive model would have taken precedence over the *a priori* scaling procedure.

With respect to the question of the exact nature of the model most appropriate for impression formation, the present results suggest that some caution is in order. On the transformed scale, the mean ratings of the combinations have been shown to be linear functions of the component adjectives. We have assumed that an adjective presented singly receives a weight of unity, and that therefore the regression weights used to predict the combination ratings from the ratings of the components directly reflect the weights determining the meaning of the combination. These observed weights are greater than .5, and therefore seemingly a weighted sum rather than either a weighted average or a summation model. Anderson's (1965, 1968a) weighted-average model necessitated the inclusion of an "initial or neutral" stimulus that also receives weight in an overall impression. In his system, the weights, including that for the neutral stimulus, are assumed to sum to unity. It seems simpler to abandon these assumptions and substitute that of the unitary weight for the single adjective.

The small and usually nonsignificant interactions indicate that an adjective has the same effect no matter which other it is paired with. This fact together with the simplicity of the relation between favorableness and the multidimensional loadings, suggest that the overlap in meaning of the two adjectives in the pair, their "redundancy," is not the source of the failure to find a simple additive effect. Two adjectives taken together result in greater polarization than the average of their separate polarizations, but not greatly so; this is not a consequence of any overlap in the meaning of the two, however.

The effect of the transformation of the scale is to make the extremes more extreme. When this was first noted, it was thought that the simple additive model might hold on the transformed scale, but the transformation is not enough to have this effect. It may, however, be enough to eliminate the diminishing returns set-size effect for adjectives after the second adjective since its form is such as to compensate for this effect as it is displayed, for example, in Anderson (1967). Thus the model he presented there, which is in part designed to take account of this effect, may not be appropriate for data on a scale transformed to additivity.

The present author also believes that the procedure employed here is one which is employed in any quantitative field. There is a continual interaction between measurements and models. Models are evolved to explain relations among measurements, and measurement methods—and apparatus—are adjusted to fit models. The textbook examples of physical measurement are the *result*, not the foundation, of a complex system of transactions between theories and measurement methods.

Perhaps anachronistically, the transformations used in this paper were found using graph paper and a hand calculator. This is clearly an undesirable state of affairs, and needs to be remedied. The MONANOVA procedure of Kruskal (1965) might have been used instead and it would be interesting to try it on the data. The freehand procedure used has the advantage of providing a smooth rather than a step-function transformation, although since the set of data points was dense enough to define the transformation rather tightly, MONANOVA might have given very similar results.

The results provide support for scaling-through-models from another direction. The high degree of relation between the numbers derived from judgments of favorableness through the additive adjective combinations model and those derived from judgments of similarity through the Euclidean distance model provide the most convincing kind of support for not only the models but the believability of the numbers derived by means of them.

The results also provide support for Cliff and Young's (1968) concepts. They suggested that the individual carries around with him an organization of a given stimulus set. They referred to this organization as a "configuration," and suggested that responses to these stimuli could be described as mathematical functions of, or operations on, the configuration. A set of such responses of a given kind to the stimuli are called a representation. They also suggested that the results of nonmetric multidimensional scaling yield an approximation to the configuration.

They went on to show a number of examples wherein it was possible to demonstrate simple, quantitative relations between the positions of the stimuli in the space determined by nonmetric multidimensional scaling and other judgments or responses. Among other things, they showed that they could find a direction in space such that the projection of the adjectives on this axis agreed highly with independent judgments on favorableness. Rosenberg, Nelson, and Vivekananthan (1968) also supported these findings. The present results extend this result to pairs of adjectives. It appears that the favorableness of a pair depends on the coordinates of the members of the pair in very close to a simple averaging fashion. The main departure from simple averaging is in the increase in polarity of pairs over single adjectives which was previously noted. The notion that multidimensional scaling results provide a general representation of a stimulus set to which other kinds of responses can be related by means of simple mathematical functions continues to receive further support.

Summary

A general additive model for relating the favorableness of adjective combinations to the component adjectives was investigated. The model was found to hold with a high degree of accuracy when the response scale was subjected to an optimizing transformation in the spirit of conjoint measurement or MONANOVA. The data thus transformed were found to be highly consistent with the favorableness of the component single adjectives and with their coordinates from a multidimensional scaling solution. The results are taken as strengthening the credibility of the general additive model and of multidimensional scaling results as means of yielding valid representations of subjective structuring of stimulus sets.

Acknowledgment

This research was supported in part by Public Health Service Institutional Research Grant 5 S05 FR07012 to the University of Southern California. Computing assistance was obtained from the Health Sciences Computing Facility, UCLA, sponsored by NIH Grant FR-3. The help of Paul Bradley in various stages of the research, particularly the data analyses, is gratefully acknowledged. The author would also like to thank the other participants in the conference, particularly the discussant Mike Burton, for a number of valuable suggestions.

References

Anderson, N. H. On the quantification of Miller's conflict theory. *Psychological Review*, 1962, **69**, 400–414. (a)

Anderson, N. H. Application of an additive model to impression formation. *Science*, 1962, **138**, 817–818. (b)

Anderson, N. H. Averaging vs. adding as a stimulus-combination rule in impression foundation. *Journal of Experimental Psychology*, 1965, **70**, 394–400.

Anderson, N. H. Averaging model analysis of set-size effect in impression formation. *Journal of Experimental Psychology*, 1967, **75**, 158–165.

Anderson, N. H. A simple model for information integration. In R. P. Abelson, E. Aronson, W. J. McGuire, T. M. Newcomb, M. J. Rosenberg, and P. H. Tannenbaum (Eds.), *Theories of cognitive consistency: A sourcebook*. Chicago, Illinois: Rand McNally, 1968. (a)

Anderson, N. H. Likableness ratings of 555 personality-trait words. *Journal of Personality and Social Psychology*, 1968, **9**, 272–279. (b)

Anderson, N. H. Application of a linear-serial model to a personality-impression task using serial presentation. *Journal of Personality and Social Psychology*, 1968, **10**, 354–362. (c)

Bock, R. D., & Jones, L. V. *The measurement and prediction of judgment and choice.* San Francisco, California: Holden-Day, 1968.

Cliff, N. Adverbs as multipliers. *Psychological Review*, 1959, **66**, 27–44.

Cliff, N., & Young, F. W. On the relation between unidimensional judgments and multidimensional scaling. *Organizational Behavior and Human Performance*, 1968, **3**, 269–285.

Dixon, W. J. (Ed.). *BMD: Biomedical computer programs.* Los Angeles, California: UCLA School of Medicine, 1964.

Ellis, B. *Basic concepts of measurement.* Cambridge, Massachusetts: Cambridge University Press, 1966.

Gollob, H. F. Impression formation and word combination in sentences. *Journal of Personality and Social Psychology*, 1968, **10**, 341–353.

Guttman, L. A general nonmetric technique for finding the smallest coordinate space for a configuration of points. *Psychometrika*, 1968, **33**, 469–506.

Helm, C. E. Successive intervals analysis of color differences. Princeton, New Jersey, Educational Testing Service, 1960. Multilithed report.

Howe, E. S. Probabilistic adverbial qualifications in adjectives. *Journal of Verbal Learning and Verbal Behavior*, 1963, **1**, 225–242.

Krantz, D. H. Conjoint measurement: The Luce-Tukey axiomatization and some extensions. *Journal of Mathematical Psychology*, 1964, **1**, 248–277.

Kristof, W. Das Cliffische Gesetz im Deutschen: Eine sprachpsychogische Unterschung. *Psychologische Forschung*, 1966, **29**, 22–31.

Kruskal, J. B. Multidimensional scaling by optimizing goodness of fit to a nonmetric hypothesis. *Psychometrika*, 1964, **29**, 1–27. (a)

Kruskal, J. B. Nonmetric multidimensional scaling: A numerical method. *Psychometrika*, 1964, **29**, 115–129. (b)

Kruskal, J. B. Analysis of factorial experiments by estimating monotone transformations of the data. *Journal of the Royal Statistical Society* 1965 (Series B, methodological), **27**, 251–263.

Lingoes, J. C. An IBM 7090 program for Guttman-Lingoes smallest space analysis—I. *Behavioral Science*, 1965, **10**, 183–184.

Lingoes, J. C. The multivariate analysis of quantitative data. *Multivariate Behavioral Research*, 1968, **3**, 61–94. (a)

Lingoes, J. C. The rationale of the Guttman-Lingoes nonmetric series: A letter to Doctor Philip Runkel. *Multivariate Behavioral Research*, 1968, **3**, 495–508. (b)

Lord, F. M., & Novick, M. R. *Statistical theories of mental test scores*. Reading, Massachusetts: Addison-Wesley, 1968.

Luce, R. D., & Tukey, J. W. Simultaneous conjoint measurement: A new type of fundamental measurement. *Journal of Mathematical Psychology,* 1964, **1,** 1–27.
Morikawa, Y., Hatano, T., Shimizu, M., Nemoto, N., Sasaki, T., & Kinoshita, T. Imi no suryo-teki kenkyu: Tangó-fukugo ni okeru imi-henyo. *Shinri-gaku Hyoron,* 1960, **4,** 61–85.
Rosenberg, S., Nelson, C., & Vivekananthan, P. S. A multidimensional approach to the structure of personality impressions. *Journal of Personality and Social Psychology,* 1968, **9,** 283–294.
Shepard, R. N. The analysis of proximities: Multidimensional scaling with an unknown distance function. I. *Psychometrika,* 1962, **27,** 125–140. (a)
Shepard, R. N. The analysis of proximities: Multidimensional scaling with an unknown distance function. II. *Psychometrika* 1962, **27,** 219–246. (b)
Sidowski, J. B., & Anderson, N. H. Judgments of city-occupation combinations. *Psychonomic Science,* 1967, **7,** 279–280.
Stevens, S. S. On the psychophysical law. *Psychological Review,* 1957, **64,** 153–181.
Young, F. W. A model for polynomial conjoint analysis algorithms. This book, Volume I.
Young, F. W., & Torgerson, W. S. TORSCA, a FORTRAN IV program for Shepard-Kruskal multidimensional scaling analysis. *Behavioral Science,* 1967, **12,** 498.

MARKETING RESEARCH APPLICATIONS OF NONMETRIC SCALING METHODS

Paul E. Green

WHARTON SCHOOL OF FINANCE AND COMMERCE
UNIVERSITY OF PENNSYLVANIA
PHILADELPHIA, PENNSYLVANIA

Frank J. Carmone[1]

UNIVERSITY OF WATERLOO
WATERLOO, ONTARIO, CANADA

Since the days of motivation research (Dichter, 1958), marketers have shown little restraint in adopting many of the models of inquiry and measurement techniques of the behavioral scientist. Projective tests, Guttman, Thurstone and Likert scaling are among the many procedures which have been used by marketing researchers in the past (Benson, 1962; Lirtzman, 1966; Richards, 1959). The semantic differential is probably familiar to the

[1] Present address: Department of Marketing, Drexel University, Philadelphia, Pennsylvania.

most fledgling of advertising agency personnel and corporate image studies using this tool have become almost routine (Clevenger, Lazier, & Clark, 1965).

Unfortunately, it has often been the case that marketing researchers' adoption of these devices has been accompanied by little adaptation to the specific conditions of use. Knowledge of a methodology's assumptions—let alone any evaluation of its relevance—frequently has been lacking. What errors have been made in the uncritical utilization of behavioral measurement techniques can only be speculated on; corporate archives yield little information to the curious outsider.

Multidimensional scaling and taxonomic techniques are currently receiving a fair amount of attention from the marketing research community. A number of consulting firms have started to offer such scaling services and at least a score of large corporations are beginning to develop internal capability for conducting multidimensional scaling studies. One firm, the DuPont Company (Doehlert, 1968) has been using nonmetric scaling methods since 1963 in the measurement of buyer perceptions and preferences.

The authors' research in the applicability of multidimensional scaling techniques to marketing problems has been somewhat less auspicious; with relatively few exceptions our studies have involved small samples of respondents (drawn from that ubiquitous army of graduate business students). Fortunately for us, few policy decisions have hung in the balance, and we have been able to try a number of things with a number of different algorithms. The methodology used in this somewhat more casual research is still evolving, but we think we have encountered a number of problems which may be of interest to methodologists and applied researchers.

The purpose of this chapter is threefold. First, we describe typical problem areas representing potential applications of multidimensional scaling to marketing research; this part of the paper is frankly speculative (and laudably brief) but may be useful in suggesting ways in which nonmetric methods can be adapted to deal with various classes of marketing problems. Second, we describe the approach and findings of some of our own pilot research dealing with marketing behavior. One study is described in some detail and others are cited more briefly as they serve to raise questions about future research directions in this field. Third, in the concluding section of the chapter we try to draw together and organize the substantive and methodological problems which have arisen in our own research. We hope that the questions raised here will be useful, both to developers of the methodology and to applications researchers aspiring to use nonmetric scaling in policy-level marketing problems.

Potential Marketing Applications

Stefflre (1968) has already commented on one of the more promising areas of application of nonmetric scaling methods—the design of new products for existing markets and the design of new markets for existing products. He refers (1968, p. 252) to a dozen corporate-level studies conducted over a period of five years using his "market structure" approach.

In a more speculative vein, (Green, Carmone, & Robinson, 1968b) have suggested a number of potential applications of nonmetric scaling procedures to a variety of problems in marketing. A few of these are described here.

Market Segmentation Analysis

A market segment is often defined as a reasonably homogeneous group of buyers who respond differently from other segments to similar marketing appeals—advertising, point-of-purchase display, product features, and so on. That is, emphasis is placed on individual differences in sales response to more or less the same set of stimuli. Theoretically, if one could identify such segments and their response functions, one might use this information in tailoring various types of sales efforts to cater to specialized groups of buyers.

It seems to us that market segments might fruitfully be described in terms of commonality of perceptual configurations and ideal point locations (Coombs, 1964) in a joint space representation of stimuli (brands, suppliers of services) and "person" points or vectors. Points of view techniques (Carroll & Chang, 1970; Tucker & Messick, 1963) might be employed to partition buyers into reasonably homogeneous segments based on similarities responses, and preference data might then be used to find ideal point locations or vector directions. The usual socioeconomic or demographic variables might subsequently be employed as correlative information on segments which are constructed originally from the analysis of similarities and preference judgments. A recently completed study of musical artists (Morris, 1969) suggested that intergroup differences in perception and preferences can be related to other characteristics of the judges.

In this approach to market segmentation, corporate sales efforts might then be viewed as attempts to (a) "move" a manufacturer's brand to a more favored region in the joint space; (b) move a cluster of ideal points toward the manufacturer's brand; or (c) reorient the entire stimulus configuration through product or service innovation.

Predicting the effect of policy changes on perception and/or preference responses is certainly no easy problem, however. Nor is much known about the relationship of sales response probability to "distance" from ideal point. At present this approach to segmentation would, at best, appear to have programmatic value for the design of future research.

Product Life-Cycle Analysis

Another area of interest to marketing researchers concerns the characterization of sales (or some other measure) of a product over time. Traditionally, product life-cycle analyses have relied on empirical curve fitting methods—usually some type of S-shaped curve—as applied to time series data. An alternative formulation of the problem might be to view each variant (brand) of a product class as a time-subscripted point in performance space. Changes in performance over time could be conceptualized as movements of the points through performance space. Such movements could reveal changes in technology as well as changes in interbrand "competitiveness" (i.e., the closeness of various brands in performance space). Furthermore, quantum changes in the state of the art could be represented as additions or deletions of axes in the performance space.

Again this approach is quite speculative, but a pilot study of the computer market has been completed with results which, after the fact, seem reasonable (Green & Carmone, 1968a). Other product classes—for example, automobiles, machine tools, electric motors, etc.—could, in principle, be subjected to the same general type of analysis.

Evaluation Functions

A third prototypical problem in marketing concerns the procedures which buyers use to "collapse" partially ordered alternatives to simply ordered ones. Coombs (1964), Dawes (1964), Shepard (1964) and Yntema and Torgerson (1961) have all discussed this problem and have suggested provocative approaches.

In both industrial and consumer purchasing, characteristics of alternative vendors or brands are most realistically viewed as multidimensional. It would seem that conjoint measurement techniques (Tversky, 1967) and various nonmetric scaling approaches (Kruskal, 1965) might be employed to examine the implicit tradeoffs which people use in mapping multidimensional criteria onto a single scale. A pilot study by Wind, Green, and Robinson (1968) has demonstrated the feasibility of this approach in industrial marketing; and one of the senior author's doctoral students has examined the problem in a consumer setting.

Marketing Audits

A favorite preoccupation of many marketing researchers concerns the auditing of product movements through the (frequently long) distribution channels from manufacturer to consumer. A variety of data-supplying services have sprung up to provide marketers with such "pipeline" information. In addition, other services provide marketers with consumer diary data which have been used in developing indexes of household brand switching and various types of market share information.

Perhaps it is not too wishful to imagine the auditing of buyer perceptions and preferences over time. Changes in stimulus (or ideal point and stimulus) configurations could, again in principle, be related to changes in competitive sales strategy. Such procedures also might be employed in tracking the progress of new product introductions. Use of consumer purchase diaries could provide a behavioral link for estimating purchase probabilities from relationships portrayed by the joint space configurations, as developed from judgments obtained from the same group of respondents. Cook and Herniter (1968) have explored this approach in the context of a simulation model of consumer behavior.

Self-Concept and Brand Preference

Self-concept theory (Rodgers & Dymond, 1954) and its relationship to brand preference are also receiving attention by marketing researchers (Birdwell, 1968). Briefly stated, the central notion is a buyer tends to choose brands whose "personalities" are compatible with his self-image. This tendency could be defined operationally in terms of distance of brands from self in, say, semantic differential space.

While this approach appears provocative and potentially useful to marketing researchers (and advertising agencies), a pilot study using automobile brand names as stimuli (Green, Maheshwari, & Rao, 1969) suggested that self-concept theory and preference entail more complex relationships than might be first imagined. The results of the pilot inquiry indicated some evidence of reaction formation. That is, for some subjects preference ranks were *negatively* correlated with distance of brand from self-concept. (The conditions under which congruence versus divergence obtain still await further investigation, however.)

OTHER APPLICATIONS

The above examples hardly exhaust the potential applicability of nonmetric scaling methods to marketing. Salesman and store image research, advertisement pretesting, media readership patterns, analysis of questionnaire data, attitudinal measurement, characterization of "opinion leaders" in new product adoption, and so on, illustrate the potential applicability of these methods to general measurement tasks in marketing.

In short, it is not difficult at all to imagine a variety of problems which could be approached using nonmetric scaling methodology. In some cases "behavioral" data (based on same-different judgments, category assignment and the like) could be used as well as subjective responses of judged similarity. Such use of behavioral data is illustrated by work by Green, Carmone, and Robinson (1968a), Kruskal and Hart (1966), Laumann and Guttman (1966), Shepard (1963), and Shepard and Carroll (1966).

It is equally easy to point out, however, the many conceptual and operational difficulties attendant upon attempts to implement this new methodology. Some of these limitations will become evident as we describe a pilot application of nonmetric scaling methods to a recurring problem in advertising research.

A Pilot Application of Nonmetric Scaling Techniques

Over the past three years the authors, aided immeasurably by the efforts of our graduate students, have conducted approximately 25 small-scale applications of nonmetric techniques. Stimulus sets have covered a wide gamut: political candidates, soft drinks, breakfast foods, graduate business schools, automobiles, cold cereals, common stocks, professional journals, T. V. programs, industrial vendors, musical artists—even ladies' underwear. Stimulus definitions have included the actual objects, object names, and profile descriptions of objects.

One study (Green & Carmone, 1968b) has been selected from this group in order to demonstrate the types of substantive problems of interest to marketing researchers as well as the methodological sequence employed. The substantive problem of this study concerned the perceptual and preference judgments of so-called "creative experts" in advertising—those people who write advertising copy and prepare ad layouts. It is generally supposed that such individuals, compared to lay individuals, are predictive experts whose ability to distinguish between good and poor advertisements is an important condition for occupational success. In the pilot study we were interested in two questions:

1. Do advertising specialists perceive and evaluate ads differently from nonspecialists?
2. If so, are their judgments of ad effectiveness "superior" to those of the nonspecialist?

Stimuli and Respondents

The stimuli of this pilot study consisted of ten print ads, all dealing with the services of a company specializing in mail order activities involving home study courses. Photographs of the ads were made comparable in size ($8\frac{1}{2} \times 11$ in.) in the experiment and appeared with only a code identifying number. For this study, we elected to use "polar extreme" advertisements, namely those found by the company's analysis to be either extremely good (the six advertisements numbered 1, 4, 5, 6, 8 and 10) or extremely poor (the four advertisements numbered 2, 3, 7 and 9). All objective evaluations were based on the company's records of coupon response after correction for position in the magazine, ad size, vehicle circulation, seasonality, and similar factors. No attempt was made to order individual advertisements within the good and poor sets, despite the rather elaborate procedures used by the company to measure their effectiveness.

The study was conducted in the Winter of 1967 and involved two groups of respondents: (a) a student (control) group made up of 22 M.B.A. students majoring in marketing at the Wharton School of Finance and Commerce; and (b) an "expert" group consisting of 12 professional advertising personnel. This latter group was composed of account executives, copy writers, and art directors who worked in the Philadelphia area. (No member of the expert group was directly associated with the advertising account.) For purposes of this comparative analysis a random sample of 12 student subjects was then chosen from the original control group of 22 (MacDiarmid, 1968).

Procedure

Data collection procedures were identical over the two respondent groups; responses were obtained on an individual basis. Each subject was shown the ten advertisements and told that each had been used in past advertising by the company. Then, following a preselected (originally randomized) order, one of the advertisements was singled out as a reference item. The subject was asked to choose that advertisement from the remaining nine which he felt was most similar to the reference advertisement. He was instructed to use any criteria which he wished but to try to maintain the same frame of reference across all comparisons. After the most similar item was chosen, this advertisement was placed faced down and the subject was asked to pick out the next most similar advertisement to the reference item, and so on, until all nine had been ranked. After this was done, a new advertisement was selected as a standard for comparison and the process was repeated until each had served as a reference item. This procedure yielded a matrix of rank-order information for all ten reference advertisements. After the similarity rankings were completed, the respondent was asked to specify the criteria which he believed he had used during all of the preceding comparisons.

The subject was next asked to rank the advertisements according to his expectation about their overall ability to elicit coupon responses (magazine unspecified). He was then told that in the past the company had placed print advertisements in the following magazines: (a) *True;* (b) *Sport;* (c) *Popular Mechanics;* (d) *Guy;* (e) *Women's World;* and (f) *Men Today.*[2] (Copies of the magazines were available for the subject to browse through in order to get an idea of the format of each.) He was then asked to rank the same ten advertisements in terms of their relative ability to elicit coupon responses in each of the six magazines in turn. This step produced a set of rank orders conditional upon the vehicle in which the advertisements were to be placed. The entire interview lasted about 45 min. including instruction time. At no time was the subject made aware of the fact that some of the advertisements were "good" while others were "poor."

Analysis

Analysis of the data reflected the major objectives of the study, which can be summarized in terms of the following research questions:

1. Does the professional advertising group "see" the advertisements differently from the student (control) group?
2. What attributes of the advertisements appear to be used in the similarity judgments made by each group?
3. Are good advertisements perceived to be more similar to each other

[2] Based on the records maintained by the mail order company, three of the magazines, *True, Sport* and *Popular Mechanics,* were chosen as representative of "good" vehicles in terms of their ability to elicit coupon responses; while the other three, *Guy, Women's World* and *Men Today,* were selected as "poor" vehicles.

than they are to bad advertisements, i.e., do we find clusters of each type in the stimulus configurations obtained from the similarities data?

4. Does the expert (professional advertising) group evaluate the advertisements differently from the control (student) group with regard to overall "preference"?

5. Do good advertisements rank higher than poor ones in the overall evaluation of each group?

6. What type of utility model best describes each group's evaluations of the advertisements?

7. Is this model—and the position of the ideal point—sensitive to the vehicle in which the advertisement is to be placed?

The main analysis was preceded by a data reduction step in which the ranked similarities were converted to pairwise proximity measures (Carmone, Green, & Robinson, 1968) yielding, for each subject, a 45-component vector which represented his rank ordering of all advertisement pairs in terms of increasing dissimilarity. The following steps were then taken:

1. Intersubject rank correlations were obtained across each subject's 45-component proximity vector. This step yielded a 24×24 symmetric matrix of rank-order correlation coefficients.

2. This correlation matrix was then submitted to the TORSCA 8 nonmetric scaling program (Young & Torgerson, 1967) for the purpose of finding a subject configuration in which interpoint distances were monotonically related to intersubject correlations with respect to the original similarity judgments. This was followed by a discriminant analysis to see if intergroup differences existed with respect to coordinate values in the respondent configuration.

3. Similarity vectors representative of each point of view were then submitted to the TORSCA 8 program and stimulus (advertisement) configurations obtained. These configurations were checked for any clustering of good versus poor advertisements.

4. From the unconditional preference vectors of each group separately, unidimensional (Thurstonian) scales were computed in order to see if good advertisements were generally scaled higher than poor ones.

5. Preference vectors for each subject in each major point of view were entered into Carroll and Chang's joint space program (1967) for the purpose of finding the type of utility model most representative of each point of view. This step also enabled us to see if the type of utility model and the position of the ideal point were sensitive to the conditional preference vectors obtained under each of the six specific magazines.

The preceding steps, as well as supporting analyses, should become clearer as the results of the study are discussed.

Study Results

Results of the nonmetric "points of view" analysis with regard to the intersubject proximity data indicated that the configuration of subjects could be represented adequately in four dimensions.[3] A two-group discriminant analysis was then conducted to see if differences existed between advertising personnel's and the control group's four-space coordinates. The results of this computation indicated that the discriminant function correctly classified 20 out of 24 subjects, which was statistically significant at the .05 level. It is well known, however, that such procedures capitalize on chance. As a precautionary step, a second discriminant analysis was run, based on an arbitrary assignment (odd versus even subject numbers) of respondents to the two groups. This check run "correctly" classified 16 out of 24 subjects; as might be expected, the function was not statistically significant.

Although the first discriminant analysis results were not particularly compelling, we provisionally accepted the hypothesis that the two groups had different points of view. But two questions remained: (a) do even more homogeneous subgroups exist *within* the expert and nonexpert groups; and, if so, (b) how different are these points of view with respect to the stimulus configurations?

An answer to the first question was sought by using a numerical clustering routine (Howard & Harris, 1966) on each group separately. Only the 20 subjects correctly classified by the discriminant function were included. The four-space coordinates of the subject configuration were again used as input data.[4]

The cluster analysis yielded two subgroups each for the expert and control groups. For purposes of further analysis these clusters were identified as:

C_1: cluster 1 of control group (six subjects);
C_2: cluster 2 of control group (four subjects);
E_1: cluster 1 of expert group (seven subjects);
E_2: cluster 2 of expert group (three subjects).

[3] Kruskal's stress measure was .04,

[4] Although not discussed here, separate TORSCA 8 scalings were also run for the misclassified subjects as based on the discriminant analysis. As might be surmised, their configurations were closer to the average subject configurations of the comparison group than to their own group.

Proximity data for the clustered subjects were aggregated by subgroup and the four sets of "raw" proximity data were submitted separately to the TORSCA 8 program in order to find configurations of the ten advertisements. Next the resulting configurations were uniformly scaled and orthogonally rotated (Cliff, 1966; Pennell & Young, 1967) to a common orientation (using the C_1 configuration as the reference configuration so as to make the task of visual comparison easier).

(a) STIMULUS CONFIGURATIONS. Application of the scaling program and subsequent rotation of the solutions resulted in the four configurations shown in Figure 1. All four multidimensional scaling solutions yielded "badness of fit" measures, Kruskal's stress (1964), between .05 and .11 in three dimensions.

Using the C_1 configuration as a reference, one can determine how "close"

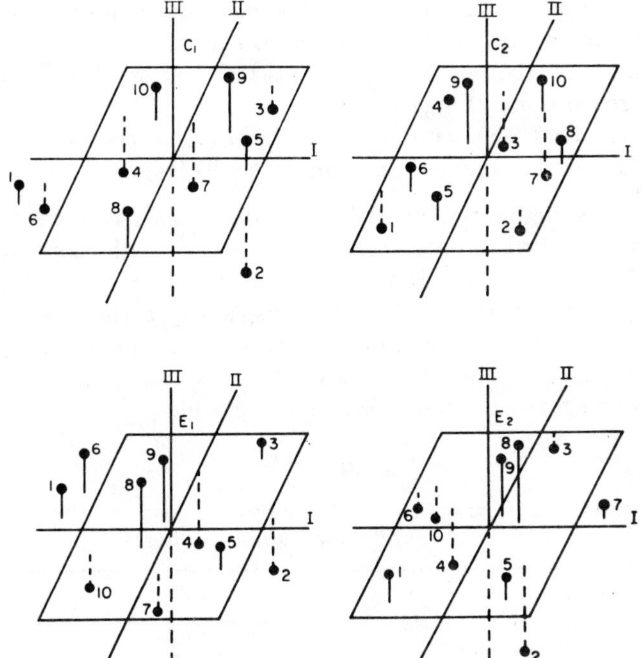

FIG. 1. Three-space configurations of ten advertisements by cluster designation. C_1: cluster one of control group (six subjects); C_2: cluster two of control group (four subjects); E_1: cluster one of expert group (seven subjects); E_2: cluster two of expert group (three subjects).

the other three are to it by computing correlations between the 45 interpoint distances of C_1 versus those of the other configurations in turn. Bearing in mind that clustering was done *within* group, it is not surprising that E_1 was closest to C_1 (an interpoint distance product-moment correlation of .61) while C_2 was farthest from C_1 (product-moment correlation of .24). For purposes of interpretation, however, all four solutions were treated as distinct "points of view."

(b) Interpretation of the scaling configurations. One of the major problems in multidimensional scaling concerns appropriate labeling of the dimensions, an extrastatistical task. In this case we had hypothesized that subjects would use two classes of criteria (possibly in combination) for discriminating among the characteristics of the advertisements. Accordingly, before the study was conducted, the advertisements had been characterized by four "property" vectors:

1. Proportion of its total area devoted to pictures or other illustrations.
2. Number of benefits listed in the advertisement.
3. Whether the theme of the advertisement stressed individual as opposed to group (family) appeals.
4. Whether the theme of the advertisement was couched in strong (hard-sell) language as opposed to weak (soft-sell) language.

The first two vectors represented physically measured characteristics, while the last two had to be developed subjectively, with each advertisement coded on a 0–1 basis. It is of interest to note that the four poor advertisements (numbers 2, 3, 7 and 9) displayed on the average (a) a higher proportion of total space devoted to pictorial material; (b) fewer benefits; (c) a greater preponderance of family appeals; and (d) weaker (soft-sell) language, than the six good advertisements.

TABLE 1

Multiple Correlation Coefficients of Property Vectors and Projections of Most Congruent Fitted Vectors in Space

		Projections		
Clusters	Correlations	1	2	3
C_1	.86	.61	.40	.89
C_2	.93	.66	.59	.49
E_1	.51	.56	.57	.70
E_2	.53	.77	.41	.61

TABLE 2

CANONICAL CORRELATIONS OF PROPERTY MATRIX AND STIMULUS CONFIGURATIONS—FIRST LINEAR COMPOUND

Clusters	Index of canonical correlation	Canonical weights of stimulus dimensions			Canonical weights of property vectors			
		1	2	3	1	2	3	4
C_1	.94	−.79	−.60	.11	−.13	.24	−.41	1.18
C_2	.99	−.06	−.61	.58	−.78	.35	−.15	.26
E_1	.86	.10	−.92	−.46	.48	.86	−.83	.15
E_2	.84	−.51	−.93	.24	−.28	.76	−.25	.62

Availability of the four property vectors enabled us to find directions in the three-space configurations of Figure 1, whose projections were most highly correlated with each property vector in turn. Table 1 shows the multiple correlation obtained by the maximum "r" procedure (Miller, Shepard, & Chang, 1964). Descriptively, we note that the control group clusters appear to emphasize the pictorial characteristics (property 1) of the advertisements more than the expert group. But, with the exception of property 1 for cluster C_2, none of the correlations is compellingly high. By fitting property vectors one at a time, however, this procedure does not take their intercorrelations into account. Accordingly, a canonical correlation was also run between the three-space coordinates of each cluster and the matrix of four property vectors.

Table 2 shows the canonical weights and index of canonical correlation for the first pair of linear compounds as found from the canonical correlations. We note descriptively that the indexes of canonical correlation, ranging from .84 for E_2 to .99 for C_2, are generally high (Note, however, that sample size is quite small.) Property vector 4 appears most prominently in cluster C_1, while property vector 1 is most prominent for C_2, vectors 2 and 3 for E_1, and vectors 2 and 4 for E_2.

It appears that no clearcut interpretation of the axes of the stimulus configurations is possible, although the property matrix in its entirety is highly correlated with the configurations. One might tentatively classify cluster C_1 respondents as employing thematic dimensions and C_2 respondents as employing "physical" dimensions. Clusters E_1 and E_2 might be classified as employing both. The above classifications must be considered provisionally inasmuch as it is quite possible that subjects could have (a) switched criteria over trials (i.e., ignored instructions to maintain the same frame of reference); (b) employed psychophysical transforms (Carroll & Chang, 1965) not captured by a linear fitting model; or (c) used criteria other than those hypothesized by the experimenter. (In view of the above caveats, and the small sample size we believe the preceding "labels," at best, are candidate hypotheses for additional experimentation with the same stimuli.)

(c) Accuracy of discrimination. Somewhat less equivocal is the answer to the more crucial question of whether the expert or the control groups tended to cluster good advertisements together and poor advertisements together, i.e., whether their similarity judgments reflected advertisement "quality." Several ways are available to answer this question. First, one can look for visual evidence of clustering in the configurations of Figure 1. Second, one can use a clustering routine to group advertisements mechanically, as based on their three-space coordinates in Figure 1. Third, one can rotate the configuration to find a vector whose projections show maximal discrimination between good and poor advertisements (not unlike the conventional application of discriminant analysis). Given the exploratory nature of this study, only the first and third approaches were used.

Examination of Figure 1 shows little visual evidence of good or poor advertisement clustering by subject clusters in either the control or expert groups. Application of the maximum "r" procedure supported this finding: the associated point multiserial correlations were .76, .59, .63 and .76, respectively, for C_1, C_2, E_1, and E_2. Not only are these correlations not compellingly high, but also there is no differential predictive ability among groups.

We conclude provisionally that (a) some moderate difference exists between the expert and control groups with respect to perceptual points of view, but (b) the configurations of neither group show high accuracy in the discrimination of good versus poor advertisements. Finally, some modest support exists for the hypothesis that the groups used both physical and thematic characteristics of the stimuli in their similarity judgments.[5]

(d) Thurstonian scaling of preference data. In order to answer the questions concerning (a) intergroup differences regarding "general" evaluation of the advertisements and (b) comparative accuracy of the expert versus control group, the overall (unconditional) preference vectors

[5] This statistical finding was supported by the overt responses made by subjects after completing the similarities task; in most cases the physical or thematic characteristics of the advertisements were mentioned as criteria which they believed they had used in making similarity comparisons.

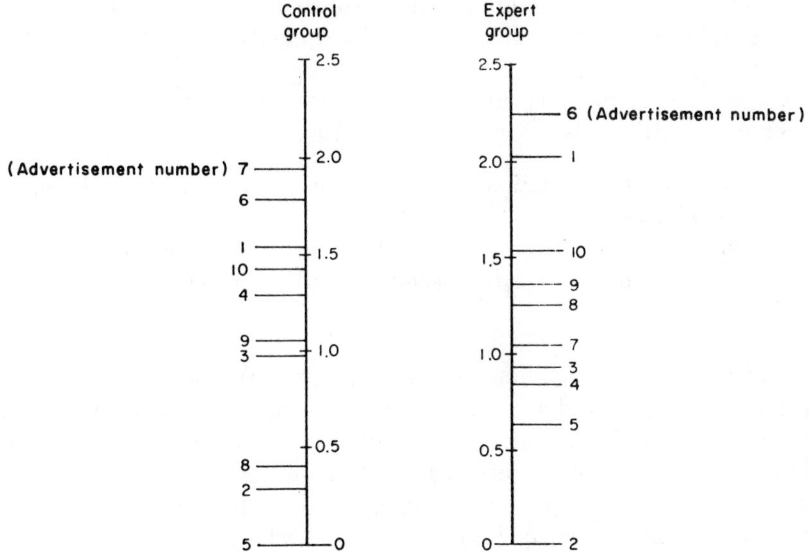

FIG. 2. Thurstonian Case V Scales for overall evaluations—control versus expert group.

of each group were analyzed separately by application of Thurstonian Case V Scaling (Hogan, 1968).

Figure 2 shows the resulting Case V scales for each group. We note that the two scales are somewhat different for the two groups. In the control group, advertisement 5 ("good") received the lowest scale value, while advertisement 7 ("poor") received the highest. In the expert group, advertisement 2 ("poor") received the lowest scale value, while advertisement 6 ("good") received the highest. Little association between the two groups was noted by the fact that the intergroup product-moment correlation between scale value pairs was only .47, which, again, is not particularly noteworthy.[6]

More interesting, however, is that neither group appeared to distinguish clearly between good and poor advertisements. This can be observed by the general dispersion of the poor ones (numbers 2, 3, 7 and 9) throughout the range of scale values in both the control and expert groups. A Mann–

[6] Lack of high correlation between group averages was supported by a separate two-way discriminant analysis of the four-space coordinates obtained from another (nonmetric) obverse analysis of intersubject correlations over the preference vectors; the results of this analysis suggested moderate intergroup differences between their (unconditional) evaluations of the advertisements.

Whitney U-test on each group indicated that neither the experts nor the control group performed significant discrimination at even the .2-alpha risk level.

These results appear to substantiate the earlier findings, leading to the observations of:

1. Moderate discrimination between groups with regard to both perception and evaluation.
2. Poor (and nondifferentiated) ability on the part of each group to separate good from poor advertisements, either perceptually or evaluatively.

(e) EFFECT OF VEHICLE ON ADVERTISEMENT EVALUATION. The last step of the analysis involved an examination of the effect of vehicle (magazine) on the rank-order judgments of the expert and control groups. That is, are evaluative judgments conditioned by type of magazine in which the advertisement is to be placed? We might expect that for some subjects a "good advertisement is good," irrespective of which magazine is to serve as a vehicle for it. Other subjects' evaluations of advertisements, however, may be conditioned by their perception of the vehicle's editorial format, audience profile, and the like; i.e., their judgments may be sensitive to the characteristics of the prospective carrier of the advertisement.

Inasmuch as the respondents were asked for both overall (unconditional) evaluations and then evaluations conditional upon six different vehicles: (a) *True*; (b) *Sport*; (c) *Popular Mechanics*; (d) *Guy*; (e) *Women's World*; and (f) *Men Today*; we had seven sets of "preference" data for each subject. So as not to confound differences in evaluation with differences in perception, this part of the analysis was also done for each cluster, C_1, C_2, E_1, and E_2, separately.

Carroll and Chang's generalization of the Coombsian unfolding model (1967) provided a relevant procedure for studying the effect of advertisement vehicle on evaluative judgment. The input to this program consisted of the scaling configuration representing each group's perception of the advertisements (Figure 1) and the average preference vectors for each group's overall evaluation and evaluations conditioned upon each of the six vehicles in turn. The program finds a joint space representation of stimuli *and* ideal points.[7] Although the procedure enables one to fit four types of evaluative models, our interest was focused on only two of those four,

[7] In this study the metric version of the program was used; as such, one assumes that utility is linearly related to the (weighted) squared distance between ideal point and stimuli.

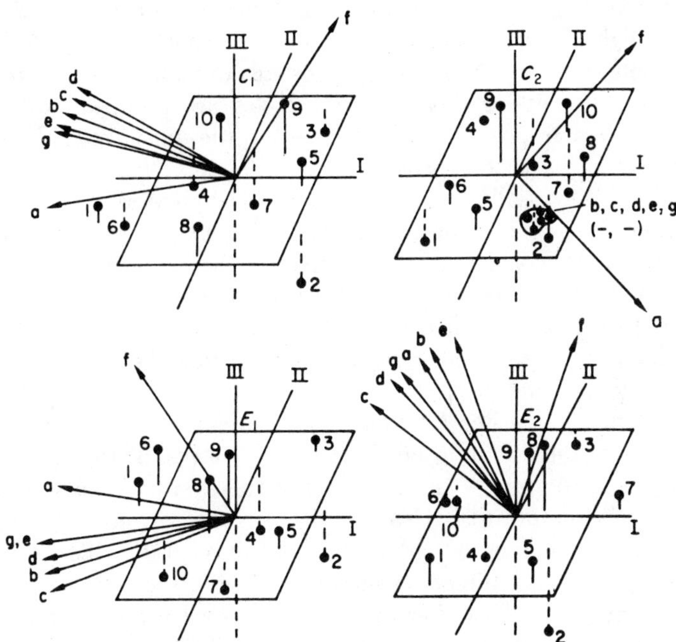

FIG. 3. Joint space configurations of stimuli and evaluations—control versus expert group. (a) Unconditioned evaluation; (b–) Evaluation conditioned by vehicle (particular magazine); *True;* (c) *Sport;* (d) *Popular Mechanics;* (e) *Guy;* (f) *Women's World;* (g) *Men Today.*

namely, the Coombsian model with equal axis weighting[8] and the vector model in which utility is assumed to increase linearly with increases along each of the dimensions of the perceptual configuration. Inasmuch as the vector model represents a special case of the ideal point model, one can determine by appropriate statistical tests whether the latter (more complex) model is required.

Figure 3 shows the results of this analysis, cluster by cluster. Looking first at the joint space configuration of cluster C_1, we note that a vector model is appropriate for describing this group's evaluations. That is, evaluations are related to the projection of each stimulus point on the

[8] Although equal weights are used, application of this model can be preceded by a rotation and differential stretching of the axes to account best for the preference data of the (grand) average subject. To maintain comparability with the configurations of Figure 1, however, this option was not used; all model fitting was based on the original multidimensional scaling solutions.

"utility" vector; projections farther out in the direction of the vector indicate higher evaluations. With the major exception of *Women's World*, we also note that conditional evaluations are not highly sensitive to vehicle; vectors for the five male-audience vehicles are grouped quite closely. Moreover, this group of vectors is closer to the unconditional evaluative vector than is the vector associated with *Women's World.*

Cluster C_2 is partially represented by an ideal point model, in this case a *negative* ideal—preference increases the farther a stimulus is from the ideal point. Again, the conditional ideal points for the male-audience magazines are quite near each other. On the other hand, both the unconditional evaluation and the evaluation conditioned by *Women's World* are better represented by vector models. Again we note that the directions of these two vectors are quite disparate.

Like cluster C_1, cluster E_1 is also represented by a vector model. Again we note that the vector conditioned by *Women's World* plots at some distance from the rest. Cluster E_2 is also represented by a vector model similar to that found for C_1 and E_1. We continue to note the somewhat anomalous positioning of the vector conditioned by *Women's World.* Otherwise, the vector directions are fairly close to each other.

In summary, for both the expert and control groups, advertisement evaluations are not highly dependent upon vehicle, with the major exception of *Women's World.* Both groups of respondents tended to view the five male-audience vehicles as fairly similar, at least insofar as advertisement evaluations were concerned. We remark in passing that in practically all instances a vector model was sufficient to portray the results. The direction cosines of the vector can be interpreted as "tradeoffs" among the three attributes (dimensions) assumed to underlie both the similarities and preference judgments. From a substantive standpoint it is difficult to make intercluster comparisons of the joint-space configurations since differences in the stimulus orientations have already been shown in Figure 1. We might say, rather tenuously, that the C_2 responses appear most anomalous, at least in terms of the type of model required to link evaluations with the stimulus configuration.

Discussion

The substantive findings of this exploratory study indicated:

1. Modest intergroup differences with respect to perceptions and evaluation of the advertisements.

2. Little ability on the part of either group to separate good from bad advertisements, either in a perceptual or evaluative context. Moreover, each group's performance was about the same.

3. With the exception of *Women's World* magazine, little dependence on vehicle as a conditioning variable in the respondents' evaluative judgments.

In view of the extremely small sample sizes employed in this study, the above results must be considered as highly tentative. In this regard, with a few exceptions, little use was made of significance tests. Indeed, we view the value of this study as much in methodological as in substantive terms. For this reason we have attempted to explicate the various analytical steps in some detail so that future studies dealing with the "predictive expert" in advertising might use some or all of these procedures. Such versions of this research would be required before anything approaching a definitive statement could be made about the predictive abilities of advertising personnel.

Finally, some additional limitations of a methodological nature should be mentioned. First, the problem of partitioning subjects into more homogeneous subsets with regard to perception is far from resolved. While one can use various clustering procedures (or discriminant analyses where prior information is available), these are rather *ad hoc* approaches. In our experience, however, homogeneity of perception has been the exception rather than the rule. Better approaches for dealing with this problem are sorely needed if one is to deal efficiently with large-scale studies in which it is highly impractical to scale each subject's similarities data. McGee (1968) has recently developed an approach which may be useful in this regard. Also, Carroll and Chang's INDSCAL model (1970) strikes us as particularly noteworthy.

Second, the dimension-labeling problem is also far from resolved, as witnessed in this pilot application. We believe that the employment of "property" vectors is a useful way to proceed but one is still plagued with the possibility of shifting criteria over respondent trials and finding the appropriate transforms for linking perceptual dimensions with property vectors. In this regard it seems that a series of experiments would be required to test hypothesized "labels" as developed from exploratory studies.

Other problems of a methodological and substantive nature come easily to mind. Rather than explore them here, in the context of a specific application, it appears more useful to discuss these problems in a more general setting. The concluding section of the paper is devoted to this topic.

Current Problems in Applying Multidimensional Scaling Techniques

Although current problems in multidimensional scaling can be looked at from several viewpoints—empirical, mathematical, or philosophical—we prefer to confine our remarks to empirical problems encountered in the application of these procedures to marketing activities. These problems and implied suggestions for future research, having come from our own work, may reflect the idiosyncratic aspects of marketing research problems, although we would like to think, that they may also be relevant to other problem areas.

For purposes of discussion the topics have been classified as problems of (a) mechanics; (b) invariance and reliability; (c) interpretatability; and (d) prediction and control. Phrased differently: How can "good" data be obtained more easily? How stable are solutions over stimulus sets, instructions, people, and time? How can the interpretative aspects of scaling solutions be improved? And, how can predictions arising out of improved interpretability be used in meeting a firm's policy objectives? Thus, our aim is ultimately prescriptive—the use of multidimensional scaling procedures as tools for the formulation and control of marketing strategy.

Problems of Mechanics

By problems of mechanics we refer to the design and testing of new procedures for collecting similarities and preference data. Older methods—triads, n-dimensional rank order, numerical ratings, tetrad comparisons—become quite laborious as the number of stimuli increase. Of course, if the analyst is content to compute association measures over a set of (prespecified) monadic scale responses (e.g., semantic differential items), such derived coefficients may be used. Two problems are associated with this latter procedure: (a) are the preselected scales exhaustive of the constructs which *could* be used by the subject and (b) how does one weight the individual scales in arriving at composite association measures?

In our own work we have tried a variety of data collection procedures (Green & Carmone, 1967). When more than one procedure is used in the same study the results have usually been stable. Procedures designed to handle large numbers (e.g., $n > 15$) of stimuli are (a) unconstrained clustering; (b) anchor point clustering; (c) hierarchical clustering; and (d) core set methods.

Unconstrained clustering, in which respondents group stimuli into similar classes, usually requires pooling responses over subjects in order to obtain requisite stability in the frequencies with which stimulus pairs are grouped together. Anchor point clustering (a variety of the pick k out of n procedure (Coombs, 1964) where each stimulus, in turn, serves as a reference item) also requires pooling of data. While hierarchical grouping—using the level at which two stimuli are grouped together as a surrogate for "distance"—does permit one to develop individual configurations, the procedure is subject to degeneracy under nonmetric methods.

In short, the practical tradeoff between handling large stimulus sets appears to involve the need to pool data over subjects. Two tentative solutions to this problem can be suggested. First, one could use a core set of stimuli which are presented to each subject along with a secondary set of stimuli which vary across subjects. Points of view could then be determined in terms of the core set and subjects' responses for the secondary set could be added later, using techniques like those suggested by Kruskal and Hart (1966) and Roskam and Lingoes (1970).

A second approach is to use some variant of the tetrad procedure in which certain comparisons are foregone. With a large number of stimuli it seems intuitively reasonable to suppose that not all comparisons are needed to fix the configuration adequately. The problem concerns how many of the tetrads to use and, just as importantly, which ones. Perhaps approaches drawn from the experimental design literature will prove to be useful here.

It seems to us that applications research will require more investigation and testing of alternative data collection procedures, particularly in dealing with large collections of stimuli. In our own work we have found some invariance of results between pair comparison and anchor point clustering procedures (Green & Rao, 1969), but such comparisons of data collection methods are only just beginning.

Invariance and Reliability Problems

A problem of particular interest to marketing researchers concerns invariance of similarities and similarities/preference configurations over (a) changes in the composition of the stimulus set; (b) different sets of instructions and scenarios; (c) different subjects at a given point in time; and (d) different occasions involving the same subject. Our pilot type research has convinced us of the need to examine all of these problems carefully.

We have found some evidence to support the notion of configuration invariance over moderate changes in the composition of the stimulus set in two different sets of stimuli, automobile brand names and T.V. programs (Green, Maheshwari, & Rao, 1969; Green & Rao, 1969). Operationally, both studies entailed the use of a core set of stimuli embedded in larger sets whose composition varied over groups of subjects. Core set invariance was checked by product-moment correlations of the derived interpoint distances. It seems reasonable to suppose, however, that the introduction of disparate stimuli could change the constructs by which more homogeneous stimuli are judged for comparative similarity. Moreover, relatively little is known regarding the effect of sequential presentation of stimulus pairs (versus full disclosure at the outset) on the resulting stimulus configurations. Cliff and Young's research (1968) appears most relevant in this respect.

The question of configuration invariance over changes in instructions and scenarios appears wide open for further study. It seems to us that similarities and preference judgments *ought* to be context-bound but attempts to prespecify attributes along which such judgments are to be elicited have not been notably successful—recall the pilot study described earlier. We suspect, however, that the fault lies with our choice of prespecified constructs. That is, in instances where these have been employed the prespecified constructs turned out to be rather highly correlated with the dimensions found in the unstructured segment (calibration phase) of the study (Green & Carmone, 1967). One idea that comes to mind concerns the "mapping of maps" in which the scenarios themselves might be scaled based on association coefficients derived from the scaled configurations obtained under each scenario.

This notion appears better able to be handled, however, by Carroll and Chang's new individual differences model (1970), a provocative approach for dealing generally with the question of individual differences of subjects, occasions, data collection methods, scenarios—in short, practically all of the problems described here. Interesting possibilities arise for combining this model with prior clustering of subjects. In this way fine-grained differences may be revealed within clusters, while among-cluster differences might also be portrayed by using representative subjects in each cluster.

The problem of invariance and instrument reliability will probably remain with us for a long time and, to us, appears central to the quest for developing subjects' central "cognitive maps" in the sense of Cliff and Young's description (1968). That is, we would like to find interconnections between representations of the "map" under changes in scenarios and stimulus set composition.

Interpretability Problems

The problem of interpretation is only just beginning after the configuration has been obtained. In the marketing field, stimuli—brands, suppliers of services, package designs, advertisements—are quite complex; simple psychophysical transforms are quite difficult to obtain in field studies.

Usually, the researcher is forced to "label" the dimensions quite subjectively, on the basis of prior knowledge of the stimulus class or rather ad hoc usage of "criteria" stated by the respondent at the conclusion of the data-gathering phase.

One could, of course, dispense with dimensional interpretations altogether and merely show the configuration in some conventional (e.g., principal components) orientation. From a policy standpoint this would be akin to making the recommendation that the brand image should be changed to make it more like brand X which presumably occupies some "favorable" position in the configuration. We feel more impelled, however, to attempt some type of spatial interpretation, at least in some instances.

In our own work we often use monadic scale responses to hypothesized constructs; directions are then found which are mostly highly correlated with outside "property" vectors (Miller *et al.*, 1964). Such approaches appear reasonable to us but underscore the need to run a sequence of experiments in order to see how well the hypothesized constructs hold up under replication. But, obtaining the candidate constructs in the first place represents an interesting problem. In this respect Kelley's repertory grid (Kelly, 1955) or similar devices can be used to develop a set of possible constructs. The candidate constructs may be reduced to a manageable subset by choosing those which appear more or less common across subjects' responses.

One of the most interesting problems incurred in the interpretation of scaling solutions concerns the configuration's structure. Torgerson (1965) and Degerman (1970) have made significant contributions to the identification of "mixtures" of classlike and dimensional structures. A number of instances have occurred in our own studies (Green, Carmone, & Fox, 1969; Green & Rao, 1969) where it appears as though the configuration can be best interpreted as a class-dimensional structure. Such structures may involve nested characteristics in which large interpoint distances are between cluster centroids (e.g., westerns and variety shows in the case of T.V. programs) and dimensional variation seems appropriate for interpreting within-cluster distances.

It seems to us that additional model-building efforts are required to portray most transparently the various types of data structures that can be obtained in empirical research. Such models could include the display of nested dimensional variation where the within-cluster dimensions are not common over clusters or where a three stage process might be involved: (a) dimensional interpretation among cluster centers; (b) classlike interpretation of the cluster characteristics themselves; and (c) idiosyncratic dimensional variation within cluster.

Prediction and Control Decisions

From the standpoint of market strategy formulation, all of the preceding problems—and additional ones—provide opportunities for future research. In order to use multidimensional scaling procedures in policy-level problems one must be able to make (at least) two types of predictions: (a) what effect a given change in a brand's physical or chemical characteristics, package design, etc., will have on its location in "perceptual" space and, ultimately, (b) what effect this will have on consumer behavior. Similar considerations relate to new product design or other strategies aimed at changing the joint-space configurations of ideal points and stimuli.

Measuring the psychophysical transforms between the "objective" dimensions and the perceived dimensions presents a formidable task. Little is known about the susceptibility of similarities and preference judgments to changes in the stimuli or to messages describing the stimuli. Many of the changes may be so minor as to produce changes in similarities judgments which are lost simply in the noise typically associated with data collection. To our knowledge no careful tests of predicted positioning of new stimuli have been carried out as yet. However, Barnett (1969) reported that Stefflre has made predictions of market share with reasonably high accuracy. It is not known to us whether he has also succeeded in predicting positions of new stimuli.

In our judgment little is known about the relationship of probability of choice to distance of stimuli from the ideal. A host of problems surround this topic, e.g., scenario dependence, utility for variety, other marketing variables affecting choice, and so on. It seems to us that joint-space portrayals of stimuli and ideal points (or vectors) provide a useful conceptualization of stimulus choice, but it is not clear to us how this concept can be translated into operational terms. One possibility, of course, is to combine the collection of similarities and preference judgments with consumer diary data (in which actual choices are recorded) for the same group of respondents. By assuming stability over fairly short time intervals, one could postulate a function relating choice probability to distance from ideal point and attempt to estimate the parameter values of the function from recorded purchase data.

Alternatively, one might try to simulate consumer brand choices from similarities and preference data obtained from a representative sample of the buying public and determine the extent to which "reasonable" probability functions predict the gross characteristics of the market, e.g., actual brand shares. Such an approach appears quite speculative at this point, however.

In short, there seems to be a wide gulf between the conceptualization of multidimensional scaling models as devices for predicting the effectiveness of marketing alternatives and their operational use in policy-level decisions. We would speculate that the consumer diary approach seems most fruitful as a way to proceed, but we can offer no evidence supporting our conjecture.

Conclusions

Our choice of problems besetting the expanded application of multidimensional scaling procedures to substantive business problems is evidently colored by our marketing research interests. Clearly, many other problems—the development of statistical significance tests, continued exploration of the philosophical aspects of similarity, the design of models for characterizing social utility, relating preference judgments for stimulus bundles to the part worths of their components—all provide challenging areas for future research. We leave to other researchers the tasks of synthesizing the many algorithms which currently exist and the development of an appropriate inferential apparatus.

However, from the applications researcher's viewpoint the prediction problem remains uppermost. Understanding a perceptual-evaluative space implies the ability to design and predict the positioning of new objects in that space. Currently, this level of comprehension is not present in most cases of practical interest to marketers.

Acknowledgments

The authors are indebted to their many graduate students who assisted on virtually every study reported here. Arun Maheshwari and Vithala R. Rao deserve special mention for their continuing participation in a variety of projects. We are also grateful for the counsel of Drs. J. D. Carroll and J. B. Kruskal of Bell Laboratories; only the authors, however, are responsible for the results of all this help.

References

Barnett, N. L. Beyond market segmentation. *Harvard Business Review*, 1969, 152–166.

Benson, P. H. A short method for estimating a distribution of consumer preferences. *Journal of Applied Psychology*, 1962, **46**, 307–313.

Birdwell, A. E. A study of the influence of image congruence on consumer choice. *Journal of Business*, 1968, **41**, 76–88.

Carmone, F. J., Green, P. E., & Robinson, P. J. TRICON—An IBM 360/65 FORTRAN IV Program for the triangularization of conjoint data. *Journal of Marketing Research*, 1968, **5**, 219–220.

Carroll, J. D., & Chang, J. -J. A general index of nonlinear correlation and its application to the interpretation of multidimensional scaling solutions. *American Psychologist* 1965, **19**, 540.

Carroll, J. D., & Chang, J. -J. Relating preference data to multidimensional scaling solutions via a generalization of Coombs' unfolding model. (Mimeographed) Bell Telephone Laboratories, Murray Hill, New Jersey. 1967.

Carroll, J. D., & Chang, J. -J. Analysis of individual differences in multidimensional scaling via an N-way generalization of "Eckart-Young" decomposition. *Psychometrika*, 1970, **35**, 283–319.

Clevenger, T. G., Lazier, A., & Clark, M. L. Measurement of corporate images by semantic differential. *Journal of Marketing Research*, 1965, **2**, 80–82.

Cliff, N. Orthogonal rotation to congruence. *Psychometrika*, 1966, **31**, 33–42.

Cliff, N., & Young, F. W. On the relation between unidimensional judgments and multidimensional scaling. *Organizational Behavior and Human Performance*, 1968, **3**, 269–285.

Cook, V. J., & Herniter, J. D. Preference measurement in a new product demand situation. R. L. King (Ed.), *Proceedings of the Denver conference of the American Marketing Association*. Chicago, Illinois: American Marketing Association, 1968. Pp. 316–322.

Coombs, C. H. *A theory of data*. New York: Wiley, 1964.

Dawes, R. M. Social selection based on multidimensional criteria. *Journal of Abnormal and Social Psychology*, 1964, **68**, 104–109.

Degerman, R. Multidimensional analysis of complex structure: Mixtures of class and quantitative variation. *Psychometrika*, 1970, **35**, 475–491.

Dichter, E. Toward an understanding of human behavior. In R. Ferber and H. Wales (Eds.), *Motivation and market behavior*. Homewood, Illinois: Richard D. Irwin, 1958. Pp. 21–31.

Doehlert, D. H. Similarity and preference mapping: A color example. In R. L. King (Ed.), *Proceedings of the Denver conference of the American Marketing Association*. Chicago, Illinois: American Marketing Association, 1968. Pp. 250–258.

Green, P. E., & Carmone, F. J. The performance structure of the computer market: A multivariate approach. *Economic and Business Bulletin*, 1968, **3**, 1–11.(a)

Green, P. E., & Carmone, F. J. Advertisement perception and evaluation: An empirical application of multidimensional scaling. Working paper, University of Pennsylvania, May 1968. (b)

Green, P. E., & Carmone, F. J. Perceptions and preferences for graduate business schools. Working paper, University of Pennsylvania, June 1967.

Green, P. E., Carmone, F. J., & Fox, L. B. Television program similarities: An application of subjective clustering. *Commentary*, 1969, **11**, 70–79.

Green, P. E., Carmone, F. J., & Robinson, P. J. A comparison of perceptual mapping via confusions data and direct similarity judgments. In R. L. King (Ed.), *Proceedings of the Denver conference of the American Marketing Association*. Chicago, Illinois: American Marketing Association, 1968. (a) Pp. 323–334.

Green, P. E., Carmone, F. J., & Robinson, P. J. Nonmetric scaling: An exposition and overview. *Wharton Quarterly*, 1968, **2**, 27–41. (b)

Green, P. E., Maheshwari, A., & Rao, V. R. Self concept and brand preferences: An empirical application of multidimensional scaling. *Journal of the Market Research Society*, 1969, **11**, 343–360.

Green, P. E., Maheshwari, A., & Rao, V. R. Dimensional interpretation and configuration invariance in multidimensional scaling: An empirical study. *Multivariate Behavioral Research*, 1969, **4**, 159–180.

Green, P. E., & Rao, V. R. T.V. show perceptions—A note on stimulus invariance in multidimensional scaling. Working paper, University of Pennsylvania, February 1969.

Hogan, J. M. W. STAT-PREF.—An IBM 360/65 FORTRAN IV Program package for unidimensional scaling of preference data. *Journal of Marketing Research*, 1968, **5**, 218–219.

Howard, N., & Harris, B. A hierarchical grouping routine—IBM 360 Program. University of Pennsylvania Computer Center, October 1966.

Kelly, G. A. *Psychology of personal constructs*. New York: Norton, 1955.

Kruskal, J. B. Multidimensional scaling by optimizing goodness of fit to a nonmetric hypothesis. *Psychometrika*, 1964, **29**, 1–27.

Kruskal, J. B. Analysis of factorial experiments by estimating monotone transformations of the data. *Journal of the Royal Statistical Society*, 1965 (Series B, methodological), **27**, 251–263.

Kruskal, J. B., & Hart, R. E. A geometric interpretation of diagnostic data from a digital machine. *Bell System Technical Journal*, 1966, **45**, 1299–1338.

Laumann, E. O., & Guttman, L. The relative association contiguity of occupations in an urban setting. *American Sociological Review*, 1966, **31**, 169–178.

Lirtzman, S. The computer and procedures for scaling attitudes. In L. Adler and I. Crespi (Eds.), *Attitude research at sea*. Chicago, Illinois: The American Marketing Association, 1966. Pp. 51–58.

MacDiarmid, J. An Application of Multidimensional Scaling to Advertising Evaluation. Unpublished MBA thesis, Wharton School of Finance and Commerce, 1968.

McGee, V. E. Multidimensional scaling of N sets of similarity measures: A nonmetric individual differences approach. *Multivariate Behavioral Research*, 1968, **3**, 233–248.

Miller, J. E., Shepard, R. N., & Chang, J. J. An analytical approach to the interpretation of multidimensional scaling solutions. *American Psychologist*, 1964, **19**, 579–580.

Morris, T. Perceptions of and preferences for musical artists: An application of multidimensional scaling. Unpublished MBA thesis, Wharton School of Finance and Commerce, 1969.

Pennell, R. J., & Young, F. W. An IBM Systems/360 Program for orthogonal least squares matrix fitting. *Behavioral Science*, 1967, **2**, 165.

Richards, E. A. A commercial application of Guttman attitude scaling techniques. *Journal of Marketing*, 1959, **22**, 166–173.

Rodgers, C. R., & Dymond, R. F. (Eds.). *Psychotherapy and personality change, coordinated studies in the client-centered approach*. Chicago, Illinois: University of Chicago Press, 1954.

Roskam, E., & Lingoes, J. C. Program for the smallest space analysis of square symmetric matrices. *Behavioral Science*, 1970, **15**, 204–205.

Shepard, R. N. Analysis of proximities as a technique for the study of information processing in man. *Human Factors*, 1963, **5**, 33–48.

Shepard, R. N. On subjectively optimum selection among multi-attribute alternatives In M. W. Shelly and G. L. Bryan (Eds.), *Human judgments and optimality*. New York: Wiley, 1964. Pp. 257–281.

Shepard, R. N., & Carroll, J. D. Parametric representation of nonlinear data structures. In P. R. Krishnaiah (Ed.), *International symposium on multivariate analysis, Dayton, Ohio,* **1965**. New York: Academic Press, 1966. Pp. 561–592.

Stefflre, V. J. Market structure studies: New products for old markets and new markets (foreign) for old products. In F. Bass, C. W. King, and E. A. Pessemier (Eds.), *Applications of the sciences in marketing management*. New York: Wiley, 1968. Pp. 251–268.

Torgerson, W. S. Multidimensional scaling of similarity. *Psychometrika*, 1965, **30,** 379–393.

Tucker, L. R., & Messick, S. An individual differences model for multidimensional scaling. *Psychometrika*, 1963, **28,** 333–367.

Tversky, A. A general theory of polynomial conjoint measurement. *Journal of Mathematical Psychology*, 1967, **4,** 1–19.

Wind, Y., Green, P. E., & Robinson, P. J. The determinants of vendor selection: The evaluation function approach. *Journal of Purchasing*, 1968, **4,** 29–41.

Yntema, D. B., & Torgerson, W. S. Man-computer cooperation in decisions requiring common sense. *IRE Transactions in Electronics*, 1961, **HFE–12**(3), 20–26.

Young, F. W., & Torgerson, W. S. TORSCA, A FORTRAN IV Program for Shepard-Kruskal multidimensional scaling analysis. *Behavioral Science*, 1967, **12,** 498.

SOME APPLICATIONS OF MULTIDIMENSIONAL SCALING TO SOCIAL SCIENCE PROBLEMS

Volney J. Stefflre

SCHOOL OF SOCIAL SCIENCES
UNIVERSITY OF CALIFORNIA
IRVINE, CALIFORNIA

This chapter deals with three interrelated topics: (a) applications of multidimensional scaling to social science problems, (b) problems in applications of multidimensional scaling, and (c) problems in application of multidimensional scaling to social science problems.

Multidimensional scaling refers here to the analysis of judged similarity data (individual or aggregate) by techniques that attempt to represent these data by a spatial configuration. Respondents' judgments of similarity or dissimilarity between pairs of items can be obtained by (a) having each respondent rate or rank all pairs of items by degree of intrapair similarity, (b) having each respondent rate or rank some pairs and aggregating these individual data into an overall set which yields a rating or ranking of all pairs, or (c) having the respondents sort items into groups on the basis of similarity and aggregating these data into an overall similarity measure for the group. The respondent is not told on what basis to judge similarity, for

FIG. 1. Spatial representation of judged similarity of sandwiches.

the judgments are elicited in order to determine this basis. These individual or aggregate data on judged similarities are then subjected to a kind of analysis which uses a metric space representation in which the reverse rank ordering of distances between items corresponds to the rank ordering of similarities.

There are many other kinds of data of interest to social scientists in addition to similarity data as well as many other possible ways to analyze

TABLE 1

COORDINATE VALUES FOR SANDWICH DATA

No.	Dimensions X	Y	Z	Sandwich
1	13.21	7.38	2.25	Chicken
2	1.85	16.10	10.54	Cheddar cheese
3	0	4.25	14.05	Peanut butter
4	4.30	0.70	17.66	Jelly
5	9.33	1.71	2.52	Egg salad
6	18.42	9.55	3.17	Ham
7	3.94	2.27	17.78	Strawberry Jam
8	7.38	4.45	18.42	Apple butter
9	16.57	15.58	14.89	Weiners
10	9.93	15.76	15.41	Pizza
11	10.97	1.76	2.41	Tuna fish salad
12	13.53	14.65	1.61	Roast Beef
13	6.29	11.97	1.56	Bacon
14	14.30	18.98	6.73	Meat Loaf
15	18.75	15.81	13.16	Sausage
16	14.56	20.31	11.62	Hamburger
17	8.96	2.27	12.73	Marshmallow fluff
18	10.52	1.23	15.83	Honey
19	20.04	11.25	7.79	Baloney
20	19.99	9.60	11.78	Spam
21	1.18	9.37	6.12	Peanut butter and bacon
22	15.75	13.36	3.00	Corned beef
23	3.88	18.02	8.67	Cheese
24	13.52	12.80	7.78	Regional long sandwich
25	0.06	10.87	13.75	Cheese spread
26	7.99	8.69	10.86	Hamburger and cheese
27	9.92	8.47	19.10	Toastems
28	3.44	5.01	13.77	Peanut butter and jelly

similarity data beside multidimensional scaling analysis. Here considerations will be given to other kinds of data well suited to multidimensional scaling analysis and also to some alternative modes of analysis of similarity data which may increase the usefulness of these data for predicting other forms of behavior.

For over ten years most of the author's research and intellectual effort has been spent pursuing the implications of several banal propositions:

1. An individual will behave similarly toward things which seem similar to him.

2. If a new item is introduced into an individual's culture, the individual will behave toward it in a manner similar to the way he behaves toward familiar items that he sees as similar to the new item.

3. The close relationship between what is psychologically similar for the individual and which things are behaved towards similarly by that individual holds across individuals and across cultures despite the wide variation between individuals and cultures as to which objects are seen as similar and in how the objects or situations are behaved towards (Stefflre, 1965, 1968, ms., a).

One way of trying to determine what an individual sees as similar to what is to ask him. By aggregating these data, one may try to determine what is similar to what for members of a particular culture. Figure 1 and Table 1 provide an example of aggregate judged similarity data on different kinds of sandwiches. For this type of study, 50 respondents are asked which is similar to what. Their data are aggregated, normalized, and transformed into a physical model using multidimensional scaling (Kruskal, 1964a,b). This kind of data stabilizes with fairly small samples of respondents (N = 30–60). To test reliabilities, the respondents are assigned numbers arbitrarily and divided into two groups. When dealing with a sample of 50, item–item similarity is calculated separately for the 25 odd-numbered and the 25 even-numbered respondents. For the last five sets of similarity data we collected, the split-half reliabilities, i.e., the correlations between the even-numbered and the odd-numbered groups, were .75, .60, .85, .80, and .77. Following the Spearman–Brown formula (e.g., see Gulliksen, 1950, Ch. 6), these figures suggest that the reliability of the data for the total groups ranged from .75 to .92.

Another way to try to learn which things are similar for an individual is to observe his behavior. Several interesting forms of aggregated data can be obtained from routine behavior patterns. These can be taken as indexes of the amount of behavioral similarity which various pairs of items elicit from members of the particular culture studied.

We have done a fair amount of work over the last few years on market research and new product development because of the availability of large scale data on patterns of individual behavior in this area and because of the opportunity for conducting large scale natural experiments through the development and introduction of new consumer products. In this context, as in many marketlike situations (see Stefflre, 1965), patterns of similarity can underly patterns of substitution and competition, i.e., objects substitute for each other or compete with each other in a single choice situation to the extent that they are seen as similar.

Several types of indexes for product–product substitution have been developed: Item-by-use matrices, patterns of preference data, and substitution patterns.

Items with the Same Uses

Table 2 shows item-by-use data for one individual. Tables 3 through 7 show the stages in the rearrangement of this matrix into clumps according to distributional similarity. Table 8 shows a 34-person aggregate data matrix rearranged into clumps according to distributional similarity.

Table 2 is the data matrix for an individual in which each row is a kind of medicine and each column is a belief-frame about when to use medicines. The informant substituted each medicine into each frame, "You take (*kind of medicine*) when you (*condition of use*)," and indicated acceptability of the sentence thus formed by a *1*, unacceptability by a blank (equivalent to a zero). For example, "You take *Bufferin* when *you have a stuffy nose*" was judged unacceptable by the informant and so the position row 1, column 2, is blank.

Table 3 shows the results of the calculation of the similarity of each row to every other row in terms of the extent to which they exhibit the same patterns of ones. This procedure measures the extent to which two belief-frames allow the same form to be placed in them resulting in acceptable statements. If r_i is the row vector of 0's and 1's from the ith row, then the similarity between rows i and j is as follows:

$$s_{ij} = \frac{r_i r_j' + r_j r_i'}{r_i r_i' + r_j r_j'}$$

(where r' is the column vector obtained by transposing the row vector r).

Table 4 shows the row–row similarity of Table 3 rearranged so that the rows similar to each other are placed near each other.

Table 5 shows the results of the calculation of the similarity of each column to every other column in terms of the distributional similarity of the belief-frames that label the columns. If c_i is the column vector of zeros and ones for the ith column, then the similarity between columns i and j is as follows:

$$s_{ij} = \frac{c_i' c_j + c_j' c_i}{c_i' c_i + c_j' c_j}$$

Table 6 shows the column–column similarity of Table 5 rearranged so that columns similar to each other are near each other.

TABLE

MEDICINES AND WHEN TO TAKE THEM

MEDICINES	ROW/COL	Bad taste in your mouth 1	Stuffy nose 2	Headache 3	Minor muscular aches 4	Tightness in your chest 5	The children have a fever 6	Can't breathe 7	In the winter 8	Sore throat 9	Hangover 10	Post-nasal drip 11	Cough 12	Indigestion 13	Feel weak 14	After you've been ill 15	During the flu season 16	Broken leg 17	The children are sick 18	Neuritis, neuralgia 19	Runny nose 20	Back ache 21
Bufferin	1			1			1		1	1	1			1		1	1		1	1	1	1
Sucrets	2	1							1	1			1									
Vicks inhaler	3		1					1	1			1					1				1	
F & F Cough drops	4	1				1			1	1		1	1				1					
Hot lemonade	5	1	1			1	1	1	1	1		1	1			1	1		1		1	
Dristan medicated room vaporizer	6		1			1		1	1			1	1								1	
Listerine throat lozenges	7	1							1	1		1	1				1					
Vicks cough drops	8	1				1			1	1		1	1				1					
Chloraseptic lozenges	9								1	1		1	1				1					
A hot toddy	10		1		1	1		1	1	1	1	1	1			1	1					1
Mentholatum	11		1		1	1		1	1				1								1	1
Seeing the doctor	12														1	1	1	1	1			1
Contac	13		1			1		1	1								1				1	
Adulton cough syrup	14					1			1			1	1								1	
Privine nasal spray	15		1					1	1												1	
Anacin	16			1			1	1	1	1	1	1		1		1	1		1	1	1	1
Ben-gay	17				1	1												1		1		1
Krex A. P. A. pain relievers	18				1				1	1		1							1	1		1
Vicks formula 44 cough discs	19					1			1			1	1									
Contac nasal mist	20		1					1	1												1	
Bromo seltzer	21													1								
Hot tea	22	1	1		1	1	1	1	1	1		1	1	1	1	1	1		1		1	1
Smith Brothers cough drops	23	1							1	1		1	1				1					
Spectrocin-T-troches	24	1							1	1		1	1				1					
Coricidin cold tablets	25					1	1		1	1		1				1	1				1	
Vicks vapo-rub	26				1	1	1	1	1			1	1								1	
Fruit juice	27	1					1		1	1	1				1	1	1		1			
Dristan nasal decongestant capsules	28		1					1	1												1	
An ice pack	29						1				1							1				1
Aspirin	30			1			1		1	1	1	1		1		1	1		1	1	1	1
Cough syrup	31					1			1			1	1									
Vitamins	32						1		1		1				1	1	1		1			
Ear drops	33																					
Alka seltzer	34										1			1								
Naso-dex	35		1					1	1										1		1	
Squibb analgesic tablets	36								1	1		1								1		
Vicks throat lozenges	37	1							1	1		1	1				1					
Neosynephrine nose drops	38		1					1	1												1	
Tetrazets antibacterial analgesic	39								1	1		1							1			
Neosynephrine nasal spray	40		1					1	1												1	
Privine nose drops	41		1					1	1												1	
Warm milk	42						1		1					1			1		1			
Murine eye drops	43																					
Vicks sinex nasal spray	44		1					1	1												1	
Cepacol throat lozenges	45	1							1	1		1	1				1					
Romilar cough lozenges	46					1			1			1	1									
F & F Lozenges	47	1							1	1		1	1				1					
Empirin compound	48			1	1		1		1	1	1	1		1		1	1		1	1		1
Calling the doctor	49						1		1	1			1				1	1	1			1
Excedrin	50			1			1		1	1	1	1		1		1	1		1	1	1	1
A. P. C. Tablets	51						1		1	1		1		1		1	1		1	1		1
Salt water gargle	52								1	1	1	1	1									
	TOTAL	12	15	5	7	15	15	17	45	26	11	29	22	10	4	13	26	4	16	9	21	14

22 In the summer	23 Feel nauseated	24 Tonsils are inflamed	25 Down and out	26 Can't breathe	27 Earache	28 The children have colds	29 Hot and cold flashes	30 Taken a chill	31 Swollen glands	32 Cold	33 Stomach ache	34 Stuffy head	35 Sinus trouble	36 Bursitis	37 Nervous	38 Hay fever	39 Upset stomach	40 Fever	41 The children are overtired	42 You are cold	43 Going to be ill	44 Wet and tired	45 Girl (boy) friend has a cold	46 Asthma	47 Laryngitis	48 Overtired	49 Sore mouth	50 The children are cranky	51 Heart burn	52 Feel a little dizzy	TOTAL
		1			1	1	1	1	1	1				1	1	1		1	1		1	1	1	1	1			1	1		31
		1				1			1	1															1		1	1			11
				1		1				1		1	1			1															12
		1				1			1	1														1	1		1	1			15
		1	1	1		1	1	1	1	1		1	1		1	1		1	1	1	1	1	1	1	1	1		1		1	36
				1		1				1		1	1			1						1		1							15
		1				1			1	1														1	1		1	1			14
		1				1			1	1														1	1		1	1			15
		1				1			1	1														1	1		1	1			13
		1	1		1		1	1	1	1		1	1	1	1			1		1		1		1	1	1	1				30
				1		1				1		1	1	1										1							15
	1	1			1	1	1	1	1	1	1					1		1			1			1	1		1			1	22
				1		1				1		1	1			1									1						13
										1														1							7
				1						1		1	1			1															9
		1			1	1	1	1	1	1				1	1	1		1	1		1	1	1	1	1			1	1		33
1														1										1							8
		1				1			1	1				1	1	1									1						15
						1				1														1	1		1	1			10
				1						1		1	1			1															9
			1																	1									1		4
	1	1	1	1	1	1	1	1	1	1	1	1	1		1	1	1	1	1		1	1		1	1	1	1	1		1	43
		1				1			1	1														1	1		1	1			14
		1				1			1	1														1	1		1	1			14
						1	1	1		1										1	1	1	1		1			1			18
						1				1				1										1				1			13
1		1				1		1	1	1								1		1	1	1	1		1	1		1			23
				1		1				1		1	1			1															10
1							1							1																	7
		1			1	1	1	1	1	1				1	1	1		1	1	1	1	1	1	1	1			1	1		33
						1				1														1	1			1			9.
1		1				1		1	1	1										1	1	1	1		1	1		1			20
1					1																			1						1	4
										1											1								1		5
				1		1				1		1	1			1															10
		1				1			1	1				1		1									1				1		13
		1				1			1	1														1	1			1			13
				1						1		1	1			1															9
		1				1			1	1								1		1					1			1			12
				1						1		1	1			1															9
				1						1		1	1			1															9
	1					1	1	1			1				1		1	1	1	1		1		1				1	1		19
1																															1
				1						1		1	1			1															9
		1				1			1	1														1	1		1	1			14
		1				1			1	1														1	1		1	1			12
		1				1			1	1														1	1		1	1			14
		1			1	1	1	1	1	1				1	1	1		1	1	1	1	1	1	1	1			1	1		33
	1	1			1	1	1	1	1	1	1					1		1			1			1	1			1		1	24
		1			1	1	1	1	1	1				1	1	1		1	1	1	1	1	1	1	1			1	1		33
		1			1	1		1	1	1				1	1	1		1	1	1	1	1	1	1	1			1	1		29
		1							1	1															1		1				10
6	4	28	4	14	11	37	13	15	28	46	4	15	15	13	11	23	2	14	7	12	14	14	10	30	32	5	15	28	10	5	823

TABLE

Row–Row Similarity Matrix of Medicines

ROW/ROW	1	2	3	4	5	6	7	8	9	10	11	12	13	14	15	16	17	18	19	20	21	22	23	24	25
1	1.00	.38	.28	.43	.69	.30	.44	.43	.45	.59	.30	.60	.32	.21	.20	.97	.21	.57	.29	.20	.11	.68	.44	.44	.61
2	.38	1.00	.26	.85	.43	.31	.88	.85	.83	.39	.31	.36	.33	.33	.20	.36	.00	.54	.67	.20	.00	.41	.88	.88	.41
3	.28	.26	1.00	.37	.50	.81	.38	.37	.40	.38	.67	.24	.88	.42	.86	.36	.00	.37	.36	.86	.00	.44	.38	.38	.40
4	.43	.85	.37	1.00	.55	.47	.97	1.00	.93	.53	.40	.43	.43	.55	.17	.46	.17	.53	.80	.17	.00	.52	.97	.97	.55
5	.69	.43	.50	.55	1.00	.59	.52	.55	.49	.73	.47	.52	.53	.33	.40	.72	.09	.43	.39	.40	.10	.86	.52	.52	.67
6	.30	.31	.81	.47	.59	1.00	.41	.47	.43	.49	.80	.22	.79	.64	.75	.38	.17	.33	.56	.75	.00	.52	.41	.41	.42
7	.44	.88	.38	.97	.52	.41	1.00	.97	.96	.50	.34	.44	.37	.48	.17	.47	.09	.55	.75	.17	.00	.49	1.00	1.00	.50
8	.43	.85	.37	1.00	.55	.47	.97	1.00	.93	.53	.40	.43	.43	.55	.17	.46	.17	.53	.80	.17	.00	.52	.97	.97	.55
9	.45	.83	.40	.93	.49	.43	.96	.93	1.00	.51	.36	.46	.38	.50	.18	.48	.10	.57	.78	.18	.00	.46	.96	.96	.52
10	.59	.39	.38	.53	.73	.49	.50	.53	.51	1.00	.53	.50	.42	.32	.31	.63	.26	.49	.40	.31	.12	.74	.50	.50	.50
11	.30	.31	.67	.40	.47	.80	.34	.40	.36	.53	1.00	.22	.71	.55	.67	.33	.43	.40	.48	.67	.00	.48	.34	.34	.30
12	.60	.36	.24	.43	.52	.22	.44	.43	.46	.50	.22	1.00	.29	.14	.13	.58	.20	.43	.31	.13	.00	.65	.44	.44	.40
13	.32	.33	.88	.43	.53	.79	.37	.43	.38	.42	.71	.29	1.00	.40	.82	.35	.10	.36	.43	.82	.00	.46	.37	.37	.45
14	.21	.33	.42	.55	.33	.64	.48	.55	.50	.32	.55	.14	.40	1.00	.38	.25	.27	.27	.71	.38	.00	.28	.48	.48	.40
15	.20	.20	.86	.17	.40	.75	.17	.17	.18	.31	.67	.13	.82	.38	1.00	.24	.00	.25	.21	1.00	.00	.35	.17	.17	.22
16	.97	.36	.36	.46	.72	.38	.47	.46	.48	.63	.33	.58	.35	.25	.24	1.00	.20	.58	.33	.24	.11	.71	.47	.47	.63
17	.21	.00	.00	.17	.09	.17	.09	.17	.10	.26	.43	.20	.10	.27	.00	.20	1.00	.35	.22	.00	.00	.16	.09	.09	.08
18	.57	.54	.37	.53	.43	.33	.55	.53	.57	.49	.40	.43	.36	.27	.25	.58	.35	1.00	.40	.25	.00	.45	.55	.55	.36
19	.29	.67	.36	.80	.39	.56	.75	.80	.78	.40	.48	.31	.43	.71	.21	.33	.22	.40	1.00	.21	.00	.38	.75	.75	.50
20	.20	.20	.86	.17	.40	.75	.17	.17	.18	.31	.67	.13	.82	.38	1.00	.24	.00	.25	.21	1.00	.00	.35	.17	.17	.22
21	.11	.00	.00	.00	.10	.00	.00	.00	.00	.12	.00	.00	.00	.00	.00	.11	.00	.00	.00	.00	1.00	.09	.00	.00	.09
22	.68	.41	.44	.52	.86	.52	.49	.52	.46	.74	.48	.65	.46	.28	.35	.71	.16	.45	.38	.35	.09	1.00	.49	.49	.52
23	.44	.88	.38	.97	.52	.41	1.00	.97	.96	.50	.34	.44	.37	.48	.17	.47	.09	.55	.75	.17	.00	.49	1.00	1.00	.50
24	.44	.88	.38	.97	.52	.41	1.00	.97	.96	.50	.34	.44	.37	.48	.17	.47	.09	.55	.75	.17	.00	.49	1.00	1.00	.50
25	.61	.41	.40	.55	.67	.42	.50	.55	.52	.50	.30	.40	.45	.40	.22	.63	.08	.36	.50	.22	.09	.52	.50	.50	1.00
26	.36	.42	.49	.57	.45	.64	.52	.57	.54	.42	.71	.17	.46	.70	.36	.43	.38	.43	.70	.36	.00	.43	.52	.52	.52
27	.67	.53	.23	.53	.68	.21	.54	.53	.50	.53	.16	.53	.28	.13	.13	.64	.06	.42	.30	.13	.07	.58	.54	.54	.68
28	.24	.29	.91	.24	.43	.80	.25	.24	.26	.30	.72	.19	.87	.35	.95	.28	.00	.32	.30	.95	.00	.38	.25	.25	.29
29	.26	.00	.00	.00	.09	.00	.00	.00	.00	.22	.18	.21	.00	.00	.00	.25	.53	.18	.00	.00	.00	.12	.00	.00	.16
30	.97	.36	.31	.46	.72	.33	.47	.46	.48	.63	.29	.58	.30	.25	.19	.97	.20	.58	.33	.19	.16	.68	.47	.47	.67
31	.30	.60	.38	.75	.40	.58	.70	.75	.73	.36	.50	.76	.45	.75	.72	.33	.24	.42	.95	.22	.00	.35	.70	.70	.52
32	.63	.45	.25	.46	.41	.23	.47	.46	.48	.48	.17	.52	.30	.15	.14	.60	.07	.40	.33	.14	.08	.51	.67	.47	.68
33	.11	.00	.00	.11	.10	.11	.11	.11	.12	.12	.11	.73	.00	.18	.00	.11	.33	.00	.14	.00	.00	.13	.11	.11	.00
34	.29	.14	.12	.10	.10	.10	.11	.10	.11	.11	.10	.15	.11	.17	.14	.26	.00	.10	.13	.14	.44	.13	.11	.11	.17
35	.24	.27	.91	.24	.43	.80	.25	.24	.26	.30	.72	.19	.87	.35	.95	.28	.00	.32	.30	.95	.00	.38	.25	.25	.29
36	.55	.58	.40	.57	.41	.36	.59	.57	.62	.37	.29	.40	.38	.30	.27	.57	.19	.86	.43	.27	.12	.36	.59	.59	.39
37	.45	.83	.40	.93	.53	.43	.96	.93	.92	.47	.34	.40	.38	.50	.18	.48	.10	.57	.70	.18	.00	.46	.96	.96	.52
38	.20	.20	.86	.17	.40	.75	.17	.17	.18	.31	.67	.13	.82	.38	1.00	.24	.00	.25	.21	1.00	.00	.35	.17	.17	.22
39	.47	.70	.33	.67	.50	.30	.69	.67	.72	.43	.27	.41	.32	.32	.19	.49	.00	.67	.55	.19	.13	.40	.69	.69	.53
40	.20	.27	.86	.17	.40	.75	.17	.17	.18	.31	.67	.13	.82	.38	1.00	.24	.00	.25	.21	1.00	.00	.35	.17	.17	.22
41	.20	.20	.86	.17	.40	.75	.17	.17	.18	.31	.67	.13	.82	.38	1.00	.24	.00	.25	.21	1.00	.00	.35	.17	.17	.22
42	.60	.20	.19	.29	.51	.24	.30	.29	.31	.37	.18	.44	.19	.15	.07	.58	.07	.24	.28	.07	.26	.55	.30	.30	.49
43	.00	.00	.00	.00	.00	.00	.00	.00	.00	.00	.00	.00	.00	.00	.00	.00	.22	.00	.00	.00	.00	.00	.00	.00	.00
44	.20	.20	.86	.17	.40	.75	.17	.17	.18	.31	.67	.13	.82	.38	1.00	.24	.00	.25	.21	1.00	.00	.35	.17	.17	.22
45	.44	.88	.38	.97	.52	.41	1.00	.97	.96	.50	.34	.44	.37	.48	.17	.47	.09	.55	.75	.17	.00	.49	1.00	1.00	.50
46	.37	.78	.33	.89	.46	.52	.85	.89	.88	.49	.44	.41	.40	.63	.19	.40	.20	.52	.91	.19	.00	.44	.85	.85	.47
47	.44	.88	.38	.97	.52	.41	1.00	.97	.96	.50	.34	.44	.37	.48	.17	.47	.09	.55	.75	.17	.00	.49	1.00	1.00	.50
48	.94	.36	.27	.46	.70	.29	.47	.46	.48	.67	.29	.59	.26	.20	.14	.94	.24	.63	.33	.14	.16	.68	.47	.47	.63
49	.69	.51	.28	.56	.63	.31	.58	.56	.59	.52	.31	.93	.32	.26	.18	.67	.19	.51	.41	.18	.00	.69	.58	.58	.52
50	.97	.35	.31	.46	.72	.33	.47	.46	.48	.63	.29	.58	.30	.25	.19	.97	.20	.58	.33	.19	.16	.68	.47	.47	.67
51	.90	.43	.29	.50	.71	.32	.51	.50	.52	.61	.27	.59	.29	.22	.16	.90	.22	.64	.36	.16	.18	.67	.51	.51	.64
52	.34	.75	.27	.72	.35	.32	.75	.72	.78	.50	.24	.31	.26	.47	.21	.37	.00	.56	.60	.21	.00	.34	.75	.75	.36

TABLE

Rearranged Row–Row Similarity Matrix of

ROW/ROW	21	34	13	44	41	40	38	20	15	35	28	3	6	11	26	14	31	19	46	37	24	23	8	4	7
21	1.00	.44	.00	.00	.00	.00	.00	.00	.00	.00	.00	.00	.00	.00	.00	.00	.00	.00	.00	.00	.00	.00	.00	.00	.00
34	.44	1.00	.11	.14	.14	.14	.14	.14	.14	.13	.13	.12	.10	.10	.11	.17	.14	.13	.12	.11	.11	.11	.10	.10	.11
13	.00	.11	1.00	.82	.82	.82	.82	.82	.82	.87	.87	.88	.79	.71	.46	.40	.45	.43	.40	.38	.37	.37	.43	.43	.37
44	.00	.14	.82	1.00	1.00	1.00	1.00	1.00	1.00	.95	.95	.86	.75	.67	.36	.38	.22	.21	.19	.18	.17	.17	.17	.17	.17
41	.00	.14	.82	1.00	1.00	1.00	1.00	1.00	1.00	.95	.95	.86	.75	.67	.36	.38	.22	.21	.19	.18	.17	.17	.17	.17	.17
40	.00	.14	.82	1.00	1.00	1.00	1.00	1.00	1.00	.95	.95	.86	.75	.67	.36	.38	.22	.21	.19	.18	.17	.17	.17	.17	.17
38	.00	.14	.82	1.00	1.00	1.00	1.00	1.00	1.00	.95	.95	.86	.75	.67	.36	.38	.22	.21	.19	.18	.17	.17	.17	.17	.17
20	.00	.14	.82	1.00	1.00	1.00	1.00	1.00	1.00	.95	.95	.86	.75	.67	.36	.38	.22	.21	.19	.18	.17	.17	.17	.17	.17
15	.00	.14	.82	1.00	1.00	1.00	1.00	1.00	1.00	.95	.95	.86	.75	.67	.36	.38	.22	.21	.19	.18	.17	.17	.17	.17	.17
35	.00	.13	.87	.95	.95	.95	.95	.95	.95	1.00	1.00	.91	.80	.72	.43	.35	.32	.30	.27	.26	.25	.25	.24	.24	.25
28	.00	.13	.87	.95	.95	.95	.95	.95	.95	1.00	1.00	.91	.80	.72	.43	.35	.32	.30	.27	.26	.25	.25	.24	.24	.25
3	.00	.12	.88	.86	.86	.86	.86	.86	.86	.91	.91	1.00	.81	.67	.48	.42	.38	.36	.33	.40	.38	.38	.37	.37	.39
6	.00	.10	.79	.75	.75	.75	.75	.75	.75	.80	.80	.81	1.00	.80	.64	.64	.58	.56	.52	.43	.41	.41	.47	.47	.41
11	.00	.10	.71	.67	.67	.67	.67	.67	.67	.72	.72	.67	.80	1.00	.71	.55	.50	.48	.44	.36	.34	.34	.40	.40	.34
26	.00	.11	.46	.36	.36	.36	.36	.36	.36	.43	.43	.48	.64	.71	1.00	.70	.73	.70	.64	.54	.52	.52	.57	.57	.52
14	.00	.17	.40	.38	.38	.38	.38	.38	.38	.35	.35	.42	.64	.55	.70	1.00	.75	.71	.63	.50	.48	.48	.55	.55	.48
31	.00	.14	.45	.22	.22	.22	.22	.22	.22	.32	.32	.39	.59	.50	.73	.75	1.00	.95	.86	.73	.70	.70	.75	.75	.70
19	.00	.13	.43	.21	.21	.21	.21	.21	.21	.30	.30	.36	.56	.48	.70	.71	.95	1.00	.91	.70	.75	.75	.80	.80	.75
46	.00	.12	.40	.19	.19	.19	.19	.19	.19	.27	.27	.33	.52	.44	.64	.63	.86	.91	1.00	.80	.85	.85	.89	.89	.85
37	.00	.11	.38	.18	.18	.18	.18	.18	.18	.26	.26	.40	.43	.36	.54	.50	.73	.70	.80	1.00	.96	.96	.93	.93	.96
24	.00	.11	.37	.17	.17	.17	.17	.17	.17	.25	.25	.38	.41	.34	.52	.48	.70	.75	.85	.96	1.00	1.00	.97	.97	1.00
23	.00	.11	.37	.17	.17	.17	.17	.17	.17	.25	.25	.38	.41	.34	.52	.48	.70	.75	.85	.96	1.00	1.00	.97	.97	1.00
8	.00	.11	.43	.17	.17	.17	.17	.17	.17	.24	.24	.37	.47	.40	.57	.55	.75	.80	.89	.93	.97	.97	1.00	1.00	.97
4	.00	.11	.43	.17	.17	.17	.17	.17	.17	.24	.24	.37	.47	.40	.57	.55	.75	.80	.89	.93	.97	.97	1.00	1.00	.97
7	.00	.11	.37	.17	.17	.17	.17	.17	.17	.25	.25	.38	.41	.34	.52	.48	.70	.75	.85	.96	1.00	1.00	.97	.97	1.00
9	.00	.11	.39	.18	.18	.18	.18	.18	.18	.26	.26	.40	.43	.36	.54	.50	.73	.78	.88	.92	.96	.96	.93	.93	.96
45	.00	.11	.37	.17	.17	.17	.17	.17	.17	.25	.25	.38	.41	.34	.52	.48	.70	.75	.85	.96	1.00	1.00	.97	.97	1.00
47	.00	.11	.37	.17	.17	.17	.17	.17	.17	.25	.25	.39	.41	.34	.52	.48	.70	.75	.85	.96	1.00	1.00	.97	.97	1.00
2	.00	.11	.33	.20	.20	.20	.20	.20	.20	.29	.29	.26	.31	.31	.42	.33	.60	.67	.78	.83	.88	.88	.85	.85	.88
52	.00	.27	.26	.21	.21	.21	.21	.21	.21	.20	.20	.27	.32	.24	.35	.47	.53	.60	.73	.70	.75	.75	.72	.72	.75
39	.13	.12	.32	.19	.19	.19	.19	.19	.19	.27	.27	.33	.30	.22	.40	.32	.57	.55	.67	.72	.69	.69	.67	.67	.69
36	.12	.22	.38	.27	.27	.27	.27	.27	.27	.35	.35	.40	.36	.29	.38	.30	.45	.43	.56	.62	.59	.59	.57	.57	.59
18	.00	.19	.36	.25	.25	.25	.25	.25	.25	.32	.32	.37	.23	.40	.43	.27	.42	.40	.52	.57	.55	.55	.53	.53	.55
12	.00	.15	.29	.13	.13	.13	.13	.13	.13	.19	.19	.24	.22	.22	.17	.14	.26	.31	.41	.40	.44	.44	.43	.43	.44
49	.00	.14	.32	.18	.18	.18	.18	.18	.18	.24	.24	.28	.31	.31	.38	.26	.42	.41	.50	.59	.58	.58	.56	.56	.58
1	.11	.28	.32	.20	.20	.20	.20	.20	.20	.24	.24	.28	.30	.30	.36	.21	.30	.29	.37	.45	.44	.44	.43	.43	.44
16	.11	.26	.35	.24	.24	.24	.24	.24	.24	.28	.28	.36	.38	.33	.43	.25	.33	.33	.40	.48	.47	.47	.46	.46	.47
30	.16	.25	.30	.19	.19	.19	.19	.19	.19	.23	.23	.31	.33	.29	.39	.25	.33	.33	.40	.48	.47	.47	.46	.46	.47
48	.16	.23	.26	.14	.14	.14	.14	.14	.14	.19	.19	.27	.29	.29	.39	.20	.33	.33	.40	.48	.47	.47	.46	.46	.47
50	.16	.25	.30	.19	.19	.19	.19	.19	.19	.23	.23	.31	.33	.29	.39	.25	.33	.33	.40	.48	.47	.47	.46	.46	.47
51	.18	.24	.29	.16	.16	.16	.16	.16	.16	.21	.21	.29	.32	.27	.39	.22	.37	.36	.44	.52	.51	.51	.50	.50	.51
5	.10	.19	.53	.40	.40	.40	.40	.40	.40	.43	.43	.50	.59	.47	.45	.33	.40	.39	.46	.53	.52	.52	.55	.55	.52
22	.09	.13	.46	.35	.35	.35	.35	.35	.35	.39	.38	.44	.52	.48	.43	.28	.35	.38	.44	.46	.49	.49	.52	.52	.49
10	.12	.11	.42	.31	.31	.31	.31	.31	.31	.30	.30	.38	.49	.53	.42	.32	.36	.40	.48	.47	.50	.50	.53	.53	.50
25	.09	.17	.45	.22	.22	.22	.22	.22	.22	.29	.29	.40	.42	.30	.52	.40	.52	.50	.47	.52	.50	.50	.55	.55	.50
32	.08	.24	.30	.14	.14	.14	.14	.14	.14	.20	.20	.25	.23	.17	.30	.15	.34	.33	.44	.48	.47	.47	.46	.46	.47
27	.07	.21	.28	.13	.13	.13	.13	.13	.13	.15	.18	.23	.21	.16	.28	.13	.31	.30	.40	.56	.54	.54	.53	.53	.34
42	.26	.17	.19	.07	.07	.07	.07	.07	.07	.14	.14	.19	.24	.18	.31	.15	.29	.28	.26	.31	.30	.30	.29	.29	.30
29	.00	.17	.00	.00	.00	.00	.00	.00	.00	.00	.00	.00	.00	.18	.20	.00	.00	.00	.00	.00	.00	.00	.00	.00	.00
17	.00	.00	.10	.00	.00	.00	.00	.00	.00	.00	.00	.00	.17	.43	.38	.27	.24	.22	.20	.10	.09	.09	.17	.17	.09
33	.00	.00	.00	.00	.00	.00	.00	.00	.00	.00	.00	.00	.11	.11	.12	.18	.15	.14	.13	.12	.11	.11	.11	.11	.11
43	.00	.00	.00	.00	.00	.00	.00	.00	.00	.00	.00	.00	.00	.00	.00	.00	.00	.00	.00	.00	.00	.00	.00	.00	.00

3

Based on When Used (Individual Data)

26	27	28	29	30	31	32	33	34	35	36	37	38	39	40	41	42	43	44	45	46	47	48	49	50	51	52
.36	.67	.24	.26	.97	.30	.63	.11	.20	.24	.55	.45	.20	.47	.20	.20	.40	.00	.20	.44	.37	.44	.94	.69	.97	.90	.34
.42	.53	.29	.00	.36	.60	.45	.00	.13	.29	.58	.03	.20	.70	.20	.20	.20	.00	.20	.08	.78	.88	.36	.51	.34	.40	.76
.40	.23	.91	.00	.31	.30	.25	.00	.12	.91	.40	.40	.06	.33	.06	.06	.19	.00	.06	.38	.33	.38	.27	.20	.31	.29	.27
.57	.53	.24	.00	.46	.75	.46	.11	.10	.24	.57	.93	.17	.67	.17	.17	.29	.00	.17	.97	.89	.97	.46	.56	.46	.50	.72
.45	.68	.43	.09	.72	.40	.61	.10	.10	.43	.41	.53	.40	.50	.40	.40	.51	.00	.40	.52	.46	.52	.70	.63	.72	.71	.35
.64	.21	.80	.00	.33	.58	.23	.11	.10	.80	.36	.43	.75	.30	.75	.75	.24	.00	.75	.41	.52	.41	.29	.31	.33	.32	.32
.52	.54	.25	.00	.47	.70	.47	.11	.11	.25	.59	.96	.17	.69	.17	.17	.30	.00	.17	1.00	.85	1.00	.47	.58	.47	.51	.75
.57	.53	.24	.00	.44	.75	.46	.11	.10	.24	.57	.93	.17	.67	.17	.17	.29	.00	.17	.97	.89	.97	.46	.56	.46	.50	.72
.54	.50	.26	.00	.68	.73	.48	.12	.11	.26	.62	.92	.18	.72	.18	.18	.31	.00	.18	.96	.88	.96	.48	.59	.48	.52	.78
.42	.53	.30	.22	.63	.36	.48	.12	.11	.30	.37	.47	.31	.43	.31	.31	.37	.00	.31	.50	.48	.50	.67	.52	.63	.61	.50
.71	.16	.72	.18	.29	.50	.17	.11	.10	.72	.29	.36	.67	.22	.67	.67	.18	.00	.67	.34	.44	.34	.29	.31	.29	.27	.24
.17	.53	.19	.21	.58	.26	.52	.23	.15	.19	.40	.40	.13	.41	.13	.13	.44	.00	.13	.44	.41	.44	.58	.83	.58	.59	.31
.46	.28	.87	.00	.30	.45	.30	.00	.11	.87	.38	.38	.82	.32	.82	.82	.19	.00	.82	.37	.40	.37	.26	.32	.30	.29	.26
.70	.13	.35	.00	.25	.75	.15	.18	.17	.35	.30	.50	.38	.32	.38	.38	.15	.00	.38	.40	.63	.40	.20	.26	.25	.22	.47
.36	.13	.95	.00	.19	.22	.14	.00	.14	.95	.27	.18	1.00	.19	1.00	1.00	.07	.00	1.00	.17	.19	.17	.14	.18	.19	.16	.21
.43	.64	.28	.25	.97	.33	.60	.11	.26	.28	.57	.48	.24	.49	.24	.24	.58	.00	.24	.47	.40	.47	.94	.67	.97	.90	.37
.38	.06	.00	.53	.20	.24	.07	.33	.00	.00	.19	.10	.00	.00	.00	.00	.07	.22	.00	.09	.20	.09	.24	.19	.20	.22	.00
.43	.42	.32	.18	.58	.42	.40	.00	.10	.32	.06	.57	.25	.67	.25	.25	.24	.00	.25	.55	.52	.55	.63	.51	.58	.64	.56
.70	.30	.30	.00	.33	.95	.33	.14	.13	.30	.43	.70	.21	.55	.21	.21	.28	.00	.21	.75	.91	.75	.33	.41	.33	.36	.60
.36	.13	.95	.00	.19	.22	.14	.00	.14	.95	.27	.18	1.00	.19	1.00	1.00	.07	.00	1.00	.17	.19	.17	.14	.18	.19	.16	.21
.00	.07	.00	.00	.16	.00	.08	.00	.44	.00	.12	.00	.00	.13	.00	.00	.26	.00	.00	.00	.00	.00	.16	.00	.14	.18	.00
.43	.58	.38	.12	.68	.35	.51	.13	.13	.38	.36	.46	.35	.40	.35	.35	.55	.00	.35	.49	.44	.49	.68	.69	.69	.67	.34
.52	.54	.25	.00	.47	.70	.47	.11	.11	.25	.59	.96	.17	.69	.17	.17	.30	.00	.17	1.00	.85	1.00	.47	.58	.47	.51	.75
.52	.54	.25	.00	.47	.70	.47	.11	.11	.25	.59	.96	.17	.69	.17	.17	.30	.00	.17	1.00	.85	1.00	.47	.58	.47	.51	.75
.52	.68	.29	.16	.67	.52	.68	.00	.17	.29	.39	.52	.22	.53	.22	.22	.49	.00	.22	.50	.47	.50	.63	.52	.67	.64	.36
1.00	.28	.43	.20	.39	.73	.30	.12	.11	.43	.38	.54	.36	.40	.36	.36	.31	.00	.36	.52	.64	.52	.39	.38	.39	.38	.35
.28	1.00	.18	.20	.68	.31	.93	.07	.21	.18	.44	.56	.13	.63	.13	.13	.48	.08	.13	.54	.40	.54	.68	.60	.63	.69	.42
.43	.18	1.00	.00	.23	.32	.20	.00	.13	1.00	.35	.76	.95	.27	.95	.95	.14	.00	.95	.25	.27	.25	.19	.24	.23	.21	.20
.20	.20	.00	1.00	.25	.00	.22	.18	.17	.00	.10	.00	.00	.00	.00	.00	.15	.25	.00	.00	.60	.00	.25	.26	.25	.17	.12
.39	.68	.23	.25	1.00	.33	.64	.11	.26	.23	.57	.48	.19	.53	.19	.19	.62	.00	.19	.47	.40	.47	.97	.67	1.00	.94	.37
.73	.31	.32	.00	.33	1.00	.34	.15	.14	.32	.45	.73	.22	.57	.22	.22	.29	.00	.22	.70	.86	.70	.33	.42	.33	.37	.53
.30	.93	.20	.22	.64	.34	1.00	.08	.24	.20	.42	.48	.14	.56	.14	.14	.46	.10	.14	.47	.44	.47	.64	.55	.64	.65	.40
.12	.07	.00	.18	.11	.15	.08	1.00	.00	.00	.00	.12	.00	.00	.00	.00	.09	.40	.00	.11	.13	.11	.11	.21	.11	.12	.00
.11	.21	.13	.17	.26	.14	.24	.00	1.00	.13	.22	.11	.14	.12	.14	.14	.17	.00	.14	.11	.12	.11	.26	.14	.26	.24	.27
.43	.18	1.00	.00	.23	.32	.20	.00	.13	1.00	.35	.26	.95	.27	.95	.95	.14	.00	.95	.25	.27	.25	.19	.24	.23	.21	.20
.38	.44	.35	.10	.57	.45	.42	.00	.22	.35	1.00	.62	.27	.72	.27	.27	.25	.00	.27	.59	.56	.59	.57	.49	.57	.62	.61
.54	.56	.26	.00	.48	.73	.48	.12	.11	.26	.62	1.00	.18	.72	.18	.18	.31	.00	.18	.96	.80	.96	.48	.59	.48	.52	.70
.36	.13	.95	.00	.19	.22	.14	.00	.14	.95	.27	.18	1.00	.19	1.00	1.00	.07	.00	1.00	.17	.19	.17	.14	.18	.19	.16	.21
.40	.63	.27	.00	.53	.57	.56	.00	.12	.27	.72	.72	.19	1.00	.19	.19	.39	.00	.19	.69	.67	.69	.53	.56	.53	.59	.64
.36	.13	.95	.00	.19	.22	.14	.00	.14	.95	.27	.18	1.00	.19	1.00	1.00	.07	.00	1.00	.17	.19	.17	.14	.18	.19	.16	.21
.36	.13	.95	.00	.19	.22	.14	.00	.14	.95	.27	.18	1.00	.19	1.00	1.00	.07	.00	1.00	.17	.19	.17	.14	.18	.17	.16	.21
.31	.48	.14	.15	.62	.29	.46	.09	.17	.14	.25	.31	.07	.39	.07	.07	1.00	.00	.07	.30	.26	.30	.62	.56	.62	.63	.07
.00	.08	.00	.25	.00	.00	.10	.40	.00	.00	.00	.00	.00	.00	.00	.00	.00	1.00	.00	.00	.00	.00	.00	.00	.00	.00	.00
.36	.13	.95	.00	.19	.22	.14	.00	.14	.95	.27	.18	1.00	.19	1.00	1.00	.07	.00	1.00	.17	.19	.17	.14	.18	.19	.16	.21
.52	.54	.25	.00	.47	.70	.47	.11	.11	.25	.59	.96	.17	.69	.17	.17	.30	.00	.17	1.00	.85	1.00	.47	.58	.47	.51	.75
.64	.40	.27	.00	.40	.86	.44	.13	.12	.27	.56	.80	.19	.67	.19	.19	.26	.00	.19	.85	1.00	.85	.40	.50	.47	.44	.73
.52	.54	.25	.00	.47	.70	.47	.11	.11	.25	.59	.96	.17	.69	.17	.17	.30	.00	.17	1.00	.85	1.00	.47	.58	.47	.51	.75
.39	.60	.19	.25	.97	.33	.64	.11	.26	.19	.57	.40	.14	.53	.14	.14	.62	.00	.14	.47	.40	.47	1.00	.67	.97	.94	.37
.38	.60	.24	.26	.67	.42	.55	.21	.14	.24	.49	.59	.18	.56	.18	.18	.56	.00	.18	.58	.50	.58	.67	1.00	.67	.68	.41
.39	.68	.23	.25	1.00	.33	.64	.11	.26	.23	.57	.48	.19	.53	.19	.19	.62	.00	.19	.47	.40	.47	.97	.67	1.00	.94	.37
.38	.69	.21	.17	.94	.37	.65	.12	.24	.21	.62	.52	.16	.59	.16	.16	.63	.00	.16	.51	.44	.51	.94	.68	.94	1.00	.36
.35	.42	.20	.12	.37	.53	.40	.00	.27	.20	.61	.70	.21	.64	.21	.21	.07	.00	.21	.75	.73	.75	.37	.41	.37	.34	1.00

4

Medicines Based on When Used (Individual Data)

9	45	47	2	52	39	36	18	12	4[illegible]	1	16	30	48	50	51	5	22	10	25	32	27	42	29	17	31	43
.00	.00	.00	.00	.00	.13	.12	.00	.00	[illegible]	.11	.11	.16	.16	.16	.18	.10	.09	.12	.09	.08	.07	.26	.00	.00	.00	.00
.11	.11	.11	.13	.27	.12	.22	.10	.15	.14	.28	.26	.26	.26	.26	.24	.10	.13	.11	.17	.24	.21	.17	.17	.00	.00	.00
.38	.37	.37	.33	.26	.32	.38	.36	.29	.32	.32	.35	.30	.26	.30	.29	.53	.46	.42	.45	.30	.28	.19	.00	.10	.00	.00
.19	.17	.17	.20	.21	.19	.27	.25	.13	[illegible]	.20	.24	.19	.14	.19	.16	.40	.35	.31	.22	.14	.13	.07	.00	.00	.00	.00
.19	.17	.17	.20	.21	.19	.27	.25	.13	[illegible]	.20	.24	.19	.14	.19	.16	.40	.35	.31	.22	.14	.13	.07	.00	.00	.00	.00
.19	.17	.17	.20	.21	.19	.27	.25	.13	[illegible]	.20	.24	.19	.14	.19	.16	.40	.35	.31	.22	.14	.13	.07	.00	.00	.00	.00
.19	.17	.17	.20	.21	.19	.27	.25	.13	[illegible]	.20	.24	.19	.14	.19	.16	.40	.35	.31	.22	.14	.13	.07	.00	.00	.00	.00
.19	.17	.17	.20	.21	.19	.27	.25	.13	[illegible]	.20	.24	.19	.14	.19	.16	.40	.35	.31	.22	.14	.13	.07	.00	.00	.00	.00
.18	.17	.17	.20	.21	.19	.27	.25	.13	[illegible]	.20	.24	.19	.14	.19	.16	.40	.35	.31	.22	.14	.13	.07	.00	.00	.00	.00
.24	.25	.25	.29	.29	.27	.35	.32	.19	[illegible]	.24	.28	.23	.19	.23	.21	.43	.38	.30	.29	.20	.18	.14	.00	.00	.00	.00
.24	.25	.25	.29	.20	.27	.35	.32	.19	[illegible]	.24	.28	.23	.19	.23	.21	.43	.38	.30	.29	.20	.18	.14	.00	.00	.00	.00
.40	.38	.38	.26	.27	.33	.40	.37	.24	[illegible]	.28	.36	.31	.27	.31	.29	.50	.44	.38	.40	.25	.23	.19	.00	.00	.00	.00
.43	.41	.41	.31	.32	.30	.36	.33	.22	[illegible]	.10	.30	.33	.29	.33	.32	.59	.52	.49	.42	.23	.21	.24	.00	.17	.11	.00
.36	.34	.34	.31	.24	.22	.29	.40	.22	[illegible]	.10	.33	.29	.29	.29	.27	.47	.48	.53	.30	.17	.16	.18	.18	.43	.11	.00
.54	.52	.52	.42	.39	.40	.38	.43	.17	[illegible]	.14	.43	.39	.39	.39	.30	.45	.43	.42	.52	.30	.28	.31	.20	.39	.12	.00
.50	.49	.48	.33	.47	.32	.30	.27	.14	[illegible]	.21	.25	.25	.20	.25	.22	.33	.28	.32	.40	.15	.13	.15	.00	.27	.18	.00
.73	.70	.70	.60	.53	.57	.45	.42	.26	.42	.30	.33	.33	.33	.33	.37	.40	.35	.36	.52	.34	.31	.29	.00	.24	.15	.00
.79	.75	.75	.67	.60	.55	.43	.40	.31	.41	.29	.33	.33	.33	.33	.36	.39	.38	.40	.50	.33	.30	.28	.00	.22	.14	.00
.88	.85	.85	.78	.73	.67	.56	.52	.41	[illegible]	.37	.40	.40	.40	.40	.44	.46	.44	.48	.47	.44	.40	.26	.00	.20	.13	.00
.92	.96	.96	.83	.70	.72	.62	.57	.40	[illegible]	.45	.48	.48	.48	.48	.52	.53	.46	.47	.52	.48	.56	.31	.00	.10	.12	.00
.96	1.00	1.00	.88	.75	.69	.59	.55	.44	[illegible]	.44	.47	.47	.47	.47	.51	.52	.49	.50	.50	.47	.54	.30	.00	.09	.11	.00
.94	1.00	1.00	.88	.75	.69	.59	.55	.44	[illegible]	.44	.47	.47	.47	.47	.51	.52	.49	.50	.50	.47	.54	.30	.00	.09	.11	.00
.93	.97	.97	.85	.72	.67	.57	.53	.43	[illegible]	.43	.46	.46	.46	.46	.50	.55	.52	.53	.55	.46	.53	.29	.00	.17	.11	.00
.93	.97	.97	.85	.72	.67	.57	.53	.43	[illegible]	.43	.46	.46	.46	.46	.50	.55	.52	.53	.55	.46	.53	.29	.00	.17	.11	.00
.96	1.00	1.00	.88	.75	.69	.59	.55	.44	[illegible]	.44	.47	.47	.47	.47	.51	.52	.49	.50	.50	.47	.54	.30	.00	.09	.11	.00
1.00	.96	.96	.83	.78	.72	.62	.57	.46	[illegible]	.45	.48	.48	.48	.49	.52	.49	.46	.51	.52	.48	.50	.31	.00	.10	.12	.00
.96	1.00	1.00	.88	.75	.69	.59	.55	.44	[illegible]	.44	.47	.47	.47	.47	.51	.52	.49	.50	.50	.47	.54	.30	.00	.09	.11	.00
.96	1.00	1.00	.88	.75	.69	.59	.55	.44	[illegible]	.44	.47	.47	.47	.47	.51	.52	.49	.50	.50	.47	.54	.30	.00	.09	.11	.00
.83	.88	.88	1.00	.76	.70	.58	.54	.36	[illegible]	.30	.36	.36	.36	.36	.40	.43	.41	.39	.41	.45	.53	.20	.00	.00	.09	.00
.78	.75	.75	.76	1.00	.64	.61	.56	.31	.41	.34	.37	.37	.37	.37	.36	.35	.34	.50	.36	.40	.42	.07	.12	.00	.00	.00
.72	.69	.69	.70	.64	1.00	.72	.67	.41	[illegible]	.47	.49	.53	.53	.53	.59	.50	.40	.43	.53	.58	.63	.39	.00	.00	.00	.00
.62	.59	.59	.58	.61	.72	1.00	.86	.40	.49	.55	.57	.57	.57	.57	.62	.41	.36	.37	.39	.42	.44	.25	.10	.19	.00	.00
.57	.55	.55	.54	.56	.67	.86	1.00	.43	.51	.57	.50	.58	.63	.58	.64	.43	.45	.49	.36	.40	.42	.24	.18	.35	.00	.00
.46	.44	.44	.36	.31	.41	.40	.43	1.00	[illegible]	.60	.58	.58	.58	.58	.59	.52	.65	.50	.40	.32	.53	.44	.21	.20	.23	.00
.59	.58	.58	.51	.41	.56	.49	.51	.83	1.00	.69	.67	.67	.67	.67	.68	.63	.69	.52	.52	.55	.60	.56	.26	.19	.21	.00
.45	.44	.44	.38	.34	.47	.55	.57	.60	.69	1.00	.97	.97	.94	.97	.90	.69	.68	.59	.61	.63	.67	.60	.24	.21	.11	.00
.48	.47	.47	.36	.37	.49	.57	.58	.58	.67	.97	1.00	.97	.94	.97	.90	.72	.71	.63	.63	.60	.64	.58	.25	.20	.11	.00
.48	.47	.47	.36	.37	.53	.57	.58	.58	.67	.97	.97	1.00	.97	1.00	.94	.72	.68	.63	.67	.64	.68	.62	.25	.20	.11	.00
.48	.47	.47	.36	.37	.53	.57	.63	.58	.47	.94	.94	.97	1.00	.97	.94	.70	.68	.67	.63	.64	.68	.62	.25	.24	.11	.00
.48	.47	.47	.36	.37	.53	.57	.58	.58	.67	.97	.97	1.00	.97	1.00	.94	.72	.68	.63	.67	.64	.68	.62	.25	.20	.11	.00
.52	.51	.51	.40	.36	.59	.62	.64	.59	.40	.90	.90	.94	.94	.94	1.00	.71	.67	.61	.64	.65	.69	.63	.17	.22	.12	.00
.49	.52	.52	.43	.35	.50	.41	.43	.52	.43	.69	.72	.72	.70	.72	.71	1.00	.86	.73	.67	.61	.68	.51	.09	.09	.10	.00
.46	.49	.49	.41	.34	.40	.36	.45	.65	.49	.60	.71	.68	.68	.68	.67	.86	1.00	.74	.52	.51	.58	.55	.12	.16	.13	.00
.51	.50	.50	.39	.50	.43	.37	.49	.50	[illegible]	.59	.63	.63	.67	.63	.61	.73	.74	1.00	.50	.48	.53	.37	.22	.26	.12	.00
.52	.50	.50	.41	.38	.53	.39	.38	.40	[illegible]	.61	.63	.67	.63	.67	.64	.67	.52	.50	1.00	.68	.68	.49	.16	.09	.00	.00
.48	.47	.47	.45	.40	.56	.42	.40	.52	[illegible]	.63	.60	.64	.64	.64	.65	.61	.51	.48	.68	1.00	.93	.46	.22	.07	.08	.10
.50	.54	.54	.53	.42	.63	.44	.42	.53	.60	.67	.64	.60	.60	.68	.69	.60	.58	.53	.60	.93	1.00	.48	.20	.06	.07	.09
.31	.30	.30	.20	.07	.39	.25	.24	.44	[illegible]	.60	.58	.62	.62	.62	.63	.51	.55	.37	.49	.46	.48	1.00	.15	.07	.09	.00
.00	.00	.00	.00	.12	.00	.10	.18	.21	.76	.26	.25	.25	.25	.25	.17	.09	.12	.22	.16	.22	.20	.15	1.00	.53	.18	.25
.10	.09	.09	.00	.00	.00	.19	.35	.20	.19	.21	.20	.20	.24	.20	.22	.09	.16	.26	.00	.07	.06	.07	.53	1.00	.33	.22
.12	.11	.11	.00	.00	.00	.00	.00	.23	[illegible]	.11	.11	.11	.11	.11	.12	.10	.13	.12	.00	.00	.07	.09	.18	.33	1.00	.40
.00	.00	.00	.00	.00	.00	.00	.00	.00	[illegible]	.00	.00	.00	.00	.00	.00	.00	.00	.00	.00	.10	.00	.00	.25	.22	.40	1.00

TABLE

COLUMN–COLUMN SIMILARITY MATRIX

COL/COL	1	2	3	4	5	6	7	8	9	10	11	12	13	14	15	16	17	18	19	20	21	22	23	24	25
1	1.00	.13	.00	.11	.30	.22	.14	.42	.63	.09	.49	.65	.09	.25	.24	.58	.00	.21	.00	.12	.08	.11	.13	.60	.25
2	.15	1.00	.00	.27	.40	.13	.94	.50	.15	.08	.73	.27	.08	.11	.21	.24	.00	.13	.00	.78	.21	.00	.11	.14	.32
3	.00	.09	1.00	.17	.00	.50	.09	.20	.32	.63	.74	.00	.67	.00	.56	.32	.00	.48	.71	.31	.53	.00	.00	.30	.00
4	.11	.27	.17	1.00	.45	.27	.33	.23	.24	.22	.78	.28	.24	.18	.30	.18	.18	.26	.38	.21	.57	.15	.19	.23	.36
5	.30	.40	.00	.45	1.00	.27	.44	.47	.29	.08	.55	.65	.08	.11	.29	.34	.11	.13	.08	.44	.28	.10	.11	.28	.32
6	.22	.13	.50	.27	.27	1.00	.25	.47	.54	.62	.41	.22	.64	.32	.79	.63	.21	.77	.50	.44	.62	.29	.32	.51	.21
7	.14	.94	.09	.33	.44	.25	1.00	.55	.19	.14	.30	.31	.15	.10	.27	.28	.00	.18	.08	.84	.26	.00	.10	.18	.29
8	.42	.50	.20	.23	.47	.47	.55	1.00	.73	.32	.78	.66	.29	.12	.41	.70	.04	.49	.30	.64	.37	.08	.12	.74	.12
9	.63	.15	.32	.24	.29	.54	.19	.73	1.00	.43	.80	.63	.39	.13	.56	.81	.07	.62	.46	.30	.50	.06	.13	.93	.20
10	.09	.03	.63	.22	.08	.62	.14	.32	.43	1.00	.30	.12	.57	.27	.67	.43	.13	.52	.50	.25	.56	.35	.00	.46	.13
11	.49	.23	.24	.28	.55	.41	.30	.78	.80	.30	1.00	.75	.31	.06	.43	.69	.00	.44	.37	.40	.37	.00	.06	.77	.18
12	.65	.27	.00	.28	.65	.22	.31	.66	.63	.12	.75	1.00	.06	.08	.17	.54	.08	.16	.00	.28	.22	.00	.15	.64	.23
13	.09	.09	.67	.24	.08	.64	.15	.29	.39	.57	.31	.06	1.00	.14	.61	.44	.00	.62	.63	.32	.58	.00	.29	.37	.29
14	.25	.11	.00	.18	.11	.32	.10	.12	.13	.27	.06	.08	.14	1.00	.47	.27	.25	.40	.00	.08	.22	.40	.50	.25	.25
15	.24	.21	.56	.30	.29	.79	.27	.41	.56	.67	.43	.17	.61	.47	1.00	.67	.12	.76	.55	.41	.67	.21	.24	.59	.35
16	.58	.24	.32	.18	.34	.63	.28	.70	.81	.43	.69	.54	.44	.27	.67	1.00	.13	.62	.34	.38	.50	.13	.27	.81	.20
17	.00	.00	.00	.18	.11	.21	.00	.04	.07	.13	.00	.08	.00	.25	.12	.13	1.00	.20	.15	.00	.44	.40	.50	.13	.00
18	.21	.13	.48	.26	.13	.77	.18	.49	.62	.52	.44	.16	.62	.40	.76	.62	.20	1.00	.64	.32	.67	.18	.40	.68	.70
19	.00	.00	.71	.38	.08	.50	.08	.30	.46	.50	.37	.00	.63	.00	.55	.34	.15	.64	1.00	.27	.70	.13	.00	.43	.00
20	.12	.78	.31	.21	.44	.44	.84	.64	.30	.25	.40	.28	.32	.08	.41	.38	.00	.32	.27	1.00	.34	.00	.08	.24	.16
21	.08	.21	.53	.57	.28	.62	.26	.37	.50	.56	.37	.22	.58	.22	.67	.50	.44	.67	.70	.34	1.00	.20	.33	.52	.22
22	.11	.00	.00	.15	.10	.29	.00	.08	.06	.35	.00	.00	.00	.40	.21	.13	.40	.18	.13	.00	.20	1.00	.00	.12	.00
23	.13	.11	.00	.19	.11	.32	.10	.12	.13	.00	.06	.15	.29	.50	.24	.27	.50	.40	.00	.08	.33	.00	1.00	.19	.25
24	.60	.14	.30	.23	.28	.51	.19	.74	.93	.46	.77	.64	.37	.25	.59	.81	.13	.68	.43	.24	.52	.12	.19	1.00	.19
25	.25	.32	.00	.36	.32	.21	.29	.12	.20	.13	.18	.23	.29	.25	.35	.20	.00	.20	.00	.16	.22	.00	.25	.19	1.00
26	.15	.97	.09	.19	.34	.14	.90	.47	.10	.00	.19	.22	.08	.11	.15	.20	.00	.13	.00	.80	.14	.00	.11	.10	.22
27	.09	.15	.63	.33	.15	.62	.21	.32	.49	.55	.55	.18	.67	.27	.75	.54	.27	.67	.60	.31	.80	.12	.40	.51	.27
28	.49	.31	.24	.23	.46	.54	.37	.88	.76	.29	.79	.54	.34	.20	.48	.79	.10	.60	.35	.48	.43	.09	.20	.80	.10
29	.16	.71	.56	.30	.29	.79	.27	.38	.51	.58	.78	.23	.61	.24	.77	.62	.35	.69	.45	.41	.74	.11	.47	.49	.35
30	.22	.20	.50	.27	.27	.87	.25	.47	.59	.62	.41	.22	.64	.42	.93	.73	.21	.84	.50	.39	.69	.19	.42	.60	.32
31	.60	.14	.30	.23	.28	.51	.18	.74	.93	.46	.77	.64	.37	.25	.59	.81	.13	.68	.43	.24	.52	.12	.19	1.00	.19
32	.41	.49	.20	.23	.46	.43	.54	.97	.72	.35	.77	.65	.29	.16	.44	.69	.08	.48	.29	.63	.40	.08	.12	.76	.12
33	.13	.11	.00	.18	.11	.32	.10	.12	.13	.00	.06	.15	.29	.50	.24	.27	.50	.40	.00	.08	.33	.00	1.00	.19	.25
34	.15	1.00	.00	.27	.40	.13	.94	.50	.15	.08	.73	.27	.08	.11	.21	.24	.00	.13	.00	.78	.21	.00	.11	.14	.32
35	.15	1.00	.00	.27	.40	.13	.94	.50	.15	.08	.73	.27	.08	.11	.21	.24	.00	.13	.00	.78	.21	.00	.11	.14	.32
36	.00	.14	.56	.60	.29	.57	.27	.39	.46	.58	.43	.17	.52	.00	.54	.36	.24	.55	.82	.35	.81	.21	.00	.44	.12
37	.17	.23	.63	.44	.23	.69	.29	.39	.54	.55	.45	.18	.76	.13	.75	.54	.00	.74	.70	.38	.72	.00	.27	.51	.40
38	.11	.68	.36	.20	.21	.47	.70	.65	.45	.29	.42	.18	.42	.15	.50	.49	.15	.62	.50	.77	.54	.00	.22	.47	.15
39	.14	.12	.00	.22	.12	.24	.11	.09	.07	.00	.06	.08	.33	.33	.13	.14	.00	.22	.00	.09	.13	.00	.67	.07	.33
40	.23	.21	.53	.29	.21	.76	.26	.44	.60	.56	.42	.22	.67	.33	.81	.65	.22	.87	.52	.34	.71	.10	.44	.62	.33
41	.19	.17	.71	.25	.17	.75	.23	.33	.46	.50	.77	.13	.84	.15	.73	.51	.00	.72	.67	.40	.61	.00	.31	.43	.31
42	.17	.15	.35	.21	.22	.67	.14	.39	.47	.52	.79	.12	.55	.25	.72	.53	.00	.64	.38	.24	.38	.22	.13	.45	.39
43	.23	.14	.53	.19	.21	.83	.19	.41	.55	.64	.77	.17	.67	.44	.89	.65	.22	.80	.52	.40	.64	.20	.33	.57	.22
44	.23	.28	.53	.29	.34	.83	.32	.47	.55	.64	.47	.22	.67	.33	.89	.65	.00	.73	.52	.46	.57	.20	.22	.52	.33
45	.18	.08	.67	.12	.16	.80	.15	.36	.50	.67	.76	.06	.60	.29	.87	.56	.00	.69	.63	.39	.50	.25	.00	.47	.14
46	.48	.22	.29	.32	.58	.49	.30	.72	.68	.29	.78	.77	.40	.12	.47	.75	.18	.48	.36	.39	.55	.11	.24	.72	.18
47	.55	.17	.27	.21	.43	.51	.20	.81	.90	.42	.82	.67	.33	.22	.58	.83	.11	.63	.39	.30	.48	.11	.17	.93	.17
48	.35	.30	.00	.33	.30	.40	.27	.20	.26	.38	.18	.22	.13	.67	.56	.32	.00	.38	.00	.15	.21	.36	.22	.30	.67
49	.67	.13	.00	.18	.40	.07	.13	.47	.59	.15	.79	.76	.08	.21	.21	.54	.11	.13	.00	.06	.21	.00	.21	.65	.21
50	.60	.09	.30	.17	.42	.65	.18	.77	.81	.36	.77	.68	.42	.19	.54	.81	.06	.59	.32	.33	.38	.12	.19	.82	.13
51	.00	.00	.67	.12	.00	.56	.07	.29	.39	.57	.31	.00	.90	.00	.52	.39	.00	.62	.74	.26	.50	.00	.14	.37	.14
52	.24	.28	.00	.17	.28	.38	.18	.12	.19	.00	.12	.22	.13	.44	.33	.26	.44	.38	.00	.15	.32	.18	.67	.24	.44

TABLE

REARRANGED COLUMN–COLUMN SIMILARITY

COL/COL	22	17	14	48	25	52	23	33	39	4	10	27	29	18	40	44	6	30	15	43	45	3	19	36	21
22	1.00	.40	.40	.36	.00	.18	.00	.00	.00	.15	.35	.12	.11	.18	.10	.20	.29	.19	.21	.20	.25	.00	.13	.21	.20
17	.40	1.00	.25	.00	.00	.44	.50	.50	.00	.18	.13	.27	.35	.20	.22	.00	.21	.21	.12	.22	.00	.00	.15	.24	.44
14	.40	.25	1.00	.67	.25	.44	.50	.50	.33	.18	.27	.27	.24	.40	.33	.33	.32	.42	.47	.44	.29	.00	.00	.00	.22
48	.36	.00	.67	1.00	.67	.40	.22	.22	.29	.33	.38	.25	.33	.38	.42	.53	.40	.50	.56	.42	.40	.00	.00	.11	.21
25	.00	.00	.25	.67	1.00	.44	.25	.25	.33	.36	.13	.27	.35	.20	.33	.33	.21	.32	.35	.22	.14	.00	.00	.12	.22
52	.15	.44	.44	.40	.44	1.00	.67	.67	.29	.17	.00	.50	.44	.38	.42	.21	.30	.40	.33	.42	.13	.00	.00	.00	.32
23	.00	.50	.50	.22	.25	.67	1.00	1.00	.67	.18	.00	.40	.47	.40	.44	.22	.32	.42	.24	.33	.00	.00	.00	.00	.33
33	.00	.50	.50	.22	.25	.67	1.00	1.00	.67	.18	.00	.40	.47	.40	.44	.22	.32	.42	.24	.33	.00	.00	.00	.00	.33
39	.00	.00	.33	.29	.33	.29	.67	.67	1.00	.22	.00	.15	.27	.22	.25	.25	.24	.24	.13	.13	.00	.00	.00	.00	.13
4	.15	.18	.19	.33	.36	.17	.18	.18	.72	1.00	.22	.33	.30	.26	.29	.29	.27	.27	.30	.19	.12	.17	.38	.60	.57
10	.35	.13	.27	.38	.13	.00	.00	.00	.00	.22	1.00	.55	.58	.52	.56	.64	.62	.62	.67	.64	.67	.63	.50	.58	.56
27	.12	.27	.27	.25	.27	.50	.40	.40	.15	.33	.55	1.00	.75	.67	.80	.64	.62	.77	.75	.72	.57	.63	.60	.58	.80
29	.11	.35	.24	.33	.35	.44	.47	.47	.27	.30	.58	.75	1.00	.69	.81	.74	.79	.86	.77	.74	.61	.56	.45	.54	.74
18	.18	.20	.40	.38	.20	.39	.40	.40	.22	.26	.52	.67	.69	1.00	.87	.73	.77	.84	.76	.80	.69	.48	.64	.55	.67
40	.10	.22	.33	.42	.33	.42	.44	.44	.25	.29	.56	.80	.81	.87	1.00	.79	.76	.90	.81	.79	.67	.53	.52	.52	.71
44	.20	.00	.33	.53	.33	.21	.22	.22	.75	.29	.64	.64	.74	.73	.79	1.00	.83	.90	.89	.79	.83	.53	.52	.52	.57
6	.29	.21	.32	.40	.21	.30	.32	.32	.24	.27	.62	.62	.79	.77	.76	.83	1.00	.87	.79	.83	.80	.50	.50	.57	.62
30	.19	.21	.42	.50	.32	.40	.42	.42	.24	.27	.62	.77	.86	.84	.90	.90	.87	1.00	.93	.90	.80	.50	.50	.50	.69
15	.21	.12	.47	.56	.35	.33	.24	.24	.13	.30	.67	.75	.77	.76	.81	.89	.79	.93	1.00	.89	.87	.56	.55	.54	.67
43	.20	.22	.44	.42	.22	.42	.33	.33	.13	.19	.64	.72	.74	.80	.79	.79	.83	.90	.89	1.00	.83	.53	.52	.44	.64
45	.25	.00	.29	.40	.14	.13	.00	.00	.00	.12	.67	.57	.61	.69	.67	.83	.80	.80	.87	.83	1.00	.67	.63	.52	.50
3	.00	.00	.00	.00	.00	.00	.00	.00	.00	.17	.63	.63	.56	.48	.53	.53	.50	.50	.56	.53	.67	1.00	.71	.56	.53
19	.13	.15	.00	.00	.00	.00	.00	.00	.00	.38	.50	.60	.45	.64	.52	.52	.50	.50	.55	.52	.63	.71	1.00	.82	.70
36	.21	.24	.00	.11	.12	.00	.00	.00	.00	.60	.58	.58	.54	.55	.52	.52	.57	.50	.54	.44	.52	.56	.82	1.00	.81
21	.20	.44	.22	.21	.22	.32	.33	.33	.13	.57	.56	.80	.74	.67	.71	.57	.62	.69	.67	.64	.50	.53	.70	.81	1.00
37	.00	.00	.13	.38	.40	.25	.27	.27	.31	.44	.55	.73	.75	.74	.80	.80	.69	.77	.75	.64	.67	.63	.70	.67	.72
41	.00	.00	.15	.29	.31	.29	.31	.31	.36	.25	.50	.70	.73	.72	.78	.78	.75	.75	.73	.70	.74	.71	.67	.55	.61
13	.00	.00	.14	.13	.29	.13	.29	.29	.33	.24	.57	.67	.61	.62	.67	.67	.64	.64	.61	.67	.60	.67	.63	.52	.58
51	.00	.00	.00	.00	.14	.00	.14	.14	.17	.12	.57	.57	.52	.62	.58	.58	.56	.56	.52	.58	.60	.67	.74	.61	.50
42	.22	.00	.25	.47	.38	.12	.13	.13	.14	.21	.52	.43	.56	.64	.69	.77	.67	.74	.72	.62	.73	.35	.38	.40	.39
11	.00	.00	.06	.18	.18	.12	.06	.06	.06	.28	.30	.35	.38	.44	.42	.47	.41	.41	.43	.37	.36	.24	.37	.43	.37
32	.08	.04	.16	.20	.12	.16	.12	.12	.04	.23	.35	.35	.37	.48	.43	.43	.43	.46	.44	.47	.36	.20	.29	.37	.40
8	.08	.04	.12	.20	.12	.12	.12	.12	.09	.23	.32	.32	.38	.49	.44	.47	.47	.47	.41	.41	.36	.20	.30	.38	.37
28	.09	.10	.20	.19	.10	.19	.20	.20	.10	.23	.29	.38	.44	.60	.51	.51	.54	.54	.48	.51	.43	.24	.35	.40	.43
47	.11	.11	.22	.27	.17	.22	.17	.17	.06	.21	.42	.47	.49	.63	.57	.52	.51	.60	.58	.57	.48	.27	.39	.40	.48
31	.12	.13	.25	.30	.19	.24	.19	.19	.07	.23	.46	.51	.49	.68	.62	.52	.51	.60	.59	.57	.47	.30	.43	.44	.52
24	.12	.13	.25	.30	.19	.24	.19	.19	.07	.23	.46	.51	.49	.68	.62	.52	.51	.60	.59	.57	.47	.30	.43	.44	.52
9	.06	.07	.13	.26	.20	.19	.13	.13	.07	.24	.43	.49	.51	.62	.60	.55	.54	.59	.56	.55	.50	.32	.46	.46	.50
16	.13	.13	.27	.32	.20	.26	.27	.27	.14	.18	.43	.54	.62	.62	.65	.65	.63	.73	.67	.65	.56	.32	.34	.36	.50
50	.12	.06	.19	.24	.13	.18	.19	.19	.13	.17	.36	.41	.49	.59	.57	.57	.65	.60	.54	.57	.53	.30	.32	.34	.38
46	.11	.18	.12	.17	.18	.29	.24	.24	.13	.32	.29	.54	.51	.48	.55	.50	.49	.53	.47	.45	.35	.29	.36	.47	.55
12	.00	.08	.09	.22	.23	.22	.15	.15	.08	.28	.12	.18	.23	.16	.22	.22	.22	.22	.17	.17	.06	.00	.00	.17	.22
49	.00	.11	.21	.20	.21	.20	.21	.21	.12	.18	.15	.23	.21	.13	.21	.14	.07	.20	.21	.14	.00	.00	.00	.07	.21
1	.11	.00	.25	.35	.25	.24	.13	.13	.14	.11	.09	.09	.16	.21	.23	.23	.22	.22	.24	.23	.10	.00	.00	.00	.08
5	.10	.11	.11	.30	.32	.20	.11	.11	.12	.45	.08	.19	.29	.13	.21	.34	.27	.27	.29	.21	.16	.00	.08	.29	.28
35	.00	.00	.11	.30	.32	.20	.11	.11	.12	.27	.08	.15	.21	.13	.21	.28	.13	.20	.21	.14	.08	.00	.00	.14	.21
34	.00	.00	.11	.30	.32	.20	.11	.11	.12	.27	.08	.15	.21	.13	.21	.28	.13	.20	.21	.14	.08	.00	.00	.14	.21
26	.00	.00	.11	.21	.22	.21	.11	.11	.13	.19	.00	.08	.15	.13	.14	.21	.14	.14	.15	.14	.08	.00	.00	.07	.14
2	.00	.00	.11	.30	.32	.20	.11	.11	.12	.27	.08	.15	.21	.13	.21	.28	.13	.20	.21	.14	.08	.00	.00	.14	.21
7	.00	.00	.10	.27	.29	.18	.10	.10	.11	.33	.14	.21	.27	.18	.26	.32	.25	.25	.27	.19	.15	.09	.08	.27	.26
20	.00	.00	.08	.15	.16	.15	.08	.08	.09	.21	.25	.31	.41	.32	.34	.46	.44	.39	.41	.40	.39	.31	.27	.35	.34
38	.00	.15	.15	.14	.15	.29	.22	.22	.08	.20	.29	.53	.50	.62	.54	.49	.47	.53	.50	.54	.42	.36	.50	.44	.54

5

of Medicine Uses (Individual Data)

26	27	28	29	30	31	32	33	34	35	36	37	38	39	40	41	42	43	44	45	46	47	48	49	50	51	52
.15	.09	.49	.16	.22	.60	.41	.13	.15	.15	.00	.17	.11	.14	.23	.19	.17	.23	.23	.18	.48	.55	.35	.67	.60	.00	.24
.97	.15	.31	.21	.20	.14	.49	.11	1.00	1.00	.14	.23	.68	.12	.21	.17	.15	.14	.28	.08	.22	.17	.30	.13	.09	.00	.20
.00	.63	.24	.56	.50	.30	.20	.00	.00	.00	.56	.63	.36	.00	.53	.71	.35	.53	.53	.67	.29	.27	.00	.00	.11	.67	.00
.19	.33	.23	.30	.27	.23	.23	.18	.27	.27	.60	.44	.20	.22	.29	.25	.21	.19	.29	.12	.32	.21	.33	.19	.17	.12	.17
.34	.15	.46	.29	.27	.29	.46	.11	.40	.40	.29	.23	.21	.12	.21	.17	.22	.21	.34	.16	.58	.43	.30	.40	.42	.00	.20
.14	.62	.54	.77	.87	.51	.43	.32	.13	.13	.57	.69	.47	.24	.76	.75	.67	.83	.83	.80	.49	.51	.40	.07	.63	.56	.39
.90	.21	.37	.27	.25	.18	.54	.10	.94	.94	.27	.29	.70	.11	.26	.23	.14	.19	.32	.15	.30	.20	.27	.13	.13	.07	.14
.47	.32	.88	.39	.47	.74	.97	.12	.50	.50	.38	.39	.65	.09	.44	.33	.39	.41	.47	.36	.72	.81	.20	.47	.77	.29	.12
.10	.49	.76	.51	.59	.93	.72	.13	.15	.15	.46	.54	.45	.07	.60	.46	.47	.55	.55	.50	.68	.90	.26	.59	.91	.33	.19
.00	.55	.29	.58	.62	.46	.35	.00	.08	.08	.58	.55	.29	.00	.56	.50	.52	.64	.64	.67	.29	.42	.38	.15	.35	.57	.00
.19	.35	.79	.38	.41	.77	.77	.06	.23	.23	.43	.45	.42	.06	.42	.37	.39	.37	.47	.36	.78	.82	.18	.55	.77	.31	.12
.22	.18	.64	.23	.22	.64	.65	.15	.27	.27	.17	.18	.18	.08	.22	.13	.12	.17	.22	.06	.77	.67	.22	.76	.63	.00	.22
.08	.67	.34	.61	.64	.37	.29	.29	.08	.08	.52	.76	.42	.33	.67	.84	.55	.67	.67	.60	.40	.33	.13	.09	.62	.90	.13
.11	.27	.20	.24	.42	.25	.16	.50	.11	.11	.00	.13	.15	.33	.33	.15	.25	.44	.33	.29	.12	.22	.67	.21	.13	.00	.44
.15	.75	.48	.77	.93	.59	.44	.24	.21	.21	.54	.75	.50	.13	.81	.73	.72	.89	.89	.87	.47	.58	.56	.21	.54	.52	.33
.29	.54	.79	.62	.73	.81	.59	.27	.24	.24	.36	.54	.49	.14	.65	.51	.53	.65	.65	.56	.75	.83	.32	.54	.91	.19	.24
.00	.27	.10	.35	.21	.13	.05	.50	.00	.00	.24	.00	.15	.00	.22	.00	.00	.22	.00	.00	.18	.11	.00	.11	.05	.00	.44
.13	.67	.60	.69	.84	.68	.48	.40	.13	.13	.55	.74	.62	.22	.87	.72	.64	.80	.73	.69	.48	.63	.38	.13	.57	.52	.19
.00	.60	.35	.45	.50	.43	.29	.00	.00	.00	.82	.70	.50	.00	.52	.67	.38	.52	.52	.63	.36	.39	.00	.00	.33	.74	.00
.80	.31	.48	.41	.39	.24	.63	.08	.78	.78	.35	.38	.77	.09	.34	.40	.24	.40	.46	.39	.39	.30	.15	.06	.33	.26	.15
.14	.80	.43	.74	.69	.52	.40	.33	.21	.21	.81	.72	.54	.13	.71	.61	.38	.64	.57	.50	.55	.48	.21	.21	.34	.50	.32
.00	.12	.09	.11	.19	.12	.08	.00	.00	.00	.21	.00	.00	.00	.10	.00	.22	.20	.20	.25	.11	.11	.36	.00	.13	.00	.15
.11	.40	.20	.47	.42	.19	.12	1.00	.11	.11	.00	.27	.22	.67	.44	.31	.13	.33	.22	.00	.24	.17	.22	.21	.19	.14	.67
.10	.51	.80	.49	.60	1.00	.76	.19	.14	.14	.44	.51	.47	.07	.62	.43	.45	.57	.52	.47	.72	.93	.30	.65	.82	.37	.24
.22	.27	.10	.35	.32	.19	.12	.25	.32	.32	.12	.40	.15	.33	.33	.31	.38	.22	.33	.14	.18	.17	.67	.21	.11	.14	.44
1.00	.08	.31	.15	.14	.10	.47	.11	.97	.97	.07	.16	.70	.13	.14	.17	.08	.14	.21	.08	.18	.13	.21	.07	.13	.00	.21
.08	1.00	.38	.75	.77	.51	.35	.40	.15	.15	.58	.73	.53	.15	.80	.70	.43	.72	.64	.57	.54	.47	.25	.23	.41	.57	.50
.31	.38	1.00	.44	.54	.80	.87	.20	.31	.31	.40	.42	.57	.10	.51	.39	.41	.51	.51	.43	.78	.87	.19	.50	.86	.34	.19
.15	.75	.44	1.00	.86	.49	.37	.47	.21	.21	.54	.75	.50	.27	.81	.73	.56	.74	.74	.61	.51	.49	.33	.21	.49	.52	.44
.14	.77	.54	.86	1.00	.60	.46	.42	.20	.20	.50	.77	.53	.24	.90	.75	.74	.90	.90	.80	.53	.60	.50	.20	.60	.54	.40
.10	.51	.80	.49	.60	1.00	.76	.19	.14	.14	.44	.51	.47	.07	.62	.43	.45	.57	.52	.47	.72	.93	.30	.65	.82	.37	.24
.47	.35	.87	.37	.46	.76	1.00	.12	.49	.49	.37	.35	.67	.04	.43	.29	.34	.47	.43	.36	.71	.82	.20	.49	.73	.79	.16
.11	.40	.20	.47	.42	.19	.12	1.00	.11	.11	.00	.27	.22	.67	.44	.31	.13	.33	.22	.00	.24	.17	.22	.21	.19	.14	.67
.97	.15	.31	.21	.20	.14	.49	.11	1.00	1.00	.14	.23	.68	.12	.21	.17	.15	.14	.28	.08	.22	.17	.30	.13	.09	.00	.20
.97	.15	.31	.21	.20	.14	.49	.11	1.00	1.00	.14	.23	.68	.12	.21	.17	.15	.14	.28	.08	.22	.17	.30	.13	.09	.00	.20
.07	.58	.40	.54	.50	.44	.37	.00	.14	.14	1.00	.67	.44	.00	.52	.55	.40	.44	.52	.52	.47	.40	.11	.07	.34	.61	.00
.15	.73	.42	.75	.77	.51	.35	.27	.23	.23	.67	1.00	.53	.31	.80	.90	.61	.64	.80	.67	.49	.47	.38	.15	.46	.67	.25
.70	.53	.57	.50	.53	.47	.67	.22	.68	.68	.44	.53	1.00	.08	.54	.50	.29	.54	.49	.42	.42	.47	.14	.11	.35	.42	.29
.13	.15	.10	.27	.24	.07	.04	.67	.12	.12	.00	.31	.08	1.00	.25	.36	.14	.13	.25	.00	.13	.06	.29	.12	.13	.17	.29
.14	.80	.51	.81	.90	.62	.43	.44	.21	.21	.52	.80	.54	.25	1.00	.78	.69	.79	.79	.67	.55	.57	.42	.21	.57	.58	.42
.17	.70	.39	.73	.75	.43	.29	.31	.17	.17	.55	.90	.50	.36	.78	1.00	.57	.70	.78	.74	.46	.39	.29	.08	.49	.74	.29
.08	.43	.41	.56	.74	.45	.34	.13	.15	.15	.40	.61	.29	.14	.69	.57	1.00	.62	.77	.73	.33	.45	.47	.07	.50	.55	.12
.14	.72	.51	.74	.90	.57	.47	.33	.14	.14	.44	.64	.54	.13	.79	.70	.62	1.00	.79	.83	.45	.57	.42	.14	.57	.58	.42
.21	.54	.51	.74	.90	.52	.43	.22	.28	.28	.52	.80	.49	.25	.79	.78	.77	.79	1.00	.83	.50	.52	.53	.14	.57	.58	.21
.08	.57	.43	.61	.80	.47	.36	.00	.08	.08	.52	.67	.42	.00	.67	.74	.73	.83	.83	1.00	.35	.48	.40	.00	.53	.60	.13
.18	.54	.78	.51	.53	.72	.71	.24	.22	.22	.47	.49	.42	.13	.55	.46	.33	.45	.50	.35	1.00	.74	.17	.58	.79	.35	.29
.13	.47	.87	.49	.60	.93	.82	.17	.17	.17	.40	.47	.47	.06	.57	.39	.45	.57	.52	.48	.74	1.00	.27	.64	.87	.33	.22
.21	.25	.19	.33	.50	.30	.20	.22	.30	.30	.11	.38	.14	.29	.42	.29	.47	.42	.53	.40	.17	.27	1.00	.20	.24	.00	.40
.07	.23	.50	.21	.20	.65	.49	.21	.13	.13	.07	.15	.11	.12	.21	.08	.07	.14	.14	.00	.58	.64	.20	1.00	.56	.00	.70
.10	.41	.86	.49	.60	.82	.73	.19	.09	.09	.34	.46	.35	.13	.57	.49	.50	.57	.57	.53	.79	.87	.24	.56	1.00	.37	.18
.00	.57	.34	.52	.54	.37	.79	.14	.00	.00	.61	.67	.42	.17	.58	.74	.55	.58	.58	.60	.35	.33	.00	.00	.37	1.00	.00
.21	.50	.19	.44	.40	.24	.16	.67	.20	.20	.00	.25	.29	.29	.42	.29	.12	.42	.21	.13	.29	.22	.40	.20	.18	.00	1.00

6

Matrix of Medicine Uses (Individual Data)

37	41	13	51	42	11	32	8	28	47	31	24	9	16	50	46	12	49	1	5	35	34	26	2	7	20	38
.00	.00	.00	.00	.22	.00	.08	.08	.09	.11	.12	.12	.06	.13	.12	.11	.00	.30	.11	.10	.00	.00	.00	.20	.09	.00	.00
.00	.00	.00	.00	.00	.00	.08	.04	.10	.11	.13	.13	.07	.13	.06	.18	.08	.11	.00	.11	.00	.00	.00	.00	.03	.00	.15
.13	.15	.14	.00	.25	.06	.16	.12	.20	.22	.25	.25	.13	.27	.19	.12	.08	.21	.25	.11	.11	.11	.11	.11	.13	.09	.15
.38	.29	.13	.00	.47	.18	.20	.20	.19	.27	.30	.30	.26	.32	.24	.17	.22	.20	.35	.30	.30	.30	.21	.30	.27	.15	.14
.40	.31	.29	.14	.38	.18	.12	.12	.10	.17	.19	.19	.20	.20	.13	.18	.23	.21	.25	.32	.32	.32	.22	.32	.27	.14	.15
.25	.29	.13	.00	.12	.12	.16	.12	.19	.22	.24	.24	.19	.26	.18	.29	.22	.20	.24	.20	.20	.20	.21	.20	.19	.15	.29
.27	.31	.29	.14	.13	.06	.12	.12	.20	.17	.19	.19	.13	.27	.19	.24	.15	.21	.13	.11	.11	.11	.11	.11	.10	.09	.22
.27	.31	.29	.14	.13	.06	.12	.12	.20	.17	.19	.19	.13	.27	.19	.24	.15	.21	.13	.11	.11	.11	.11	.11	.10	.08	.22
.31	.36	.33	.17	.14	.06	.04	.09	.10	.06	.07	.07	.07	.14	.13	.13	.08	.12	.14	.12	.12	.12	.13	.12	.11	.09	.08
.44	.25	.24	.12	.21	.28	.23	.23	.23	.21	.23	.23	.24	.18	.17	.32	.28	.18	.11	.45	.27	.27	.19	.27	.33	.21	.20
.55	.50	.57	.57	.52	.30	.35	.32	.29	.47	.46	.46	.43	.43	.36	.29	.12	.15	.09	.08	.08	.08	.00	.08	.14	.25	.29
.73	.70	.67	.57	.43	.35	.35	.32	.38	.47	.51	.51	.49	.54	.41	.54	.18	.23	.09	.15	.15	.15	.08	.15	.21	.31	.53
.75	.73	.61	.52	.56	.38	.37	.38	.44	.49	.49	.49	.51	.62	.49	.51	.23	.21	.16	.29	.21	.21	.15	.21	.27	.41	.50
.74	.72	.62	.62	.64	.44	.48	.49	.60	.63	.68	.68	.62	.62	.59	.48	.16	.13	.21	.13	.13	.13	.13	.13	.19	.32	.62
.80	.78	.67	.58	.69	.42	.43	.44	.51	.57	.62	.62	.60	.65	.57	.55	.22	.21	.23	.21	.21	.21	.14	.21	.25	.34	.54
.80	.79	.67	.58	.77	.47	.43	.47	.51	.52	.52	.52	.55	.65	.57	.50	.22	.14	.23	.34	.28	.28	.21	.29	.33	.46	.49
.69	.75	.64	.56	.67	.41	.43	.47	.54	.51	.51	.51	.54	.63	.65	.49	.22	.07	.22	.27	.13	.13	.14	.13	.25	.44	.47
.77	.75	.64	.56	.74	.41	.46	.47	.54	.60	.60	.60	.59	.73	.60	.53	.22	.20	.22	.27	.20	.20	.14	.20	.25	.39	.53
.75	.73	.61	.52	.72	.43	.44	.41	.48	.58	.59	.59	.56	.67	.54	.47	.17	.21	.24	.29	.21	.21	.15	.21	.27	.41	.50
.64	.70	.67	.58	.62	.37	.47	.41	.51	.57	.57	.57	.55	.65	.57	.45	.17	.14	.23	.21	.14	.14	.14	.14	.17	.40	.54
.67	.74	.60	.60	.73	.36	.36	.36	.43	.48	.47	.47	.50	.56	.53	.35	.06	.00	.18	.16	.08	.08	.08	.09	.15	.39	.42
.63	.71	.67	.67	.35	.24	.20	.20	.24	.27	.30	.30	.32	.32	.30	.29	.00	.00	.00	.00	.00	.00	.00	.00	.03	.31	.36
.70	.67	.63	.74	.38	.37	.29	.30	.35	.39	.43	.43	.46	.34	.32	.36	.00	.00	.00	.08	.00	.00	.00	.00	.01	.27	.50
.67	.55	.52	.61	.40	.43	.37	.38	.40	.40	.44	.44	.46	.36	.34	.47	.17	.07	.00	.29	.14	.14	.07	.14	.27	.35	.44
.72	.61	.59	.50	.38	.37	.40	.37	.43	.48	.52	.52	.50	.50	.38	.55	.22	.21	.08	.28	.21	.21	.14	.21	.25	.34	.54
1.00	.90	.76	.67	.61	.45	.35	.39	.42	.47	.51	.51	.54	.54	.46	.49	.18	.15	.17	.23	.23	.23	.16	.23	.21	.38	.53
.90	1.00	.84	.74	.57	.37	.29	.33	.39	.39	.43	.43	.46	.51	.49	.46	.13	.08	.19	.17	.17	.17	.17	.17	.23	.40	.50
.76	.84	1.00	.90	.55	.31	.29	.29	.34	.33	.37	.37	.39	.44	.42	.40	.06	.08	.09	.08	.08	.08	.08	.08	.15	.32	.42
.67	.74	.90	1.00	.55	.31	.29	.29	.34	.33	.37	.37	.39	.39	.37	.35	.00	.00	.00	.00	.00	.00	.00	.00	.07	.25	.42
.61	.57	.55	.55	1.00	.39	.34	.39	.41	.45	.45	.45	.47	.53	.50	.33	.12	.07	.17	.22	.15	.15	.08	.15	.14	.24	.29
.45	.37	.31	.31	.39	1.00	.77	.78	.79	.82	.77	.77	.80	.69	.77	.78	.75	.59	.49	.55	.23	.23	.19	.23	.30	.40	.42
.35	.29	.29	.29	.34	.77	1.00	.97	.87	.82	.76	.76	.72	.69	.73	.71	.65	.49	.41	.46	.49	.49	.47	.49	.54	.63	.67
.39	.33	.29	.29	.39	.78	.97	1.00	.88	.81	.74	.74	.73	.70	.77	.72	.66	.47	.42	.47	.50	.50	.47	.50	.55	.64	.65
.42	.39	.34	.34	.41	.79	.87	.88	1.00	.87	.80	.80	.76	.79	.86	.78	.64	.50	.49	.46	.31	.31	.31	.31	.37	.48	.57
.47	.39	.33	.33	.45	.82	.82	.81	.87	1.00	.93	.93	.90	.83	.87	.74	.67	.64	.55	.43	.17	.17	.13	.17	.20	.30	.47
.51	.43	.37	.37	.45	.77	.76	.74	.80	.93	1.00	1.00	.93	.81	.82	.72	.64	.65	.60	.28	.14	.14	.10	.14	.18	.24	.47
.51	.43	.37	.37	.45	.77	.76	.74	.80	.93	1.00	1.00	.93	.81	.82	.72	.64	.65	.60	.28	.14	.14	.10	.14	.18	.24	.47
.54	.46	.39	.39	.47	.80	.72	.73	.76	.90	.93	.93	1.00	.81	.81	.68	.63	.59	.63	.29	.15	.15	.10	.15	.19	.30	.45
.54	.51	.44	.39	.53	.69	.69	.70	.79	.83	.81	.81	.81	1.00	.81	.75	.54	.54	.58	.34	.24	.24	.20	.24	.28	.38	.49
.46	.49	.42	.37	.50	.77	.73	.77	.86	.87	.82	.82	.81	.81	1.00	.79	.68	.56	.60	.42	.09	.09	.10	.09	.13	.33	.35
.49	.46	.40	.35	.33	.78	.71	.72	.78	.74	.72	.72	.68	.75	.79	1.00	.77	.58	.48	.58	.22	.22	.18	.22	.30	.39	.42
.18	.13	.06	.00	.12	.75	.65	.66	.64	.67	.64	.64	.63	.54	.68	.77	1.00	.76	.65	.65	.27	.27	.22	.27	.31	.28	.18
.15	.08	.08	.00	.07	.59	.49	.47	.50	.64	.65	.65	.59	.54	.56	.58	.76	1.00	.67	.40	.13	.13	.07	.13	.13	.06	.11
.17	.19	.09	.00	.17	.49	.41	.42	.49	.55	.60	.60	.63	.58	.60	.48	.65	.67	1.00	.30	.15	.15	.15	.15	.14	.12	.11
.23	.17	.08	.00	.22	.55	.46	.47	.46	.43	.28	.28	.29	.34	.42	.58	.65	.40	.30	1.00	.40	.40	.34	.40	.44	.44	.21
.23	.17	.08	.00	.15	.23	.49	.50	.31	.17	.14	.14	.15	.24	.09	.22	.27	.13	.15	.40	1.00	1.00	.97	1.00	.94	.78	.68
.23	.17	.08	.00	.15	.23	.49	.50	.31	.17	.14	.14	.15	.24	.09	.22	.27	.13	.15	.40	1.00	1.00	.97	1.00	.94	.78	.68
.16	.17	.08	.00	.08	.19	.47	.47	.31	.13	.10	.10	.10	.20	.10	.18	.22	.07	.15	.34	.97	.97	1.00	.97	.90	.80	.70
.23	.17	.08	.00	.15	.23	.49	.50	.31	.17	.14	.14	.15	.24	.09	.22	.27	.13	.15	.40	1.00	1.00	.97	1.00	.94	.78	.68
.29	.23	.15	.07	.14	.30	.54	.55	.37	.20	.18	.18	.19	.28	.18	.30	.31	.13	.14	.44	.94	.94	.90	.94	1.00	.84	.70
.38	.40	.32	.26	.24	.40	.63	.64	.48	.30	.24	.24	.30	.38	.33	.39	.28	.06	.12	.44	.78	.78	.80	.78	.84	1.00	.77
.53	.50	.42	.47	.29	.42	.67	.65	.57	.47	.47	.47	.45	.49	.35	.42	.18	.11	.11	.21	.68	.68	.70	.68	.70	.77	1.00

TABLE

REARRANGEMENT OF ORIGINAL DATA MATRIX (MEDICINES AND MEDICINE

		In the summer	Broken leg	Feel weak	Over-tired	Down and out	Feel a little dizzy	Feel nauseated	Stomach ache	Upset stomach	Minor muscular aches	Hangover	Earache	Hot and cold flashes	The children are sick	Fever	Wet and tired	The children have a fever	Taken a chill	After you've been ill	Going to be ill
	ROW/COL	22	17	14	48	25	52	23	33	39	4	10	27	29	18	40	44	6	30	15	43
Bromo seltzer	21					1															
Alka seltzer	34											1									1
Contac	13																				
Vicks Sinex nasal spray	44																				
Privine nose drops	41																				
Neosynephrine nasal spray	40																				
Neosynephrine nose drops	38																				
Contac nasal mist	20																				
Privine nasal spray	15																				
Naso-dex	35																				
Dristan nasal decongestant capsules	28																				
Vicks inhaler	3																				
Dristan medicated room vaporizer	6																1				
Mentholatum	11										1										
Vicks vapo-rub	26										1							1			
Adulton cough syrup	14																				
Cough syrup	31																				
Vicks formula 44 cough discs	19																				
Romilar cough lozenges	46																				
Vicks throat lozenges	37																				
Spectrocin-T-troches	24																				
Smith Brothers cough drops	23																				
Vicks cough drops	8																				
F & F cough drops	4																				
Listerine throat lozenges	7																				
Chloraseptic lozenges	9																				
Cepacol throat lozenges	45																				
F & F Lozenges	47																				
Sucrets	2																				
Salt water gargle	52											1									
Tetrazets antibacterial analgesic	39														1	1					
Squibb analgesic tablets	36														1						
Krex A. P. A. pain relievers	18										1				1						
Seeing the doctor	12		1	1			1	1	1				1	1	1	1			1	1	1
Calling the doctor	49		1				1	1	1				1	1	1	1		1	1		1
Bufferin	1											1	1	1	1	1	1	1	1	1	1
Anacin	16											1	1	1	1	1	1	1	1	1	1
Aspirin	30											1	1	1	1	1	1	1	1	1	1
Empirin compound	48										1	1	1	1	1	1	1	1	1	1	1
Excedrin	50											1	1	1	1	1	1	1	1	1	1
A. P. C. Tablets	51												1		1	1	1	1	1	1	1
Hot lemonade	5				1	1	1							1	1	1	1	1	1	1	1
Hot tea	22			1	1	1	1	1	1	1	1		1	1	1	1	1	1	1	1	1
A hot toddy	10				1	1					1	1	1	1		1	1		1	1	
Coricidin cold tablets	25													1			1	1	1	1	1
Vitamins	32	1		1	1							1			1		1.	1	1	1	1
Fruit juice	27	1		1	1							1			1	1	1	1	1	1	1
Warm milk	42							1	1	1				1	1	1	1	1	1		
An ice pack	29	1	1									1		1				1			
Ben-gay	17	1	1								1										
Ear drops	33	1					1						1								
Murine eye drops	43	1																			
	TOTAL	6	4	4	5	4	5	4	4	2	7	11	11	13	16	14	14	15	15	13	14

7

USE FRAMES) ON BASIS OF ROW–ROW, COLUMN–COLUMN SIMILARITY

Girl (boy) friend has a cold 45	Headache 3	Neuritis, neuralgia 19	Bursitis 36	Backache 21	Nervous 37	The children are overtired 41	Indigestion 13	Heartburn 51	You are cold 42	Post-nasal drip 11	You have a cold 32	In the winter 8	The children have a cold 28	Laryngitis 47	Swollen glands 31	Tonsils are inflamed 24	Sore throat 9	During the flu season 16	The children are cranky 50	Asthma 45	Cough 12	Sore mouth 49	Bad taste in your mouth 1	Tightness in your chest 5	Sinus trouble 35	Stuffy head 34	Can't breathe 26	Stuffy nose 2	Can't breathe 7	Runny nose 20	Hay fever 38	TOTAL
							1	1	1																							4
							1	1			1																					5
											1	1	1	1			1						1	1	1	1	1	1	1	1		13
											1	1													1	1	1	1	1	1	1	9
											1	1													1	1	1	1	1	1	1	9
											1	1													1	1	1	1	1	1	1	9
											1	1													1	1	1	1	1	1	1	9
											1	1													1	1	1	1	1	1	1	9
											1	1													1	1	1	1	1	1	1	9
											1	1	1												1	1	1	1	1	1	1	10
											1	1	1												1	1	1	1	1	1	1	10
										1	1	1	1					1							1	1	1	1	1	1	1	12
										1	1	1	1							1	1			1	1	1	1	1	1	1	1	15
			1	1							1	1	1							1	1			1	1	1	1	1	1	1		15
			1							1	1	1	1						1	1	1			1					1	1		13
										1	1	1								1	1			1						1		7
										1	1	1	1	1					1	1	1			1								9
										1	1	1	1	1					1	1	1	1		1								10
										1	1	1	1	1	1	1			1	1	1	1		1								12
										1	1	1	1	1	1	1	1	1	1	1	1		1									13
										1	1	1	1	1	1	1	1	1	1	1	1	1	1									14
										1	1	1	1	1	1	1	1	1	1	1	1	1	1									14
										1	1	1	1	1	1	1	1	1	1	1	1	1	1	1								15
										1	1	1	1	1	1	1	1	1	1	1	1	1	1	1								15
										1	1	1	1	1	1	1	1	1	1	1	1	1	1									14
										1	1	1	1	1	1	1	1	1	1	1	1	1										13
										1	1	1	1	1	1	1	1	1	1	1	1	1	1									14
										1	1	1	1	1	1	1	1	1	1	1	1	1	1									14
											1	1	1	1	1	1	1		1		1	1	1									11
										1	1	1		1	1	1	1				1	1										10
									1	1	1	1	1	1	1	1	1		1													12
		1	1					1		1	1	1	1	1	1	1	1														1	13
		1	1	1	1					1	1	1	1	1	1	1	1														1	15
				1							1		1	1	1	1		1		1		1									1	22
				1							1	1	1	1	1	1	1	1	1	1	1										1	24
1	1	1	1	1	1	1	1	1			1	1	1	1	1	1	1	1	1	1										1	1	31
1	1	1	1	1	1	1	1	1		1	1	1	1	1	1	1	1	1	1	1									1	1	1	33
1	1	1	1	1	1	1	1	1	1	1	1	1	1	1	1	1	1	1	1	1										1	1	33
1	1	1	1	1	1	1	1	1	1	1	1	1	1	1	1	1	1	1	1	1											1	33
1	1	1	1	1	1	1	1	1	1	1	1	1	1	1	1	1	1	1	1	1										1	1	33
1		1	1	1	1	1	1	1	1	1	1	1	1	1	1	1	1	1	1	1											1	29
1					1	1			1	1	1	1	1	1	1	1	1	1	1	1	1		1	1	1	1	1	1	1	1	1	36
				1	1	1	1			1	1	1	1	1	1	1	1	1	1	1	1	1	1	1	1	1	1	1	1	1	1	43
			1	1	1				1	1	1	1		1	1	1	1	1		1	1	1		1	1	1		1	1			30
1									1	1	1	1	1	1			1	1	1					1						1		18
1									1		1	1	1	1	1	1		1	1													20
1									1		1	1	1	1	1	1	1	1	1				1									23
					1	1	1	1	1			1	1					1	1	1												19
			1	1																												7
		1	1	1																1				1								8
																				1												4
																																1
10	5	9	13	14	11	9	10	10	12	29	46	45	37	32	28	28	26	26	28	30	22	15	12	15	15	15	14	15	17	21	23	823

TABLE

SNACKS AND WHEN TO CONSUME

		33 Anytime I was thirsty	32 With pie	18 For breakfast	12 In the morning	41 When I want something sweet	08 For dessert	03 For a low calorie lunch	43 Coffee break	21 For very special occasions	13 As an appetizer	40 With cheese	15 With soup	14 For a quick lunch	25 Three or four times a day	46 After a party
48	Beer	24	4	0	0	3	2	1	2	8	4	21	8	5	7	9
25	Milk	33	30	29	31	6	8	18	18	5	3	14	23	23	28	16
35	Raisins	0	1	7	11	11	12	16	8	1	5	2	2	6	10	6
10	Jello	6	4	1	5	22	33	29	8	7	10	3	12	21	6	8
08	Canned fruit	8	5	16	17	21	32	21	3	6	12	8	12	23	7	5
09	Leftovers	0	2	0	3	0	1	8	1	0	3	11	22	31	7	10
24	A pickle	3	2	2	4	1	0	23	4	4	14	8	14	14	6	6
05	A bowl of soup	4	4	2	4	1	0	30	5	6	22	20	18	34	4	5
07	Cottage cheese	1	1	5	6	1	5	34	3	3	16	10	11	29	5	5
12	Hard boiled eggs	1	1	15	23	0	0	33	6	4	11	9	17	31	5	8
47	Fresh fruit	8	1	28	30	17	32	30	11	14	19	11	14	25	23	6
40	Apples	8	3	11	19	13	25	27	13	2	4	14	10	20	18	6
26	Candy bars	1	1	2	5	31	23	0	22	7	2	3	4	14	8	11
17	Ice cream	7	30	0	2	26	34	1	12	25	3	4	5	10	12	14
49	Donuts	1	0	28	32	23	27	0	27	5	3	1	4	8	9	8
45	Cherry pie	1	10	9	9	27	32	0	15	22	2	6	11	13	5	8
31	Pastries	0	5	15	21	27	29	1	22	25	3	3	6	12	8	8
18	A piece of cake	1	3	12	8	29	34	0	20	26	3	6	11	14	11	12
04	Cookies	0	5	7	13	28	31	4	25	20	3	1	5	9	14	11
42	Hard candy	2	2	1	2	28	18	2	11	12	3	2	2	1	13	8
11	Coca cola	10	12	1	4	23	2	0	18	13	6	15	11	11	14	17
50	Sausage sticks	0	2	10	7	3	0	7	3	6	19	10	19	20	7	8
55	Cheese flavored popcorn	0	0	1	2	3	2	1	6	4	10	9	7	4	9	8
09	Carmel corn	1	1	2	4	17	6	1	8	5	5	2	1	1	6	7
19	Fiddle-Faddles (like Cracker Jacks)	0	0	1	3	17	6	3	11	10	8	5	3	4	8	7
21	Popcorn	1	1	0	2	4	3	2	5	7	11	10	4	1	6	8
54	Nabisco Snacks—chipsters, shapes	0	1	1	2	3	1	4	9	5	15	18	18	5	8	8
20	Fritos	1	1	0	2	2	2	2	12	10	17	19	20	10	9	12
15	Bugles	0	1	2	5	2	1	4	11	9	15	12	17	6	9	8
01	Potato chips	1	0	0	2	0	0	1	10	13	17	18	20	8	7	9
02	Pretzels	1	0	0	1	0	0	3	9	13	16	10	7	5	6	10
03	Nuts	1	3	0	2	2	10	1	8	20	18	6	2	2	9	9
27	Peanuts	0	0	0	2	4	5	3	13	11	18	4	2	5	10	12
33	Meat flavored snacks	0	2	4	2	1	0	7	8	12	19	21	22	21	8	9
59	Daisys	0	0	0	6	3	3	2	7	7	13	11	13	5	9	6
50	Shoe string potatoes	0	1	2	5	1	1	2	5	7	11	10	23	12	7	7
51	Cheese and crackers	0	0	3	3	2	6	15	4	11	19	22	24	21	7	7
52	A meaty snack	0	0	3	3	3	0	9	6	9	14	20	21	22	6	10
16	Cheese	1	19	7	8	2	13	20	10	18	23	18	16	24	13	13
29	Cold cuts—salami, bologna	1	2	4	4	1	1	18	8	7	14	23	23	32	5	6
06	Sandwich	0	5	5	7	2	1	15	10	6	11	27	31	33	6	13
30	A hamburger sandwich	1	5	3	4	2	1	8	7	6	4	24	27	34	4	10
23	Hot dogs	1	2	2	3	1	0	10	4	4	6	14	25	31	6	4
25	Potato chips and sour cream	1	0	1	0	1	1	1	0	15	17	13	7	6	4	7
40	Pizza	0	0	1	1	2	1	1	4	4	7	18	13	25	5	10
22	French fries	0	0	2	3	0	1	1	4	3	4	6	16	16	4	4
37	Beef jerky	0	2	1	2	0	1	14	4	5	11	8	10	15	6	5
41	Peanut butter and jelly sandwich	3	1	7	6	14	2	1	4	0	4	2	18	30	4	5
40	Rolls	1	0	24	26	6	6	3	16	14	7	12	22	13	7	6
14	Toastems	0	1	29	31	16	9	6	8	2	4	2	5	8	4	2
13	Presweetened breakfast cereal	0	0	31	32	14	0	4	1	2	2	2	0	5	1	2
44	Instant breakfast	4	0	31	31	7	1	22	0	2	2	2	1	14	4	2
34	Sardines	0	0	1	1	2	0	13	3	8	20	6	8	17	1	3
36	Spaghetti-O's	0	1	0	1	1	0	0	0	1	4	7	7	22	3	3
38	Herring	0	1	3	4	0	0	11	1	9	21	5	5	11	2	3
66	Other	5	4	9	11	9	10	13	10	7	14	9	13	12	5	13

[a] Odd-numbered respondents versus even-numbered respondents (split-half reliability .87).

8

THEM (AGGREGATE DATA)[a]

31 To go with a sandwich	30 When I'm working	47 When I'm shopping	53 With tea	20 With coffee	51 With milk	52 "Raiding the refrigerator"	49 When I'm nervous	09 Mostly in the afternoon	38 When I go camping	35 When I'm out	48 When I'm visiting someone	36 When I'm babysitting	22 Late at night	06 Almost anytime of the day	42 To kill my appetite	17 When I'm in a Rush	50 In cool weather	54 For men	39 For adults	28 Without tea	23 On warm days	16 For women
22	7	7	1	2	1	21	13	11	24	24	23	9	22	6	9	10	19	31	32	29	31	20
31	20	17	11	14	16	28	14	12	24	21	17	26	28	30	20	27	25	25	26	30	30	29
5	12	5	8	5	11	9	9	16	21	11	9	15	15	21	20	18	20	22	25	29	20	26
20	9	11	12	10	16	24	10	12	9	17	17	15	18	20	18	20	21	21	29	27	31	31
19	5	6	14	9	12	23	10	9	21	12	12	12	12	21	14	25	21	24	29	28	27	28
12	6	3	14	17	25	26	15	11	14	3	8	9	19	16	15	24	24	27	29	27	22	27
31	8	9	7	6	8	24	10	14	23	16	12	13	12	11	14	19	20	29	30	31	25	27
33	7	11	13	6	23	10	7	13	20	19	11	9	12	12	17	25	30	29	30	25	11	28
17	6	10	13	8	15	19	7	9	9	13	12	10	9	15	19	19	20	22	28	26	23	30
22	8	4	13	14	19	22	8	10	24	10	7	10	13	21	19	20	20	26	28	26	24	29
24	23	11	8	9	12	23	16	16	28	20	14	26	23	32	25	27	20	25	29	28	30	31
20	22	11	6	4	13	20	17	14	30	15	12	25	20	31	25	25	19	26	30	27	30	31
13	23	23	7	10	19	12	17	20	29	22	16	27	20	23	25	27	25	25	28	30	23	27
14	10	22	13	16	12	28	17	21	9	31	30	30	26	18	19	19	18	29	28	28	34	27
11	15	16	20	29	28	14	12	8	18	21	19	18	19	20	17	25	26	25	29	29	23	29
19	6	14	21	29	27	21	11	14	11	21	22	19	22	16	17	18	23	26	29	25	24	28
12	12	17	27	29	28	18	13	12	11	22	28	20	20	20	21	20	24	25	30	23	22	29
18	13	11	26	31	32	21	15	17	17	28	30	30	27	19	21	22	24	28	28	24	25	29
15	18	12	29	31	33	12	12	22	30	18	30	28	25	26	20	22	25	24	28	26	23	26
4	20	14	4	5	7	5	16	14	20	19	17	25	17	19	18	19	20	22	26	28	23	26
30	27	28	3	1	2	23	19	18	24	27	27	29	22	25	21	22	24	29	29	26	33	28
9	8	8	11	12	15	16	11	15	22	18	14	18	17	14	15	19	21	28	27	28	21	26
7	10	7	8	6	9	7	14	15	17	18	20	23	18	14	15	18	19	24	25	30	21	24
7	15	6	10	6	10	4	13	18	15	18	13	25	16	18	16	16	18	22	22	28	20	22
13	13	7	10	7	10	8	14	17	18	19	18	26	20	21	17	18	22	21	26	29	24	23
8	14	10	7	7	12	8	14	16	19	20	19	24	25	13	13	15	23	25	27	30	20	27
14	11	9	11	9	14	10	13	16	22	19	20	21	19	15	19	20	20	26	27	30	23	27
24	16	14	9	9	13	11	15	19	26	21	23	29	21	22	19	23	23	28	31	32	23	26
19	11	7	11	8	13	9	12	21	18	18	21	28	20	17	16	19	22	29	30	30	23	25
32	17	7	4	3	9	8	15	15	27	22	26	29	25	19	19	20	23	28	29	29	21	27
12	14	10	6	4	10	9	16	15	23	20	23	26	24	18	15	18	23	28	29	28	24	26
6	13	9	7	5	7	9	16	15	24	22	24	27	21	18	19	16	24	29	30	30	23	26
4	20	15	6	5	8	8	17	15	24	19	24	27	20	21	21	21	23	29	30	31	21	27
9	12	9	10	13	19	17	12	15	19	17	19	16	22	18	21	20	22	29	30	27	22	27
15	10	8	11	6	10	4	12	15	20	15	19	24	16	18	15	17	20	23	28	27	24	28
23	10	7	12	6	12	11	13	11	23	15	16	19	16	15	15	21	21	27	28	29	23	26
11	11	7	16	12	17	15	16	15	22	18	17	23	23	15	23	22	22	27	31	29	26	28
11	9	9	14	11	20	20	15	17	20	17	17	19	21	17	20	23	21	30	29	28	24	28
25	10	12	15	11	16	19	15	14	25	20	23	21	21	22	23	23	20	30	29	27	23	30
13	7	9	18	19	24	30	14	14	28	15	16	18	19	15	20	26	22	29	31	27	26	27
15	13	20	24	30	29	24	14	17	29	25	19	23	23	18	19	32	26	30	29	29	28	27
11	11	22	16	27	27	15	9	13	25	23	15	13	15	17	15	18	25	30	32	28	25	26
6	7	18	15	20	21	16	8	14	29	24	17	12	12	13	14	22	26	30	27	28	25	27
14	3	6	11	7	7	13	12	14	10	18	24	17	17	10	18	12	20	28	28	31	23	29
3	5	14	13	12	14	10	11	16	8	24	15	18	20	14	16	16	23	26	27	28	19	26
25	6	14	10	11	13	8	11	13	16	21	14	13	13	9	16	12	22	29	29	27	21	26
8	10	7	9	13	11	11	11	15	23	12	9	12	12	12	17	17	20	25	27	27	22	20
12	7	7	16	17	25	15	11	14	22	5	11	14	17	18	19	27	22	18	18	28	23	24
8	11	12	21	27	23	11	13	11	15	23	17	12	14	18	17	22	22	28	28	26	22	28
4	2	3	21	24	27	9	5	3	12	6	7	10	13	15	10	18	23	22	25	26	19	26
3	0	3	10	19	30	7	5	1	22	3	6	8	11	10	12	17	16	20	23	29	25	27
6	4	3	4	7	21	7	9	2	15	6	5	9	9	11	16	25	18	20	26	27	22	29
6	3	4	6	7	10	10	7	12	13	10	7	9	12	9	13	16	18	24	27	25	19	24
7	2	3	9	10	14	6	7	9	14	5	7	7	7	9	12	15	21	17	19	25	13	22
9	4	6	7	6	5	8	5	10	9	11	8	9	0	4	12	9	15	24	25	25	15	21
11	8	10	12	9	16	12	12	11	16	13	14	18	14	16	14	15	16	16	20	14	11	14

TABLE 8 (Continued)

		10 For kids	34 After school	29 In between meals	01 Watching T.V.	05 Just by itself	19 As a snack	24 In the evenings	26 Little get togethers	37 At parties	04 To nibble on	07 With a coke	02 While drinking beer	11 To go along with a drink	44 At a bar	45 With cocktails	27 With dips
48	Beer	2	10	25	31	26	17	29	28	29	8	0	26	5	26	7	12
25	Milk	33	28	27	26	27	25	30	23	16	6	0	1	2	3	2	8
35	Raisins	29	25	26	24	31	28	15	12	13	31	12	2	6	1	2	2
10	Jello	31	22	21	20	27	21	25	16	16	11	5	1	3	2	2	2
08	Canned fruit	25	20	20	13	27	24	20	10	10	8	4	1	3	0	0	0
09	Leftovers	18	20	17	16	21	22	21	8	4	18	24	16	14	1	2	5
24	A pickle	24	20	21	14	17	26	20	20	20	25	11	9	8	4	3	7
05	A bowl of soup	28	14	7	12	26	12	16	7	7	4	14	1	6	3	2	0
07	Cottage cheese	18	10	14	8	14	19	14	14	10	9	8	0	3	1	2	5
12	Hard boiled eggs	22	15	18	17	19	21	17	14	11	16	14	15	12	7	4	4
47	Fresh fruit	29	29	30	31	32	33	28	20	19	30	7	0	2	1	1	5
40	Apples	30	31	31	31	33	32	26	15	14	30	9	0	2	0	1	2
26	Candy bars	33	29	29	28	32	32	25	20	16	29	16	2	6	5	4	1
17	Ice cream	34	32	26	30	33	28	31	30	26	12	16	0	6	2	2	1
49	Donuts	30	23	25	25	26	27	19	19	19	19	13	3	14	2	1	3
45	Cherry Pie	26	24	22	25	25	27	29	23	21	12	11	2	13	1	1	1
31	Pastries	26	23	25	26	27	28	26	27	30	22	12	3	12	2	2	2
18	A piece of cake	29	28	25	29	28	29	30	33	30	23	18	3	14	2	2	2
04	Cookies	33	32	32	31	31	32	29	29	26	31	18	4	17	2	1	3
42	Hard candy	27	30	28	29	30	26	24	21	26	27	9	1	5	3	3	1
11	Coca cola	30	31	29	32	32	23	27	31	29	10	23	0	7	15	8	17
50	Sausage sticks	13	19	22	21	22	23	23	22	22	21	23	24	22	14	14	15
55	Cheese flavored popcorn	28	25	26	31	25	29	24	26	24	30	27	27	27	14	12	12
09	Carmel corn	31	27	27	30	31	28	23	20	23	31	25	14	21	7	3	2
19	Fiddle-Faddles (like Cracker Jacks)	32	27	27	30	28	31	28	28	25	34	28	18	20	10	9	12
21	Popcorn	33	25	27	34	28	30	31	25	27	34	29	27	29	18	13	9
54	Nabisco snacks—chipsters, shapes	25	23	25	30	26	28	28	29	30	30	27	28	27	20	19	27
20	Fritos	30	31	29	34	29	31	31	31	29	34	31	31	32	21	21	20
15	Bugles	30	27	28	30	25	31	25	26	28	32	31	28	29	16	14	25
01	Potato chips	31	30	29	33	24	31	32	33	34	34	32	32	31	27	21	34
02	Pretzels	27	28	27	33	28	31	33	32	34	33	31	33	31	29	22	19
03	Nuts	25	27	29	33	29	30	33	34	33	34	28	31	31	30	28	7
27	Peanuts	31	29	29	33	31	32	28	30	32	34	29	32	27	24	21	10
33	Meat flavored snacks	20	21	25	28	24	30	25	28	28	29	28	23	24	17	17	15
59	Daisys	25	24	23	23	22	24	26	30	27	27	28	22	26	10	13	22
50	Shoe string potatoes	26	22	20	21	23	26	24	20	21	24	29	27	25	13	11	15
51	Cheese and crackers	20	27	27	30	27	30	29	29	29	30	27	28	28	18	21	20
52	A meaty snack	20	22	24	29	25	29	28	25	28	26	30	29	28	13	16	14
16	Cheese	22	23	26	26	25	31	26	30	28	28	22	27	20	18	19	16
29	Cold cuts—salami, bologna	22	21	19	19	19	25	21	28	26	19	28	27	22	8	12	13
06	Sandwich	28	28	15	28	25	24	22	24	26	18	32	29	26	14	8	5
30	A hamburger sandwich	30	19	9	20	25	21	22	22	19	9	33	25	23	9	5	5
23	Hot dogs	34	18	14	15	21	19	18	22	15	11	31	24	16	7	3	5
25	Potato chips and sour cream	16	19	22	26	19	24	26	28	31	26	28	22	28	15	22	25
40	Pizza	27	17	15	27	25	26	30	27	27	19	30	28	26	11	9	7
22	French fries	29	14	15	16	22	21	21	15	16	23	29	19	16	8	3	8
37	Beef jerky	11	14	17	16	20	24	20	12	12	21	19	22	19	8	8	8
41	Peanut butter and jelly sandwich	31	23	21	25	20	28	12	9	8	11	22	7	11	2	3	0
40	Rolls	20	18	18	15	20	21	25	19	18	15	12	5	13	2	3	2
14	Toastems	30	20	11	14	24	20	8	8	5	20	12	3	11	1	1	1
13	Presweetened breakfast cereal	33	14	11	11	21	14	0	0	5	15	5	0	5	1	1	0
44	Instant breakfast	15	7	5	12	24	13	6	2	6	2	0	1	2	1	1	1
34	Sardines	11	10	11	9	12	16	13	12	14	12	14	18	16	7	9	6
36	Spaghetti-O's	26	9	4	7	13	14	13	4	6	5	16	2	10	1	1	1
38	Herring	6	6	13	9	10	15	16	11	14	11	9	11	15	4	12	5
66	Other	11	14	17	10	15	15	14	13	15	11	17	15	13	10	11	12

Table 7 shows the original data matrix for one individual rearranged into clusters (that are based on the separate row–row and column–column calculations described above) such that both rows which are similar to each other and columns which are similar to each other are near each other.

Table 8 is similar to Table 7 but displays group data. It shows an aggregate data matrix in which each row is a kind of snack and each column is a belief-frame about when to eat snacks.

If we split the arbitrarily numbered respondents who form the group for a given aggregate data matrix into an even-numbered half and an odd-numbered half, the split-half reliabilities for our last five studies are .77, .91, .85, .93, and .88. Following the Spearman–Brown formula (e.g., see Gulliksen, 1950, Ch. 6), these figures suggest that reliability of the data from these item-by-use matrices ranged from .83 to .97 for the total groups. Stefflre, Reich, and McClaran (1971) presented some interindividual correlations for this type of data in a number of languages. For normal respondents with a 50 × 50 matrix, a typical interindividual correlation was .70; with a 25 × 25 matrix, the median of 423 correlations was .59. Schizophrenics or respondents under the influence of drugs exhibited lower interindividual correlations.

Items Marked X by the Same Individuals (X = Liked, Respected, Feared, Etc.)

Figure 2 shows a physical model of trips *liked* by the same individuals ($N = 200$) from a correlation matrix based on preference data. The reliability of correlation matrices of this size and type run around .75 if the odd-numbered respondents' matrix is correlated with that for the even-numbered respondents.

Patterns of Substitution from Panel Purchase Data (Where Available)

With this type of data, we can see the patterns of brand-switching or the shifts in the individual family purchase bundles from one time period to the next (Buzzell, 1964, pp. 217 ff. reviews briefly some of the early variations of switching models from Markov to Casbah).

We have found it useful to work with aggregate judged similarity data ($N \approx 50$) and aggregate data ($N = 200$–10,000) on substitution among items. The data relating judged similarity to item–item substitution is

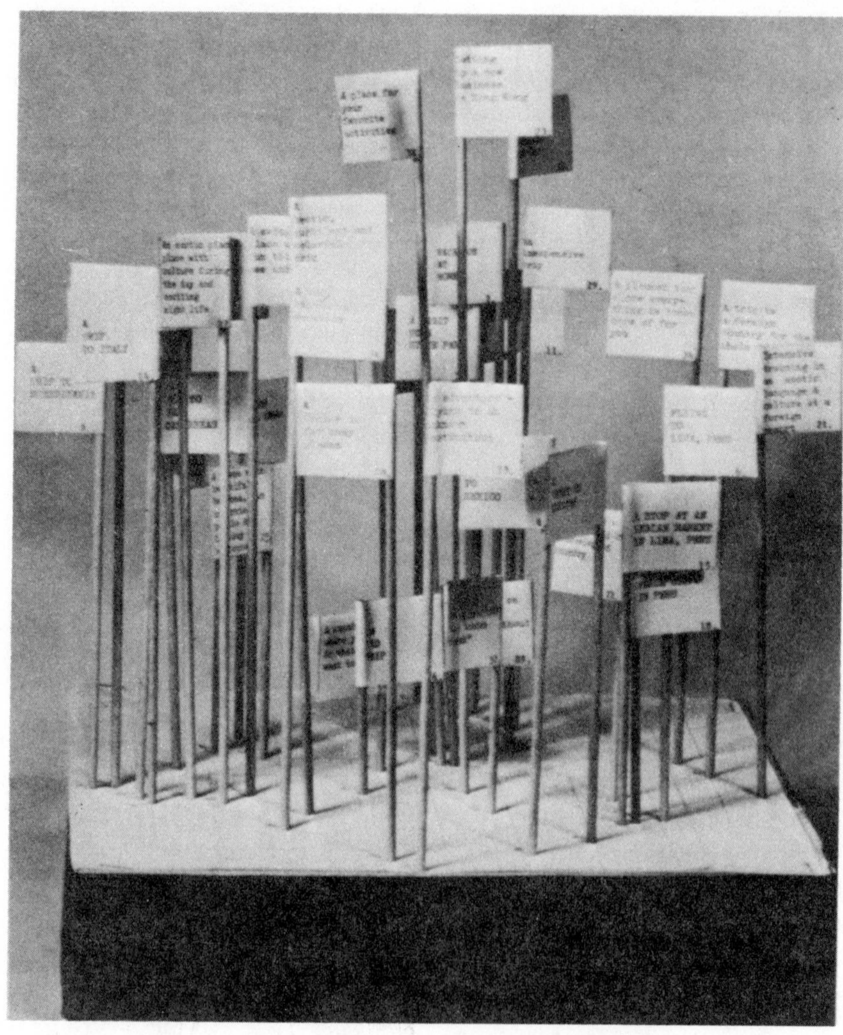

Fig. 2. Spatial representation of trip preferences.

fairly consistent. Figure 3 shows some 1961 data on judged similarity and brand switching ($N \approx 3000$) for 12 brands of cigarettes and Figure 4 shows data on judged similarity and substitution for toilet soap. The substitution index for toilet soap was obtained by combining product–product similarity-in-use rankings from data like those in Figure 2 with product–product preference correlations like those in Figure 3. Products

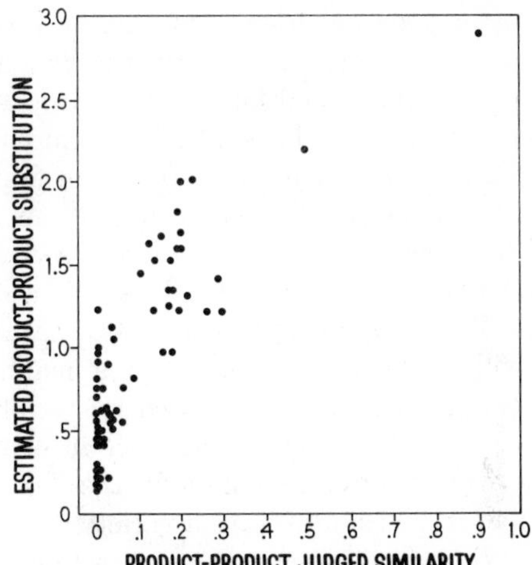

FIG. 3. Judged similarity and brand switching of cigarettes (rank correlation $\rho = .74$).

are treated as more substitutable and competitive if they (a) are seen as appropriate for the same uses, and (b) are liked by the same individuals. The Brown, Cardozo, Cunningham, Salmon, and Sultan report (1968, pp. 439 ff., 461–463) contains a description of one of our other early projects and presents in detail some of our data on judged similarity and brand–brand substitution in the coffee market. For this project, several years panel-purchase diaries for estimating patterns of substitution and competition were available.

Judged similarity in the above examples is a useful indicator of larger scale patterns of routine behavior in a culture and a spatial representation

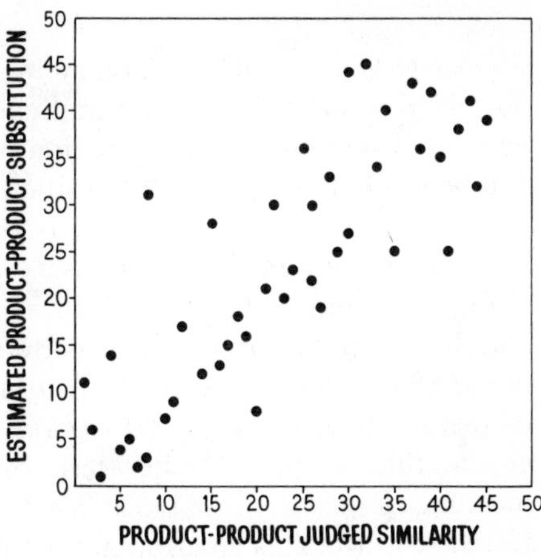

FIG. 4. Relation of product substitution and product similarity for toilet soap (rank correlation $\rho = .82$).

of judged similarity data offers a succinct summary of complex patterns of behavioral similarity. In this manner, we have studied cross-culturally perception of and behavior towards approximately 20 different sectors of the world of objects, ranging from coffee to Peace Corps volunteers; and we have found in support of the first proposition stated above that the relation between judged similarity and similarity in routine behavior holds in varying degrees in all these sectors. The lowest correlation was .45, the highest was .85, and the median, .70.

The second proposition states that a new item introduced into a culture will be behaved towards in a manner similar to the behavior toward familiar items that are seen by members of the culture as similar to the new item. It provides us with an experimental test of our understanding of the features that underly the descriptive regularities mentioned above and it is also useful for a variety of practical applications.

In order to discuss the propositions further, it is relevant to differentiate *items* and *descriptions*. My own bias in approaching the question of why an individual in a culture sees certain things as similar and different and why he sees a new thing as exhibiting a particular pattern of similarity to familiar things is to view the answer to this question as having two separable levels.

(1) *Items*. The *X*s see this new item as similar to other things because of the way they encode it (describe it to themselves).

(2) *Descriptions*. The *X*s encode this new thing (describe it to themselves) in a particular manner because it has a certain set of physical characteristics and configurations over time, was presented in such and such a way, etc.

On one level, then, the inquiry into why a particular item fits where it does in a similarity structure and elicits a particular pattern of behavior, or the attempt to design a new item which when introduced into a culture will be located in a particular position in the similarity structure and therefore will elicit certain behavior, is the search for a description that will perform as the item has been observed to or is desired to perform.

Figure 5 and Tables 9 and 10 show examples of some aspects of the search for a description which performs according to prediction. We surmised that in Quechua (an Indian language), Peace Corp workers might be described as *yanapakuqgringokuna* [*yanapakugkuna* is a reciprocal work group, that is, people who work together to help each other, and the meaning of *gringo* is obvious (Stefflre and McClaran, 1971)] and then tested the fit of this description for Cuzqueños by measuring the similarity of *yanapakuqgringokuna* to *voluntarios del cuerpo de paz.* Similarity was measured by (a) a role by behavior matrix, (b) a judged similarity matrix, and then (c) by comparing the location of these roles in the physical model of a correlation matrix based on having 500 Cuzqueños rank a group of 31 roles according to how much they thought each role was contributing to improvement in the quality of life in Cuzco.

The results of the comparison of *yanapakuqgringokuna* to *voluntarios del cuerpo de paz* were as follows: (a) it was second most similar in expected

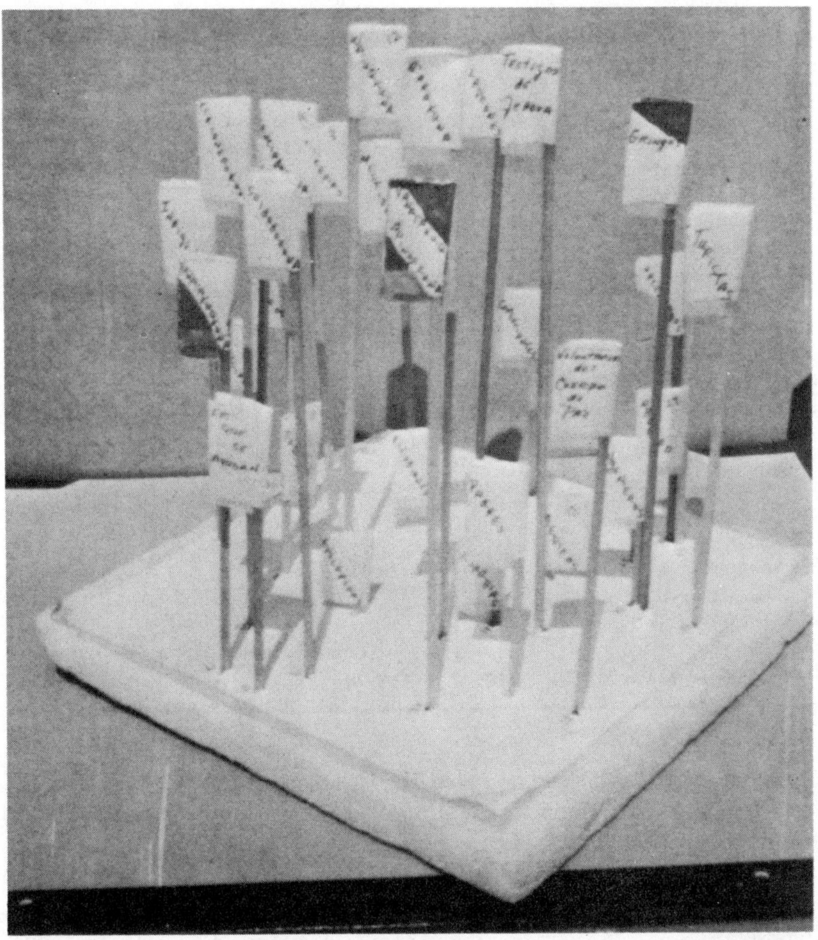

FIG. 5. Spatial representation of Peace Corps versus other types of people: A spatial model of the correlation matrix.

TABLE 9

RANKING OF PEACE CORPS VOLUNTEERS WITH OTHER TYPES OF PEOPLE

Most similar to peace corps volunteers		
1	Testigos de Jehova	Jehova's Witnesses
2	Gringos	Gringos
3	Soldados	Draftees
4	*Yanapakuqgringokuna*	*Gringos who mutually help*
5	Turistas	Tourists
6	Guardias	Policemen
7	Padres	Priests
8	Ingenieros	Engineers
9	Los que ayudan	Those who help
10	Q'arkuna	Young men city slickers
11	Maestros	Teachers
12	Yanapakuqkuna	Those who help each other
13	Abogados	Lawyers
14	Estudiantes	Students
15	Adinerados	Wealthy people
16	Enfermeras	Nurses
17	Hacendados	Landowners
18	Comerciantes	Merchants
19	Médicos	Doctors
20	Licenciadukuna	Army 'graduates'
21	Personerokuna	Village representatives
22	Campesinos	Peasants
23	Ladrones	Thieves
24	Parteras	Midwives
25	Indígenas	Indians
26	Cholos	Creoles, natives
27	Watuqkuna	Diviners
28	Mestizos	Mestizos
29	Obreros	Laborers
30	Placeras	Female plaza vendors
Least similar to peace corps volunteers		

behavior of the 53 roles compared in the role by behavior matrix, (b) it was the most similar of the 27 roles compared in the judged similarity work, and (c) it had the fourth highest correlation of the 31 roles ranked in terms of contributing improvement to life in Cuzco. Table 9 shows the ranking of the roles by their correlation with *voluntarios del cuerpo de paz.* and Figure 5 shows their positioning in a spatial model of the correlation matrix. (Table 10 shows the coordinates for the model.)

From these results we can surmise that the components concatenated by infixing *gringo* in *yanapakuqkuna* make a combination that roughly positions like *voluntarios del cuerpo de paz*. We can also surmise that if we "built" some people seen by our respondents as matching the description *yanapakuqgringokuna* they would position and perform approximately like this description.

TABLE 10

PEACE CORPS DATA COORDINATES

	Dimension				
No.	X	Y	Z	People	
1	1.05	5.98	9.42	Turistas	Tourists
2	19.22	15.67	6.68	Médicos	Doctors
3	10.35	2.97	13.16	Ingenieros	Engineers
4	13.45	2.13	10.93	Testigos de Jehova	Jehova's Witnesses
5	8.99	5.68	18.36	Obreros	Laborers
6	13.87	4.81	3.50	Guardias	Policeman
7	0	6.53	9.45	Campesinos	Peasants
8	9.10	8.84	20.51	Ladrones	Thieves
9	3.61	16.46	13.86	Comerciantes	Merchants
10	12.94	7.01	1.07	Soldados	Draftees
11	13.73	10.74	20.01	Watuqkuna	Diviners
12	11.42	20.54	13.66	Adinerados	Wealthy people
13	.47	12.20	9.58	Gringos	Gringos
14	4.22	6.84	.23	Voluntarios del cuerpo de paz	Peace Corps
15	8.74	14.49	2.32	Yanapakuqkuna	Those who help each other
16	11.50	7.63	19.25	Abogados	Lawyers
17	17.49	18.10	10.30	Enfermeras	Nurses
18	6.97	15.79	4.63	Mestizos	Mestizos
19	18.96	2.93	9.92	Padres	Priests
20	10.57	5.40	1.86	Licenciadukuna	Army 'graduates'
21	19.41	16.17	11.22	Parteras	Midwives
22	15.44	10.82	12.81	Q'arkuna	Young men city slickers
23	3.51	2.13	10.66	Indígenas	Indians
24	4.21	15.70	12.55	Personerokuna	Village representatives
25	10.70	6.74	1.34	Yanapakuqgringokuna	Gringos who mutually help
26	16.70	15.60	14.48	Estudiantes	Students
27	13.78	17.73	14.82	Hacendados	Landowners
28	1.47	15.34	14.77	Placeras	Female plaza vendors
29	20.48	8.16	10.79	Maestros	Teachers
30	5.53	0.41	12.29	Cholos	Creoles, natives
31	8.80	17.14	2.27	Los que ayudan	Those who help

TABLE 11

COMPARISON OF (1) RATING OF PRODUCT (A NEW COFFEE) ON DESCRIPTIVE SCALE, AND (2) CORRELATION OF PREFERENCE FOR THE PRODUCT WITH PREFERENCE FOR DESCRIPTION

Coffee	(1) Ratings ($N = 100$)	(2) Preference correlations ($N = 600$)
(1) Light	64.00	(2) +.071
(2) Clean	61.00	(3) +.062
(3) Friendly clean	60.50	(4) +.052
(4) Friendly	57.66	(1) +.088
(5) Mild	57.66	(5) +.049
(6) Bright flavorful	56.16	(7) −.025
(7) Lively	52.66	(6) +.011
(8) Strong	46.66	(8) −.049

$\rho = .80 (p < .05)$.

If, however, we wish to move to a more basic level of analysis, our problem becomes one of actually creating the thing that matches the description and therefore elicits the behavior desired.

One example of this problem of translating descriptions into things can be found in some early work we did several years ago on coffee. The manufacturer wished to add another brand of coffee to increase his corporate share of the market in a region where it was low and, particularly, to do so at the expense of two major competitors. We found a description—or rather a set of descriptions—of a coffee which should serve this purpose, and then we were faced with the problem of building a coffee (by varying bean selection and roasting processes) to fit these descriptions.

The process used to evolve such a coffee was rather complicated but can be summarized as systematically testing the fit of varied stimuli against description and preference until one combination has been selected that fits the description better than any competitive product. The column entitled "Ratings" in Table 11 shows the fit of the product to a set of eight descriptions.

The preference correlations column in Table 11 shows the correlation between preference for this product and preference for each of these descriptions in a 600-person national sample. Figure 6 shows a spatial

FIG. 6. Spatial representation of preference patterns for brands of coffee and coffee characteristics.

representation of the patterns of preference for this new blend of coffee in the national sample. Brands of coffee and coffee characteristics near each other are those liked by the same people.

What happened in this research was quite straightforward (a) a description was found that performed as the manufacturer desired, (b) a product was built that (i) was seen by consumers as matching the description and (ii) was liked in the large-scale test by the people who liked the descriptions it was built to match.

The client then decided to put the product in another part of the country

TABLE 12

COMPARISON PREDICTED AND OBTAINED PERCENTAGE (SHARE) OF MARKET IN TEST MARKET FOR NEW COFFEE

	Predicted %	Obtained %
1 Share	4.	5.1
2 Business from:		
brand M	38.	36.35
brand W	11.	2.3
brand C	8.	10.5
brand B	5.5	5.
brand A	5.5	9.6
brand L	4.	4.1
brand N	4.	3.

than had been its original target.[1] We tested its description in that new region and gave the client our guess as to its performance. Table 12 compares this prediction with what in fact happened during the product's first 38 weeks in test market (combining panel data adjusted for warehouse withdrawals with a telephone survey).

Since the first project of building a new coffee, we have done three others of the same type. At present we also work to evolve advertising, packaging, etc., all selected to fit a particular description whose performance in the earlier part of the research has been as the manufacturer desired.

We also have five experimental cases in which we (a) found out how people described a product under development (four cases) or just introduced it into a test market (one case), then (b) tested the product's description in a 1500-person sample, and finally (c) obtained data on the product's performance in the regional or national market in which we had tested its description. Figure 7 shows the predictions of the performance for the five different products and their actual performance in the market. In four of the five cases, the predictions were within ±30% of the volume obtained by the product.

The aim of this digression has been to show one use to which the fit between judged similarity and large scale patterns of routine behavior, on the one hand, and the performance of descriptions and the things that

[1] This project was written by our client as a Harvard Business School Case M266, 1967 and reprinted in Brown *et al.*, 1968 as Ch. 19, Pp. 439–466. My manuscript, *New Products and New Enterprises: An Experiment in Applied Social Science*, (Stefflre, ms.,b) describes some problems in applied research of this type.

match them, on the other, can be put; and to show the heuristic value of spatial models both in representing these structures and in determining which features lead items to be located as they are in the structures. Though most work of this kind that has been done to date has been in marketing, the general processes are applicable to development problems, political campaigns, etc. (e.g., Mauser, this volume).

In the work described above, the modes of representation used assume a Euclidean metric space as representing the aggregate similarity structure and the aggregate patterns of similarity in behavior.

While the assumption of a metric space[2] underlying these structures is useful in some respects, in other respects it is misleading. The major problem in representing aggregate–aggregate data (i.e., similarity judgments aggregated across individuals and across responses, using either patterns of behavior or choice measures as surrogates for patterns of behavior) by a metric space has to do with the relationship between features and preferences.

The present author is inclined to believe that in using an appropriate distance measure for psychological similarity, the triangle inequality would be violated fairly frequently. It is of course possible to use distance measures which force this assumption never to be violated, e.g., numbers ranging from .5 to 1 (J. Boyd, personal communication).

This violation occurs in two ways (a) some items (things or verbal descriptions) reside in two disjoint spaces simultaneously, and (b) three-

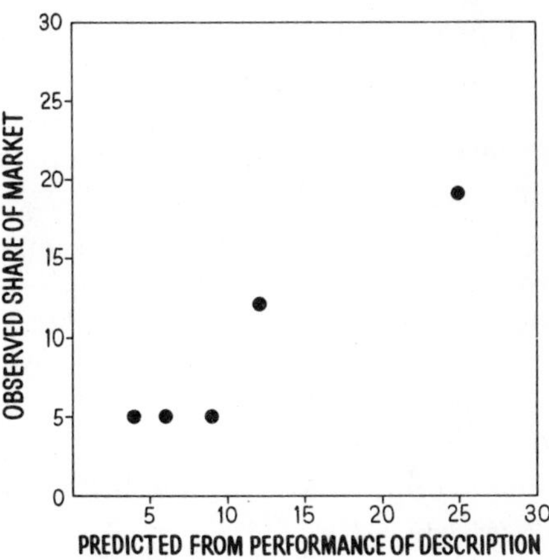

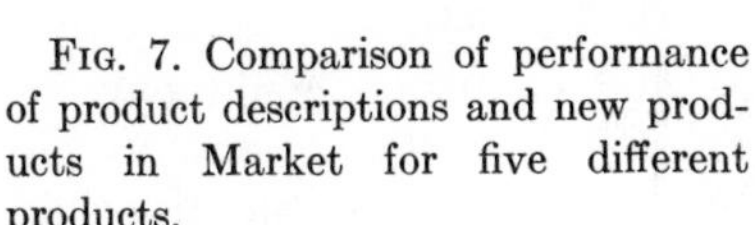
FIG. 7. Comparison of performance of product descriptions and new products in Market for five different products.

[2] A metric space is commonly defined as one in which three assumptions are met (a) $A_DA = 0$ if and only if $A =$ A, (b) $A_DB = B_DA$ (symmetry), (c) $A_DB + B_DC \geq A_DC$ (the triangle inequality).

dimensional representations of disparate sets of complex natural stimuli force a common space and understate dimensionality enough to approximate (a) above.

A simple example of (a) above is found in words with multiple meanings, e.g., *light* contrasts with *dark* in one sense and with *heavy* in another. This example may seem irrelevant; however, further examination shows that it is indeed pertinent. Multiple meanings in language can range from homonyms (e.g., different, unrelated words sounding the same, such as *board* and *bored*) to multiple meanings of the same word (e.g., various senses of the same word such as "not all *men* are *men*" or slight shifts in meaning of a word in a new context such as "the atomic *submarine* Nautilus"). The degree of interrelatedness of pairs of appearances of the same form is essentially a continuous dimension. *Light* in the context dark contrasts with one set of terms *dark* and can be defined semantically as the intersection of one set of features, while in its other use, it contrasts with and is defined in terms of another set of features.

The form itself when presented, for example, as a free association stimulus, is responded to out of context in both ways by respondents; and thus as an object in a similarity structure, it resides jointly in two spaces. Its contrasts *dark* and *heavy* each reside in one of these spaces. A synonym for *light* in one space would be *well illuminated* and in the other *not weighty* and clearly these two phrases are not synonymous.

A physical object may exhibit the same kind of multiple meaning. As a *bowl* an object fits in one space, as a *chalice* the same object fits in another.

The argument here is not just that individuals differ in the frame of reference they impute to the same object, but that the same individual will differ in the space treated as relevant to a particular object from context to context and that individual differences may only reflect differing salience in contexts.

The examples chosen here are extreme and confusion could only be avoided in such cases by subscripts—$light_1$, $light_2$, or $thing_B$, $thing_C$—but the phenomenon is continuous and ubiquitous. A and B may be similar for one reason, B and C similar for another, and A and C share nothing. I think of this as the "you can't get there from here" phenomenon in which the triangle inequality appears to be violated (e.g., James, 1890, p. 578). *Bright* is similar to *light*, and *not weighty* is similar to *light*, but *bright* and *not weighty* share *little*.

By attempting to jam the similarities into a common space in a metric space analysis and, further, by reducing the complexity of the space to a workable number of dimensions, problems appear in the heuristic value of the spatial representation as a help in determining the features underlying item placement.

As soon as coordinates are specified and a physical model built, the question "What does up mean?" emerges. One answer is "Up means the things that are high." Another is "Up is a synesthetic dimension including both light in weight and bright in illumination." Or, one we prefer is "There are no dimensions, just labeled regions—up on one end of the space may mean something very different from up on the other—and to test your understanding of how to go where, build new things and see if they go where you expect." Alternative interpretations are not to be resolved by analysis but by experimentation.

A second assumption of the current work on metric space which makes the author nervous is that location uniquely determines preference—not just which people like a thing more, but also how many people like it. Several joint models (Carroll, this volume; Carroll & Chang, 1964, 1967, 1970; Coombs, 1964; Doehlert, 1968; Doehlert & Hoerl, 1967) have been suggested in which it is inferred not only where items are located, but also where each individual's ideal point resides in the space.

While our own work in this area has been quite crude, we are at present as pessimistic about the prospects of an algorithm of this type as we are about using the spatial coordinates of a metric representation as a formula for constructing new objects. What we have found fairly frequently is that two new items which are quite near each other in free judged similarity or behavioral similarity may be differentially preferred.

An example may illustrate the possibility of the lack of correspondence between position and preference. If we present twelve pictures, ten of different people and two prints of the same dog photo to be judged on similarity, the two dog pictures will probably turn out to be quite similar. If we look at preference data both pictures will probably tend to be liked by the same individuals. If one is a good print, however, and the other not so good, their absolute levels of preference may differ rather more than their similarity in location would indicate. Another way to say this is that judged similarity may predict correlations between the preferences for items better than the cross-products of the items preferences or their levels of preference. We have analyzed several cases in which judged similarity correlated with items correlations in preferences .64, .45, and in which it correlated with cross-products .002 and .06.

A number of examples of this kind have caused me to change my point of view from one which considers location as uniquely determining both (a) level of and (b) pattern of preference to one which considers that location determines the pattern of preference, but that the level of preference is determined partly by location and partly by G, a general level of preference evaluation. Items rather than points in space represent (a) nodules with a specified level of preference, (b) occupying a particular position in the space.

Let it suffice in this context to say that we have found metric space models useful heuristics in describing regularities in aggregate–aggregate data and in positioning new items, but we have not yet found an algorithm for doing the latter that is satisfactory.

For other kinds of data we suspect the metric space assumptions may prove even more troublesome. In individual data, similarities can shift radically as various contexts call different features into salience so that individual similarity data at one point in time represent a metric space (Shepard, 1964), while at another point in time they represent a different metric space. This kind of change seems quite antithetical to the whole notion of spatial representation. Aggregate free response judged similarity data aggregate these contexts by aggregating individuals; pattern of behavior data or choice data aggregate these data across individuals and contexts.

Due to the perverse and/or delightful flexibility in sequential behavior on the part of human beings, several first-rate workers who did early work on similarity and spatial representation of the mind have shifted to means–ends process models (Abelson, 1954; Abelson & Carroll, 1965; Abelson, Aronson, McGuire, Newcomb, Rosenberg & Tannenbaum, 1968; Miller, Galanter and Pribram, 1960; Miller & Nicely, 1955).

In addition to assuming stability of the structure, the spatial representation assumes that an element is an element. However, as saliency among dimensions shifts, i.e., as the spatial configuration appropriate for one context flows into that for another, an element in the space takes on a new set of properties (e.g., a *bowl* becomes a *chalice*). In working with aggregate data, the change in similarity as a function of context poses a problem. Consider the following case: Items A and B are more similar than items A and C and hence generally elicit more similar patterns of behavior, yet there may go undetected a single crucial behavior or context in which A and C may prove more similar (e.g., legal cases).

These properties of the mind—shifting contexts shifting salient features, and shifting features transforming elements—seem quite unspatial. Even if we freeze the data at one point in time and look at them in terms of the metric space assumptions, there are still problems. $A_D A = 0$ suggests that there is nothing closer to A than A, but consider confusions in recognition experiments in which a single incorrect stimulus may be selected more often than the correct stimulus. Such a situation suggests that if we take confusions as a measure of distance, $A_DA' < A_DA$ and $A_DA \neq 0$. A_DB and B_DA symmetry frequently seems to be violated in data on judged similarity and confusions. An imperfect example of an X may be more often judged as similar to a prototypic X than vice versa. Confusions data often indicate similar asymmetries. The triangle inequality ($A_DB + B_DC \geq A_DC$) and its problems were considered above. At this point let it suffice to say that though A is similar to B (a red apple and a red Cadillac) and B is similar to C (a red apple and an orange), A and C (a red Cadillac and an orange) may be more dissimilar than a strict reading of Schwartz might suggest.

This is not to suggest that by appropriate manipulations of our data collection and data analysis we cannot force a metric space, but only to suggest that while such manipulation may be useful for specific practical or theoretical purposes their utility is limited and provisional.

The present author's own notion of the reality of the phenomenon with which we deal—the individual mind and its aggregated analog, the group mind or collective representations (Durkheim, 1915)—is that its structure is discrete, and combinatorial rather than continuous and geometric, looking more like a dictionary, thesaurus, and a grammar than a three-space (Stefflre, Reich, and McClaran, 1971). It is composed of elements and relations and each element can be represented as a description list of the elements to which it exhibits specified classes of relations. (This alternative type of development can be seen in the works of Goodman, 1951; Tyler, 1969; Minsky, 1968; Hartmanis & Stearns, 1966.)

The basic structure is that of a multigraph (Berge, 1962; Harary, Norman, & Cartwright, 1965; Ore, 1963), though the data we deal with are usually spatial representations of the similarity structure obtained in aggregate free judged similarity; e.g., frozen slices of individual data with the elements on the description list at a particular salience aggregated into a collective representation.

I am inclined to believe that a multigraph description will allow us (a) to calculate from it the spatial configuration, and (b) offer us a model with more flexibility and generality than a spatial approach.

In summary, then, it has been suggested that multidimensional scaling methods have a real utility in describing patterns of similarity and patterns in the similarity of behavior elicited by things or events. They are a powerful descriptive tool for studying regularities in the patterns of behavior of aggregates and are of some help, if used heuristically, in determining *what* features put new items *where* in structures of this kind.

Some problems in the use of these methods stem from the shifting nature of psychological salience in an individual through time and the fact that many crucial behaviors one may wish to predict can hinge on the presence or absence of particular features rather than overall similarity.

A spatial configuration, while not a very good model for the structure of the individual or group mind or of the society, does provide a useful device for working on special problems.

References

Abelson, R. P. A technique and a model of multidimensional attitude scaling. *Public Opinion Quarterly*, 1954, **19**, 405–418.

Abelson, R. P., Aronson, E., McGuire, W. J., Newcomb, T. M., Rosenberg, M. J., & Tannenbaum, P. H. (Eds.) *Theories of Cognitive Consistency: A Sourcebook*, Chicago, Illinois: Rand McNally, 1968.

Abelson, R. P., & Carroll, J. D. Computer simulation of individual belief systems. *The American Behavioral Scientist*, 1965, **8**(9), 24–30.

Berge, C. *The theory of graphs and its applications*. London: Metheuen, 1962.

Brown, M. P., Cardozo, R. N., Cunningham, M. W., Salmon, W. J., & Sultan, R. G. *Problems in marketing*. (4th ed.) New York: McGraw-Hill, 1968.

Buzzell, R. *Mathematical models and marketing management*. Cambridge, Massachusetts: Harvard University Press, 1964.

Carroll, J. D. Individual differences and multidimensional scaling. This book, Volume I.

Carroll, J. D., & Chang, J. -J. Non-parametric multidimensional analysis of paired-comparisons data. Paper presented at the joint meeting of the Psychometric and Psychonomic Societies, Niagara Falls, October 1964.

Carroll, J. D., & Chang, J. -J. Relating preference data to multidimensional scaling solutions via a generalization of Coombs' unfolding model. Paper presented at meeting of Psychometric Society, Madison, Wisconsin, April 1967.

Carroll, J. D., & Chang, J. -J. Analysis of individual differences in multidimensional scaling via an N-way generalization of "Eckart-Young" decomposition, *Psychometrika*, 1970, **35**, 283–319.

Coombs, C. H. *A theory of data*. New York: Wiley, 1964.

Doehlert, D. H. Similarity and preference mapping: A color example. In R. L. King (Ed.), *Proceedings of the Denver conference of the American Marketing Association*. Chicago, Illinois: American Marketing Association, 1968. Pp. 250–258.

Doehlert, D. H., & Hoerl, A. E. Finding the preferred regions in multidimensional space. Spring Program of the Psychometric Society, Madison, Wisconsin, 1967.

Durkheim, E. *Elementary forms of religious life*. London: Allen & Unwin, 1915.

Goodman, N. *The structure of appearance*. Cambridge, Massachusetts: Harvard University Press, 1951.

Gulliksen, H. *Theory of mental tests*. New York, Wiley, 1950.

Harary, F., Norman, R. Z., & Cartwright, D. *Structural models: An introduction to the the theory of directed graphs*. New York: Wiley, 1965.

Hartmanis, J., & Stearns, R. E. *Algebraic structure theory of sequential machines*. Englewood Cliffs, New Jersey: Prentice-Hall, 1966.

James, W. *Principles of psychology*. New York: Dover, 1890.

Kruskal, J. B. Multidimensional scaling by optimizing goodness of fit to a nonmetric hypothesis. *Psychometrika*, 1964, **29**, 1–27. (a)

Kruskal, J. B. Nonmetric multidimensional scaling: A numerical method. *Psychometrika*, 1964, **29**, 115–129. (b)

Mauser, G. A structural approach to predicting patterns of electoral substitution. This book, Volume II.

Miller, G. A., Galanter, G., & Pribram, K. H. *Plans and the structure of behavior*. New York: Holt-Dryden, 1960.

Miller, G. A., & Nicely, P. E. An analysis of perceptual confusions among some English consonants. *Journal of the American Acoustical Society*, 1955, **27**, 338–352.

Minsky, M. (Ed.) *Semantic information processing*. Cambridge, Massachusetts: MIT Press, 1968.

Ore, O. *Graphs and their uses*. New York: Random House, 1963.

Shepard, R. N. Attention and the metric structure of the stimulus space. *Journal of Mathematical Psychology*, 1964, **1**, 54–87.

Stefflre, V. J. Simulation of people's behavior toward new objects and events. *The American Behavioral Scientist*, 1965, **8**(9), 12–15.

Stefflre, V. J. Market structure studies: __ New products for old markets and new markets (foreign) for old products. In F. M. Bass, C. W. King, & A. Pessemier (Eds.), *Application of the sciences in marketing management*. New York: Wiley, 1968. Pp. 251–268.

Stefflre, V. J. *Language and behavior*. Unpublished manuscript. (a)

Stefflre, V. J. *New Products and New Enterprises: An Experiment in Applied Social Science*. Unpublished manuscript. (b)

Stefflre, V. J., & McClaran, M. *A study of the perception of Peace Corps volunteers and their activities by Spanish and Quechua speakers in Cuzco and Chimbote, Peru*. (Revision of a 1967 Peace Corps report), in press.

Stefflre, V. J., Reich, P., & McClaran, M. Some eliciting and computational procedures for descriptive semantics. In P. Kay (Ed.), *Explorations in mathematical anthropology*. Cambridge, Massachusetts. MIT Press, 1971.

Tyler, S. A. (Ed.) *Cognitive anthropology*. New York: Holt, Rinehart, & Winston, 1969.

A STRUCTURAL APPROACH TO PREDICTING PATTERNS OF ELECTORAL SUBSTITUTION

Gary A. Mauser

L'INSTITUT D'ÉTUDES COMMERCIALES
UNIVERISTÉ DES SCIENCES SOCIALES
UNIVERSITÉ DE GRENOBLE
GRENOBLE, FRANCE

Consider the problem of predicting patterns of competition or substitution for any new candidate in an election with at least two candidates. Clearly, the new candidate need not draw votes equally from each of the original candidates. If the new candidate draws disproportionately from the old candidates even though he draws a small proportion of the vote, he can alter the outcome of the electron.

This problem may be illustrated by looking at the recent Presidential election. George Wallace introduced a new political party, the American Independent Party as it was known in most states, into the usual two-party contest for the American Presidency and drew almost 14% of the popular vote. During the campaign it was an open question from whom Wallace would draw more votes and why. Optimistic Democrats argued that Wallace would draw more heavily from Nixon because they both appealed to "the Goldwater vote," but Republican leaders hoped that Wallace would hurt Humphrey more because they both appeared to lower-class Democrats. Since in any close election even a minor candidate can influence, indeed sometimes even determine, the outcome of the election, it is important to learn how to predict the influence of new candidates on the election.

A model will be developed empirically in this paper to describe the underlying structure in the 1968 Presidential election in California and used to predict the pattern of substitution for several hypothetical new candidates in this election. "Structure" refers to the similarity relationships among the candidates and potential candidates in an electoral contest. Following Downs (1957) and Converse (1966), political candidates are represented by points in a multidimensional space, so that the similarity of any pair of candidates is mapped onto their proximity in the model. It is not necessary to assume all of the properties of multidimensional space in order to represent electoral structure spatially. It is only necessary to assume that the structure can be embedded in a suitable dimensionality.

In this model, voters are hypothesized to share a common system of beliefs about the political world which underlies their perceptions of and preferences for candidates and political parties. To be sure, there are important differences between distinct social groupings in the polity, nevertheless, a common conceptual framework exists for the vast majority of the members. Each voter is considered to choose that candidate in an election who is nearest to his ideal.

The approach taken here to understanding electoral substitution rests upon three interlocking assertions borrowed from psycholinguistics:

1. objects *substitute* for each other in a single choice situation, such as an election, to the extent that they are seen as *similar*;

2. if a new item is introduced into the situation, an individual will act towards it in a manner that is similar to the way he acts towards familiar items that he sees the new item as similar to, and

3. the close relationship between what is psychologically similar for the individual and which things are behaved towards similarly by that individual holds across individuals and across cultures despite the wide variation between individuals and cultures in which objects or situations are seen as similar and in how the objects or situations are behaved towards (Stefflre, this volume). One example of this relationship can be seen in predicting patterns of preference. If candidate x' is seen as being basically similar to candidate x whom the voter already knows and prefers more than do most voters, he will probably prefer candidate x' more than most voters (i.e., the candidates will substitute for each other to some extent), or alternatively, if candidate x' is seen as similar to candidate y

whom the voter dislikes more than most voters, he will probably dislike candidate x' more than do most voters. This is not to say that candidates that are seen as similar (e.g., as Republicans) will be behaved towards in the same way (e.g., voted for) by all voters. The hypothesis only asserts that if a voter prefers Republican x he will also prefer Republican x' in the event that he sees x' as essentially similar to x.

The assertion that similar candidates substitute remains tautological unless independent measures are used to determine (a) the extent to which candidates are seen as similar to each other, and (b) the extent to which candidates substitute for each other in the election. In this paper similarity and substitutability were measured on separate samples of voters drawn from the same target population and interrelated to test this proposition. The first sample determined the perceived similarity of the candidates, while the second sample determined the pattern of preferences for candidates across voters, and substitutability was measured in the third sample by draw ratios.

The first sample judged the relative similarity of a set of Presidential candidates and a model was developed to represent the aggregate similarity structure. Hypotheses were then made about the features of the candidates which led them to position where they did in the similarity structure. The candidates were ranked by the respondents in the second sample in terms of their preferences for President and a model of the substitution structure was derived from the patterns of the intercorrelated rankings. The hypotheses about which of the candidates would compete with each other were then tested and new hypotheses generated. To explore how features of candidates determine their position in the substitution structure, hypothetical candidates composed of a few selected features were introduced in the preference interview. The hypothetical candidates should position close to actual candidates that share the specified features.

To predict the influence of a few selected new candidates on the 1968 Presidential election, the respondents in a third, and relatively large, sample were asked to rank eight Presidential candidates (both actual and hypothetical). Since the outcome of an election between any subset of these candidates may be simulated, not only new candidates can be included in the election, but also alternatives to the old candidates can be considered. While the emphasis here is primarily descriptive, the utility of this analysis for evaluating electoral strategies prior to an election should be obvious.

The techniques used to measure: (a) the similarity of items or events, (b) the items' substitutability in a choice situation, and (c) the extent to which similarity can predict substitutability have been developed by V.

Stefflre to measure the similarity and substitutability of objects in general and are described more fully elsewhere (Stefflre, ms.; Stefflre, 1965; Stefflre and Wendell, 1966).

Nonmetric multidimensional scaling (MDS) procedures were used to display the similarity and substitution data in a spatial model. This approach was originally developed by Shepard (1962a, b) to analyze proximity data and was later extended by Kruskal (1964a, b). This approach was selected primarily for its relatively low compression of the data coupled with its capability for allowing complex relationships to be easily conceptualized. Since a very large range of structures can be embedded in a k-dimensional space (Torgerson, 1965), MDS techniques are particularly useful for exploring new structures. Nevertheless, the spatial model may not be adequate to display the underlying structure. To evaluate the spatial representation, Rapoport and Fillenbaum (this book, Volume II) and Shepard (this book, Volume II) have suggested comparing the dimensional model with an analysis of a very different basic nature, particularly with a nondimensional schema. Thus, the hierarchical clustering procedure developed by Johnson (1967) was used to independently analyze the judged similarity data and then was compared with the dimensional model.

The MDS and clustering techniques will be used here as data reduction procedures only and not as direct models for the underlying structures. These techniques will be used as exploratory tools and the nature of the structure will be inferred from the constraints made upon the shape or character of the configuration that can be generated. The distinction between the MDS model and the nature of the structure is particularly useful to make because not all of the assumptions of either scaling model, whether many-valued dimensions or hierarchical organization, may apply to the structure of this domain.

As is characteristic of almost all multidimensional scaling procedures, the intent of the Shepard–Kruskal analysis is to represent the set of proximity measures geometrically in such a way that the interpoint distances in the scaling model best correspond inversely to the order of the original proximities. This approach is termed nonmetric because it assumes that the proximities were measured on an ordinal scale (i.e., they are unique up to a monotonic transformation), but that the resulting interpoint distances satisfy the requirements of a ratio scale (i.e., they are unique up to multiplication by a positive constant).

The basic data for the MDS procedure and the cluster analysis are measures of the relative proximity of object pairs. Suitable measures have been developed for the relative similarity of political candidates and for the degree to which candidates will substitute for each other.

The Kruskal procedure uses an iterative algorithm to find the best fitting correspondence between the ranked proximity measures and the interpoint distances. The degree to which the interpoint distances are not a monotonic function of the proximity measures is expressed in a measure, called "stress," of the overall goodness of fit of the model. Stress is a normalized sum of squared deviations and can be thought of as analogous to the standard error of estimate in a regression analysis.

Johnson's (1967) clustering procedure is one of a class of numerical procedures for defining categories and constructing taxonomic frameworks on the basis of proximity data. His procedure constructs hierarchical systems of clusterings using either of two different clustering methods, *connectedness* or *diameter*. Both methods begin by considering each object as a separate cluster and then merge the most similar pair of objects in the matrix at each step. The methods differ however in how a new proximity function is defined for the newly merged entry. The connectedness method uses the minimum of the two entries, while the diameter method uses the maximum. The two clusterings have simple interpretations: the diameter method minimizes the diameter of the cluster (i.e., the largest intracluster proximity) and the connectedness method minimizes the chain distance for each new item (i.e., the distance from the new item to the cluster).

Method and Results

Selecting the Political Candidates

In order to describe the structure of any domain, the first task must be to define the domain of interest. The researcher must clearly state the domain he is interested in and how the primitive content is selected. This necessarily involves more than arbitrarily selecting elements that suit the researcher's convenience or fancy. Inasmuch as the analysis of the structure depends upon the interrelationships of the elements within that domain, it is critical that the entire range of elements which naturally occur in that domain be included in the study (Brunswik, 1956; Black & Metzger, 1965).

Since this study is concerned with contemporary American Presidential politics, and specifically with the 1968 Presidential election, names of widely known people who were seen as relevant to this election were included in this study. To construct this list, a small heterogeneous sample of voters was asked to "Name people who are candidates in, or who are otherwise relevant to, the Presidential election this year (1968)." Almost all of the names mentioned by these voters, with the addition of a few names to emphasize potentially important themes in the campaign, were included

TABLE 1

LABELS AND NAMES USED IN JUDGED SIMILARITY AND SMALL SCALE PREFERENCE INTERVIEWS

1 BROWN	= Edmund G. "Pat" Brown	14 RAFF	= Maxwell Rafferty
2 CARML	= Stokely Carmichael	15 REAGN	= Ronald Reagan
3 DRKSN	= Everett Dirksen	16 ROCKY	= Nelson A. Rockefeller
4 IKE	= Dwight D. Eisenhower	17 SCHMT	= John G. Schmitz
5 GOLDW	= Barry M. Goldwater	18 SPOCK	= Dr. Benjamin Spock
6 HUMPH	= Hubert Humphrey	19 STVSN	= Adlai Stevenson
7 LBJ	= Lyndon B. Johnson	20 UNRUH	= Jesse M. Unruh
8 JFK	= John F. Kennedy	21 WALLC	= George Wallace
9 RFK	= Robert F. Kennedy	22 WARRN	= Earl Warren
10 KING	= Martin Luther King, Jr.	23 WELK	= Lawrence Welk
11 LNDSY	= John V. Lindsay	24 WESTY	= Gen. William C. Westmoreland
12 MC C	= Eugene J. McCarthy	25 YORTY	= Samuel Yorty
13 NIXON	= Richard Nixon	26 IDEAL	= my ideal candidate for President[a]

[a] "My Ideal candidate" was used only in JSI.

in this study (See Table 1). This list was used in the Judged Similarity Interview (JSI) and, with the exception of the Ideal candidate, was also used in the Small Scale Preference Interview (SSPI).

In addition to the names of actual politicians, a class of "hypothetical candidates" were introduced in the preference interviews. The hypothetical candidates (or descriptions) consisted of short phrases describing plausible classes of candidates and were constructed to discover which features determine positioning in the substitution structure. To ensure plausibility all features were drawn from the voters' comments about candidates in the JSI. A wide variety of features were included: e.g., assertions about what the candidate could or would do if elected, about what kind of person he is, who his supporters are, and his political experience. Several diverse strategies were used to fashion plausible or well-formed candidates out of these features. Candidates were devised (a) to take a clear stand on salient policy questions, (b) to exhibit a definite personality, (c) to stand on campaign slogans, (d) to appeal directly to certain groups, or (e) to match important actual politicians. Candidates that are seen as sharing the same essential characteristics should be treated similarly. Thus, it should be possible to infer a candidate's most important features from the hypothetical candidates who position close to him in the substitution structure. New candidates should position close to old candidates with whom they are seen as sharing essential characteristics. Table 2 shows the list of descriptions used in the Small Scale Preference Interview (SSPI).

Eight of the most competitive and diverse candidates—names and descriptions—were selected from the list in the SSPI to be presented to the 1500-person sample in the Large Scale Preference Interview (LSPI). These candidates are shown in Table 3.

TABLE 2

LABELS AND DESCRIPTIONS USED IN SMALL SCALE PREFERENCE INTERVIEW (SSPI)

26	FINEX	= A President we could be proud of who would set a fine example.
27	EXREP	= An experienced, mature Republican who is running for President again.
28	POVTY	= A candidate who wants to eliminate poverty and slums in the United States.
29	CHRST	= A good Christian American who could set a good example for the country as President.
30	WAR	= A candidate who wants an honorable end to the Vietnam war.
31	JOBS	= A President who guarantees a job with a decent wage for everybody.
32	PTRT	= A patriotic American who would be a strong leader as President.
33	LBLDM	= A liberal Democratic nominee who supports organized labor.
34	WNWAR	= A President who can win the Vietnam war.
35	COPS	= A President who would support the police and stop the courts from coddling criminals.
36	VP	= The Vice President of the United States and the Democratic nominee for President.
37	WITHD	= A candidate who wants the United States to immediately withdraw from Vietnam.
38	UNITE	= A President who could unite the nation and heal our troubled cities.
39	RIOTS	= A President who wouldn't be afraid to stop Negro rioters and student anarchists.
40	STDUP	= A man who is willing to stand up for his beliefs regardless of the consequences.
41	ENTRP	= A Republican nominee who supports the free enterprise system and fiscal responsibility in government.
42	NUCLR	= A candidate who would use nuclear weapons if necessary to win the Vietnam war.
43	PEACE	= A President who will sincerely search for peace.
44	RACST	= A candidate who will work to end white racism in the United States.
45	POLIT	= The incumbent President who is a shrewd politician and who would continue pretty much the same policies as before.
46	LAW	= A candidate who will enforce law and order in our cities.
37	STOPB	= An idealistic intellectual who wants the United States to unconditionally stop bombing North Vietnam.
48	STATE	= A candidate who believes in states' rights: that the states should be able to handle their own racial problems.
49	CUTTX	= A President who would cut federal spending and reduce taxes.
50	YNGS	= A young, dynamic Senator who believes in civil rights and who appeals to the youth and to the minorities.

TABLE 3

LABELS AND CANDIDATES USED IN LARGE SCALE PREFERENCE INTERVIEW (LSPI)

1	LBJ	= Lyndon Johnson
2	HUMPH	= Hubert Humphrey
3	NIXON	= Richard Nixon
4	ROCKY	= Nelson Rockefeller
5	WLLCE	= George Wallace
6	RFK	= A candidate like Robert Kennedy
7	RIOTS	= A candidate who would not be afraid to stop Negro rioters and student anarchists
8	WAR	= A candidate who wants an honorable end to the Vietnam War

RESPONDENTS

To be able to understand naturally occurring social phenomena, one very useful approach is to interview individuals who are involved in the events of interest. Since the focus here is on electoral competition, this means that the target population should be those voters who actually cast a ballot in the selected contest. But predicting which voters go to the pools on election day out of those who could go has proven to be a very difficult problem (Berelson, Lazarsfeld, & McPhee, 1954; Campbell, Converse, Miller, & Stokes, 1960; Pool, Abelson, & Popkin, 1964). No simple rule has been formulated which is particularly successful in predicting turnout in more than a few elections. In view of the difficulty of sampling the population of citizens who actually voted, the target population was California registered voters.

Rather than attempting to predict the national vote, this study was concerned with predicting the Presidential vote for a single state because of the unique role that each state plays in electing the President of the United States. Historically, the President has not been elected by direct popular vote but by a weighted sum of the states in the Electoral College. The state vote goes to the candidate who received a plurality in that state, usually on a "winner take all" basis, although there have been a few exceptions to this rule. Consequently, the state is the most appropriate political unit for studying the role of political perceptions in patterns of candidate substitution. This is not to say that the national vote for President could not be predicted using this approach, but only that such a prediction would have to depend upon a weighted sum of the estimates for each state in a manner similar to that used by Pool *et al.* (1964).

Prior to the 1968 Presidential election, three separate samples of California registered voters were drawn and interviewed. The first sample consisted of 65 respondents (*R*s) who were asked to judge the similarity of a set of politicians (the Judged Similarity Sample or JSS). Of the *R*s, 36 were interviewed in July and 29 in September. In the second sample 193 *R*s rank-ordered a list of names and descriptions (the Small Scale Preference Sample or SSPS), which was drawn during September and October. The third and last sample was interviewed during the four days preceding the General Election in November and consisted of 1500 registered voters who rank-ordered eight candidates for President (the Large Scale Preference Sample or LSPS).

The first two samples were only crudely representative of California voters. A loose quota system was used to balance these samples with respect to major socioeconomic factors. The primary variables considered were race, religion, party affiliation, county of residence, and income level.

Small samples were drawn for the first two interviews, not only for economic reasons, but also because these similarity measures were expected to be stable across people.

The third and last sample was drawn to estimate the number of votes each candidate would receive in the Presidential election. Of the California registered voters, 1500 were selected using a probability sampling procedure and were interviewed over the telephone at my request by Hooper, Inc. This survey was conducted in two distinct stages: first, four replicated samples of telephone numbers of private households were selected from telephone books throughout the state using a multistage probability sampling procedure (Kish, 1965); next, interviewers called the selected households in search of a registered voter to interview. The procedure used is discussed elsewhere much more fully than is possible here (Mauser, 1970).

Measuring the Perceived Similarity of Candidates

To measure the perceived similarity of the political names, 65 *R*s in th first sample were given the list of political candidates (see Table 1) an asked for each name, "Is there anybody on the list that you feel is simila to______in any way?" Each name in turn served as a reference item in thi question frame (this procedure is called anchor point clustering). The lis was presented in reverse order to half of the sample. Up to four judgmen were accepted for each name. The *R* was not required to justify his sele tions in any way at this point, but simply to indicate who he sees as simil to whom. If a name was not familiar to a respondent, it was dropped from his list. The description at the bottom of the list, "my ideal candidate," was presented to the *R* as a hypothetical or imaginary person who "would be everything that you would want in a candidate for President." After all similar names have been paired, the *R* was asked to indicate in what way he saw the members of each pair as similar, or, in other words, what features they shared. All responses were recorded *verbatim*.

An index was developed to assess the relative similarity of the candidates—as seen by the electorate as a whole or by any significant subgroup. Since this study was primarily concerned with predicting patterns of competition in the aggregate, no attempt was made to examine the similarity structure of individual *R*s. The binary similarity judgments (similar, not-similar) of the *R*s were aggregated to yield similarity matrices for Democratic voters ($N = 27$), Republican voters ($N = 23$), the odd-numbered *R*s ($N = 33$), the even-numbered *R*s ($N = 32$), in addition to the matrix for all *R*s ($N = 65$). The frequency with which each candidate was judged to be similar to any other candidate is shown for all *R*s in Appendix 1.

To normalize these raw scores in terms of the familiarity of the candidates, an index of object similarity in a population was used (Stefflre, ms.). The index can be expressed as

$$s_{ij} = \frac{f_{ij} + f_{ji}}{f_{i.} + f_{j.} + f_{.i} + f_{.j}} \tag{1}$$

where s_{ij} is the relative similarity of a pair of candidates, f_{ij} is the frequency with which candidate i is judged to be similar to candidate j, f_{ji} is the frequency with which candidate j is judged to be similar to candidate $f_{i.}$ is the total frequency candidate i was judged to be similar to any other candidate, $f_{.i}$ is the total frequency any other candidate was judged to be similar to candidate i, and in identical fashion $f_{j.}$ and $f_{.j}$ are defined for candidate j. This expression yields a number which theoretically ranges between 0 and .5 to indicate relative similarity. The normalized similarity indices for all respondents are shown in Appendix 2.

The index was developed to force the following conditions. First, the similarity of a candidate pair is proportional to the total number of judgments made about either candidate. Since more familiar candidates are more similar than less familiar candidates to any other candidate simply because they are mentioned more frequently, in order to compare candidate pairs in terms of relative similarity, similarity must be made independent of familiarity. Thus, assuming that familiarity is directly related to the frequency with which a candidate is mentioned, the relative similarity of a candidate pair was divided by the sum of those candidates' marginals. To the extent that samplings of candidates and voters are representative of their respective domains, this is not an unreasonable assumption. Second, the similarity of candidate pairs is symmetrical (i.e., $s_{ij} = s_{ji}$). Symmetry is necessary if the index is to be considered a proximity measure. Correlations of .950 to .980 have been found between this measure and the raw similarity scores on ten different data sets (Stefflre, ms.).

The features voters ascribed to each of the candidates were used to interpret the patterns in the similarity and substitution structures. A list was compiled of all the comments made about each candidate when he was paired with the others in the similarity task. For example, Eisenhower was often paired with General Westmoreland because they were both seen as "patriotic Americans" and as "generals." These features then appear on the description lists of both Eisenhower and Westmoreland. Table 4 shows an example of George Wallace's characteristics as seen by Republican voters, while Table 5 shows examples of Robert Kennedy's characteristics as seen by Democratic voters. These description lists were then content-analyzed to determine (a) the general classes of features that were ascribed to each candidate, and (b) the frequency with which each candidate was described by comments in each of the feature classes. The features which determine positioning *vis-a-vis* the other candidates in the substitution structure were then inferred from the features shared by other candidates who positioned similarly in the judged similarity MDS configuration. Due to the supplemental nature and the excessive length of the content analysis it cannot be presented here. For further details see Mauser (1970).

Measuring Candidate Preference Patterns

To measure the relative preference for each of the potential candidates, 203 *R*s in a second sample were asked to rank-order the lists of names and hypothetical candidates (i.e., descriptions) on the basis of "How likely you would be to vote for______if he were a candidate for President." First, *R*s ranked from 1 to 25 the list of names and then the list of descriptions. Tables 1 and 2 show the list of 25 names and 25 descriptions used for all *R*s in the SSPS. The list was presented in reverse order to half the sample. To help the *R* rank these lists, he was given a set of alphabetically arranged cards, with one name on each. The *R* was instructed to first rank the 5 cards on top of the deck, and then to insert each of the remaining 20 cards in the preferred order for President with respect to those cards already ordered. *R*s were asked not to omit any candidates. This step provided

TABLE 4

CHARACTERISTICS OF GEORGE WALLACE MENTIONED BY REPUBLICAN VOTERS IN JUDGED SIMILARITY SAMPLE (JSS) SEPTEMBER, 1968

Carmichael	Wallace is an intelligent radical, Carmichael is a basic radical. Intelligent—radical—gilds the lily basic radical—stands with might, like going to "switch you."
	Extremists—polarized—want to use violent means to achieve an end or change something they don't like.
	Both are racists. Neither one tries to see any good in opinions other than their own.
	Both want to take all our freedom starting a little at a time. Both are too extreme in the measures they are trying for.
	Trying to wreck the country—Carmichael thru the Blacks—Wallace thru the Whites.
Goldwater	Straighten things out instead of fooling around. Believe in strong armed riot control. Both believe in upholding the police and cut out a lot of this foreign spending.
Humphrey	Both running for President. Both losing.
King	Both want to rule, take a little freedom away and slowly work to take it all. Both are two-faced as can be.
	King was for the Blacks and stirred them up. Wallace stirs up Whites.
McCarthy	Strongly opinionated about platforms. Wallace is going to save South for Whites by not putting up with civil rights movements. McCarthy is unyielding, like when he lost to Nixon, like Wallace is going to lose to Nixon.
Nixon	Running for President. Dislike Humphrey.
	They don't have the showmanship. In person they give out a warmth, but on TV, they just don't have it. They have loyal supporters in groups of people who know them personally, but on TV, they don't come across.
	Republicans. Running for President. Stronger domestic law enforcement.
Rafferty	Excel in their ability to confound masses of middle class voters. Emotions and distortions of fact seem to be the vanguard of their attacks on other opinion.
	Does the same things as Rafferty in an unsophisticated way. He thinks he is right. Wallace does not have the worldliness to lead the country. The way he handled his state would indicate he could not gain respect of world for any higher office, being so dictatorial—but not sophisticated.
Rockefeller	Running for President.
Schmitz	In that they represent some of the narrowest and dangerously conservative thinking of any politicians in the U.S. today. Both have immediate and oversimplified solutions to grave problems of today.
Unruh	Both are power-hungry for political office.
	They take opposite sides in their political opinions, they take opposite sides of a situation.
Warren	Both are men that will say what they think regardless of whether they'll be popular or not, they'll still do what they want to do.
Yorty	Against some of this integration. Believe in a little bit more law and order. At least they'll come out and say it whether they're popular or not.
	Both believe in enforcing law and order.
Ideal	(If he lives up to what he says, and I believe he would) to get back law and order in this country to where it should be, so you can walk down the streets safely anytime.

TABLE 5

Characteristics of Robert Kennedy Mentioned by Democratic Voters in Judged Similarity Sample (JSS) September, 1968

Brown	RFK being young had the potential to become a Pat Brown in terms of his accomplishments—help unify the country like Brown did for California. RFK was starting and Brown was the end: young and old.
John Kennedy	They are from the same family. Have the same family feeling. Care for children. Bring up kinds broadly. Dynastic idea.
	Brothers, Catholics, Democrats.
	Idealistic, charismatic quality. Leadership.
	Had a real interest in helping their country. At least if they were competitive, they had something to give to their country.
	Brothers, popular, charismatic; good politicians; know how to work with and manipulate people; progressive urban concerned Democrats; liberal and peace loving.
	Dedicated public servants. Sacrificed their talents and capabilities for the improvement overall of the country.
	Peace in Vietnam. Equality for all races.
King	Crusaders, had a great deal of potential that was never tapped; both were willing to take a chance against public feeling or pressures.
	Leadership quality. Care about people.
	Both men of peace. Peaceful solutions to Negro problem.
	Workers. Go beyond the system (beyond the framework) right to the people, to the problem.
Lindsay	They've so many abilities, but more than that, it comes out and hits you. Charisma.
McCarthy	Believe in idea of peace in Vietnam.
Rockefeller	Looking for a new liberalism in their parties. Out for discovering new and better ways of doing things.
	Use personality (theirs) well. They exploit it. Advertising image. Opportunistic.
	Have a female reaction—give me the impression of being able to influence the female population. Both men of wealth.
Spock	Both say what they believe in gut level—whether it's popular or not.
Stevenson	Idealistic. They have up-dated New Deal Liberalism by expanding foreign policy with more of an international concept of coexistence.
	Both had greatness—statesmanship. Don't just think of the country, but for the people, the individuals. They had love.
Unruh	Both peace advocates and try to further their political well-being.
	Worked together in RFK's campaign—try hard at being politicians; sometimes have a ruthless image—willing to compromise for party expediency and personal gain; progressively liberal Democrats.
	Unruh announced JFK for President. Both liberal, both against war in Vietnam. For equality for all.
	Organizationalists—believe in planning everything.
Warren	Humanitarian interest—give equal opportunity to all people.
	Criticized for divergent views from mainstream of American thought.
	Controversy—always in the eye of the public, so they just retreated.

TABLE 5 (Continued)

Warren	Liberal views. Fair, sincere. Against discrimination. For equality for all.
	Secure, fair, unbiased, sincere.
	Realization of legal rights of minorities. Far-sighted—can see where things will lead.
Yorty	Disliked by large segments. Pragmatists.
Ideal	Because like his his brother John, took stance on issues. Had convictions. Tried to get at causes behind riots, give Negroes some self-respect, don't just put them on welfare.
	He seems to have had real empathy for people who were down-trodden today. He really seemed to care.
	Capable of achieving idealistic ends with practical means. Far-sighted.

estimates of the relative preferences within each of the two lists of possible candidates. Finally, *R*s were presented with all possible (25 × 25) name-description pairs and asked to indicate which of the candidates in each pair they would prefer to vote for. Again, they were asked not to omit any.

*R*s were dropped from the study if they omitted more than 2% of the total name-description pair choices or more than two of the candidates in either of the ranking tasks. In this way, 10 *R*s were dropped, leaving 193 who successfully completed the interview.

For each individual *R*, candidates (i.e., both names and descriptions) were assigned a score in terms of their rank within their own class and the frequency with which they were chosen in preference to a candidate of the other class. This score allowed preference rankings for candidates to be calculated for each individual *R*—across all candidates (rankings from 1 to 50) and within lists of names or descriptions (rankings from 1 to 25). In case of ties, that candidate who was either ranked higher than or chosen in preference to the other candidate was assigned the higher rank.

A measure of the extent to which candidates are ranked similarly across *R*s was constructed to test the original proposition that candidates judged to be similar are (a) preferred by the same people and (b) substitute for each other in a single choice situation. Considering that candidates with high variability will draw more votes in an election than will candidates with low variability (Thurstone, 1959, Ch. 13), an index of the relative substitutability of candidate pairs in a single choice situation can be constructed by setting the covariance of the preference for the candidates proportional to their joint variability. The Pearson correlation coefficient satisfactorily meets this criterion.

The preference rankings were then intercorrelated across *R*s to provide a measure of the pattern of preferences across voters ("preference correlations"). To provide indices of candidate pattern of preference for the electorate as a whole and for significant subgroups, separate preference correlation matrices were constructed for the Democrats ($N = 81$), the Republicans ($N = 79$), the Independents ($N = 33$), the odd-numbered *R*s ($N = 97$), the even-numbered *R*s ($N = 96$), in addition to the matrix for all *R*s together ($N = 193$). To indicate which names or descriptions would substitute for each other, the rankings *within* each class of candidates (i.e., the 1 to 25 rankings) were intercorrelated. All preference correlations used in this paper involving both names and descriptions are based upon these "within" rankings. In order to consider these correlations as proximity data, they had to be standardized by adding one to each correlation, forcing the index to range between 0 and 2. The standardized preference correlations are shown in Appendix 3 for all *R*s.

Reliability of the Measures

Before further analysis of the similarity or pattern of preference structures is possible, the stability of these measures must first be tested. To do this, the samples were split into subsamples, the similarity and pattern of preference measures calculated separately for each, and the subsamples intercorrelated. These subsamples were formed by placing *R*s in each of the samples in one of two subgroups ("odd" or "even") on the basis of an arbitrary assignment of numbers from 1 to N (the number of *R*s). In addition *R*s were also classified on the basis of party affiliation: Democratic, Republican, or Independent. (A voter was assigned to the Independent category if he did not specify a party of if he specified some party other than Democratic or Republican).

If there is widespread agreement about which candidates are judged to be similar to each other, or have similar patterns of preference correlations within a population, then random samples drawn from the population should differ from one another only by sampling error. The odd/even correlations in Table 6 show that a moderately strong and reliable correlation exists across all voters about patterns of candidate similarity and preference (all correlations are significantly different than zero at the $p < .001$ level using the critical-ratio z-test).[1] Not only are all odd/even correlations significantly different from zero, but with only one exception, they can account for at least half of the variance. At the same time, the stronger hypothesis that the subgroups are random samples from the same

[1] All tests of significance were drawn from Hays (1963).

TABLE 6

SPEARMAN RHO SAMPLE STABILITY CORRELATIONS FOR THE JUDGED SIMILARITY ($N = 65$) AND THE SMALL SCALE PREFERENCE ($N = 193$) SAMPLES

Judged similarity:	Odd/Even	Demo/Repub	Demo/Indep	Repub/Indep
All names of candidates plus "ideal" ($k = 26$)	0.707	0.648	0.640	0.552
Preference correlation:	**Odd/Even**	**Demo/Repub**	**Demo/Indep**	**Repub/Indep**
Names of candidates only ($k = 25$)	0.894	0.419	0.024	−0.022
Candidate descriptions only ($k = 25$)	0.868	0.716	0.678	0.657
Candidate names and descriptions ($k = 50$)	0.494	0.328	0.298	0.276

population can be rejected at the $p < .001$ level for all subgroups using the Wilcoxon test for matched groups. While there is little agreement ($r = .494$, $r^2 = .24$) about which descriptions have the same preference patterns as which names; in general, there is moderate support for the stability of the measures of judged similarity and preference pattern.

As expected, there is less agreement across party lines than between the odd/even samples. With only two exceptions out of twelve, however, all correlations between parties are significantly different than zero at the $p < .001$ level using the critical-ratio z-test. The lack of agreement is particularly striking in the preference patterns of known candidates with one another. While there is considerable agreement ($r = .894$, $r^2 = .80$) between the odd/even samples about the patterns of candidate preference, there is much less agreement, but still significant ($r = .419$, $r^2 = .16$) between Democrats and Republicans, and no agreement whatsoever between members of either of the major parties and the Independents ($r_{DI} = .024$, $r^2_{DI} = .004$; $r_{RI} = -.022$, $r^2_{RI} = .004$). Given the wide diversity of voters in this third category and their small number, such a low correlation does not seem surprising. The relatively low agreement between members of the two major parties about patterns of preference suggests that there might be two distinct subgroups within the electorate with distinctly different notions about which candidates substitute for each other. If this is true, generalizations based upon the model for the entire electorate would not be applicable to subgroups of voters.

To explore the possibility of distinct subgroups in the electorate, the *R*s rather than the candidates were scaled in a manner analogous to inverse factor analysis. A random sample of 45 *R*s was drawn from the preference sample. The preference rankings for the 25 candidate names were intercorrelated across candidates for each voter, yielding a 45 × 45 correlation matrix. A correlation indicates how similar are one voter's rankings to another's. These correlations were then used as input for MDS analysis. Figure 1 shows the two-dimensional plot of the resulting configuration.

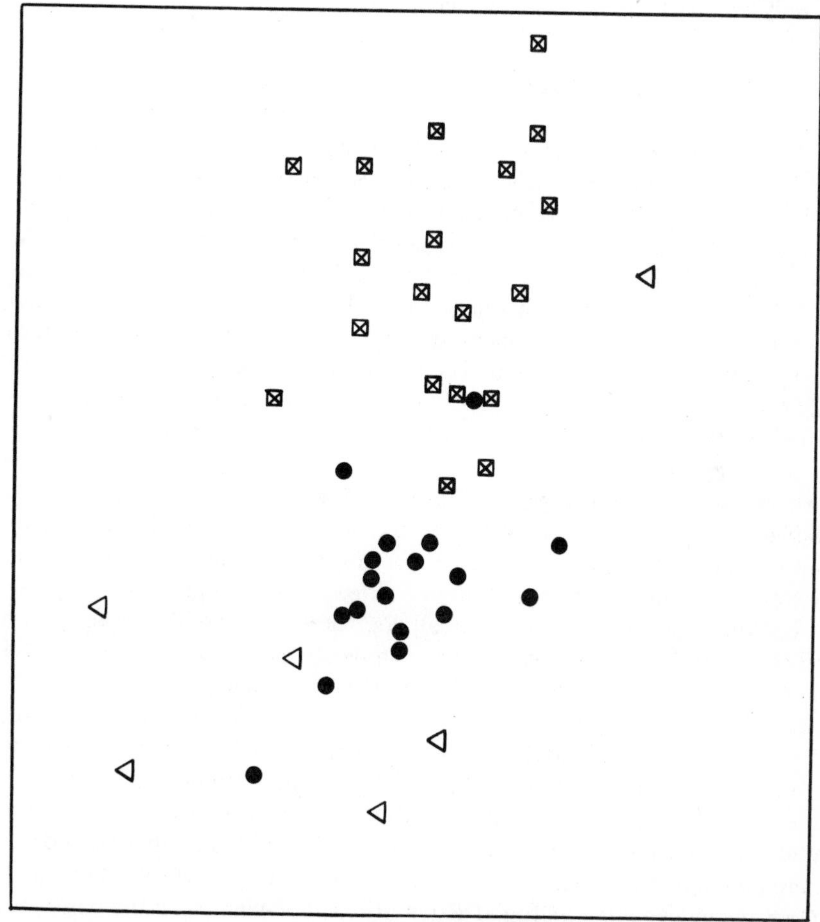

FIG. 1. Two-dimensional plot of the inverse M-D-SCAL for voter × voter preference correlations (stress = .132). Solid circles are Democratic voters, crossed squares are Republican voters, and open triangles are Independent voters.

The stress for this configuration is .132, which is very low for 45 points (considerably less than that expected for random data). Inspecting the plot shows quite clearly that two clusters of voters can be distinguished. Of the possible voter characteristics, only party affiliation allows a simple partitioning of the voters into the two observable clusters. All Democrats (except for two) are on the left, and all Republicans (except for two) are on the right, with the Independents scattered around the periphery of both clusters. This plot suggests that different models may be needed to represent the patterns of candidate substitution in elections limited to members of only one party (e.g., primary elections).

Interrelating Similarity and Pattern of Preference

To be able to predict the substitution pattern for any new candidate with specified features, an interlocking series of relationships must be substantiated. First, a strong relation between the indices of candidate similarity and pattern of preference must be demonstrated, and next, the capability of these indices to predict the substitution patterns in the election must be verified. In this section, the first of these questions, that of the strength of the relationship between judged similarity and pattern of preference, is examined. Further questions are deferred until after the MDS analysis when it will be possible to examine the entire series of questions in more depth.

One way to approach the first question is to simply intercorrelate the two measures. This can be done because the feature of interest in both indices is their relative magnitude, and the indices have been suitably normalized. Table 7 shows the results of intercorrelating the similarity and pattern of preference matrices for the three classes of *R*s.

Looking first at the results for all *R*s, there is a significant and quite reliable correlation between relative similarity and candidate pattern of preferences. (The correlations with M.E.V. less than 7 are significantly different from zero, with $p < .001$, using a two-tailed t-test). Moreover, there is a dramatic and progressive increase in this correlation as the unfamiliar candidates are eliminated. The few judgments which are made about the little-known candidates only serve to introduce noise into the analysis and thereby attenuate the true correlation. Unfamiliar candidates were eliminated by setting a minimum value for expected cell frequencies assuming independent marginal distributions. For example, if the minimum expected value (M.E.V.) is set at the mean cell frequency (i.e., at four comparisons for all voters), all of the comparisons for Schmitz and Yorty are eliminated, as are many of the cells for Carmichael, Dirksen, and a few

TABLE 7

SPEARMAN RANK ORDER CORRELATION COEFFICIENTS BETWEEN JUDGED SIMILARITY AND INTERCORRELATED PREFERENCE RANKINGS OF 25 NAMES OF HYPOTHETICAL PRESIDENTIAL CANDIDATES[a]

Respondents	Minimum expected values for cell frequencies								
	0	1	2	3	4	5	6	7	8
All voters	.534 (300)	[b]	[b]	[b]	.635 (201)	.718 (117)	.758 (60)	.846 (25)	.800 (4)
Democratic voters	−.028 (300)	−.030 (266)	−.016 (145)	−.416 (21)					
Republican voters	−.014 (300)	−.027 (253)	−.017 (106)						

[a] The number of cells with expected values higher than the indicated minimum expected value, which were used in each correlation, is in parentheses.
[b] Not calculated.

others. The correlation continues to increase until it reaches its upper limit (when the minimum expected value is seven), leaving only the most well-known candidates to be compared (e.g., Goldwater, John Kennedy, King, and Reagan).

In striking contrast to the results for all respondents, the correlation between similarity and pattern of preference collapses to zero when *R*s are divided by political party. When a relationship between two variables disappears with the introduction of a third variable, classic sociological analysis holds that the third variable is responsible for the original relationship (Rosenberg, 1968, Ch. 2). This implies that the *R*'s party affiliation is the major determinant of the relationship between similarity and pattern of preference. If this is so, Democratic and Republican candidates should form partisan clusters only when all *R*s are pooled and should not do so within parties. An examination of the MDS configurations supports this conjecture. For all *R*s together there are distinct clusterings of candidates by party in both similarity and in pattern of preference structures; this clustering is particularly polarized in the pattern of preference structure. For *R*s of the same party affiliation, partisan clusters can be seen only in the similarity structures, but not in the pattern of preference structures.

Multidimensional Scaling Structures

The features which determine placement in the underlying substitution structure must be discovered in order to be able to make predictions about how any new candidate will be behaved towards in an election. The MDS configurations allow hypotheses to be generated about which features are important in substitution. Preliminary hypotheses about the nature of substitution were made from both the patterns of candidate similarity and the knowledge about which features the candidates shared and tested against the patterns of preference configuration. New hypotheses were then made about what features could lead candidate preferences to distribute as they do. Then these were tested against the similarity configuration and description lists. After a few such cycles, final hypotheses were then made about the nature of substitution in the Presidential election and about how certain new candidates would be behaved towards.

All MDS configurations referred to in this study were constructed using Kruskal's iterative program M-D-SCAL (Kruskal, version 3, May 1967) which has been modified for use on the IBM 1130.[2] Since the indices of perceived similarity and pattern of preference are proximity data, they were used as input to the MDS and clustering routines. The following M-D-SCAL parameters were used throughout this paper: the secondary approach to ties, stress form 1, and the Euclidean metric. All configurations were generated by starting at a maximum number of dimensions of five or six and proceeding, in decrements of one, to a usual minimum of two dimensions.

To be able to use MDS techniques, the researcher must decide which dimensionality is the most suitable for display. Shepard (this book, Volume II) argues that it is rarely justifiable to use more than three dimensions, for the clarity and simplicity inherent in such "natural" models far outweigh the added explanatory power gained by increased dimensionality. The following criteria were used to select the most suitable dimensionality within the natural models: (a) minimizing the dimensionality necessary to obtain a suitable goodness of fit, (b) maximizing the interpretability of the resulting configuration, and (c) testing the goodness of fit with that expected for random data. First, the stress-dimensionality curves were inspected for an "elbow" (i.e., a point beyond which any further increase in dimensionality yields little decrease in stress). No elbow was found which could distinguish between the two possible dimensionalities. Next, the configurations were examined to see which were more interpretable. In general, the

[2] Most of the programs used in this paper were either written or modified by David Napior for the IBM 1130.

TABLE 8

COMPARISON OF STRESSES FOR OBSERVED CONFIGURATIONS WITH EXPECTED VALUES OF STRESSES FOR MONTE CARLO CONFIGURATONS

	Measures			
	Judged similarity ($k = 26$) No. of dimensions		Pattern of preference ($k = 50$) No. of dimensions	
Samples	3	2	3	2
Expected values for Monte Carlo data, $E(S)$	.228	.323	.280	.374
Confidence limit (E(S) − .030)	.198	.293	.250	.344
All voters	.183	.295[a]	.113	.160
Democrats	.176	.249	.234	.329
Republicans	.192	.290	.230	.329
Independents	.204[a]	.277	—	—
Even-numbered *R*s	.188	.283	—	—

[a] Stress not significantly different than random data.

three-dimensional configurations appeared more reasonable than the two-dimensional configurations. Finally, the stresses of the configurations were compared with those expected from random data.

To determine if the stresses were significantly different than those for random data, Monte Carlo techniques were used to estimate the expected values for a random permutation of rankings following Stenson and Knoll (1969). Their procedures were replicated for sets of 26 points. The stresses for the observed configurations were compared with the estimates for corresponding random permutations (see Table 8). Adopting their "conservative rule" (Stenson & Knoll, 1969, p. 125) and using the largest range width for any sample distribution in my data (.015), only configurations more than twice this distance away from the expected value for the random distribution were considered significantly different than random data. Only one of the eight configurations in each dimensionality was not significantly different than random. Since the only aberrant three-dimensional configuration is that of the Independents (a small group with a very low interrespondent agreement), while the deviant configuration in two-dimensions is that of all respondents, the three-dimensional model describes the data more satisfactorily than the two-dimensional model.

The three-dimensional configurations were used throughout this paper to represent the similarity and pattern of preference structures. Figures 2 and 3 show the pictures of the three-dimensional configurations for all voters; the coordinates of these configurations are shown in Appendixes 4 and 5.

(a) Similarity structure. The circular or spherical shape of the similarity configuration is particularly striking. However, it is probably an artifact of the MDS procedure's overdependence upon the larger dis-

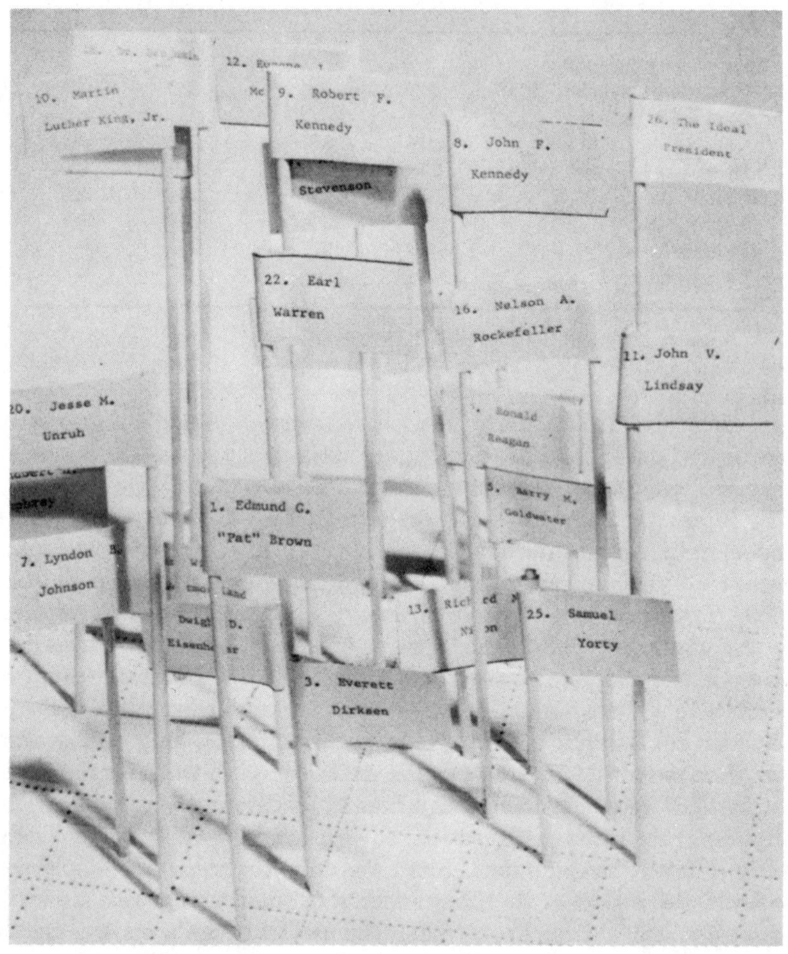

Fig. 2. Three-dimensional judged similarity configuration for all voters (N = 63 Rs; k = 26 candidates; stress = .183).

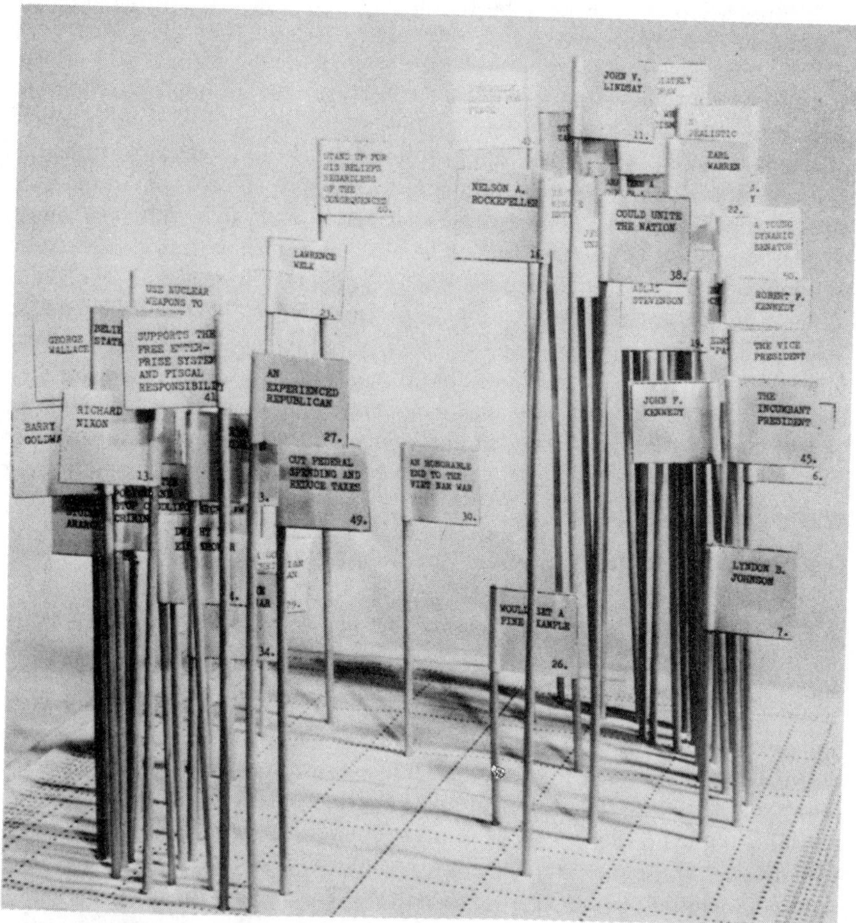

FIG. 3. Three-dimensional pattern of preference configuration for all voters ($N = 193$ Rs; $k = 50$ candidates; stress $= .113$).

similarities to determine the shape of the configuration and the relatively small proportion of very similar candidates in this domain.

Despite this artifact, the MDS configuration is readily interpretable. While it is possible to pass many explanatory dimensions through this structure, there appear to be two orthogonal dimensions which span the four major clusters and are the major determinants of the structure:

1. dimension one: from Johnson and Unruh to Goldwater, Reagan, and Rafferty;

2. dimension two: from Robert Kennedy and McCarthy to Eisenhower and Nixon.

Both dimensions extend between Democratic and Republican clusters. The first is primarily an ideological "left-right" or "liberal-conservative" dimension in the sense that opponents advocate different governmental policies on the basis of relatively coherent principles. The second dimension also involves a liberal-conservative distinction, but in a different sense, that of a posture towards change. The advocates of liberal reform (foreign or domestic) are arrayed against the defenders of the status quo. This dimension also seems to involve a young/old cleavage. The third dimension, extending from Carmichael and Spock to Lindsay and Yorty, is not very interpretable. The two interpretable dimensions consist of three ordered categories: the two extremes and a neutral middle category. Candidates within any of these categories do not appear to be ordered with respect to that dimension. This trichotomy may be attributable to any of the following possible causes:

1. the voters do not make any finer discriminations beyond this rough trichotomy;
2. finer discriminations are lost in the noisy data collection methods; or
3. finer discriminations are lost in compressing the data into the artificially spherical display.

Interpretation of the structure in terms of orthogonal dimensions ignores a considerable amount of potentially important information. An alternative approach is to search for interpretable clusters in the MDS configuration, without requiring the existence of polar clusters, and to consider the structure as a set of more or less mutually exclusive and exhaustive classes. This approach can be very fruitful, particularly if the clustering scheme is not reified, and instead is viewed as only one of many alternative ways to think of the underlying structure. In this respect it is important to remember that new candidates conceivably could position *between* existing clusters.

To locate such tightly knit clusters, the input similarities were used to check proximity in the MDS configuration. Since statistical error might place dissimilar candidates close to each other in the configuration, candidates were considered to be clustered if and only if they had a high degree of similarity to the other candidates they positioned close to in the configuration. This approach yields seven clusters in the similarity configuration:

1. Goldwater, Nixon, Rafferty, Reagan, (Wallace);
2. Eisenhower, Westmoreland, Welk;

3. Johnson, Humphrey, Brown, Unruh, Warren;
4. Dirksen, Yorty;
5. Rockefeller, Lindsay, the Ideal candidate, (John F. Kennedy);
6. Robert Kennedy, Stevenson, McCarthy, John F. Kennedy, (King);
7. Carmichael, Spock, King, Wallace.

(Schmitz is excluded from the clustering scheme because too few people knew who he was). The parentheses indicate a candidate's weaker membership in a second cluster.

To evaluate the adequacy of the dimensional assumptions for displaying the candidate similarities, Johnson's (1967) hierarchical clustering procedure was used to analyze the same input and was compared with the three-dimensional MDS configuration. If the order in which the candidates are clustered in the hierarchical clustering procedure is ignored, then the diameter method and the MDS configuration yield very similar clusterings. Furthermore, the clusterings in the similarity configurations for either the Democratic or Republican voters alone substantially agree with the one for all voters together. This agreement provides considerable support for validity of the three-dimensional configuration as a representation of the underlying structure.

To interpret these clusters, the important features of the candidates were inferred from the transcripts of their descriptions in the JSI.

The Goldwater cluster contains those candidates who are seen as willing to use armed force (police or military) to enforce authority. They are seen for example as wanting to "stop communist aggression in Vietnam," as "(believing) in . . . law and order" and as "disgusted with student sit-ins . . . would get rid of the riff-raff types." They are described as "conservative Republicans," "right-wingers," or as "very patriotic," and are seen as moralistic and frugal. While Wallace is described as "believing in the same things (as Reagan)," he is not seen as being in the same class of candidates as these because he is seen as "an extremist," "a racist," and therefore not supporting the proper authority.

The Eisenhower group is as patriotic as the Goldwater cluster and is seen as "military," but the Eisenhower cluster is also seen as "grandfatherly, sentimental," and as appealing to older people.

Dirksen and Yorty are seen as minor professional politicians and also as "misplaced actors."

The Rockefeller cluster is seen as nonpartisan, "idealistic," and humanitarian. Its members have the sophistication of "wealthy Easterners" and are "statesmen."

The Robert Kennedy cluster is composed of "liberal Democrats" who are seen as having a strong charismatic appeal—particularly to youth and to the ethnic minorities. While sharing the concern with domestic issues of the Johnson cluster, and the principles of the crusaders in the Carmichael cluster, the Kennedy group has in addition the sophistication of the Rockefeller cluster. There is an aura of tragedy about them for they are seen as the noble leaders of losing causes, particularly RFK and King.

The Johnson cluster is seen as the "old-fashioned liberals" and as "Democrats" who are primarily concerned with domestic issues such as "welfare" and "discrimination." They are also seen as "unattractive," "politicians," and as supporting the Vietnam war.

The Carmichael group is simultaneously seen as "just the opposite" of the Goldwater cluster and as sharing their most important characteristics. Except for Wallace, the Carmichael group is seen as "radical left-wingers" while the Goldwater cluster is "conservative." All of the candidates in the Carmichael cluster are described as "extremists" and as "causing riots by their public appearances." But because of their intense concern with the same issues, particularly those having to do with Negroes or with Vietnam, the two groups are seen as quite similar. Both groups are described as pro-violence and as "militant."

(b) THE PATTERN OF PREFERENCE STRUCTURE. If candidates judged to be similar are preferred by the same voters, then the basic underlying structure should be the same for both judged similarity and preference correlations. The same clusters should be observable in both MDS configurations and the same dimensions should span them. The relative importance of the features might differ due to the different roles that they play in similarity and substitution, causing clusters to be stretched or compressed, any other difference would indicate that some new factor—not present in the similarity structure—was operating in the preference pattern structure.

Figure 3 shows the three-dimensional configuration of the preference patterns for all voters. The coordinates are given in Appendix 5. In striking contrast to the spherical nature of the similarity configuration, the pattern of preference structure is polarized between two long clusters with very few candidates in between. At one extreme there are the opponents of the Vietnam war, the civil rights activists, the advocates of liberal reform, and all of the Democrats except Wallace and Yorty. Some of the descriptions which cluster at this pole are "A candidate who wants the U.S. to immediately withdraw from Vietnam," "A candidate who wants to end white racism in the U.S.," and "A candidate who wants to eliminate poverty and slums in the U.S." At the other end there are the advocates of escalating the war, the fiscal conservatives, the supporters of stricter "law and order" police policies, and almost all of the Republicans except Rockefeller and Lindsay. Some of the descriptions which cluster about this pole are "A President who can win the Vietnam war," "A President who would cut federal spending and reduce taxes," and "A candidate who will enforce law and order in our cities." There are only a few candidates who do not polarize; e.g., Rockefeller, Lawrence Welk, "A President who could be proud of and who would set a fine example," and "A President who could unite the nation and heal our troubled cities." The candidates in this central or neutral area are not particularly highly preferred. They range in popularity from Lawrence Welk, who has an average rank close to twenty-fourth, to "A candidate who could unite the nation. . . ," who has one of the highest average ranks. Candidates position in the central region because they elicit general agreement about their preference—at whatever level of popularity.

The axis of polarization is a "left-right" or "liberal-conservative" dimension, in terms of both domestic and foreign policy questions, and in terms of attitudes towards social change, coupled with a Democratic–Republican split. As expected, the Democratic candidates were seen as more liberal than the Republicans and preferred by Democratic voters; while the Republicans were seen as more conservative and preferred by Republican voters. This axis appears to be identical to a collapsed form of the two primary dimensions in the similarity configuration.

A second dimension, orthogonal to the first, extends from Carmichael to Johnson, within the Democratic cluster, and from Wallace to Dirksen, within the Republican cluster. This dimension appears to be between the same kinds of descriptions in both clusters, that is between the audacious, militant critics of the federal government to the cautious, more diplomatic national leaders. While this dimension can be easily seen in the similarity structure, it did not emerge as a third dimension orthogonal to the first two dimensions in the similarity configuration.

The polarization of the pattern of preferences is primarily due to the intense polarization of partisan feeling just prior to a national election. Candidate similarity is much more stable and resistant in this respect.

By embedding the clusters that were developed for the similarity structures into the pattern of preference configuration, it is easy to see that the clustering scheme remains intact. Welk and Yorty are the only candidates who are not tightly grouped with their original clusters. Except for a distortion in the direction of the audacity dimension, the clusters are almost identical in both similarity and in pattern of preference.

Predicting Patterns of Electoral Substitution

In order to test hypotheses about patterns of electoral substitution for any new candidate with specified features, the third and last sample was drawn the week before the election. Since it is impossible to directly measure electoral substitution (only the voters' first choices are officially recorded in an election), this sample is the only available approximation of the actual situation. While the first two samples were used to develop preliminary hypotheses and, thus, could be small and only loosely representative, the last sample had to be relatively large and truly representative of the target population to be able to test the preliminary hypotheses and to generalize these results to the target population. Fifteen-hundred voters were drawn from California and asked to rank order eight candidates for President. (The selection procedures are described in an earlier section of this paper). *R*s were asked to rank the eight candidates on the basis of "How likely you would be to vote for______if he were a candidate for President." Interviews were conducted over the telephone. Since it is very difficult to reliably rank more than four items over the telephone, the eight candidates were presented in six sets of four candidates each. All candidates were presented to each respondent. A balanced lattice design was used to present all possible permutations within these four sets and selections of sets of size four to the sample. The candidates included in this interview are shown in Table 3. After *R*s ranked the candidates, they were asked a few questions about their political and socioeconomic background.

The rankings were used to estimate the proportion of the vote each candidate would get in an election between subsets of the candidates. The frequency with which a candidate is ranked higher than the others in the selected contest was used to estimate the frequency with which he would be voted for in an actual election. Thus, it is possible to simulate the outcome of any election—actual or hypothetical—between any subset of the candidates.

Table 9 shows the predicted and observed outcomes of the California popular vote for the three major candidates in the 1968 Presidential election. The LSPS is remarkably close to the actual election results and it is even closer to the division of the two-candidate contest.

The extent to which candidate A will substitute for candidate B can be defined as the extent to which candidate A draws votes from candidate B in a single choice situation. This is a relatively crude measure but it enables the central hypothesis to be tested for the Humphrey–Nixon contest. Consider this pair of candidates as the kernel of a series of three-person electoral contests. Inserting each of the possible "new" candidates into this

TABLE 9

PREDICTING THE CALIFORNIA POPULAR VOTE FOR ALL THREE MAJOR CANDIDATES IN THE 1968 PRESIDENTIAL ELECTION

	Small scale preference sample (SSPS)		
Humphrey	Nixon	Wallace	Total
90 (0.466)	89 (0.461)	14 (0.073)	193 (1.000)
	Large scale preference sample (LSPS)		
Humphrey	Nixon	Wallace	Total
519 (0.447)	549 (0.473)	93 0.080)	1161 (1.000)
	Official election results[a]		
Humphrey	Nixon	Wallace	Total
3,244,318 (0.451)	3,467,664 (0.482)	487,270 (0.068)	7,199,232 (1.001)

[a] As reported in the *Statement of Vote,* Office of the Secretary of State, December 1968.

kernel one at a time produces as many three-person contests as there are new candidates. Since the outcomes of these hypothetical contests can be simulated, it is easy to calculate the proportion of the vote lost by each of the candidates in the original kernel to each of the new candidates.

The difference between the proportions that each of the old candidates lose to a new candidate is a simple measure of the relative substitutability of the new candidate in the three-candidate situation. To be able to test the hypothesis that similar candidates substitute in the Humphrey–Nixon contest, parallel measures of differential similarity and differential preference correlation were developed by taking the difference of the new candidate's similarity or preference correlation with each of the original candidates. For example, George Wallace is judged to be more similar to Nixon than to Humphrey (0.019 − 0.034 = −0.015), and his rankings are more correlated with Nixon's than with Humphrey's (0.661 − 1.161 = −0.500). Hence, Wallace should draw proportionately more from Nixon than from Humphrey, which is exactly what happened (6 − 8% = −2%). This is shown in Table 10.

TABLE 10

1968 PRESIDENTIAL ELECTION IN CALIFORNIA: SIMULATED USING THE LARGE SCALE PREFERENCE SAMPLE

No. of times ranked second	No. of times ranked first			
	Nixon	Humphrey	Wallace	Row Totals
Nixon	—	438	54	492
Humphrey	407	—	39	446
Wallace	142	81	—	223
Column totals	549	519	93	1161
Column percentage	47.3%	44.7%	8.0%	
Original Totals (two-person contest)	603	558		
Percentage loss	8%	6%		

TABLE 11

PREDICTING SUBSTITUTION PATTERNS OF HYPOTHETICAL THIRD CANDIDATES IN THE HUMPHREY–NIXON KERNEL CONTEST FROM SIMILARITY INDICES

Hypothetical third candidate	Similarity indices		
	Differential similarity (JSS)	Differential preference correlation (SSPS)	Differential substitutability (LSPS)
Lyndon Johnson	+.149[c]	+.980	+27%
Nelson Rockefeller	−.004	−.001	+15%
George Wallace	−.150	−.500	−2%
Robert Kennedy	+.010	+.083	+41%
Riots[a]	[d]	+.017	+2%
War[b]	[d]	−.061	+9%

[a] Hypothetical candidate described as "not (being) afraid to stop Negro rioters and student anarchists."

[b] Hypothetical candidate described as "(wanting) an honorable end to the Vietnam war."

[c] Positive scores indicate that the third candidate is more similar to (or substitutes more for) Humphrey than Nixon, while negative scores indicate greater similarity to (or substitutability for) Nixon than Humphrey.

[d] No descriptions were included in the judged similarity interviews.

It is now possible to test the entire chain of interrelationships between the measures of similarity and substitution: (a) candidates judged to be similar should substitute for each other, and should be preferred by the same voters more than less similar candidates, and (b) candidates whose patterns of preference are similar should substitute more for each other than candidates whose patterns of preference are less similar. Table 11 shows the differential similarity, differential preference correlation, and differential substitutability of each of the six possible third candidates in the Humphrey–Nixon contest that were included in the LSPS. Differential similarity predicts the rank of the differential preference correlations perfectly ($\rho = 1.000$), and is a fairly good predictor of the order of the differential substitutability ($\rho = .800$). Differential preference correlation has a moderate relationship with differential substitution ($\rho = .657$). If all of the candidates in the SSPS are considered, there is a correlation of $\rho = .830$ ($t = 6.811$; r = 23; $p < .001$) between the differential relative similarity and the differential preference correlations in the Humphrey–Nixon contest. While this hardly constitutes conclusive proof, given the size of the candidate sample, the data definitely support the central hypothesis that similar candidates substitute for each other in an election situation.

It is interesting to speculate about conceivable elections rather than the one which actually occurred. Using the candidate rankings to estimate the proportion of vote in hypothetical elections, a few such speculative contests are shown in Tables 12 through 15. Contrary to what some reputable political observers predicted, Nixon would have beaten Humphrey by an even larger margin had Wallace not been in the contest. To put this a little differently, if Wallace could have drawn even more votes than he actually did, say as much as 30% of the total vote in California, he would have

TABLE 12

"Nixon–Humphrey" Contest in California: Simulated Using Large Scale Preference Sample

No. of times ranked second	No. of times ranked first		
	Nixon	Humphrey	Row Totals
Nixon	—	558	558
Humphrey	603	—	603
Column totals	603	558	1161
Column percentages	51.9%	48.1%	

TABLE 13

"NIXON–HUMPHREY–RIOTS"[a] CONTEST IN CALIFORNIA: SIMULATED USING THE LARGE SCALE PREFERENCE SAMPLE

No. of times ranked second	No. of times ranked first			
	Nixon	Humphrey	Riots	Row totals
Nixon	—	185	160	345
Humphrey	122	—	159	281
Riots[a]	321		—	535
Column totals	443	399	319	1161
Column percentages	38.1%	34.4%	27.5%	
Original totals (two-person contest)	603	558		
Percentage loss	26%	28%		

[a] "Riots" is a hypothetical third candidate who is described as "a President who wouldn't be afraid to stop Negro rioters and student anarchists."

swung the state to Humphrey given the same draw ratio. It is also interesting to consider what would have happened if the major parties had nominated different candidates. If Johnson had not withdrawn from the contest, and had attempted to win another term as President, he would have fared even worse than Humphrey against Nixon. The best candidate that the Democrats could have nominated—against any Republican—would have been "somebody like Robert Kennedy."

TABLE 14

"NIXON–RFK–WALLACE" CONTEST IN CALIFORNIA: SIMULATED USING THE LARGE SCALE PREFERENCE SAMPLE

No. of times ranked second	No. of times ranked first			
	Nixon	RFK	Wallace	Row totals
Nixon	—	533	41	574
RFK	358	—	38	396
Wallace	96	95	—	191
Column totals	454	628	79	1161
Column percentages	39.1%	54.1%	6.8%	
Original totals (two-person contest)	495	666		
Percentage loss	8%	5%		

TABLE 15

"NIXON–LBJ–WALLACE" CONTEST IN CALIFORNIA: SIMULATED USING LARGE SCALE PREFERENCE SAMPLE

No. of times ranked second	No. of times ranked first			
	Nixon	LBJ	Wallace	Row Totals
Nixon	—	425	56	481
LBJ	435	—	38	473
Wallace	127	80	—	207
Column totals	562	505	94	1161
Column percentages	48.4%	43.5%	8.1%	
Original totals (two-person contest)	618	543		
Percentage loss	9%	6%		

The accuracy of the predictions made from the preference samples can be evaluated by comparing them with the election results. Table 16 shows the mean absolute differences and the square root of the mean squared deviations of the predicted from the observed proportions for the three major candidates. Clearly, the LSPS can predict the actual election returns (note that the mean absolute deviation and the root mean square are both less than 1%). The vote for George Wallace deviates the most from the

TABLE 16

THE SUCCESS OF PREDICTING THE PROPORTION OF THE VOTE FOR EACH OF THE THREE MAJOR CANDIDATES IN THE PRESIDENTIAL ELECTION FOR EACH OF THE PREFERENCE SAMPLE ESTIMATES

Sample from which estimate was calculated	Source of criterion	Mean absolute difference	Root mean square of the difference
Large Scale Preference Sample (LSPS)	Official election results[a]	0.008	0.009
Small Scale Preference Sample (SSPS)	Official election results[a]	0.014	0.015
Small Scale Preference Sample (SSPS)	Large Scale Preference Sample (LSPS)	0.013	0.014

[a] As Reported in the *Statement of Vote, State of California, General Election, November 5, 1968.*

prediction. Fewer people voted for him than had said they would. Considering only the results of the two-candidate contest, the predictions even more closely approximate the official results.

This success compares quite favorably with similar predictions made by the major pollsters. In the 1968 election, only Gallup had a mean absolute deviation of less than 1% from the national Presidential popular vote (both Harris and Sindlinger had mean absolute deviations of 1.4%), and the best media sponsored poll of the California popular vote, the State Poll, had a mean absolute deviation of 3.7% (the data for these comparisons came from Crossley & Crossley, 1969).

Discussion

The objectives of this paper were to (a) describe the similarity and substitution structures underlying the 1968 Presidential election, (b) test the hypothesis that similar candidates substitute for each other, and (c) discover the features which determine placement in the underlying structure so as to be able to predict for any new candidate of specified features: (i) where he would place in the similarity and substitution structures, and (ii) his substitution pattern in the election.

Multidimensional scaling models were developed to describe the similarity and substitution structures in the election. The features which determine placement in this structure were inferred from the description lists generated in the Judged Similarity Interview and from the multidimensional scaling configurations. New candidates should position in the substitution structure close to old candidates with whom they are seen as sharing essential characteristics. While it is conceivable for a new candidate to differ from the old candidates so radically that he redefines the nature of the structure, it is very unlikely. It is much more likely that such a candidate would be seen and treated similarly to other "radicals," such as Carmichael or Wallace, or else ignored as was Pat Paulson.

The hypothesis that candidates seen as similar will substitute more for each other in an election than will candidates judged as less similar was supported. Support was found for the entire chain of necessary interrelations. First, within the broad domain of people relevant to the Presidential election, a strong and reliable correlation was found between judged similarity and patterns of candidate preference. Those candidates which clustered together in the similarity structure also clustered together in the pattern of preference structure, and two of the three major dimensions in the similarity configuration were also observed in the substitution configuration and determined most of the structure. Second, for the Humphrey–Nixon–Candidate X contest set, new candidates who were judged to be relatively more similar to or who had a more similar pattern of preference to one of the original candidates substituted more for (i.e., drew more votes from) that candidate than did less similar candidates.

APPENDIX 1

Observed Judged Similarity Frequencies for All Voters

		26	16	24	4	13	5	14	15	21	10	2	18	22	20	1	6	7	3	9	8	11	19	12	25	17	23
26	IDEAL	0	5	1	6	7	5	1	8	5	6	1	4	5	0	0	0	1	1	6	23	5	18	9	0	0	0
16	ROCKY	2	0	4	2	3	4	0	4	0	3	2	0	4	0	1	4	3	0	6	11	11	6	2	0	0	1
24	WESTY	0	2	0	34	2	11	4	7	6	1	1	1	0	0	0	2	14	0	1	0	1	0	0	1	2	1
4	IKE	0	2	25	0	18	7	4	6	3	2	0	1	6	0	3	3	9	8	1	9	2	2	0	0	0	9
13	NIXON	0	10	4	20	0	21	11	22	3	0	0	1	2	0	3	7	4	5	1	2	4	4	3	9	0	0
5	GOLD	2	3	7	7	14	0	25	31	18	0	2	1	1	0	2	2	3	4	1	3	1	3	4	4	3	2
14	RAFF	0	0	5	3	7	24	0	21	24	1	6	2	1	3	0	0	3	3	0	0	2	2	1	6	9	1
15	REAGAN	1	7	2	4	16	27	18	0	19	0	2	0	1	0	5	2	0	2	2	5	1	4	4	10	5	5
21	WALLACE	0	1	3	1	6	22	20	15	0	4	18	3	2	3	1	2	0	2	2	0	0	1	4	10	7	0
10	KING	1	0	0	0	0	0	2	0	4	0	18	23	4	1	2	5	8	1	22	17	4	5	6	1	0	2
2	CARML	0	0	0	0	0	6	10	1	23	28	0	22	1	1	1	0	0	0	2	0	0	1	1	0	0	0
18	SPOCK	0	1	3	1	0	2	4	0	3	28	23	0	3	1	1	1	1	0	7	3	1	5	12	0	1	2
22	WARREN	2	9	3	4	3	2	0	1	0	7	5	3	0	5	14	2	6	4	6	9	3	12	4	1	0	0
20	UNRUH	0	2	0	2	2	1	5	2	2	0	3	0	6	0	16	10	15	11	16	3	3	1	3	8	0	1
1	BROWN	0	4	0	4	4	0	1	2	2	0	2	1	17	14	0	26	13	4	4	2	1	6	2	7	0	3
6	HUMPH	0	7	1	2	14	0	0	0	3	3	1	1	3	7	17	0	21	4	5	6	2	13	11	1	0	5
7	LBJ	0	7	7	9	2	0	4	2	5	6	0	1	6	11	14	21	0	11	0	6	0	2	1	6	0	1
3	DIRK	0	2	2	9	8	7	3	3	0	0	0	0	2	8	4	9	6	0	2	2	4	5	1	6	0	4
9	RFK	0	8	0	1	1	1	2	2	3	21	5	4	7	13	1	0	1	2	0	30	5	8	11	4	0	0
8	JFK	0	10	0	7	2	2	3	3	0	13	0	1	8	4	6	1	4	0	29	0	14	20	5	1	0	1
11	LINDS	1	26	1	3	2	1	1	5	0	2	0	1	2	1	2	1	0	1	14	13	0	2	6	14	0	1
19	STEVENSN	1	7	0	4	2	5	2	1	3	4	0	7	10	2	3	9	2	8	8	18	8	0	17	0	0	0
12	MC CARTH	0	6	1	3	4	3	0	5	2	8	2	12	3	5	3	5	1	2	18	8	5	16	0	4	0	0
25	YORTY	0	3	1	1	5	6	14	14	11	1	0	0	1	6	8	0	6	3	4	0	15	1	3	0	4	2
17	SCHMITZ	0	0	1	0	1	4	7	3	5	0	0	1	0	1	0	0	0	0	0	0	0	0	0	0	0	1
23	WELK	0	0	3	8	2	0	3	16	0	1	2	4	0	1	1	3	1	5	0	1	3	4	2	5	1	0

APPENDIX 2

Normalized Judged Similarity Indices for All Voters

	BROWN	CARML	DIRK	IKE	GOLD	HUMP	LBJ	JFK	RFK	KING	LINDS	MC CARTH	NIXON
WN	0.000	0.014	0.040	0.028	0.007	0.183	0.114	0.031	0.018	0.008	0.014	0.022	0.028
ML	0.014	0.000	0.000	0.000	0.031	0.004	0.000	0.000	0.030	0.200	0.000	0.014	0.000
K	0.040	0.000	0.000	0.080	0.046	0.063	0.082	0.007	0.017	0.004	0.027	0.015	0.060
	0.028	0.000	0.080	0.000	0.050	0.020	0.072	0.056	0.007	0.007	0.022	0.011	0.147
D	0.007	0.031	0.046	0.050	0.000	0.007	0.011	0.016	0.006	0.000	0.008	0.026	0.122
P	0.183	0.004	0.063	0.020	0.007	0.000	0.172	0.024	0.017	0.032	0.013	0.067	0.083
	0.114	0.000	0.082	0.072	0.011	0.172	0.000	0.036	0.003	0.055	0.000	0.008	0.023
	0.031	0.000	0.007	0.056	0.016	0.024	0.036	0.000	0.199	0.104	0.109	0.048	0.014
	0.018	0.030	0.017	0.007	0.006	0.017	0.003	0.199	0.000	0.155	0.076	0.111	0.007
G	0.008	0.200	0.004	0.007	0.000	0.032	0.055	0.104	0.155	0.000	0.026	0.056	0.000
DS	0.014	0.000	0.027	0.022	0.008	0.013	0.000	0.109	0.076	0.026	0.000	0.051	0.026
CARTH	0.022	0.014	0.015	0.011	0.026	0.067	0.008	0.048	0.111	0.056	0.051	0.000	0.028
ON	0.028	0.000	0.060	0.147	0.122	0.083	0.023	0.014	0.007	0.000	0.026	0.028	0.000
F	0.003	0.069	0.027	0.026	0.171	0.000	0.027	0.010	0.007	0.011	0.013	0.004	0.067
GAN	0.026	0.012	0.020	0.034	0.186	0.007	0.006	0.025	0.013	0.000	0.022	0.032	0.130
KY	0.022	0.012	0.009	0.017	0.028	0.049	0.044	0.084	0.057	0.014	0.182	0.036	0.053
MITZ	0.000	0.000	0.000	0.000	0.038	0.000	0.000	0.000	0.000	0.000	0.000	0.000	0.006
CK	0.009	0.232	0.000	0.008	0.011	0.009	0.009	0.015	0.044	0.220	0.010	0.112	0.004
VENSN	0.036	0.004	0.061	0.023	0.028	0.086	0.015	0.134	0.058	0.034	0.045	0.135	0.022
UH	0.140	0.020	0.102	0.008	0.003	0.076	0.116	0.028	0.119	0.004	0.019	0.038	0.008
LACE	0.011	0.177	0.009	0.015	0.139	0.019	0.018	0.000	0.017	0.029	0.000	0.024	0.034
REN	0.145	0.030	0.032	0.044	0.011	0.022	0.054	0.067	0.054	0.046	0.025	0.032	0.021
K	0.024	0.012	0.065	0.095	0.010	0.046	0.011	0.009	0.000	0.016	0.025	0.011	0.010
TY	0.000	0.005	0.012	0.279	0.075	0.014	0.101	0.000	0.004	0.004	0.011	0.005	0.028
TY	0.069	0.000	0.048	0.004	0.038	0.004	0.053	0.004	0.032	0.008	0.144	0.032	0.059
AL	0.000	0.004	0.005	0.023	0.031	0.000	0.004	0.079	0.021	0.030	0.032	0.039	0.028

	RAFF	REAGAN	ROCKY	SCHMITZ	SPOCK	STEVENSN	UNRUH	WALLACE	WARREN	WELK	WESTY	YORTY	IDEAL
WN	0.003	0.026	0.022	0.000	0.009	0.036	0.140	0.011	0.145	0.024	0.000	0.069	0.000
ML	0.069	0.012	0.012	0.000	0.232	0.004	0.020	0.177	0.030	0.012	0.005	0.000	0.004
K	0.027	0.020	0.009	0.000	0.000	0.061	0.102	0.009	0.032	0.065	0.012	0.048	0.005
	0.026	0.034	0.017	0.000	0.008	0.023	0.008	0.015	0.044	0.095	0.279	0.004	0.023
D	0.171	0.186	0.028	0.038	0.011	0.028	0.003	0.139	0.011	0.010	0.075	0.038	0.031
P	0.000	0.007	0.049	0.000	0.009	0.086	0.076	0.019	0.022	0.046	0.014	0.004	0.000
	0.027	0.006	0.044	0.000	0.009	0.015	0.116	0.018	0.054	0.011	0.101	0.053	0.004
	0.010	0.025	0.084	0.000	0.015	0.134	0.028	0.000	0.067	0.009	0.000	0.004	0.079
	0.007	0.013	0.057	0.000	0.044	0.058	0.119	0.017	0.054	0.000	0.004	0.032	0.021
G	0.011	0.000	0.014	0.000	0.220	0.034	0.004	0.029	0.046	0.016	0.004	0.008	0.030
DS	0.013	0.022	0.182	0.000	0.010	0.045	0.019	0.000	0.025	0.025	0.011	0.144	0.032
CARTH	0.004	0.032	0.036	0.000	0.112	0.135	0.038	0.024	0.032	0.011	0.005	0.032	0.039
ON	0.067	0.130	0.053	0.006	0.004	0.022	0.008	0.034	0.021	0.010	0.028	0.059	0.028
F	0.000	0.133	0.000	0.099	0.025	0.015	0.033	0.163	0.004	0.020	0.042	0.082	0.003
GAN	0.133	0.000	0.042	0.043	0.000	0.017	0.006	0.116	0.007	0.093	0.035	0.091	0.034
KY	0.000	0.042	0.000	0.000	0.004	0.056	0.008	0.004	0.063	0.008	0.036	0.012	0.045
MITZ	0.099	0.043	0.000	0.000	0.015	0.000	0.009	0.073	0.000	0.025	0.026	0.028	0.000
CK	0.025	0.000	0.004	0.015	0.000	0.053	0.005	0.025	0.030	0.038	0.022	0.000	0.018
VENSN	0.015	0.017	0.056	0.000	0.053	0.000	0.013	0.015	0.095	0.019	0.000	0.004	0.077
UH	0.033	0.006	0.008	0.009	0.005	0.013	0.000	0.021	0.055	0.013	0.000	0.068	0.000
LACE	0.163	0.116	0.004	0.073	0.025	0.015	0.021	0.000	0.009	0.000	0.040	0.087	0.019
REN	0.004	0.007	0.063	0.000	0.030	0.095	0.055	0.009	0.000	0.000	0.016	0.009	0.040
K	0.020	0.093	0.008	0.025	0.038	0.019	0.013	0.000	0.000	0.000	0.028	0.043	0.000
TY	0.042	0.035	0.036	0.026	0.022	0.000	0.000	0.040	0.016	0.028	0.000	0.010	0.005
TY	0.082	0.091	0.012	0.028	0.000	0.004	0.068	0.087	0.009	0.043	0.010	0.000	0.000
AL	0.003	0.034	0.045	0.000	0.018	0.077	0.000	0.019	0.040	0.000	0.005	0.000	0.000

APPENDIX

STANDARDIZED PREFERENCE

	1	2	3	4	5	6	7	8	9	10	11	12	13	14	15	16	17	18	19	20	21	22	23	24	25
1	2.00	1.20	0.76	0.62	0.57	1.41	1.30	1.24	1.23	1.31	1.09	1.28	0.54	0.59	0.48	0.99	0.81	1.20	1.23	1.18	0.74	1.25	0.94	0.65	0.8
2	1.20	2.00	0.73	0.46	0.65	0.96	0.87	0.99	1.15	1.53	1.09	1.20	0.51	0.69	0.58	0.78	0.92	1.42	1.03	1.28	1.03	1.22	1.20	0.72	0.8
3	0.76	0.73	2.00	1.33	1.47	0.72	0.78	0.70	0.61	0.72	0.90	0.70	1.30	1.31	1.37	1.03	1.02	0.71	0.73	0.71	1.16	0.80	0.91	1.22	1.0
4	0.62	0.46	1.33	2.00	1.53	0.75	0.93	0.86	0.75	0.46	0.67	0.58	1.49	1.44	1.50	1.02	1.15	0.58	0.76	0.58	1.06	0.70	0.95	1.37	1.2
5	0.57	0.65	1.47	1.53	2.00	0.54	0.69	0.61	0.49	0.52	0.74	0.58	1.64	1.55	1.64	1.03	1.08	0.66	0.66	0.52	1.34	0.56	0.93	1.26	1.1
6	1.41	0.96	0.72	0.75	0.54	2.00	1.69	1.36	1.41	1.20	0.99	1.23	0.56	0.64	0.52	1.00	0.81	0.98	1.32	1.23	0.66	1.14	0.80	0.73	0.7
7	1.30	0.87	0.78	0.93	0.69	1.69	2.00	1.28	1.25	1.03	0.85	1.07	0.71	0.76	0.66	0.93	0.93	0.81	1.20	1.13	0.75	1.02	0.77	0.93	0.96
8	1.24	0.99	0.70	0.86	0.61	1.36	1.28	2.00	1.75	1.19	1.04	1.38	0.68	0.59	0.52	0.96	0.83	0.98	1.37	1.13	0.67	1.19	0.71	0.68	0.69
9	1.23	1.15	0.61	0.75	0.49	1.41	1.25	1.75	2.00	1.34	1.09	1.36	0.58	0.54	0.51	0.92	0.89	1.15	1.24	1.25	0.56	1.26	0.79	0.61	0.67
10	1.31	1.53	0.72	0.46	0.52	1.20	1.03	1.19	1.34	2.00	1.14	1.39	0.49	0.49	0.46	0.91	0.76	1.42	1.24	1.31	0.66	1.31	0.98	0.59	0.64
11	1.09	1.09	0.90	0.67	0.74	0.99	0.85	1.04	1.09	1.14	2.00	1.14	0.86	0.80	0.87	1.20	0.93	1.24	1.09	1.09	0.80	1.18	0.88	0.81	0.81
12	1.28	1.20	0.70	0.58	0.58	1.23	1.07	1.38	1.36	1.39	1.14	2.00	0.57	0.50	0.56	1.02	0.76	1.34	1.18	1.21	0.75	1.25	0.93	0.57	0.72
13	0.54	0.51	1.30	1.49	1.64	0.56	0.71	0.68	0.58	0.49	0.86	0.57	2.00	1.50	1.67	1.11	1.00	0.63	0.68	0.64	1.17	0.67	0.93	1.30	1.19
14	0.59	0.69	1.31	1.44	1.55	0.64	0.76	0.59	0.54	0.49	0.80	0.50	1.50	2.00	1.58	0.95	1.27	0.64	0.61	0.58	1.32	0.57	1.08	1.37	1.26
15	0.48	0.58	1.37	1.50	1.64	0.52	0.66	0.52	0.51	0.46	0.87	0.56	1.67	1.58	2.00	1.01	1.16	0.61	0.50	0.50	1.32	0.55	1.18	1.40	1.27
16	0.99	0.78	1.03	1.02	1.03	1.00	0.93	0.96	0.92	0.91	1.20	1.02	1.11	0.95	1.01	2.00	0.94	1.00	0.98	1.07	0.76	1.07	0.88	0.90	0.86
17	0.81	0.92	1.02	1.15	1.08	0.81	0.93	0.83	0.89	0.76	0.93	0.76	1.00	1.27	1.16	0.94	2.00	0.84	0.81	0.99	1.13	0.77	1.11	1.18	1.04
18	1.20	1.42	0.71	0.58	0.66	0.98	0.81	0.98	1.15	1.42	1.24	1.34	0.63	0.64	0.61	1.00	0.84	2.00	1.06	1.27	0.83	1.32	1.10	0.57	0.76
19	1.23	1.03	0.73	0.76	0.64	1.32	1.20	1.37	1.24	1.24	1.09	1.18	0.68	0.61	0.50	0.98	0.81	1.06	2.00	1.25	0.74	1.18	0.81	0.76	0.84
20	1.18	1.28	0.71	0.58	0.52	1.23	1.13	1.13	1.25	1.31	1.09	1.21	0.64	0.58	0.50	1.07	0.99	1.27	1.25	2.00	0.78	1.24	0.93	0.71	0.84
21	0.74	1.03	1.16	1.06	1.34	0.66	0.75	0.67	0.56	0.66	0.80	0.75	1.17	1.32	1.32	0.76	1.13	0.83	0.74	0.78	2.00	0.67	1.22	1.29	1.24
22	1.25	1.22	0.80	0.70	0.56	1.14	1.02	1.19	1.26	1.31	1.18	1.25	0.67	0.57	0.55	1.07	0.77	1.32	1.18	1.24	0.67	2.00	0.82	0.76	0.75
23	0.94	1.20	0.91	0.95	0.93	0.80	0.77	0.71	0.79	0.98	0.88	0.93	0.93	1.08	1.18	0.88	1.11	1.10	0.81	0.93	1.22	0.82	2.00	1.03	1.15
24	0.65	0.72	1.22	1.37	1.26	0.73	0.93	0.68	0.61	0.59	0.81	0.57	1.30	1.37	1.40	0.90	1.18	0.57	0.76	0.71	1.29	0.76	1.03	2.00	1.42
25	0.80	0.84	1.09	1.21	1.13	0.78	0.96	0.69	0.67	0.64	0.81	0.72	1.19	1.26	1.27	0.86	1.04	0.76	0.84	0.84	1.24	0.75	1.15	1.42	2.00
26	1.09	0.93	0.93	0.98	0.85	1.10	1.23	1.06	0.99	0.90	1.03	0.96	0.88	1.01	0.91	1.02	1.11	0.97	1.06	0.99	1.04	1.09	1.04	1.00	1.06
27	0.73	0.67	1.22	1.43	1.45	0.74	0.85	0.72	0.75	0.72	0.97	0.68	1.62	1.31	1.53	1.13	1.08	0.75	0.69	0.66	0.99	0.84	0.88	1.16	1.04
28	1.32	1.34	0.78	0.58	0.64	1.18	1.04	1.18	1.24	1.37	1.10	1.30	0.57	0.60	0.56	0.93	0.84	1.37	1.21	1.25	0.92	1.22	1.03	0.71	0.96
29	0.89	0.93	1.06	1.22	1.11	0.92	1.07	0.96	0.95	0.75	0.82	0.83	1.04	1.21	1.15	0.90	1.28	0.86	0.81	0.84	1.08	0.84	1.12	1.18	1.18
30	1.15	0.93	0.86	0.98	0.95	1.09	1.10	1.19	1.09	0.96	0.94	1.18	0.92	0.98	0.94	0.94	0.98	0.93	1.11	1.07	0.95	0.89	0.98	0.94	1.05
31	1.22	1.56	0.75	0.54	0.62	1.09	0.97	1.14	1.27	1.39	1.11	1.22	0.58	0.65	0.55	0.95	0.84	1.46	1.18	1.30	0.91	1.28	1.14	0.68	0.81
32	0.84	0.72	1.20	1.34	1.27	0.83	1.07	0.83	0.83	0.67	0.83	0.71	1.22	1.32	1.32	0.93	1.10	0.66	0.75	0.75	1.13	0.85	1.05	1.36	1.32
33	1.37	1.31	0.91	0.64	0.59	1.22	1.20	1.16	1.24	1.29	1.08	1.23	0.60	0.65	0.61	0.91	0.91	1.27	1.21	1.31	0.78	1.22	1.00	0.67	0.91
34	0.77	0.76	1.17	1.33	1.33	0.77	0.99	0.91	0.87	0.80	0.82	0.78	1.29	1.27	1.31	0.92	1.21	0.63	0.81	0.82	1.10	0.82	0.93	1.25	1.12
35	0.69	0.53	1.32	1.50	1.54	0.82	0.95	0.73	0.59	0.48	0.79	0.62	1.47	1.52	1.61	1.01	1.15	0.55	0.65	0.57	1.31	0.54	1.11	1.38	1.26
36	1.31	1.10	0.72	0.72	0.51	1.57	1.45	1.31	1.34	1.31	1.07	1.21	0.63	0.61	0.53	0.99	0.87	1.10	1.32	1.36	0.71	1.30	0.82	0.77	0.70
37	1.26	1.50	0.77	0.55	0.62	1.03	0.84	1.10	1.22	1.50	1.16	1.28	0.62	0.66	0.58	1.02	0.84	1.56	1.22	1.27	0.80	1.38	0.97	0.62	0.73
38	1.10	0.91	0.94	1.00	0.91	1.08	1.01	1.07	1.07	1.04	1.23	1.07	0.99	0.85	0.87	1.07	0.76	1.07	1.16	1.09	0.87	1.04	0.92	1.01	0.96
39	0.72	0.54	1.31	1.48	1.46	0.83	0.91	0.81	0.66	0.45	0.76	0.66	1.44	1.43	1.54	1.01	1.15	0.52	0.71	0.62	1.34	0.65	1.10	1.42	1.24
40	0.94	1.16	0.99	0.91	0.99	0.81	0.84	0.85	0.84	1.03	0.91	1.02	0.91	0.94	1.01	0.96	1.15	1.15	0.98	1.03	1.09	1.03	1.16	1.16	1.11
41	0.64	0.62	1.30	1.34	1.44	0.73	0.76	0.76	0.65	0.66	1.11	0.77	1.54	1.37	1.51	1.14	1.04	0.83	0.78	0.68	1.07	0.75	0.87	1.18	1.09
42	0.76	0.98	1.06	1.16	1.31	0.84	0.93	0.75	0.78	0.91	0.76	0.76	1.27	1.21	1.30	0.96	1.15	0.73	0.75	0.83	1.31	0.75	1.11	1.20	1.09
43	1.12	1.13	0.84	0.74	0.77	1.01	0.92	1.14	1.21	1.15	1.28	1.25	0.73	0.76	0.70	1.11	1.02	1.27	1.27	1.21	0.74	1.09	1.06	0.82	0.98
44	1.21	1.39	0.67	0.52	0.62	1.19	1.00	1.08	1.24	1.47	1.22	1.36	0.65	0.59	0.56	1.06	0.82	1.41	1.17	1.38	0.84	1.25	1.02	0.65	0.80
45	1.21	1.06	0.97	0.82	0.73	1.36	1.41	1.13	1.09	1.23	1.02	1.08	0.81	0.74	0.77	1.08	0.79	0.97	1.18	1.21	0.82	1.18	0.88	0.84	0.77
46	0.78	0.55	1.27	1.44	1.39	0.83	0.95	0.93	0.82	0.50	0.85	0.66	1.40	1.39	1.42	1.13	1.10	0.57	0.87	0.70	1.13	0.64	0.97	1.29	1.30
47	1.27	1.49	0.76	0.54	0.57	1.14	0.91	1.18	1.28	1.51	1.21	1.35	0.57	0.57	0.50	0.99	0.85	1.46	1.22	1.34	0.79	1.47	0.97	0.63	0.63
48	0.70	0.84	1.24	1.31	1.42	0.65	0.69	0.77	0.67	0.70	0.82	0.77	1.30	1.37	1.40	0.86	1.06	0.80	0.82	0.69	1.43	0.77	1.10	1.32	1.14
49	0.78	0.79	1.21	1.25	1.29	0.84	0.85	0.95	0.80	0.72	1.02	0.92	1.23	1.33	1.20	1.01	1.06	0.80	0.92	0.74	1.17	0.81	0.88	1.18	1.10
50	1.26	1.26	0.70	0.58	0.49	1.41	1.17	1.40	1.57	1.49	1.16	1.40	0.58	0.56	0.47	0.94	0.77	1.30	1.30	1.37	0.65	1.32	0.88	0.55	0.71

3

CORRELATIONS FOR ALL VOTERS

26	27	28	29	30	31	32	33	34	35	36	37	38	39	40	41	42	43	44	45	46	47	48	49	50
1.09	0.73	1.32	0.89	1.15	1.22	0.84	1.37	0.77	0.69	1.31	1.26	1.10	0.72	0.94	0.64	0.76	1.12	1.21	1.21	0.78	1.27	0.70	0.78	1.26
0.93	0.67	1.34	0.93	0.93	1.56	0.72	1.31	0.76	0.53	1.10	1.50	0.91	0.54	1.16	0.62	0.98	1.13	1.39	1.06	0.55	1.49	0.84	0.79	1.26
0.93	1.22	0.78	1.06	0.86	0.75	1.20	0.91	1.17	1.32	0.72	0.77	0.94	1.31	0.99	1.30	1.06	0.84	0.67	0.97	1.27	0.76	1.24	1.21	0.70
0.98	1.43	0.58	1.22	0.98	0.54	1.34	0.64	1.33	1.50	0.72	0.55	1.00	1.48	0.91	1.34	1.16	0.74	0.52	0.82	1.44	0.54	1.31	1.25	0.58
0.85	1.45	0.64	1.11	0.95	0.62	1.27	0.59	1.33	1.54	0.51	0.62	0.91	1.46	0.99	1.46	1.31	0.77	0.62	0.73	1.39	0.57	1.42	1.29	0.49
1.10	0.74	1.18	0.92	1.09	1.09	0.83	1.22	0.77	0.82	1.57	1.03	1.08	0.83	0.81	0.73	0.84	1.01	1.19	1.36	0.83	1.14	0.65	0.84	1.41
.23	0.85	1.04	1.07	1.10	0.97	1.07	1.20	0.99	0.95	1.45	0.84	1.01	0.91	0.84	0.76	0.93	0.92	1.00	1.41	0.95	0.91	0.69	0.85	1.17
1.06	0.72	1.18	0.96	1.19	1.14	0.83	1.16	0.91	0.73	1.31	1.10	1.07	0.81	0.85	0.76	0.75	1.14	1.08	1.13	0.93	1.18	0.77	0.95	1.40
0.99	0.75	1.24	0.95	1.09	1.27	0.83	1.24	0.87	0.59	1.34	1.22	1.07	0.66	0.84	0.65	0.78	1.21	1.24	1.09	0.82	1.28	0.67	0.80	1.57
0.90	0.72	1.37	0.75	0.96	1.39	0.67	1.29	0.80	0.48	1.31	1.50	1.04	0.45	1.03	0.66	0.91	1.15	1.47	1.23	0.50	1.51	0.70	0.72	1.49
1.03	0.97	1.10	0.82	0.94	1.11	0.83	1.08	0.82	0.79	1.07	1.16	1.23	0.76	0.91	1.11	0.76	1.28	1.22	1.02	0.85	1.21	0.82	1.02	1.16
0.96	0.68	1.30	0.83	1.18	1.22	0.71	1.23	0.78	0.62	1.21	1.28	1.07	0.66	1.02	0.77	0.76	1.25	1.36	1.08	0.66	1.35	0.77	0.92	1.40
0.88	1.62	0.57	1.04	0.92	0.58	1.22	0.60	1.29	1.47	0.63	0.62	0.99	1.44	0.91	1.54	1.27	0.73	0.65	0.81	1.40	0.57	1.30	1.23	0.58
1.01	1.31	0.60	1.21	0.98	0.65	1.32	0.65	1.27	1.52	0.61	0.66	0.85	1.43	0.94	1.37	1.21	0.76	0.59	0.74	1.39	0.57	1.37	1.33	0.56
0.91	1.53	0.56	1.15	0.94	0.55	1.32	0.61	1.31	1.61	0.53	0.58	0.87	1.54	1.01	1.51	1.30	0.70	0.56	0.77	1.42	0.50	1.40	1.20	0.47
1.02	1.13	0.93	0.90	0.94	0.95	0.93	0.91	0.92	1.01	0.99	1.02	1.07	1.01	0.96	1.14	0.96	1.11	1.06	1.08	1.13	0.99	0.86	1.01	0.94
1.11	1.08	0.84	1.28	0.98	0.84	1.10	0.91	1.21	1.15	0.87	0.84	0.76	1.15	1.15	1.04	1.15	1.02	0.82	0.79	1.10	0.85	1.06	1.06	0.77
0.97	0.75	1.37	0.86	0.93	1.46	0.66	1.27	0.63	0.55	1.10	1.56	1.07	0.52	1.15	0.83	0.73	1.27	1.41	0.97	0.57	1.46	0.80	0.80	1.30
1.06	0.69	1.21	0.81	1.11	1.18	0.75	1.21	0.81	0.65	1.32	1.22	1.16	0.71	0.98	0.78	0.75	1.27	1.17	1.18	0.87	1.22	0.82	0.92	1.30
0.99	0.66	1.25	0.84	1.07	1.30	0.75	1.31	0.82	0.57	1.36	1.27	1.09	0.62	1.03	0.68	0.83	1.21	1.38	1.21	0.70	1.34	0.69	0.74	1.37
1.04	0.99	0.92	1.08	0.95	0.91	1.13	0.78	1.10	1.31	0.71	0.80	0.87	1.34	1.09	1.07	1.31	0.74	0.84	0.82	1.13	0.79	1.43	1.17	0.65
1.09	0.84	1.22	0.84	0.89	1.28	0.85	1.22	0.82	0.54	1.30	1.38	1.04	0.65	1.03	0.75	0.75	1.09	1.25	1.18	0.64	1.47	0.77	0.81	1.32
1.04	0.88	1.03	1.12	0.98	1.14	1.05	1.00	0.93	1.11	0.82	0.97	0.92	1.10	1.16	0.87	1.11	1.06	1.02	0.88	0.97	0.97	1.10	0.88	0.88
1.00	1.16	0.71	1.18	0.94	0.68	1.36	0.67	1.25	1.38	0.77	0.62	1.01	1.42	1.16	1.18	1.20	0.82	0.65	0.84	1.29	0.63	1.32	1.18	0.55
1.06	1.04	0.96	1.18	1.05	0.81	1.32	0.91	1.12	1.26	0.70	0.73	0.96	1.24	1.11	1.09	1.09	0.98	0.80	0.77	1.30	0.63	1.14	1.10	0.71
2.00	0.83	0.91	1.32	0.91	1.02	1.24	1.01	0.89	0.91	1.10	0.99	1.00	0.93	1.01	0.83	0.84	0.97	0.87	1.01	0.89	0.96	0.81	0.98	0.88
0.83	2.00	0.63	1.02	0.90	0.72	1.08	0.74	1.19	1.21	0.84	0.73	0.98	1.16	0.80	1.51	1.18	0.75	0.72	0.97	1.18	0.67	1.12	1.14	0.77
0.91	0.63	2.00	0.80	1.31	1.45	0.71	1.29	0.68	0.66	1.09	1.30	1.08	0.68	1.05	0.52	0.71	1.34	1.48	0.89	0.71	1.23	0.70	0.76	1.22
1.32	1.02	0.80	2.00	0.98	0.98	1.29	0.88	1.16	1.09	0.85	0.74	0.82	1.10	1.07	0.95	1.04	0.90	0.78	0.75	1.09	0.71	0.91	1.01	0.73
0.91	0.90	1.31	0.98	2.00	1.05	0.95	1.07	1.01	0.99	0.95	0.80	0.96	1.01	0.90	0.90	0.81	1.26	1.00	0.85	1.10	0.82	0.85	0.89	0.95
1.02	0.72	1.45	0.98	1.05	2.00	0.71	1.43	0.70	0.57	1.12	1.34	0.96	0.54	1.01	0.63	0.78	1.23	1.32	1.05	0.54	1.31	0.68	0.77	1.24
1.24	1.08	0.71	1.29	0.95	0.71	2.00	0.80	1.21	1.31	0.72	0.61	1.04	1.27	1.09	1.04	1.09	0.84	0.64	0.80	1.25	0.56	1.12	1.08	0.60
1.01	0.74	1.29	0.88	1.07	1.43	0.80	2.00	0.75	0.63	1.28	1.27	0.89	0.58	0.98	0.67	0.80	1.11	1.21	1.25	0.64	1.28	0.63	0.63	1.35
0.89	1.19	0.68	1.16	1.01	0.70	1.21	0.75	2.00	1.35	0.78	0.68	0.76	1.33	0.81	1.11	1.31	0.74	0.62	0.84	1.30	0.72	1.09	1.11	0.77
0.91	1.21	0.66	1.09	0.99	0.57	1.31	0.63	1.35	2.00	0.58	0.51	0.84	1.71	0.86	1.29	1.34	0.63	0.48	0.76	1.58	0.50	1.42	1.24	0.46
1.10	0.84	1.09	0.85	0.95	1.12	0.72	1.28	0.78	0.58	2.00	1.07	0.99	0.66	0.78	0.69	0.89	1.00	1.16	1.59	0.68	1.31	0.69	0.77	1.45
0.99	0.73	1.30	0.74	0.80	1.34	0.61	1.27	0.68	0.51	1.07	2.00	1.01	0.51	1.09	0.78	0.82	1.16	1.34	1.04	0.54	1.71	0.75	0.78	1.34
1.00	0.98	1.08	0.82	0.96	0.96	1.04	0.89	0.76	0.84	0.99	1.01	2.00	0.94	0.93	1.00	0.71	1.24	1.16	0.99	0.94	0.98	0.95	0.99	1.07
0.93	1.16	0.68	1.10	1.01	0.54	1.27	0.58	1.33	1.71	0.66	0.51	0.94	2.00	0.88	1.18	1.27	0.69	0.51	0.69	1.60	0.48	1.45	1.25	0.49
1.01	0.80	1.05	1.07	0.90	1.01	1.09	0.98	0.81	0.86	0.78	1.09	0.93	0.88	2.00	0.90	0.84	1.11	1.15	0.87	0.84	1.01	1.07	0.90	0.87
0.83	1.51	0.52	0.95	0.90	0.63	1.04	0.67	1.11	1.29	0.69	0.78	1.00	1.18	0.90	2.00	1.08	0.77	0.73	0.98	1.22	0.70	1.24	1.30	0.78
0.84	1.18	0.71	1.04	0.81	0.78	1.09	0.80	1.31	1.34	0.89	0.82	0.71	1.27	0.84	1.08	2.00	0.64	0.83	0.91	1.15	0.85	1.15	1.07	0.79
0.97	0.75	1.34	0.90	1.26	1.23	0.84	1.11	0.74	0.63	1.00	1.16	1.24	0.69	1.11	0.77	0.64	2.00	1.35	0.83	0.92	1.10	0.77	0.80	1.13
0.87	0.72	1.48	0.78	1.00	1.32	0.64	1.21	0.62	0.48	1.16	1.34	1.16	0.51	1.15	0.73	0.83	1.35	2.00	1.06	0.54	1.37	0.66	0.65	1.39
1.01	0.97	0.89	0.75	0.85	1.05	0.80	1.25	0.84	0.76	1.59	1.04	0.99	0.69	0.87	0.98	0.91	0.83	1.06	2.00	0.69	1.19	0.84	0.84	1.29
0.89	1.18	0.71	1.09	1.10	0.54	1.25	0.64	1.30	1.58	0.68	0.54	0.94	1.60	0.84	1.22	1.15	0.92	0.54	0.69	2.00	0.53	1.33	1.17	0.57
0.96	0.67	1.23	0.71	0.82	1.31	0.56	1.28	0.72	0.50	1.31	1.71	0.98	0.48	1.01	0.70	0.85	1.10	1.37	1.19	0.53	2.00	0.77	0.76	1.37
0.81	1.12	0.70	0.91	0.85	0.68	1.12	0.63	1.09	1.42	0.69	0.75	0.95	1.45	1.07	1.24	1.15	0.77	0.66	0.84	1.33	0.77	2.00	1.29	0.62
0.98	1.14	0.76	1.01	0.89	0.77	1.08	0.63	1.11	1.24	0.77	0.78	0.99	1.25	0.90	1.30	1.07	0.80	0.65	0.84	1.17	0.76	1.29	2.00	0.83
0.88	0.77	1.22	0.73	0.95	1.24	0.60	1.35	0.77	0.46	1.45	1.34	1.07	0.49	0.87	0.78	0.79	1.13	1.39	1.29	0.57	1.37	0.62	0.83	2.00

APPENDIX 4

JUDGED SIMILARITY CONFIGURATION FOR ALL VOTERS. THE FINAL CONFIGURATION OF TWENTY-SIX POINTS IN THREE DIMENSIONS WITH STRESS 0.183

	I	II	III
BROWN	−0.183	−1.006	0.034
CARML	−0.784	0.797	0.343
DIRK	−0.009	−0.716	−0.656
IKE	−0.232	−0.189	−0.879
GOLD	0.376	0.501	−0.716
HUMPH	−0.656	−0.654	−0.049
LBJ	−0.455	−0.776	−0.279
JFK	0.420	−0.272	0.820
RFK	−0.113	−0.162	0.927
KING	−0.666	0.244	0.778
LINDS	0.905	−0.423	0.287
MC CARTH	−0.002	0.261	0.817
NIXON	0.543	−0.042	−0.745
RAFF	0.117	0.739	−0.592
REAGAN	0.581	0.453	−0.529
ROCKY	0.815	−0.242	0.316
SCHMITZ	0.224	1.276	−0.427
SPOCK	−0.664	0.592	0.634
STEVENSN	0.299	−0.010	0.702
UNRUH	−0.410	−0.898	0.255
WALLACE	−0.112	0.855	−0.300
WARREN	−0.028	−0.688	0.591
WELK	−0.965	0.019	−0.493
WESTY	−0.453	0.265	−0.965
YORTY	0.654	−0.458	−0.514
IDEAL	0.796	0.535	0.636

APPENDIX 5

PATTERN OF PREFERENCE CONFIGURATION FOR ALL VOTERS. THE FINAL CONFIGURATION OF FIFTY POINTS IN THREE DIMENSIONS WITH STRESS 0.113

	I	II	III
01 BROWN	0.582	0.738	−0.101
02 CARML	0.038	0.849	0.568
03 DRKSN	−0.320	−0.939	−0.191
04 IKE	−0.447	−0.846	−0.487
05 GOLDW	−0.656	−0.898	−0.170
06 HUMPH	0.875	0.422	−0.294
07 LBJ	0.680	0.267	−0.675
08 JFK	0.776	0.500	−0.249
09 RFK	0.751	0.643	0.038
10 KING	0.573	0.741	0.467
11 LNDSY	0.460	−0.040	0.804
12 MC C	0.659	0.608	0.370
13 NIXON	−0.536	−0.977	−0.130
14 RAFF	−0.770	−0.703	−0.286
15 REAGN	−0.756	−0.785	−0.207
16 ROCKY	0.378	−0.660	0.509
17 SCHMT	−0.853	0.106	−0.345
18 SPOCK	0.239	0.687	0.742
19 STVSN	0.866	0.301	0.097
20 UNRUH	0.513	0.706	0.231
21 WALLC	−0.977	−0.292	−0.043
22 WARRN	0.738	0.374	0.508
23 WELK	−0.851	0.403	0.159
24 WESTY	−0.777	−0.518	−0.415
25 YORTY	−0.800	−0.203	−0.505
26 FINEX	0.175	0.219	−0.858
27 EXREP	−0.229	−1.041	0.045
28 POVTY	0.246	0.874	0.330
29 CHRST	−0.516	0.052	−0.807
30 WAR	−0.171	0.673	−0.542
31 JOBS	0.208	0.899	0.378
32 PTRT	−0.545	−0.396	−0.712
33 LBLDM	0.441	0.860	0.040
34 WNWAR	−0.382	−0.623	−0.719
35 COPS	−0.683	−0.767	−0.382
36 VP	0.919	0.414	−0.083
37 WITHD	0.424	0.629	0.733
38 UNITE	0.652	−0.395	0.431
39 UNAFR	−0.681	−0.719	−0.424
40 STDUP	−0.688	0.416	0.494
41 ENTRP	−0.336	−1.006	0.138
42 NUCLR	−0.857	−0.473	0.166
43 PEACE	0.099	0.461	0.720
44 RACST	0.422	0.637	0.615
45 POLIT	0.975	0.044	−0.183
46 LAW	−0.484	−0.760	−0.447
47 STOPB	0.632	0.578	0.605
48 STATE	−0.768	−0.724	0.076
49 CUTTX	−0.044	−0.936	−0.279
50 YNG S	0.805	0.592	0.271

Acknowledgments

This research was supported in part by a National Foundation Doctoral Dissertation Support Grant (NoGS 2070). The author wishes to take this opportunity to thank Volney Stefflre, Martin Stefflre, David Napior, and Joe Harding for their critical examination of the ideas that went into earlier drafts of this paper and their many hours of friendly help. Without their efforts this paper could not have been written.

References

Berelson, B., Lazarsfeld, P., & McPhee, W. *Voting*. Chicago, Illinois: University of Chicago Press, 1954.

Black, M., & Metzger, D. Ethnographic description and the study of law. In L. Nader (Ed.), *The ethnography of law. American Anthropologist Special Issue,* 1965, **67,** (6, Pt. 2) 141–165.

Brunswik, E. *Perception and the representative design of psychological experiments.* Berkeley, California: University of California Press, 1956.

Campbell, A., Converse, P., Miller, W., & Stokes, D. *The American voter*. New York: Wiley, 1960.

Converse, P. The problem of party distances in models of voting change. In M. K. Jennings and L. H. Zeigler (Eds.), *The electoral process*. Englewood Cliffs, New Jersey: Prentice-Hall, 1966. Pp. 175–207.

Crossley, A., & Crossley, H. Polling in 1968. *Public Opinion Quarterly,* 1969, **33,** 1–16.

Downs, A. *An economic theory of democracy*. New York: Harper & Row, 1957.

Hays, W. *Statistics for Psychologists*. New York: Holt, Rinehart, & Winston, 1963.

Johnson, S. C. Hierarchical clustering schemes. *Psychometrika,* 1967, **32,** 241–254.

Kish, L. *Survey sampling*. New York: Wiley, 1965.

Kruskal, J. B. Multidimensional scaling by optimizing goodness of fit to a nonmetric hypothesis. *Psychometrika,* 1964, **29,** 1–27. (a)

Kruskal, J. B. Nonmetric multidimensional scaling: A numerical method. *Psychometrika,* 1964, **29,** 115–129. (b)

Kruskal, J. B. How to use MD-SCAL, a multidimensional scaling program, May 1967. Bell Telephone Laboratories program use instructions.

Mauser, G. A. A structural approach to predicting patterns of electoral substitution: a study of the 1968 Presidential contest in California, Unpublished doctoral dissertation, University of California, Irvine, 1970.

Office of the Secretary of State, *Statement of vote, state of California,* General Election, November 5, 1968. Sacramento, California: State Printing Office, December, 1968.

Pool, I., Abelson, R., & Popkin, S. *Candidates, issues, and strategies*. Boston, Massachusetts: MIT Press, 1964.

Rapoport, A., & Fillenbaum, S. Experimental analysis of semantic structures. This book, Volume II.

Rosenberg, M. *The logic of survey analysis*. New York: Basic Books, 1968.

Shepard, R. N. The analysis of proximities: multidimensional scaling with an unknown distance function. I. *Psychometrika,* 1962, **27,** 125–140. (a)

Shepard, R. N. The analysis of proximities: multidimensional scaling with an unknown distance function. II. *Psychometrika,* 1962, **27,** 219–246. (b)

Shepard, R. N. A taxonomy of some principal types of data and of multidimensional methods for their analysis. This book, Volume I.

Stefflre, V. Simulation of people's behavior toward new objects and events. *The American Behavioral Scientist*, 1965, **8**(9), 12–15.

Stefflre, V. Some applications of multidimensional scaling to social science problems. This book, Volume II.

Stefflre, V. *Language and Behavior*. Unpublished manuscript.

Stefflre, V., & Wendell, M. A study of the perceptions of Peace Corps Volunteers and their activities by Spanish and Quechua speakers in Cuzco and Chimbote, Peru. Prepared for the Peace Corps under subcontract with the Simulmatics Corporation, Contact number PC-80-1506. 1966.

Stenson, H., & Knoll, R. Goodness of fit for random rankings in Kruskal's nonmetric scaling procedure. *Psychological Bulletin*, 1969, **71**, 122–126.

Stokes, D. Spatial models of party competition. In A. Campbell, P. Converse, W. Miller, & D. Stokes (Eds.), *Elections and the political order*. New York: Wiley, 1966. Pp. 161–179.

Thurstone, L. *The measurement of values*. Chicago, Illinois: University of Chicago Press, 1959.

Torgerson, W. Multidimensional scaling of similarity. *Psychometrika*, 1965, **30**, 379–393.

DIFFERENCES IN PERCEIVED SIMILARITY OF NATIONS

Myron Wish

BELL TELEPHONE LABORATORIES, INC.
MURRAY HILL, NEW JERSEY

Morton Deutsch and Lois Biener

TEACHERS COLLEGE, COLUMBIA UNIVERSITY
NEW YORK, NEW YORK

This paper reports a study which is part of a program of research that is directed both toward characterizing the ways different kinds of people conceive of nations and their interrelations and toward understanding the conditions which give rise to different types of conceptions. The research reported here was guided by methodological as well as by substantive questions. We were interested in determining whether INDSCAL (Carroll & Chang, 1970; Carroll, this book, Volume I), a new procedure for analyzing individual differences in multidimensional structures, could be fruitfully applied to the understanding of different individuals' conceptions of nations. Since most previous investigations of the "dimensions of nations" have dealt with objective measures of nations or aggregate judgments (Cattell, 1941; Klingberg, 1941; Wish, 1964; Adelman & Morris, 1965; Banks & Gregg, 1965; Gregg & Banks, 1965; Russett, 1966; Robinson &

Hefner, 1967; Sawyer, 1967; Rummel, 1967), one cannot determine from these studies how relevant the dimensions are to any particular subject. Two dimensions that account for the same percentage of variance may differ in the sense that they account for different subjects' variance. Alternatively, one dimension may be moderately important to all subjects, while another is very important to a few subjects and irrelevant to the rest. Our concern with such considerations influenced our choice of data collection methods and data analysis procedures.

Substantively, we wished to see how much difference there was in the underlying dimensions used to characterize nations among different groups of students; e.g., students from developed and underdeveloped countries, students with opposed viewpoints on the war in Vietnam, and males and females. We, of course, expected that students would not necessarily agree in their characterizations of all nations. But this lack of full agreement might reflect a different set of underlying dimensions, or different weights being placed on the dimensions, or different judgments of where a nation fits on a given dimension.

Experimental Design

Subjects

For the study, 90 subjects from 15 different countries volunteered. All but a few were Columbia University students and the great majority were in graduate school. Subjects were primarily recruited by means of posters placed in the International House and Foreign Student Center at Columbia. They were run in six groups of 10–20 each from mid-August to mid-October, 1968. Included in the sample were seven or more subjects from each of eight countries (Colombia, U.K., France, India, Korea, Thailand, U.S.A., and Yugoslavia) and three or fewer subjects from each of several other countries. Subjects were paid $7.50 for the 2–4 hours it took to complete a questionnaire. Only the data from the 75 subjects who were from the eight nations listed above will be discussed. Although these subjects may be reasonably representative of foreign students at Columbia University, it is unlikely that they are representative of the student or general population in these nations.

Stimuli

Most of the nations selected for this study (Table 1) were used in previous studies of nation perception (Wish, 1964, 1971; Robinson & Hefner, 1967).

TABLE 1

NATIONS USED IN SIMILARITY AND SEMANTIC DIFFERENTIAL RATING TASKS

Brazil	France	Poland
China (mainland)	Greece	U. S. S. R.
Congo	India	South Africa
Cuba	Indonesia	Spain
Egypt	Israel	U. S. A.
U. K.	Japan	West Germany
Ethiopia	Mexico	Yugoslavia

These nations span the multidimensional spaces obtained in most prior studies concerned with objective or subjective characteristics of nations. However, the stimuli do not represent a random sample of all nations in the world. Since it was important for subjects to have some familiarity with most of the countries, we primarily chose countries that are large in population and/or size.

TASKS IN THE QUESTIONNAIRE

(a) SIMILARITY RATINGS. Subjects gave ratings on a nine-point scale with regard to the degree of overall similarity between numerous pairs of nations. As shown below, larger numbers were used to indicate greater similarity between the nations of a particular pair.

1	2	3	4	5	6	7	8	9
Extremely dissimilar				Moderately similar				Extremely similar

Although similarity judgments were obtained for all possible pairs of nations, each subject judged the similarity of only 150 of the 210 pairs. Every subject responded to each of the 90 pairs in which the U.S.A., Spain, Congo, U.S.S.R., and China were included. These five countries span the multidimensional space obtained from previous studies (Wish, 1964, 1971; Robinson & Hefner, 1967). The pairs that do not include the "core" countries were randomly divided into four mutually exclusive and exhaustive subsets of 30 pairs each. Any particular individual responded to all pairs in two of the four subsets. In addition to the 150 judgments concerning the similarity between pairs of nations, each subject also evaluated the degree of similarity between each country and his hypothetical "ideal country."

TABLE 2

SEMANTIC DIFFERENTIAL SCALES

Rating: 1	9
I dislike	I like
Poor	Rich
Aggressive	Peaceful
Weak	Powerful
Collectively oriented	Individualistically oriented
Internally divided	Internally united
Nonindustrialized	Industrialized
Small	Large
Deteriorating	Progressing
Little influence on culture of other nations	Much influence on culture of other nations
Little opportunity for change in individual's social status	Much opportunity for change in individual's social status
Unstable	Stable
Bad	Good
People have few rights	People have many rights
Illiterate population	Highly educated population
Population dissatisfied	Population satisfied

(b) SEMANTIC DIFFERENTIAL RATINGS. After judging the similarities of nations to each other, subjects rated the same nations on the bipolar scales listed in Table 2. The order of the scales, poles, and nations were balanced in the study. Graphical responses on the scales were converted to ratings ranging from 1 for the left pole to 9 for the right pole (as listed in Table 2).

(c) OTHER ITEMS. Tables 3 and 4 show two shorter items from the questionnaire. The first deals with the political alignment of nations (in the event of a large scale war within the next five years). The second is an attitudinal item in which each subject was asked to check the statement that corresponds best with his opinion regarding the action that the U.S.A. should take in Vietnam. Also included in the questionnaire were items dealing with perceived friendship among nations, characterizations of nations, sortings of nations with regard to several contexts and criteria,

TABLE 3

POLITICAL ALIGNMENT SORTING[a]

In the event that the U. S. A. is involved in a large scale war in the next five years, who do you think will be the principal enemy?

Using the list of countries, sort them into the following five categories in regard to the hypothetical war discussed above. Each country should appear in one and only one category.

Military ally of U. S. A.

Sympathetic to U. S. A., but not militarily involved

Military ally of enemy of U.S.A.

Sympathetic to enemy of U. S. A., but not militarily involved

Neutral or uninvolved

[a] Odd-numbered ratings from 1 to 9 were assigned to these categories in order to derive a bipolar scale similar to those in Table 2. Higher numbers indicated greater alignment with the U. S. A.

preferences among presidential candidates, factual information about nations, and biographic and demographic information about the subjects.

The INDSCAL procedure was used to analyze the data on nation similarities. Since the procedure is so new we shall now briefly describe its basic aims and assumptions.

TABLE 4

OPINION ITEM REGARDING THE WAR IN VIETNAM

Opinions vary about what the U. S. A. should do with regard to the war in Vietnam. Check the statement[a] which most clearly represents your opinion.

__________The U. S. A. should provide enough support to the military to achieve a military victory in Vietnam even if this entails the use of nuclear weapons.

__________The U. S. A. should provide enough support to the military to achieve a military victory in Vietnam but it should not be the first to use nuclear weapons.

__________The U. S. A. should continue essentially the same policy as it is now following.

__________The U. S. A. should be willing to make far more concessions to Hanoi and the Vietcong than it has so far, in order to bring about a negotiated peace in Vietnam.

__________The U. S. A. should start to withdraw from Vietnam recognizing that it had no right to intervene.

[a] Subjects who endorsed the last statement were classified as doves; subjects who endorsed the fourth statement were classified as moderates; and subjects who endorsed either the first, second, or third statement were classified as hawks.

The INDSCAL Model

The usual input to INDSCAL is a set of similarity or dissimilarity matrices which pertain to the same stimuli. Each matrix comes from a single subject, or other data source such as an experimental condition (see Wish & Carroll, 1971). In INDSCAL, as in other multidimensional scaling procedures, (Torgerson, 1958; Shepard, 1962; Kruskal, 1964a, b; Coombs, 1964; Young & Torgerson, 1967; Guttman, 1968), it is assumed that these similarities are related to distances in some latent psychological space. INDSCAL differs from most other scaling procedures in that it determines the relative importance, or weight, of each dimension to every subject. The dimension weights for a particular subject indicate how much each dimension should be stretched so that the distances between stimuli will correlate as highly as possible with his similarities data.[1] The formula relating distances for a particular subject to the stimulus coordinates and dimension weights is given below:

$$d_{jk}^{(i)} = \left(\sum_{t=1}^{r} w_{it}(x_{jt} - x_{kt})^2 \right)^{1/2}$$

where $d_{jk}^{(i)}$ is the distance between stimulus j and stimulus k for subject i, w_{it} is the weight of dimension t for subject i, and x_{jt} and x_{kt} are the coordinates of the two stimuli on dimension t.

If we consider a new set of y-coordinates for subject i such that $y_{jt}^{(i)} = x_{jt}(w_{it})^{1/2}$, then $d_{jk}^{(i)}$ is the ordinary Euclidean distance between j and k for subject i in the space defined by the y's.

When the dimensions of the group stimulus space are appropriately normalized,[2] the square of a subject's weight on a particular dimension indicates the proportion of variance[3] in his similarities data which can be accounted for by that dimension. The aim of the program is to determine (by means of an iterative least squares procedure) the stimulus coordinates (plotted in a *"group" stimulus space*) and the subject weights (which can be plotted in a *subject space*) that account for as much total variance in all subjects' data as possible. In this process the program finds the orientation of axes that maximizes the goodness-of-fit measure. On the basis of analyses for many different sets of data, it appears that the unrotated dimensions from INDSCAL are easier to interpret than those obtained from multi-

[1] The correlation is actually between scalar products derived from the similarities and distances by means of a procedure described in Torgerson (1958).

[2] The dimensions are normalized so that the sum of squared coordinates on each stimulus dimension equals 1.

[3] The squared weight for a dimension underestimates the proportion of variance accounted for if the stimulus dimensions are correlated.

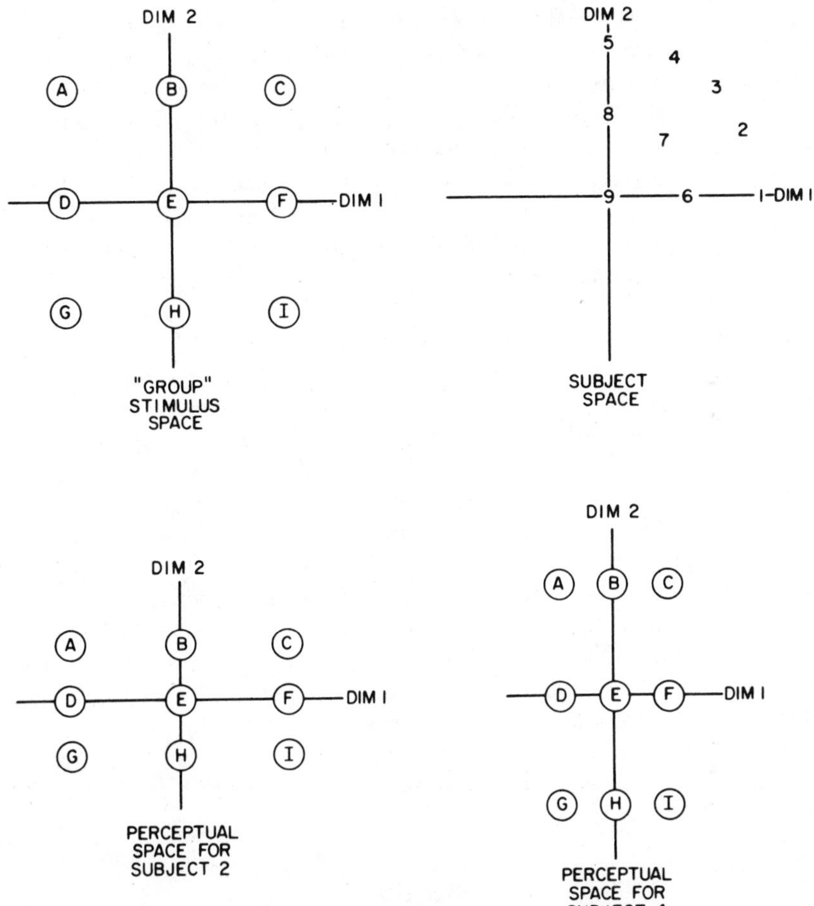

FIG. 1. Hypothetical example illustrating INDSCAL model. Weights from *subject space* (upper right) are applied to dimensions of *"group" stimulus space* (upper left) to produce individual perceptual spaces for subjects such as 2 (lower left) and 4 (lower right).

dimensional scalings of averaged data or from factor analyses. INDSCAL, therefore, is particularly valuable when one does not know the dimensions ahead of time.[4]

[4] Except for a rotation and weighting of dimensions, a multidimensional solution for averaged similarities data is generally quite similar to the *"group" stimulus space* from an INDSCAL analysis (See Horan, 1969). One can therefore, save considerable computer time by using a solution for averaged similarities as a starting configuration for INDSCAL.

Although it is assumed that the subjects use a common set of dimensions, some of the dimensions may have little or no importance to some subjects. Since the dimensions that have the highest weights for some subjects can have zero or near-zero weights for other subjects, the model allows for considerable variation in multidimensional structures.

Figure 1 illustrates the kind of output provided by INDSCAL. The spaces shown in these figures are hypothetical and do not represent the results of an actual analysis. The *"group" stimulus space* shows the location of stimuli on both dimensions, while the *subject space* shows the weights of dimensions 1 and 2 to nine hypothetical subjects (as indicated by the projections of their points on the axes of the *subject space*). While only the first dimension is relevant to subjects 1 and 6, and only the second dimension is relevant to subjects 5 and 8, both dimensions are relevant to subjects 2, 3, 4, and 7. The distance of a subject from the origin is approximately equal to the correlation between his original similarities data and the stimulus distances on his appropriately weighted space. Since the points for the first five subjects are further from the origin than those of the other four, these dimensions would account for their data the best. None of Subject 9's data could be accounted for by these dimensions since his point is precisely at the origin. The bottom diagrams illustrate how the stimulus space would look if the dimensions were stretched in proportion to the weights of Subjects 2 and 4. Subject 2's *perceptual space* shows more horizontal than vertical variation since he has a higher weight on the first than on the second dimension. The vertical stretching of Subject 4's *perceptual space* shows that the second dimension is more salient to him (more highly weighted) than the first.

Results

The similarities data could not be directly analyzed by INDSCAL since the procedure at the time required that every subject's matrix of similarities (or dissimilarities) be complete.[5] (As stated previously, only 150 of the 210 possible pairs were responded to by any single subject). We therefore used the following procedure to obtain a complete matrix (of Euclidean distances, which can be regarded as measures of dissimilarity) for every subject. The original similarities data for each subject were analyzed individually by means of Kruskal's (1964a, b) nonmetric multidimensional scaling procedure (which does allow for missing data). Four dimensions were sufficient to account for the data of any single subject. Specifically,

[5] There are now several variations of INDSCAL, one of which (INDSCALM) allows for missing data.

the four-dimensional configurations for all but two of the subjects had stress (SFORM 1) values (Kruskal, 1964a) less than .08 and two-thirds of the configurations had stresses below .05. The Euclidean distances between every pair of stimulus points for a particular subject were computed from the coordinates of that subject's multidimensional scaling solution. The set of 75 complete matrices of Euclidean distances, one for each subject, served as input to the INDSCAL procedure.[6]

Four dimensions accounted for 41% of the variance in all subjects' data. (In other words, 41% was the average percentage of variance accounted for in a matrix from a single subject). The percentage of variance accounted for in every single subject's matrix was greater than that obtained for any of 24 hypothetical subjects whose data were randomly generated by a computer (and analyzed by INDSCAL). Thus, there appeared to be at least some structure (as opposed to purely random variation) in every subject's matrix. (A discussion of the reliability of an INDSCAL solution and of other methodological issues involving INDSCAL is reported in Wish & Carroll, in press.)

Although only 41% of the total variance was accounted for by these four dimensions, there did not seem to be any other dimensions which many subjects had in common. In this regard INDSCAL analyses in five and six dimensions did not provide any further insight into the data and the additional variance accounted for was no more than would be expected by chance. Some explanations for the large residual variance are (a) low reliability of similarities data from single individuals; (b) relatively unique dimensions (relevant to only a few subjects or stimuli); and (c) individual differences with respect to these dimensions which cannot be accounted for by the INDSCAL model without bringing in many more dimensions; e.g., differences in the spacing or ordering of stimuli on the dimensions and differences in the relationships among the dimensions.

Interpretation of Dimensions

The stimulus coordinates on the *unrotated* dimensions from the four-dimensional INDSCAL analysis are given in Table 5.[7] Figure 2 shows a

[6] Analyses of other data in which similarity judgments were made for all stimulus pairs (Wish, 1969) indicated that INDSCAL analyses of the original similarities data and INDSCAL analyses of the prescaled data give almost identical results. Moreover, prescaling the data resulted in only a negligible improvement in the goodness-of-fit measure.

[7] As is frequently the case, there are some moderate correlations between pairs of dimensions from this analysis. Dimension 2 correlates .46 with dimension 4 and .33 with dimension 1. All other correlations are below .20.

TABLE 5

STIMULUS COORDINATES ON NORMALIZED INDSCAL DIMENSIONS

	Dim 1: Political alignment	Dim 2: Economic development	Dim 3: Geography and population	Dim 4: Culture and race
U. S. A.	.290	.334	.172	.160
U. K.	.263	.310	.096	.192
West Germany	.261	.326	.141	.204
France	.175	.223	−.050	.155
Israel	.168	.108	−.169	.212
Japan	.120	.115	.456	.106
South Africa	.069	.268	−.283	−.493
Greece	.065	−.092	−.197	.290
Spain	.189	−.038	−.178	−.026
Brazil	.212	−.186	.016	−.168
Mexico	.196	−.156	.016	−.083
Ethiopia	−.012	−.296	−.353	−.039
India	−.064	−.295	.250	−.102
Indonesia	−.052	−.301	.268	−.123
Congo	−.086	−.283	−.237	−.442
Egypt	−.215	−.220	−.204	−.076
China	−.403	−.114	.399	−.174
Cuba	−.283	−.080	−.082	−.212
Yugoslavia	−.234	.051	−.033	.226
Poland	−.308	.126	−.131	.299
U.S.S.R.	−.353	.201	.102	.094

plot of the first two dimensions. The interpretation "political alignment" given to the first dimension was based on the fact that nations aligned with the U.S.A. (the pro-Western nations) and nations aligned with U.S.S.R. or China (the pro-Communist nations) are at opposite extremes. Since the more developed nations generally project higher on the vertical dimension, dimension 2 was labeled "economic development."

Interpretation of the third and fourth dimensions (Figure 3) presented some difficulties. Our predilections were to interpret the plane as a whole since both dimensions reflect geography, culture, race, and other associated characteristics. It is what is left after political and economic considerations have been accounted for! Nevertheless, for convenience of reference the labels "geography and population" and "culture and race" were assigned to the third and fourth dimensions, respectively. On the left side of the third dimension are the four African countries followed by three countries (Greece, Israel, and Spain) that are geographically very close to Africa. At the opposite extreme of the third dimension are the four Far Eastern, or

Oriental, countries. In addition to contrasting certain geographical regions, the third dimension dichotomizes the countries with respect to population. Thus, except for a couple of comparisons involving France, all of the countries higher than Yugoslavia on the third dimension exceed all of the other countries in population. With a larger sample of countries it is likely that there would be one dimension distinguishing the Far Eastern from the African countries and another dimension based on population. The countries that are high on the fourth dimension are European, but not Spanish, in geography, culture, or origin. Instead of "culture and race" the fourth

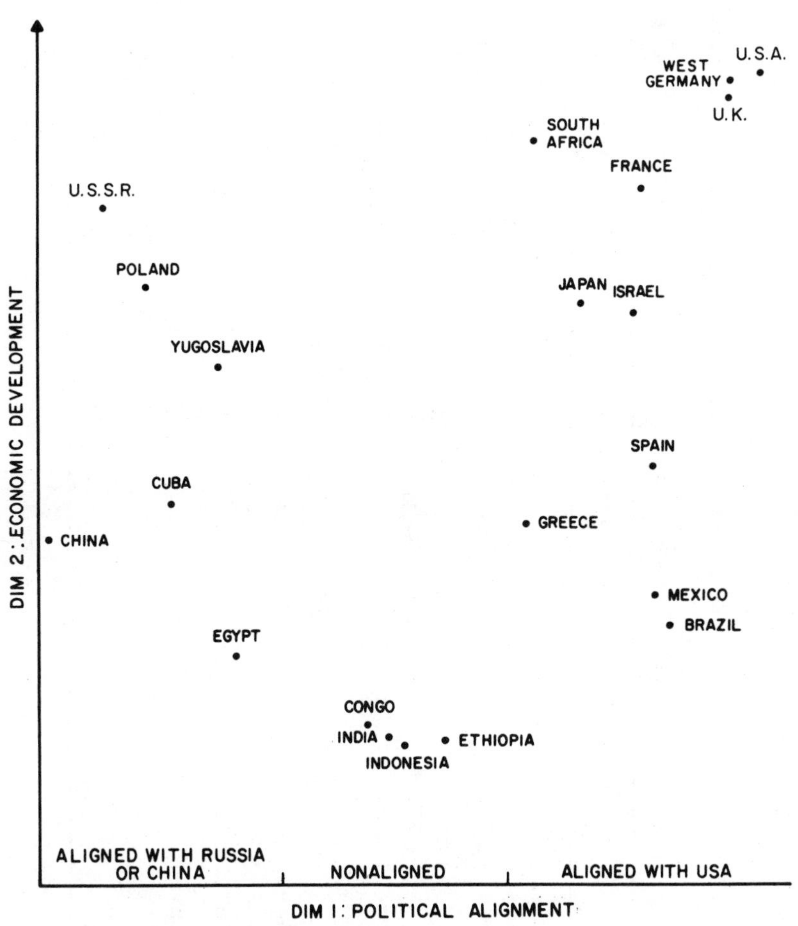

FIG. 2. Dimensions 1 and 2 of *"group" stimulus space* for total group.

TABLE 6

MEAN RATINGS OF TWENTY-ONE NATIONS ON EIGHTEEN BIPOLAR SCALES

	USA	U.K.	W.G.	FRA	ISR	JAP	S.A.	GRE	SPA	BRA	MEX
Aligned with U.S.A.	9.00	8.52	8.12	7.24	7.36	7.16	6.00	6.92	6.62	6.42	6.78
Individualistic	7.36	5.80	5.92	5.57	3.11	4.88	6.64	5.85	6.09	5.59	5.21
Peaceful	4.45	6.71	5.67	5.75	3.33	6.36	5.12	6.20	6.36	6.81	6.99
Many rights	7.53	7.92	6.37	6.11	6.35	6.60	2.88	3.21	3.40	4.37	4.55
I Like	7.45	7.65	6.52	6.40	6.13	6.77	3.64	6.43	5.47	6.48	6.39
Good	6.61	7.17	6.25	6.07	5.71	6.91	3.41	4.81	4.16	5.16	5.72
Similarity to ideal	5.45	5.77	4.71	5.38	4.38	5.24	2.15	3.64	2.89	3.06	3.48
Can change status	7.52	5.83	6.16	5.71	6.23	6.71	2.75	3.69	3.47	3.93	4.09
Stable	7.23	7.69	7.00	5.44	6.52	7.43	4.59	3.45	5.47	3.57	5.15
Population satisfied	6.08	6.64	6.71	5.57	6.56	6.53	3.43	3.81	4.36	3.56	4.57
Internally united	4.75	6.89	6.32	5.11	7.57	7.21	2.76	4.19	4.45	4.25	5.72
Cultural influence	7.44	6.83	5.43	6.43	5.37	5.91	3.24	6.17	5.03	3.63	4.67
Educated population	8.11	7.92	7.85	6.75	6.59	6.89	3.43	4.56	4.37	3.03	3.25
Rich	8.79	7.19	7.76	6.36	6.16	7.35	6.29	3.56	3.49	4.17	3.81
Industralized	8.84	8.25	8.29	6.63	6.13	8.25	5.63	3.65	3.92	3.81	3.97
Powerful	8.91	6.52	7.07	6.08	5.87	7.03	4.71	2.97	3.05	3.77	3.41
Progressing	6.60	5.28	7.64	5.96	7.61	8.03	4.72	4.49	4.33	5.91	5.71
Large	8.83	4.04	5.57	5.56	1.92	5.01	5.72	2.97	4.55	7.24	5.40

TABLE 6 (Continued)

	ETH	INDI	INDO	CON	EGY	CHI	CUB	YUG	POL	U.S.S.R.
Aligned with U.S.A.	5.64	6.04	5.12	4.98	3.56	1.12	2.06	3.86	3.22	2.66
Individualistic	5.16	4.57	5.45	5.69	4.11	2.03	2.59	2.64	2.41	1.53
Peaceful	6.84	6.79	4.81	4.75	3.08	2.43	3.65	6.60	5.71	3.72
Many rights	4.08	4.57	3.32	2.96	3.76	2.05	2.89	4.09	3.13	2.57
I Like	6.16	6.24	5.20	4.76	5.07	4.23	4.97	6.47	5.57	5.32
Good	5.40	5.51	4.32	3.84	4.19	3.87	4.41	5.53	4.85	5.01
Similarity to ideal	2.65	2.90	2.52	1.65	2.52	2.73	2.92	3.93	3.25	3.97
Can change status	3.55	3.37	3.59	3.01	3.52	3.24	3.71	4.37	3.99	4.28
Stable	5.39	4.97	3.36	2.36	4.13	4.47	4.53	6.23	6.61	7.29
Population satisfied	4.84	3.53	3.88	3.52	4.47	3.84	4.29	5.59	4.92	5.55
Internally united	5.88	3.44	3.67	2.60	5.63	4.20	6.05	6.04	6.27	6.81
Cultural influence	3.08	5.63	3.17	2.99	5.01	5.19	3.97	3.72	3.57	6.60
Educated population	2.75	2.45	2.76	2.17	3.00	3.35	3.73	5.37	6.07	7.05
Rich	2.97	2.13	3.39	3.09	3.37	3.08	3.59	3.96	4.57	7.13
Industralized	2.48	3.04	3.03	2.16	3.48	4.65	3.77	5.00	5.87	7.91
Powerful	2.79	3.59	3.41	2.61	3.71	6.97	3.49	3.76	3.92	8.53
Progressing	5.39	5.56	5.15	4.53	4.68	6.39	5.68	6.36	5.79	7.81
Large	4.07	8.11	5.27	5.39	5.11	8.67	1.95	4.13	4.48	8.84

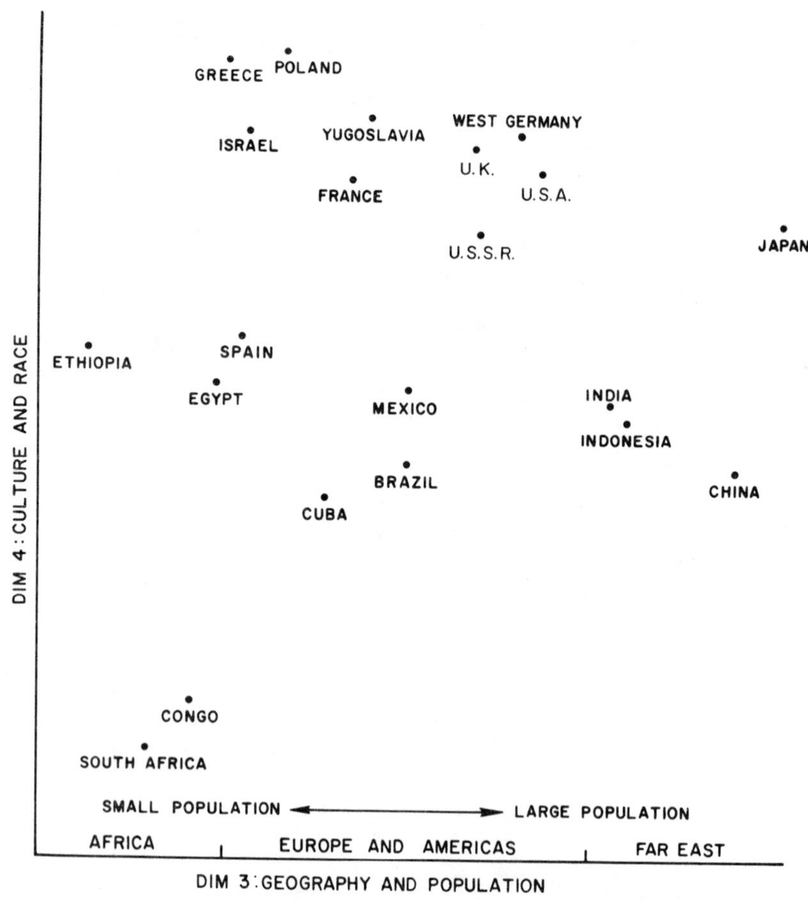

Fig. 3. Dimensions 3 and 4 of *"group" stimulus space* for total group.

dimension could possibly have been interpreted as "European–non-European," "north–south," or "light–dark."

Correlations of INDSCAL Dimensions with Mean Ratings on 18 Bipolar Scales

Table 6, which shows the mean ratings of each nation on 18 bipolar scales,[8] and Table 7, which lists the correlations of each INDSCAL dimen-

[8] The "similarity to ideal" scale is based on subjects' ratings of how similar the countries are to their respective "ideals." The "aligned with U. S. A." was derived from the political alignment sorting described in Table 3.

TABLE 7

CORRELATIONS OF INDSCAL DIMENSIONS WITH MEAN RATINGS OF NATIONS ON EIGHTEEN BIPOLAR SCALES

	Dim. 1: Political alignment	Dim. 2: Economic development	Dim. 3: Geography and population	Dim. 4: Culture and race	Multiple correlation
1 Aligned with U. S. A.	.965	.379	.012	.299	.974
2 Individualistic	.818	.103	−.124	−.159	.876
3 Peaceful	.500	−.043	−.065	.201	.596
4 Many rights	.740	.535	.273	.499	.874
5 I like	.606	.301	.246	.700	.890
6 Good	.556	.482	.395	.660	.861
7 Similarity to ideal	.498	.735	.390	.736	.940
8 Can change status	.548	.676	.384	.631	.885
9 Stable	.233	.755	.318	.641	.846
10 Population satisfied	.350	.703	.241	.708	.842
11 Internally united	.022	.423	.116	.672	.698
12 Cultural influence	.321	.546	.415	.560	.738
13 Educated population	.336	.890	.268	.741	.973
14 Rich	.461	.906	.255	.405	.936
15 Industrialized	.316	.924	.407	.537	.975
16 Powerful	.142	.748	.556	.356	.885
17 Progressing	−.000	.461	.544	.434	.715
18 Large	−.099	.056	.522	−.203	.614

sion with mean ratings on each scale, provide additional support for the interpretations we have given to the dimensions. (The grouping of scales in these tables is based on factor analyses of the rating scales.) The multiple correlations in the last column of Table 7 show how well mean ratings on each scale can be predicted from the four optimally weighted INDSCAL dimensions.

The first dimension, as its name would suggest, correlates most highly (.965) with mean ratings on the "aligned with U.S.A." scale. The correlation between the first dimension and the "individualistic" scale is lower since some nations aligned with the U.S.A. (such as Israel) are rated as more collectively oriented than some nations aligned with U.S.S.R. or China (such as Egypt). The first dimension also has moderately high positive correlations with several socially desirable, or evaluative-type, scales (e.g., scales 3 to 8) indicating that the subjects in our sample tend to favor the non-communist countries. The second dimension correlates very highly with scales directly concerned with economic development—.924 with "industrialized," .906 with "rich," and .890 with "educated population." There are also moderate correlations between the second dimension and scales that are indirectly associated with economic development (such as the "stable," "powerful," "similarity to ideal," and "population satisfied" scales). Since none of the rating scales is specifically concerned with geography, culture, or race, there are no correlations in the .80's or .90's between the scales and the last two dimensions. The scales most highly correlated with the third dimension are concerned with power and size. In fact, the third dimension correlates .80 with the actual population of these countries. The fourth dimension correlates moderately with scales that seem to reflect favorable internal conditions, or perhaps domestic tranquility, in the countries; e.g., "population satisfied," "united," "similarity to ideal," and "stable." Not shown in Table 8 is the correlation of .83 between mean latitude of the countries and their projections on the fourth dimension.

The high multiple correlations for most of the rating scales show that a variety of measures can be predicted with a high degree of success from the INDSCAL dimensions. Many of these characteristics probably had some influence on the similarity ratings. However, 5 of the 18 scales—"peaceful", "united," "cultural influence," "progressing," and "large"—have multiple correlations in the .60's and .70's. These relatively low correlations (and other evidence in the data which will not be discussed here) suggest that these 5 characteristics are not very salient in subjects' judgments of similarities among nations.

Subgroup Differences in Weights for Dimensions

Attention will now be focused on subgroup differences in the relative weights of the stimulus dimensions. The Vietnam opinion question (Table 4) was used to classify subjects as doves, moderates, or hawks. Table 8, which provides a sex × attitude classification for each of the eight nationality subgroups, shows that there are considerable differences in sex and attitude distribution among the eight nationality subgroups. The "dove"–"non-dove" split is 1 to 18 for the Koreans and Thais, and 28 to 28 for the other six nationalities combined. U.K., Yugoslavia, and Korea are represented predominantly by males, while all but one of the nine Thais are female. While the male–female split is fairly equal (21–18) among subjects from the more underdeveloped countries, males outnumber females 27–9 among subjects from the more developed countries. In order to avoid some of the confounding between sex, attitude, and nationality, we divided the

TABLE 8

SEX × ATTITUDE CLASSIFICATION WITHIN EACH NATION

	Male			Female		
Nationality	Dove	Mod.	Hawk	Dove	Mod.	Hawk
American (U. S. A.)	2	1	1	3	1	0
British	5	5	1	1	0	0
French	2	3	1	1	2	0
Yugoslav	3	1	2	1	0	0
Developed nations:	12	10	5	6	3	0
Colombian	2	3	0	3	1	0
Indian	3	4	0	2	2	0
Korean	0	4	4	0	1	1
Thai	0	1	0	1	4	3
Underdev. nations:	5	12	4	6	8	4

subjects into eight subgroups according to a three-way classification: dove or non-dove, male or female, and from a developed or an underdeveloped nation.

Table 9 shows the mean weights on the INDSCAL dimensions for 16 subgroups. Comparisons of each male subgroup with the female subgroup that immediately follows show that, on the average, males have higher weights on both the political and the economic dimensions. Characteristics of the government (dimensions 1 and 2) appear to be more important for the males, whereas characteristics more associated with the people (dimensions 3 and 4) seem to have relatively greater salience for the females.

The last column of Table 9 shows, for each subgroup, the mean weight on the first dimension divided by the mean weight on the second dimension. The higher this ratio, the greater the importance of "political alignment" relative to "economic development." Comparisons of each "dove" group with the "non-dove" group which is the same on the other two classification variables (Groups 1 and 5, 2 and 6, 3 and 7, and 4 and 8) show in every instance that the ratio is higher for "non-doves" than for "doves." Not shown in this table is the fact that the ratio based on all "moderates" (1.15) is about midway between the ratios for "doves" (0.77) and "hawks" (1.68). Table 9 also shows that the ratio is higher for females than for males (Group 2 > Group 1; Group 4 > Group 3; Group 6 > Group 5; Group 8 >

TABLE 9

MEAN WEIGHTS OF INDSCAL DIMENSIONS FOR SIXTEEN SUBGROUPS

		N	Dim. 1: Political alignment	Dim. 2: Economic development	Dim. 3 : Geography and population	Dim. 4: Culture and race	Mean Weight on Dim. 1 / Mean Weight on Dim. 2
1	Dove-M-developed	12	.237	.383	.247	.175	0.62
2	Dove-F-developed	6	.223	.313	.158	.216	0.71
3	Dove-M-underdev.	5	.302	.300	.172	.191	1.01
4	Dove-F-underdev.	6	.273	.260	.253	.225	1.05
5	Non-dove-M-developed	15	.316	.350	.211	.247	0.90
6	Non-dove-F-developed	3	.229	.107	.344	.087	2.14
7	Non-dove-M-underdev.	16	.346	.259	.234	.207	1.34
8	Non-dove-F-underdev.	12	.263	.119	.250	.282	2.21
9	Americans (U. S. A.)	8	.217	.280	.205	.242	0.78
10	British	12	.304	.435	.221	.155	0.70
11	French	9	.219	.244	.292	.184	0.90
12	Yugoslavs	7	.323	.342	.169	.271	0.94
13	Colombians	9	.322	.246	.191	.202	1.31
14	Indians	11	.303	.244	.250	.184	1.24
15	Koreans	10	.371	.243	.238	.200	1.53
16	Thais	9	.223	.140	.242	.338	1.59

Group 7) and is higher for subjects from "underdeveloped" countries than for subjects from "developed" countries (Group 3 > Group 1; Group 4 > Group 2; Group 7 > Group 5; Group 8 > Group 6).

The difference between "doves" and "non-doves" with regard to the relative importance of "political alignment" and "economic development" was also observed in a pilot study (Wish, 1971). Elsewhere (Wish, 1971) it is shown that "political alignment" is a highly evaluative dimension since it correlates highly (positively or negatively) with most subjects' ratings of nations on the "similarity to ideal" and "I like" scales, and is also the most important dimension of friendship among nations. Thus, the high salience of "political alignment" to the "non-doves" suggests that evaluative, or affective, considerations are particularly relevant to them. Other evidence for evaluative responding by the "non-doves" (Wish, Deutsch, & Biener, 1970) is the fact that "political alignment" is also more relevant to the "non-doves" than to the "doves" when rating nations on the bipolar scales.

The relatively high salience of "political alignment" for females might also reflect a more evaluative, or affective, orientation. However, there is not as much supplementary evidence supporting this conjecture for females as for "non-doves" (see Wish, 1970). The relatively low weights on the "economic development" dimension for subjects from "underdeveloped" countries are hard to understand. Perhaps these subjects deemphasize (subconsciously) "economic development" in order to minimize the differences between "underdeveloped" countries such as theirs and the countries they regard as more "ideal," the "developed" countries. It is consistent with theories of balance to consider one's own nation to be similar to those one regards as more desirable. It is also conceivable that the differences between subjects from "developed" and "underdeveloped" countries relate to different criteria for selecting students in these countries.

The differences in patterns of weights for the eight nationality subgroups are largely accounted for by the classification variables. Thus, the fact that American, British, French, and Yugoslav students weight the second dimension more than the first while students from Colombia, India, Korea, and Thailand weight the first dimension more than the second shows the difference between subjects from "developed" and "underdeveloped" countries with regard to the relative importance of "political alignment" and "economic development." Higher weights for British and Yugoslav than French and American subjects on the first two dimensions relate to the higher percentages of males in the British and Yugoslav samples. Differences in dimension weights for Koreans and Thais also relate to the sex distribution in the subsamples. Finally, the greater importance of "economic development" for Colombians and Indians than for Koreans and Thais can be explained by the greater proportion of "doves" among the Colombian and Indian subgroups.

INDSCAL Analysis for Different Subgroups

Table 9 provided comparisons of subgroups with respect to the same set of dimensions. In order to determine the degree to which subgroups differed in terms of the dimensions they used in judging similarities among nations, separate INDSCAL analyses were done for a large number of subgroups. The discussion which follows concerns five of these subgroups—male doves, male moderates, male hawks, female doves, and female non-doves.

The multiple correlations shown in Table 10 indicate the degree to which a dimension from the total group's INDSCAL configuration can be linearly predicted from the four optimally weighted dimensions from a particular subgroup's INDSCAL solution. All of the multiple correlations are greater than .800 and only three are below .890. Thus the dimensions from the total group analysis are represented quite well in the configurations for each of these subgroups.[9]

Examination of the subgroups' configurations did reveal some interesting differences among subgroups however. The greatest differences appeared to be between the male doves and the female non-doves, particularly with regard to the first two dimensions. A plot of the first two dimensions (unrotated) from the INDSCAL analysis for Male Doves (shown in Figure

TABLE 10

Multiple Correlations between Dimensions from Total Group INDSCAL Analysis and INDSCAL Configurations for Five Subgroups

		INDSCAL dimensions for total group (dependent variables)			
Subgroup	*N*	Dim 1	Dim 2	Dim 3	Dim 4
Male doves	17	.930	.983	.937	.846
Male moderates	22	.983	.970	.964	.929
Male hawks	9	.965	.937	.836	.893
Female doves	12	.920	.944	.903	.900
Female non-doves	15	.980	.803	.952	.949

[9] This conclusion also applies to the configurations for the eight nationality subgroups.

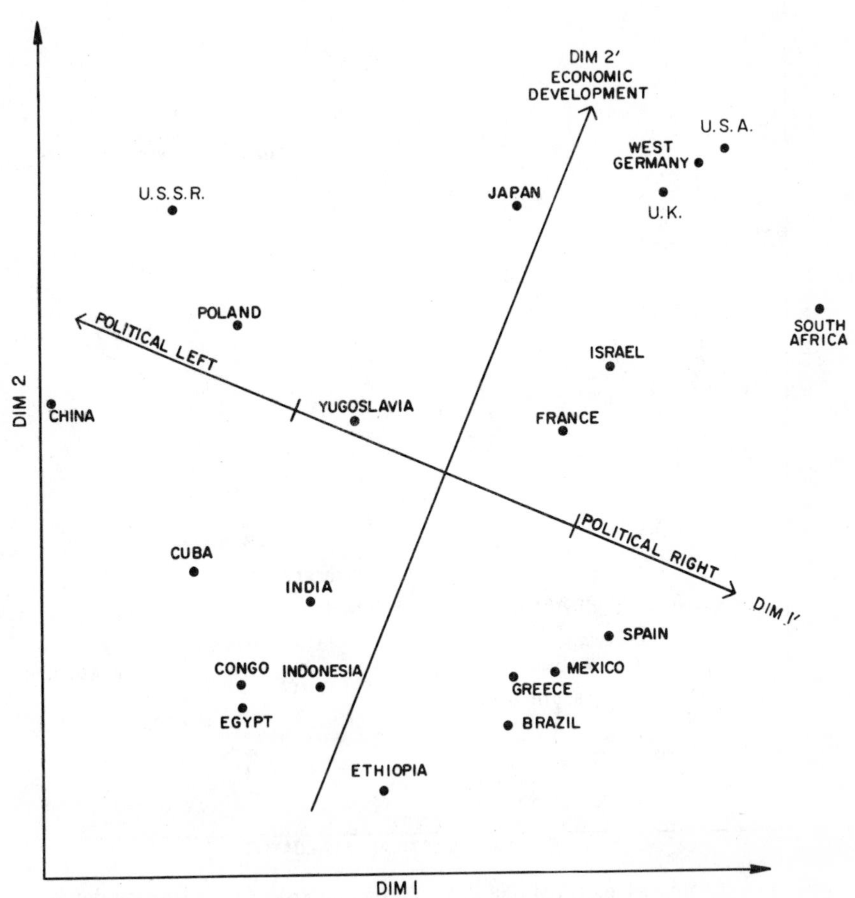

FIG. 4. Dimensions 1 and 2 of "*group*" *stimulus space* for male doves.

4) indicates that a slight rotation of the axes can bring out more clearly the political and economic dimensions in the configuration. The rotated "Economic Development" (Dim 2′) strongly resembles the second dimension in the configuration for the total group. However, the rotated political dimension (Dim 1′) reflects ideology more than alignment, since it goes roughly from the political left to the political right.[10]

Perhaps the most striking difference between the configurations for male

[10] Rotation of axes may be necessary if there is not much variation among subjects in the patterns of dimension weights.

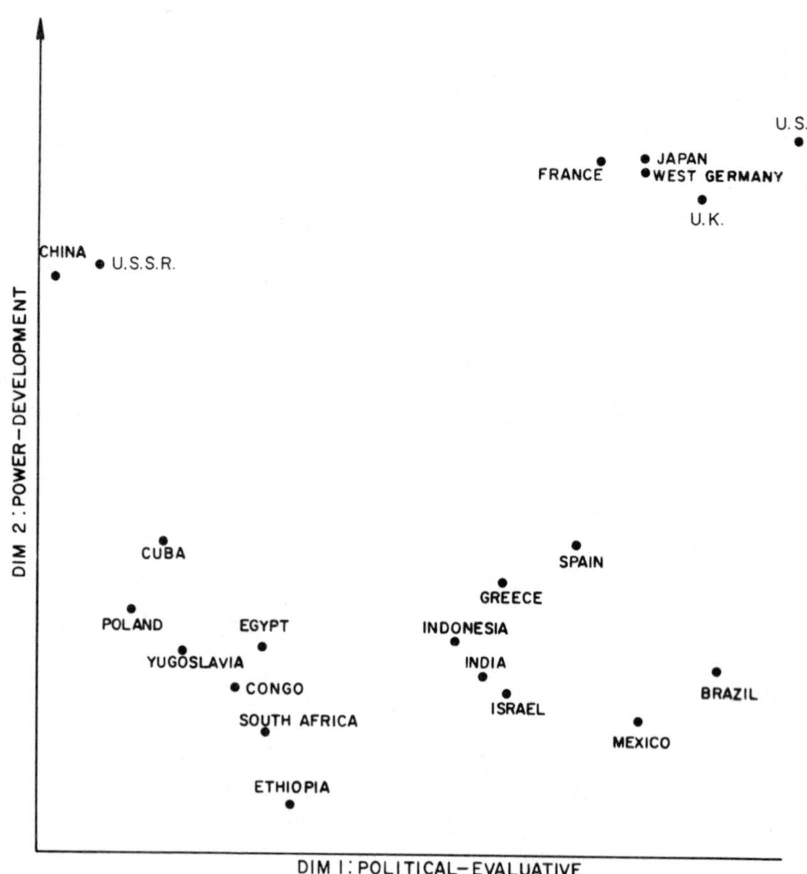

FIG. 5. Dimensions 1 and 2 of "*group*" *stimulus space* for female non-doves.

doves and female non-doves (Figure 5) is that the configuration for the latter group shows much tighter clustering, indicating less differentiation among nations. The first dimension for female non-doves is labeled "political-evaluative" since it correlates .93 with the "political alignment" dimension from the total group INDSCAL analysis and correlates .87 with ratings by these subjects on the "I like" scale. The second dimension for female non-doves appears to refer more to power than development, since the correlation between this dimension and ratings by these subjects on the "power," "industrialized," and "rich" scales are .85, .82, and .71, respectively.

Although the dimensions from the INDSCAL configuration for all subjects are not optimal for every subgroup, they do represent a compromise which reasonably reflects the respective dimensions of most subgroups. The rather high communality among subgroups with regard to the dimensions relevant to the similarities among nations provides some justification for the comparison of subgroups in terms of a common set of dimensions.

Discussion and Conclusions

Several conclusions seem warranted by the results of this study. In terms of the methodological queries that we had posed at the outset of our investigation, it seems evident that INDSCAL can be fruitfully applied to the understanding of individual differences in conceptions of nations. There seems to be sufficient communality in the underlying dimensions employed in characterizing nations for meaningful comparisons to be made of how salient or important the different dimensions are for various groups of people.

Substantively, our data indicate that the subjects' judgments of the similarity among nations are based, primarily on four dimensions which we interpreted as "political alignment" (or ideology), "economic development," "geography and population," and "culture and race." The labeling of the dimensions was facilitated and supported by the correlations with other data, mainly obtained from the rating scales. Thus, dimension 1 was labeled "political alignment" (or ideology), because it correlated .97 with ratings the subjects made of the political alignment of nations with respect to the U.S.A. (in case of a large-scale war in the next five years). The dimension labeled "economic development" correlated .92 with ratings of "industrialization" and .91 with ratings on a "rich–poor" scale. It was more difficult to label the third and fourth dimensions because a number of characteristics were confounded with them. We selected labels "geography and population" and "culture and race" that seemed to describe the obtained distributions on the respective dimensions. There was some correlational support also for labeling the fourth dimension "north–south" or "domestic tranquility" since it correlated .83 with mean latitudes of the countries and also had moderately high correlations with several scales which reflected favorable domestic conditions.

Despite the considerable heterogeneity of our subject population, consistent differences in conceptual structures were obtained as a function of political orientation, sex, and country of origin. The importance, or weight, of "political alignment" relative to "economic development" was consistently greater for "hawks," females, and students from "underdeveloped" countries than for "doves," males, and students from "developed" countries. We would like next to determine how much the conceptual structures of subjects would vary if they were asked to view nations from various perspectives—e.g., from the perspective of a tourist, of a military strategist, of an international civil servant, or of an export–import trader. On the basis of pilot study results (Wish, 1971), we suspect that the conceptual structures of some subjects would vary considerably as a function of the particular perspective that was momentarily dominant while those of others would remain relatively unchanged. It seems worthwhile to identify the major types of perspectives on nations, to investigate how much variation there would be as a function of perspective, and to study what factors lead one or another type of perspective to be dominant. These are tasks that will guide some of our future research.

Acknowledgments

The research reported in this paper was partially supported by a National Science Foundation Grant GS-302, "Elements of Conflict Resolution," whose principal investigator is Morton Deutsch.

References

Adelman, I., & Morris, C. T. A factor analysis of the interrelations between social and political variables and per capita gross national product. *Quarterly Journal of Economics* 1965, **79,** 555–578.

Banks, A. S., & Gregg, P. M. Grouping political systems: Q-factor analysis of a cross-polity survey. *American Behavioral Scientist,* 1965, **9,** 3–6.

Carroll, J. D. Individual differences and multidimensional scaling. This book, Volume 1.

Carroll, J. D., & Chang, J. J. Analysis of individual differences in multidimensional scaling via an N-way generalization of "Eckart-Young" decomposition. *Psychometrika,* 1970, **35,** 283–319.

Cattell, R. B. The dimensions of culture patterns by factorization of national characteristics. *Journal of Abnormal and Social Psychology,* 1949, **44,** 443–469.

Coombs, C. H. *A theory of data.* New York: Wiley, 1964.

Gregg, P. M., & Banks, A. S. Dimensions of political systems: Factor analysis of a cross-polity survey. *American Political Science Review,* 1965, **59,** 602.

Guttman, L. A general nonmetric technique for finding the smallest coordinate space for a configuration of points. *Psychometrika,* 1968, **33,** 469–506.

Horan, C. B. Multidimensional scaling: Combining observations when individuals have different perceptual structures. *Psychometrika,* 1969, **34,** 139–165.

Klingberg, F. L. Studies in measurement of the relations among sovereign states. Psychometrika, 1941, **6,** 335–352.

Kruskal, J. B. Multidimensional scaling: A numerical method. *Psychometrika,* 1964, **29,** 1–27. (a)

Kruskal, J. B. Multidimensional scaling by optimizing goodness of fit to a nonmetric hypothesis. *Psychometrika,* 1964, **29,** 115–129. (b)

Robinson, J. P., & Hefner, R. Multidimensional differences in public and academic perceptions of nations. *Journal of Personality and Social Psychology,* 1967, **9,** 251–259.

Rummel, R. J. Research communication: some attributes and behavioral patterns of nations. *Journal of Peace Research,* 1967, **2,** 196–206.

Russett, B. M. Delineating international regions. In J. D. Singer (Ed.) Empirical studies of international relations: *International yearbook of political behavior research,* Vol. 7. New York: Free Press, 1966.

Sawyer, J. Dimensions of nations: Size, wealth, and politics. *American Journal of Sociology,* 1967, **73,** 145–172.

Shepard, R. N. The analysis of proximities: Multidimensional scaling with an unknown distance function. I, II. *Psychometrika,* 1962, **27,** 125–140, 219–246.

Torgerson, W. S. *Theory and methods of scaling.* New York: Wiley, 1958.

Wish, M. Multidimensional scaling of similarities among nations. Detroit Area Study report, 1964 (Mimeo).

Wish, M. Individual differences in perceived dissimilarity among stress patterns of English words. Paper presented at Psychonomic Society meetings, October 1969.

Wish, M. Comparisons among multidimensional structures of nations based on different measures of subjective similarity. In L. von Bertalanffy and A. Rapoport (Eds.), *General systems.* Vol. 15. 1970, 55–65.

Wish, M. Individual differences in perceptions and preferences among nations. In C. W. King and D. Tigert (Eds.), *Attitude research reaches new heights.* Chicago: American Marketing Association, 1971. Pp. 312–328.

Wish, M., & Carroll, J. D. Multidimensional scaling with differential weighting of dimensions. In F. R. Hudson, D. A. Kendall, & P. Tǎutu (Eds.), *Mathematics in the archaeological and historical sciences,* Edinburgh: Edinburgh University Press, 1971. Pp. 150–167.

Wish, M., & Carroll, J. D. Applications of INDSCAL to studies of human perception and judgment. In E. C. Carterette & M. P. Friedman (Eds.), *Handbook of perception,* New York: Academic Press, in press.

Wish, M., Deutsch, M., & Biener, L. Differences in conceptual structures of nations: An exploratory study, *Journal of Personality and Social Psychology,* 1970, **16,** 361–373.

Young, F. W., & Torgerson, W. S. TORSCA, a FORTRAN IV program for Shepard-Kruskal multidimensional scaling analysis. *Behavioral Science,* 1967, **12,** 498.

AUTHOR INDEX

Numbers in italics refer to the pages on which the complete references are listed.

A

B

C

D

E

F

G

H

J

K

L

SUBJECT INDEX

A

B

C

T

U

V

W

5
6
C 7
D 8
E 9
F 0
G 1
H 2
I 3
J 4